CURRENT THEMES IN TROPICAL SCIENCE

Chief Editor: THOMAS R. ODHIAMBO, I.C.I.P.E. *Nairobi*

Volume 3

Caste Differentiation in Social Insects

Other Pergamon publications of interest

Books

ENGELMANN Physiology of Insect Reproduction

HINTON Biology of Insect Eggs, 3-volume set

KERKUT & GILBERT Comprehensive Insect Physiology, Biochemistry and Pharmacology, 13-volume set

LÜSCHER Phase and Caste Determination in Insects

MATSUDA Morphology and Evolution of the Insect Abdomen

OBENCHAIN & GALUN The Physiology of Ticks

SAUNDERS Insect Clocks, 2nd Edition

SHORROCKS Drosophila

SUTTON Woodlice

VON FRISCH Twelve Little Housemates

WHITEHEAD & BOWERS Natural Products for Innovative Pest Management

Journals*

INSECT BIOCHEMISTRY
INSECT SCIENCE AND ITS APPLICATION
INTERNATIONAL JOURNAL FOR PARASITOLOGY
INTERNATIONAL JOURNAL OF INSECT MORPHOLOGY AND EMBRYOLOGY
JOURNAL OF INSECT PHYSIOLOGY

*Free specimen copies available on request

Caste Differentiation in Social Insects

Guest Editors

J. A. L. WATSON
CSIRO Division of Entomology, Canberra, Australia

B. M. OKOT-KOTBER
International Centre of Insect Physiology and Ecology, Nairobi

and

CH. NOIROT
Laboratory of Zoology, University of Dijon, Dijon, France

PERGAMON PRESS

OXFORD · NEW YORK · TORONTO · SYDNEY · PARIS · FRANKFURT

U.K.	Pergamon Press Ltd., Headington Hill Hall, Oxford OX3 0BW, England
U.S.A.	Pergamon Press Inc., Maxwell House, Fairview Park, Elmsford, New York 10523, U.S.A.
CANADA	Pergamon Press Canada Ltd., Suite 104, 150 Consumers Rd., Willowdale, Ontario M2J 1P9, Canada
AUSTRALIA	Pergamon Press (Aust.) Pty. Ltd., P.O. Box 544, Potts Point, N.S.W. 2011, Australia
FRANCE	Pergamon Press SARL, 24 rue des Ecoles, 75240 Paris, Cedex 05, France
FEDERAL REPUBLIC OF GERMANY	Pergamon Press GmbH, Hammerweg 6, D-6242 Kronberg-Taunus, Federal Republic of Germany

---

First edition 1985

Library of Congress Cataloging in Publication Data

Main entry under title:
Caste differentiation in social insects.
(Current themes in tropical science; v. 3)
"Based on the International Study Workshop on Termite Caste
Differentiation, held at the International, Centre of Insect
Physiology and Ecology (ICIPE), in Nairobi, Kenya, on 7th–12th
November 1982"—Pref.
    1. Termites—Behavior—Congresses.   2. Insect societies—
Congresses.   3. Insects—Behavior—Congresses.
I. Watson, J. A. L.   II. International Study Workshop on
Termite Caste Differentiation (1982: International Centre of
Insect Physiology and Ecology)   III. Series.

British Library Cataloguing in Publication Data

Caste differentiation in social insects—
(Current themes in tropical science; v. 3)
1. Insects—Behaviour   2. Social behaviour in animals
I. Watson, J. A. L.   II. Series
595.7′051   QL496
ISBN 0-08-030783-3

Printed in Great Britain by A. Wheaton & Co. Ltd, Exeter

Preface

This book is based on the International Study Workshop on Termite Caste Differentiation, held at the International Centre of Insect Physiology and Ecology (ICIPE), in Nairobi, Kenya, on 7–12 November 1982.

The Workshop had its origins in the realization that, in the decade that had elapsed since the last comprehensive reviews of caste development in termites had appeared, much new information had been gathered, and new perspectives gained. There had been an increased emphasis on the study of termite caste systems in warmer areas of the world, where termites are diverse and abundant. A reappraisal was needed, one that would not only involve termite caste differentiation, but also development in other groups of social insects, particularly the social Hymenoptera which, being abundant in cold-temperate regions, are in many ways better known; the Workshop was designed to provide that reappraisal.

It is particularly appropriate that the Workshop, and this volume, should be dedicated to the memory of Martin Lüscher. It was he who, some three decades ago, set on its feet the infant study of causal mechanisms in termite caste differentiation and who, at the ICIPE, sought to rear it to a healthy maturity. His tragic death in 1979 robbed the science of a personal contribution that he could have made, but the impetus of his work has continued. It is also appropriate that the ICIPE should have convened the Workshop; it is the institution at which Lüscher sought new perspectives on the castes of termites, and it is also in Africa where, two hundred years ago, Smeathman, in amazement, first observed the workings of termite societies.

ICIPE, Nairobi, February 1983

J. A. L. WATSON
B. M. OKOT-KOTBER
CH. NOIROT
Guest Editors

Foreword

The series of publications under the general title of CURRENT THEMES IN TROPICAL SCIENCE was launched in 1982 by the publication in November of that year, of the book, *Physiology of Ticks* (edited by Frederick D. Obenchain and Rachel Galun). "The series has been established to remove the lack of a common forum for the presentation of critical reviews of new research being carried on, and new syntheses being forged among, the various facets of insect science as well as the application of these new insights into the solution of the numerous problems related to tropical insects (and their close arthropod relatives)", as was stated in the Foreword to *Physiology of Ticks*. The new series is particularly focused on the tropical insect and arthropod phenomena, the main criteria for a particular field of choice being its timeliness, its scientific and technological concerns, its impact on socio-economic development, or the crucial nature of the current advances in the particular facet.

The second volume in this series, *Natural Products for Innovative Pest Management* (edited by David L. Whitehead and B. L. Bowers), recently published, follows closely on the foundation established by the first and inaugural volume. The present volume in this series, *Caste Differentiation in Social Insects (With Emphasis on Termites)*, follows the footsteps of the two pioneer volumes.

The book is largely arranged around papers presented during an International Study Workshop on Termite Caste Differentiation, sponsored by the International Centre of Insect Physiology and Ecology (ICIPE), and held in Nairobi from 7–12 November 1981. Under the chairmanship of Dr J. A. L. Watson of CSIRO, Australia, 25 participants and 11 countries presented a colossal amount of new information gained in recent years especially on insect caste systems in the tropics. A few chapters in this book were invited from non-participants. The 27 chapters are arranged in 4 main sections: Pathways of Caste Development in Principal Termite Groups (6 chapters), Environment and Caste Composition Regulation (8 chapters), Hormones and Caste Determination (7 chapters), and Caste Differentiation in Other Social Insects (5 chapters). The whole presentation is preceded by a first section, a memorial chapter on Prof. Dr Martin Lüscher (1917–1979), in whose memory both the International Study Workshop and this book are dedicated. In a moving ceremony on the grounds of ICIPE's Duduville International Guest Centre in Nairobi, the venue of the International Study Workshop, Mrs Noemi Lüscher, accompanied by her son (Dr Lüscher Jr.) and his young wife, unveiled the sculpture of her late husband during the Workshop. The late Professor Lüscher was, until his death on 10 August 1979, the Head of the Department of Zoophysiology at the University of Berne, in Switzerland. He was a very close friend of the ICIPE right from its establishment in April 1970. He was among the first group of world renowned scientists who were appointed Visiting Directors of Research at the ICIPE. In his case, he had responsibility for endocrinological work; and, in 1971, he helped in establishing the Grassland Termites Research Programme, in which a great deal of research on termite caste differentiation in higher termites was undertaken. His outstanding leadership and great contribution to termite research at the ICIPE is remembered with fondness and warmth.

This book on *Caste Differentiation in Social Insects* is not a mere compendium of field observations or experimental data. For the first time ever, a panoramic presentation has been made on various facets of caste differentiation in a group of social insects in some depth (termites) as well as a comparative discussion of this question in other social insects (bees, ants and wasps). The complexity of post-embryonic developmental pathways in both higher and lower termites are well covered. Views regarding the evolutionary status of lower termites are discussed, as well as the controversial issues pertaining to question as to whether a "worker caste" exists among the Kalotermitidae, or the question as to whether the "reproductive caste" has an early and rigidly expressed origin in this group as is the case in the higher termites. The environmental influence as an important factor in caste differentiation is explored thoroughly in both lower and higher termites. In a similar vein, control mechanisms for the formation of the reproductives (primary, secondary, or replacement) are elucidated in some detail, pointing out the differences in these mechanisms within the same families or between the latter; these differences sometimes being seemingly contradictory, but none the less pointing to the complexity of the mechanisms involved. The role of pheromones as an environmental messenger for the control of differentiation is clearly evidenced and, in this respect, the new information on soldier control in the higher termites begins to complete the overall picture in this segment of our knowledge. The book does, indeed, represent a major signpost in our search for a comprehensive understanding of the old biological problem of caste differentiation. We commend it to our readers.

Our warmest appreciations go to the three Guest Editors—Dr J. A. L. Watson, of CSIRO, Australia; Dr Moses Okot-Kotber, of the ICIPE, and Professor Ch. Noirot of the Department of Zoology, University of Dijon, France—for their patience and thoroughness in putting together the various presentations into a coherent book, which in our hope will become the standard work on caste differentiation for many years to come. Mrs Serah W. Mwanycky, the Associate Editor for this series of books, undertook painstaking supportive editorial work, and our special gratitude goes to her.

Our sincere thanks go to Miss Dorcas T. Adhiambo and Mrs Esther Opere, who undertook all the secretarial work essential for the preparation of the manuscripts for this book.

Finally, we wish to dedicate this book to Prof. Dr Martin Lüscher, a termite biologist and insect physiologist who contributed so much to international scientific cooperation.

Nairobi 15 July 1983

Thomas R. Odhiambo
Editor-in-Chief
Current Themes in Tropical Science

Contents

Section C. Environment and Caste Composition Regulation 105

Section D. Hormones and Caste Determination 219

Section E. Caste Differentiation in Other Social Insects 329

Section A
In Memoriam

CHAPTER 1

In Memoriam Martin Lüscher (1917–1979): His Contributions to Insect Physiology and Sociobiology

J. DE WILDE*

Department of Entomology, Agricultural University, Wageningen, The Netherlands

CONTENTS

1.1 INTRODUCTION

It is certainly fitting that, on an evening during our symposium, we sit together and commemorate Professor Martin Lüscher, whose untimely death on 9 August 1979, at the age of 62, has been such a shock to his relatives and friends, but no less to the International Community of Insect Physiologists.

He was at the height of his performance, sometimes attending two, three or more International Meetings, Symposia or Congresses, during one summer, releasing a constant flow of publications, and at the same time preparing for a more quiet phase of his life, when more and more of his work would be shifted

* Prof. Dr J. De Wilde suddenly passed away on 5 October 1983.

from the laboratory to his home. He had gradually surrounded himself with a number of collaborators who had grown to the level of independent and internationally renowned scientists.

Had his institute been built out to a size to accommodate several chairs, several professors of animal physiology and behaviour would now have continued the work he had initiated; but as it was, until the last day, he had to be satisfied with a minimum of staff and administrative help.

Nevertheless, it would seem to the outer world that the flow of scientific output by this group could only be performed by a larger personnel and sophisticated housing provisions, so varied was his approach in concept as well as in technology. But Lüscher was far from being an empire builder. His belief was in research rather than administration, and when technology was not available at his institute, he preferred to seek cooperation with specialized laboratories elsewhere. And in his thematical approach he found constant inspiration, as Leuthold (1980) has stated, in the awe and respect at the incomprehensible and beautiful features of the organisms of his study. Those were mainly termites, and later on he extended his interests to honey bees.

1.2 EARLIER WORKS

It would certainly not be due to dwell in my survey on the details of Martin Lüscher's personal life and his development as a biologist, as so much more qualified accounts have been given by Mrs Lüscher (1980) and by Leuthold (1980). I may only state that his Ph.D. in Zoology was guided by Rudolf Geigy in Basel. In his thesis he discussed his experiments on the determination of larval and adult features in the cloth moth, *Tineola bisselliella*. This study of developmental physiology was certainly an excellent way to be introduced into the problems of insect differentiation and development, a field in which Lüscher remained interested for the rest of his life.

It may be remembered that Rudolf Geigy (1931), who had an unconventional approach to the study of insect metamorphosis, had been able to demonstrate that in *Drosophila*, localized irradiation of the cleaving egg, results in either larval or adult defects, depending on the time of treatment. Lüscher (1944) confirmed these data for *Tineola*, and thereby showed that the early programming of larval and adult features is of wider application within the domain of the Holometabola.

As an assistant of Lehmann in Berne, he successively worked on topics of amphibian developmental physiology, and especially regeneration, a subject he continued to study during his stay with Wiggleworth in Cambridge, England, in the years following the end of the Second World War. But this time the experimental animal was *Rhodnius prolixus* (Lüscher, 1948) and its study marked the beginning of a long-lasting scientific relation and friendship with the nestor of Insect P'ıysiology, whose standard treatise, *The Principles of Insect Physiology*, he later translated into German.

1.3 TERMITE BIOLOGY

1.3.1 Communication—the pheromone concept

Following the stay in Cambridge, Lüscher went to Paris where a sojourn at the Laboratoire d'Evolution des Etres Organisés with P. P. Grassé introduced him into the domain of the termites. Grassé and Noirot (1946a, b) had started work on social polymorphism in the colonies of the European termite *Kalotermes flavicollis*, and had developed some interesting hypotheses on the way castes were determined. Lüscher immediately recognized that the numerical regulation of caste individuals required an extensive system of communication and feedback mechanisms and, as optical stimuli were excluded, the probability of chemosensory communication was evident.

This was in contrast with the prevailing conceptions centring around the state of nutrition, or around the so called "group effects" of a hypothetical nature (Grassé, 1949). The most likely mechanism, best supported by experimental evidence, is the effect of token substances released by the differentiated castes, which have been referred to in literature as ectohormones, sociohormones, and, most recently by the more generally-accepted term of pheromones, proposed by Karlson & Lüscher (1959).

Extending the experiment of Light (1944) with *Zootermopsis*, Lüscher could show that in *Kalotermes*, the inhibitory pheromone of the primary sexuals, preventing the formation of replacement reproductives, is released by the anus. He established by further experiments that the larvae pass on the pheromone by oral intake and anal release, in the frame of proctodaeal trophallaxis common in termites (Lüscher, 1955a, b).

The inhibitory effect of reproductives on the development of their own castes finds a parallel in the development of soldiers.

Stimulating tokens are also present. In *Kalotermes*, male sexuals stimulate the transformation of female larvae into replacement reproductives, and this effect can even be obtained by extracts of the heads of functioning males (Lüscher, 1964). Together with Springhetti (1970), Lüscher could demonstrate that in the same species, reproductives activate the formation of soldiers.

The isolation and identification of the various pheromones instrumental in caste regulation of termites is certainly a challenging task for future workers. The regulative effects I discussed were established in the lower termites, but recent observations on the higher termites point to similar mechanisms. With *Macrotermes michaelseni*, in the framework of the termite programme of ICIPE,

Lüscher tried to test the inhibitory effects of the royal pair on nymph formation. But these effects may be somewhat obscured by the huge size of the colonies (Lüscher, 1976).

1.3.2 Caste determination

Caste differentiation depends on specific "trigger" stimuli acting during sensitive periods. Their relation to the determination of patterns is not a direct one. Reprogramming is part of ontogenetic determination, leading to the development of caste features. According to Hadorn (1967) determination is the programming of the developmental potential by activation of specific groups of genes. Juvenile hormone (JH) is at the base of this control in caste polymorphism. Extrinsic control of caste differentiation is mediated therefore, through the environmental impact of JH levels. Much of the above statement is based on work done by Lüscher and his co-workers, and although recent work on social Hymenoptera was necessary to allow for generalization of the mechanism, Lüscher's work on *Kalotermes* has provided the primary impetus (Lüscher, 1974a).

It also gave a physiological explanation for the phenomenon of competence. It had struck the investigators that the larvae or nymphs of *Kalotermes* are not always able to develop, under the proper stimulations, into replacement reproductives, but can only do so during early spring and summer. The volume of their corpora allata (CA) is much reduced during these periods, and Lüscher (1974b) could show that a low CA activity is a requirement for competence. After competence has been obtained and the adult moult is induced, the CA increase in size, which is related to their activity in reproduction.

With soldier formation it is different. Larvae and nymphs can be induced to change into presoldiers by increasing their JH levels. Competence is generally prevailing, and is only suppressed when soldiers are already abundant. After presoldiers are formed, they automatically moult into soldiers, a caste with reduced CA activity.

I only briefly relate Lüscher's experiments with prothoracic glands and their hormone, ecdysone; they did not reveal any specific effect on caste induction, but merely interfered with the time of moulting. They thereby sometimes interfered with the above-mentioned effects of JH, in an indirect manner.

As regards the higher termites, the ICIPE Termite Programme has marked a period rich in new and interesting findings, though sometimes baffling and at the same time puzzling.

I omitted in my former discussion the ingenious techniques developed by Lüscher for rearing termite colonies in captivity in such a way that their functions were open to biological observation and experiment. This was already a feature of his earliest work with *Kalotermes*, but became even more essential in his studies of *Macrotermes*, where huge mounds and stone-hard building elements are prohibitive of any detailed work on caste determination and behaviour.

Bühlman (1977a, b) has been instrumental in solving the essential problems and devising the *in vitro* culture of microcolonies showing all the essential features of the natural colony.

A first and all-important question was, whether caste determination in the higher termites is blastogenic, i.e. already prevailing in the egg stage.

Termite eggs are rich in JH, but their content is varying throughout the seasons. These fluctuations are paralleled by the haemolymph JH titre of the physogastric queen varying more than tenfold in the course of the year. Such queens have multilobed CA, divaricating in the cavities of neck and thorax.

Caste formation in the higher termites is much more rigid than in the lower groups, and regressive moults are absent. In some cases it has been established that the decision to develop into one of the neuter forms (soldier, worker) occurs in the first larval instar.

Lüscher (1976) initiated research to test several hypotheses with respect to the relation between the JH content of the egg and the formation of nymphs in *Macrotermes*. His aim was to decide whether or not, as suggested by some authors, the induction of nymphs would already occur during embryonic development, a process known as blastogenic caste formation. With a great deal of care he started collecting data on JH content of the egg following a seasonal pattern; he passed away from life before this work could be completed.

It has to be understood that in this line of thought, endocrine induction of blastogenic caste formation would be similar to caste determining endocrine induction in a growing larva. This comparison is purely speculative and a complete fixation of a developmental program as is present in holometabolous insects has never been demonstrated in termites. In fact, even in the social Hymenoptera, caste induction takes place in the course of larval life (de Wilde & Beetsma, 1982). In higher termites, deviation from the developmental programme is observed under strenuous conditions such as removal of reproductives (Bordereau, 1975). Also, there are several ways in which a first instar larva can still increase JH content, and already by this fact we may conclude that blastogenic caste determination in termites has not been proven.

Beautiful additions to our knowledge of endocrine caste determination have been given by some of Lüscher's African students. Wanyonyi (1974), whose untimely death has been such a loss, was able to demonstrate that external application of increasing doses of JH and a JH analogue to larvae of *Zootermopsis* subsequently leads to the inhibition of reproductive development, to regressive development, and to presoldiers and worker-like forms. We are now waiting for the determination of JH titres in normal development of these castes. During this Symposium, another African student, Dr Okot-Kotber has presented more evidence on the higher termite, *Macrotermes michaelseni*.

1.3.3 Functions of termite colonies

It has been said that a colony of social insects is in a sense a superorganism. In these creatures, the physiological functions of the individual are paralleled by social functions. During his stay in Ivory Coast, on one of the foreign visits he made before settling in Berne, Lüscher became acquainted with the elaborate nest structures built by *Macrotermes natalensis*. In the chimneys and inner channels of the termite mound he recognized a system of ventilation with regulation of oxygen tension, temperature and humidity, functioning through the temperature gradient at the outline of the nest (Lüscher, 1955a, b). But the Termite Programme he developed with Sands at ICIPE provided further opportunities, and foraging and nest building were two of the fields in which outstanding progress was made.

Grassland termites were found to compete with cattle or wild herbivores, and food intake by a full-sized colony of *Macrotermes michaelseni* was found to be equivalent to that of a large antelope. Leuthold and his students found that harvester termites orientate their way home by means of their optical sense (Leuthold *et al.*, 1976).

Building behaviour was studied under Lüscher's guidance by Bruinsma, and very remarkable facts were found, especially in the construction of pillars and queen cells. This work suggests that the fatbody of a termite queen is in fact functioning as a pheromone gland, the building pheromone being released through the abdominal stigmata. A gradient is thereby created at which the building termites measure the distance at which the cell wall has to be constructed, with respect to the body of the queen (Bruinsma & Leuthold, 1977).

I could go on entertaining you with the remarkable outcome of their observations, made possible by Bühlmann's microcolony rearing method mentioned before.

1.3.4 The ICIPE programme on grassland termites

It was in the beginning of 1972 that some members of the ICIPE Board were meeting in Oxford with John Pringle to evaluate research proposals, and among them a rather elaborate one by Martin Lüscher, to be supported by the Swiss National Science Foundation Fund to study communication and caste development in grassland termites. It was clear right from the first moment that the new Director of Research had rather strict financial and other requirements, and we were worried whether he was planning to go his own way or was prepared to integrate his work in the kind of scientific developmental aid which we had in mind when founding ICIPE.

It has been our lucky fate that we decided to go along with Lüscher. Though strictly adhering to his principles of responsibility in guiding the research, he has been collaborating with the Board in an excellent way, and has managed to extend the termite work both in the physiological and the ecological sphere. Sharing the directorship of research with a termite ecologist such as Sands and assisted by a behaviour specialist such as Leuthold, he was able to attract very competent people and at the same time to do a considerable job in training young African biologists in the painstaking research he had developed. This group has been one of the best organized at ICIPE, and his critical attitude has resulted in a very high quality of work. For example, Darlington's and Lapage's contributions towards the understanding of termite populations and their foraging activity in a semi-arid ecosystem (Kajiado, Kenya) have been enormous and unparalleled in this region. Oloo, another young African scientist contributed much towards the understanding of mechanisms of foraging behaviour of grass-feeders, *Trinervitermes* etc.

Lüscher annually spent several months at ICIPE, and among his efforts is a film on colony life in *Macrotermes* which has become famous. Due acknowledgement should be made to Mrs Lüscher who has assisted her husband during these stages and shared his work in every respect. When in 1970 Lüscher ended his role as a Director of Research, his task was taken over by Noirot.

During the 7 years, Lüscher has given very dedicated guidance and has obtained very considerable support from outside, to the benefit of ICIPE. It is therefore due that a statue has been erected here to commemorate his great merits to this Institute.

1.4 ENDOCRINE REGULATION IN BLATTIDAE

Termites are uniquely unsuitable for the study of the endocrine regulation of body functions. In isolation they survive for only a short time, and when released in a colony after having been operated on, they are invariably eaten by the other members. Even to fix a termite in a colony for the purpose of individual observation, leads to a considerable mortality. Therefore, Lüscher chose to study endocrine processes in the related group, the Blattidae. For several reasons, this group can be considered to be taxonomically very close to termites. Their individual development, their symbiont-dependent digestive functions, their nocturnal habits with corresponding tegumental features are all in line with this concept. *Nauphoeta cinerea* and *Leucophaea maderae* became the species of his study. First in association with Lüscher and Engelmann (1955), later on with Wyss-Huber and Lüscher (1972) and finally with Lüscher and Lanzrein (1976), he embarked on a series of studies which mainly concerned the regulation of CA function and the endocrine control of metabolism, vitellogenesis, and the differential effect of JH in ontogenesis and reproduction.

The fact that three and later even more JH were found to exist, and their presence at various rates in different developmental stages, led Lüscher to investigate whether these hormones had a differential effect on larval development and adult reproduction with some initially positive results, which are now questionable in the light of more recent experience. But very interesting was Lüscher's finding (Lüscher *et al.*, 1971) that the fatbody of the cockroach after allatectomy starts to synthesize a protein not found under normal conditions. In my laboratory, similar results had been obtained by De Loof in the Colorado beetle, and the term "short-day proteins" had been applied to denote this category.

In this research, Lüscher profoundly proved to be an insect physiologist. Here he could bring his endocrine work in level with the international progress, and participate in the study of problems belonging to the frontiers of our science. It was especially Lanzrein among his students who gradually carried this line on her own and is now setting forth the rich tradition. Inevitably, the factors regulating the JH titre came under study, and an overall picture was drawn of morphometrical and physiological parameters of the endocrine regulation of oocyte maturation (Lanzrein *et al.*, 1978; Lanzrein *et al.*, 1981). Also, the ecdysteroids and JH present in the egg, and their role in embryogenesis were given due attention (Imboden *et al.*, 1978).

1.5   HONEY BEE WORKER FUNCTIONS—THEIR ENDOCRINE CONTROL

Through his relations with the Swiss Bee Research Station at Liebefeld-Berne, Lüscher became acquainted with social functions in honey bees analogous to those he had studied in termites. Gradually, the termite work more and more enriched the bee research, and this has led to very interesting discoveries. As worker bees are morphologically identical, but show a successive shift in behavioural functions, the term polyethism was introduced, and the physiological states concerned were subjected to endocrine studies. Publication of this work started in 1974.

It so happened that in my department in Wageningen, Wirtz (1973) had shown in his thesis that caste differentiation in the honey bee was based on the haemolymph titre of JH, the sensitive period being at the end of the third day of larval life. Low JH titres result in the development of worker bees, high titres in queen development.

After Lüscher's findings in termites, this was the second case in which JH was shown to be involved in caste differentiation. But this time the situation was more complicated. After the sensitive period has elapsed, several larval moults take place, and only at the subsequent pupal and adult moult, there are time lapses and caste features showing the fulfilment of the programme. Normally, for the pupal and adult moult to take place, a low JH titre is required. It thus appears that in the honey bees, JH induces programmes comprising various activities of the CA.

During adult life, in the honey bee, as said above, a series of functions is performed, from cell cleaning to foraging. With some variability, this program is carried out in every worker bee and it is this form of age-polyethism that Lüscher with research workers from Liebefeld-Bern such as Rutz, Gerig and Wille, started out to investigate endocrinologically. They thereby found that a high JH titre is responsible for the transition from "hive bee" to "field bee" and suppresses the activity of glands characteristic for hive bees, such as the hypopharyngeal glands and the wax glands (Rutz *et al.*, 1977).

Interesting enough, in the Wageningen laboratory the matter was approached from a different direction, but with the same outcome. After discovering the JH-induced queen differentiation, we realized that here a real danger was presented by the juvenoid insecticides we helped to develop for many years. We therefore fed whole colonies with diets containing JH analogues and found that some analogues would not do any harm, but others disorganized the colony, the worker bees ceasing to feed the larvae. This brought us to making independently the same discovery as reported by the Swiss group, providing a beautiful confirmation of this very important effect (Beetsma & ten Houten, 1975).

In subsequent work, the Swiss group found that winter bees, which are in a diapause-like condition, are characterized by a very low JH titre in the hemolymph (Fluri *et al.*, 1977). Further work was on queen pheromones (Lüscher & Walker, 1963), vitellogenic protein synthesis and its dependence on JH, and some nutritive aspects.

1.6   AN EVALUATION OF LÜSCHER'S CONTRIBUTIONS TO INSECT PHYSIOLOGY, ESPECIALLY REGARDING SOCIAL INSECTS

When I try to survey the panorama of Lüscher's work and Lüscher's impact on the work of others, my feelings are of respect, understanding and sympathy. I may freely say so, since my own approach to insect physiology has grown from the same sources and in many cases had led to results similar to his own. In the foregoing account the audience has found some examples.

I may therefore state that Lüscher was a typical organismal physiologist, who drew his inspiration from the insect as a whole, and, in his case, from the insect as a member of a society. He had the strength of mind to fix the goals of his research, and to continue his approach for a lifetime.

He thereby has enlightened our picture of communication and caste formation in the considerable complexity of colonies even of the lower termites, and when he passed away, he had already a strong foothold in the higher termites.

If he had lived, promises were that he would have succeeded in unravelling the considerably complicated relations in this group a good deal further.

Lüscher and his group deepened their endocrinological knowledge by the study of Blattidae and subsequently broadened our knowledge on endocrine regulations in termites and their dependence on stimuli inside and outside the colony. In doing so, their contribution to environmental endocrinology has been considerable.

Despite of a great deal of continuity, Lüscher's approach had much flexibility, and this was especially shown in the way he built out and helped to conduct the termite programme of ICIPE. His attitude was not at all alien to the ecologist and the taxonomist, with whom he shared on the one hand the great inspiration provided by working in an ecosystem and on the other a considerable precision in his performance.

Lüscher has pursued the role of hormones in termite polymorphism and the role of pheromones, of which he was a nominator, in termite communication. He subsequently closed the bridge by showing that pheromones have their impact on termite differentiation via their effect on the endocrine system. In doing so, Lüscher stretched the impact of hormones to the utmost. He showed the vapour tension of JH to have important effects and he tried to study the hypothesis that JH, next to being a hormone, is also a pheromone. It is characteristic of his approach that he also studied unlikely possibilities and unattractive hypothesis, which gave his work a great deal of objectivity and candour. And when the outcome was negative, he drew his conclusions.

In my account, I have purposely concentrated on Lüscher's share in the modern development of termite biology, and have not named the many important contributions of workers from different nations, without whose impact his work would have been less fruitful or perhaps non-existing. But to-day I want to put Martin Lüscher in the limelight.

If our handbooks nowadays contain less vague conceptions, less unproven theoretical mechanism, and less incomprehensible relations in the field of termite biology and physiology, this is for a considerable part due to the virtue of Martin Lüscher.

1.7 SUMMARY

An account is given of the scientific work of Martin Lüscher and its importance to insect physiology and sociobiology. Mention is made of his contributions to our knowledge of polymorphism and polyethism in termites and in the honey bee and his work on communication within the termite colony and its importance to the regulation of caste development.

Stress is laid on the significance of the Grassland Termite Programme of ICIPE founded and guided by Lüscher, and its impact on our knowledge of foraging, nutrition, building activity and the regulation of caste development in the higher termites.

The research of Lüscher and his co-workers on the endocrine regulation of growth and reproduction in the Blattidae is reviewed and its importance for our understanding of similar processes in termites is stressed.

1.8 REFERENCES

Beetsma J. & ten Houten A. (1975) Effects of juvenile hormone analogues in the food of honeybee colonies (*Apis mellifera L.*). *Z. angew. Ent.* **77,** 292–300.

Bordereau C. (1975) Determinisme des castes chez le termites supérieurs: mise en évidence d'un controle royal dans la formation de la caste sexuee chez *Macrotermes bellicosus* Smeathman (Isoptera, Termitidae). *Insectes Sociaux* **22,** 363–374.

Bruinsman O. & Leuthold R. H. (1977) Information involved in the building behaviour of *Macrotermes subhyalinus* (Rambur). Proc. 8th Int. Congr. IUSSI, Wageningen, pp. 257–258.

Bühlmann G. (1977a) The study of caste differentiation in the higher termites. In: *Advances in Medical, Veterinary and Agricultural Entomology in Eastern Africa* (C. P. F. de Lima, ed.) pp. 107–110. Nairobi, Kenya.

Bühlmann G. (1977b) The development of the incipient colony and egg adaptation experiments in the termite *Macrotermes subhyalinus*. Proc. 8th Int. Congr. IUSSI, Wageningen, pp. 259–261.

De Wilde J. & Beetsma J. (1982) The physiology of caste development in social insects. *Adv. Insect Physiol.* **16,** 167–246.

Fluri P., Wille H., Gerig L. & Lüscher M. (1977) Juvenile hormone and the determination of winter bee physiology. (*Apis mellifera*). Proc. 8th Int. Congr. IUSSI, Wageningen, pp. 28–29.

Geigy R. (1931) Erzeugung rein imaginaler Defekte durch ultraviolette Eibestrahlung bei *Drosophila melanogaster. Roux Arch. Entw. Mech. Organ.* **125,** 406–447.

Grassé P. P. (1949) Ordre des Isoptères ou termites. In: *Traite de Zoologie* (P. P. Grassé, ed.), Vol. 9, pp. 408–544. Masson, Paris.

Grassé P. P. & Noirot Ch. (1946a) La production des sexués neoténiques chez le termite á cou jaune (*Calotermes flavicollis*). *Inhibition germinale et inhibition somatique. C.R. Acad. Sci. Paris* **223,** 869–871.

Grassé P. P. & Noirot Ch. (1946b) Le polymorphisme social du termite a cou jaune (*Calotermes flavicollis F.*). *La production des soldats. C.R. Acad. Sc. Paris* **223,** 929–931.

Hadorn, E. (1967) Dynamics of determination. In: *Major Problems in Developmental Biology* (M. Locke, ed.), pp. 85–104. Academic Press, New York.

Imboden H., Lanzrein B., Delbecque J. P. & Lüscher M. (1978) Ecdysteroids and juvenile hormone during embryogenesis in the ovoviviparous cockroach *Nauphaeta cinerea. Gen. Comp. Endocrinol.* **36,** 628–635.

Karlson P. & Lüscher M. (1959) Pheromone. Ein Nomenklaturvorschlag fur eine Wirkstoffklasse. *Naturwiss.* **46,** 63–64.

Lanzrein B., Lüscher M., Gentinetta V. & Fehr. R. (1978) Correlation between haemolymph juvenile hormone titer, corpus allatum volume and corpus allatum *in vivo* and *in vitro* activity during oocyte maturation in a cockroach (*Nauphaeta cinerea*). *Gen. Comp. Endocrinol.* **36,** 339–345.

Lanzrein B., Wilhelm R. & Buscho J. (1981) On the regulation of the corpora allata activity in adult females of the ovoviviparous cockroach *Nauphaeta cinerea*. *Juvenile Hormone Biochemistry,* pp. 147–160. Elsevier, North Holland.

Leuthold R. (1980) Martin Lüscher. *Nature* **284,** 197–198.

Leuthold R. H., Bruinsma O. & van Huis A. (1976) Optical and pheromonal orientation and memory for homing distance in the harvester termite *Hodotermes mossambicus* (Hagen). *Behav. Ecol. Sociobiol.* **1,** 127–139.

Light S. F. (1944) Experimental studies on ectohormonal control of the development of supplementary reproductives in the termite genus *Zootermopsis*. University of California *Publ. Zool.* **43,** 418–1347.

Lüscher M. (1944) Experimentelle Untersuchungen ueber die larvale and imaginale Determination im Ei der Kleidermotte (*Tineola biselliella* Hum.). *Rev. Suisse Zool.* **51,** 531–627.

Lüscher M. (1948) The regeneration of legs in *Rhodnius prolixus* (Hemiptera). *J. Exp. Biol.* **25,** 334–343.

Lüscher M. (1955a) Zur Frage der Uebertragung sozialer Wirkstoffe bei Termiten. *Naturwissenschaften* **42,** 186.

Lüscher M. (1955b) Der Sauerstoffverbrauch bei Termiten und die Ventilation des Nestes bei *Macrotermes natalensis* (Haviland). *Acta Tropica* **12,** 289–307.

Lüscher M. (1964) Die spezifische Wirkung männlicher und weiblicher Ersatzgeschlechtstieren bei der Termite *Calotermes flavicollis* (Fabr.). *Insectes Sociaux* **11,** 79–90.

Lüscher M. (1974a) Kasten und Kastendifferenzierung bei niederen Termiten. In: *Sozialpolymorphismus bei Insekten* (G. H. Schmidt, ed.), pp. 695–739. Wiss. Verl. Ges., Stuttgart.

Lüscher M. (1976) Evidence for an endocrine control of caste determination in higher termites. Symp. Phase and Caste Determination in Insects, pp. 91–104. Pergamon Press, Oxford and New York.

Lüscher M. and Engelmann F. (1955) Ueber die Steuerung der corpora allata Funktion bei der Schabe *Leucophaea maderae*. *Rev. Suisse Zool.* **62,** 649–657.

Lüscher M. and Lanzrein B. (1976) Differential effects of the three Juvenile Hormones (JH I, II, III) in the cockroach *Nauphaeta cinerea*. Actualites sur les hormones d'invertebres, pp. 435–440. Coll. Int. CNRS no. 251.

Lüscher M. and Walker I. (1963) Zur Frage der Wirkungsweise der Königinnenpheromone bei der Honigbiene. *Rev. Suisse Zool.* **70,** 304–311.

Lüscher M., Buhlmann G. and Wyss-Huber M. (1971) Juvenile hormone and protein synthesis in adult female cockroaches. *Mitt. Schweiz. Ent. Ges.* **44,** 197–206.

Lüscher-Stoecklin N. (1980) Lebenslauf in: Martin Lüscher, Professor der Zoologie an der Universität Bern, 1917–1979. Memorial Edition, Bern.

Rutz W., Imboden E. R., Jaycox H., Wille H., Gerig L. & Lüscher M. (1977) Juvenile hormone and polyethism in adult worker honeybees (*Apis mellifera*). Proc. 8th Int. Congr. IUSSI, Wageningen, pp. 26–27.

Springhetti A. (1970) Influence of the king and queen on the differentiation of soldiers in *Calotermes flavicollis* (Fabr.) (Isoptera). *Monit. Zool. Ital. N.S.I.* **4,** 99–105.

Wanyonyi K. (1974) The influence of the juvenile hormone analogue ZR 512 (Zoecon) on caste development in *Zootermopsis nevadensis* (Hagen) (Isoptera). *Insectes Sociaux* **21,** 35–44.

Wirtz P. (1973) Differentiation in the honey bee larva. Meded. Landb. Hogesch. Wageningen, pp. 73–75, 155 pp.

Wyss-Huber M. and Lüscher M. (1972) *In vitro* synthesis and release of proteins by fat body and ovarian tissue of *Leucophaea maderae* during the sexual cycle. *J. Ins. Physiol.* **18,** 689–710.

Section B

Pathways of Caste Development in Principal Termite Groups

CHAPTER 2

Genetic Relations Among Castes in Lower Termites

PETER LUYKX

Department of Biology, University of Miami, Coral Gables, Florida 33124, U.S.A.

CONTENTS

2.1 INTRODUCTION

The non-reproductive castes of social insects provide our best example of altruism at the level of the individual, for these castes, often highly modified in form and behaviour, are also often completely sterile. The specialized genes that are expressed in these specialized individuals therefore cannot be passed on to their offspring, for they have no offspring. Such genes are nevertheless present in all colonies, and undoubtedly in all members of all colonies. When such genes are expressed, they cannot be transmitted to the next generation; in order to be transmitted, they cannot be expressed. How do such genes ever come to be a fixed part of the evolutionary heritage of a species, when the individuals whose fitness is presumably increased by their presence—as would be measured by an increased reproductive output—never express them?—when their expression automatically means decreased fitness—sterility—of the individual that expresses them?

Charles Darwin (1896) provided an answer with an analogy: "Breeders of cattle wish the flesh and fat to be well marbled together: an animal thus characterized has been slaughtered, but the breeder has gone with confidence to the same stock and has succeeded"; and, more directly, ". . . slight modifications of structure or of instinct, correlated with the sterile condition of

17

certain members of the community, have proved advantageous: consequently the fertile males and females have flourished, and transmitted to their fertile offspring a tendency to produce sterile members with the same modification".

For the Hymenoptera, with their haplodiploid mechanism of sex-determination, a more precisely formulated answer to this general question was provided by Hamilton (1964). He pointed out, first, that the fitness of an individual can be more properly defined to include not only his own lifetime reproductive output, but also that of his relatives—so that a gene that he possesses even if he is sterile can be effectively transmitted if his close relatives (parents, siblings, etc., who also share some of his genes) have enough offspring at least to compensate for his sterility. The conditions necessary for a sterile altruist's gene to increase in a population are given by Hamilton's well-known formula $b/c > 1/r$, i.e., the ratio of benefit (to the relative) to cost (to the altruist) must be greater than the reciprocal of the degree of relatedness. Secondly, with the hymenopteran haplodiploid mechanism of sex-determination, where females—sisters—arising from fertilized diploid eggs make up the vast majority of the individuals in a colony, the genetic relatedness of the individuals in the colony to each other is greater than that of any female to her own offspring. This is because all sisters share the same full set of genes they received from their haploid father, as well as half the genes, on average, that they received from their mother. With this pattern of inheritance, a female might forego having her own offspring, with whom she shares only half her genes, for the sake of behaving in such a way as to have more sisters, with whom she shares three-quarters of her genes.

2.2   GENETIC RELATIONS

Until recently the mechanism of sex-determination in termites was totally unknown (White, 1976). It was recognized that males as well as females are diploid, however, and so the reasoning developed for the Hymenoptera, based on male haploidy–female diploidy, did not seem likely to apply to the termites. There are nevertheless other circumstances in which higher relatedness between siblings than between parent and offspring may occur. Under special conditions of inbreeding, where the king and queen are themselves inbred but unrelated, their offspring may be highly heterozygous and more closely related to each other than to their parents (Hamilton, 1972; Bartz, 1979). But these ideas were based on uncertain assumptions about population structure and levels of inbreeding in termites, and the genetic basis for the evolution of eusociality in termites remained problematical.

It was therefore exciting to find (Syren & Luykx, 1977) that many of the lower termites do in fact have a highly unusual sex-chromosome system, one that would give higher degrees of relatedness between same-sex siblings than between parents and offspring, even in the absence of inbreeding (Luykx & Syren, 1979; Lacy, 1980). For example, in *Incisitermes schwarzi* (Kalotermitidae) around Miami, Florida, both males and females have a diploid number of 32, with half the chromosomes behaving like sex-chromosomes in their mode of transmission to offspring: 8 Xs and 8 Ys in males, and 16 Xs in females. Half the genetic material is therefore sex-linked. Recent studies indicate that the Y chromosomes carry active genes homologous to those in the X chromosomes (Luykx, 1981), and therefore, apart from infrequent crossing-over between Xs and Ys, a king transmits to all of his sons the same set of Y-linked genes, and to all of his daughters the same set of X-linked genes. The result is that male and female members of a colony are expected to be more closely related to siblings of the same sex than to their own offspring, as far as sex-linked genes are concerned. Under these conditions, sex-linked altruistic genes would be favoured if they directed the behaviour of the individual bearing them so as to result in the production of more siblings of the same sex. For the case in which half of the genes are sex-linked, the pattern of transmission of genes from the royal pair to their offspring gives the genetic relations shown in Fig. 2.1. Even if the effect is not as strong with multiple sex chromosomes as it is with haplodiploidy, the analogy with the Hymenoptera is striking: individuals in the colony are more closely related to their same-sex siblings than they would be to their own offspring.

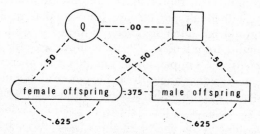

Fig. 2.1. Genetic relations within a colony where half the genes are sex-linked.

It has been objected that while this may be true for siblings of the same sex, it is not true for the termite colony as a whole. With an equal number of males and females, the high degree of relatedness among same-sex siblings is exactly balanced by a low degree of relatedness among opposite-sex siblings; the average relatedness is then 0.5, not any higher than that between parents and offspring. But as the observations described below demonstrate, sex-ratios in termite colonies are variable, and the relatedness among siblings of the predominant sex might outweigh the others. It is also conceivable, although the idea may seem far-fetched, that colonies are internally organized in such a way that the behaviour of soldiers of a particular sex benefits primarily workers of the same sex—for example, the sexes of all castes in a colony might be spatially segregated.

To explore further the genetic implications of multiple sex chromosomes, and to evaluate their possible role in the evolution of altruism in termites, a cytogenetic survey of several species of lower termites was undertaken, along with a more intensive study of the sex-ratio, population biology, and genetics of *I. schwarzi*.

The cytogenetic survey of kalotermitids in Florida showed that four species carry multiple sex-chromosomes while five other species apparently do not (Luykx & Syren, 1979). Furthermore, in the two species studied most extensively (*I. schwarzi* and *Kalotermes approximatus*), the number of chromosomes tied up in sex-linkage varies considerably (Syren & Luykx, 1981; Luykx & Syren, 1981). Surveys of higher termites by Vincke and Tilquin (1978) revealed that in that group there are typically four sex-chromosomes in a diploid number of 42. In contrast to the Hymenoptera, the unusual sex-determining system in Isoptera is not universal, and is even variable within species. These observations weaken the case for the importance of multiple sex-chromosomes in the evolution of isopteran eusociality, although it could be argued that many species have only secondarily lost the multiple sex-chromosome system.

A census of 51 complete colonies of *I. schwarzi* collected in the Miami area, ranging in size from two (the reproductive pair only) to over 1000 individuals (mean size = 250 individuals per colony), showed that in 37 colonies the male–female ratio did not differ significantly from 1.0, while in 14 colonies (27%) it did, ranging from 0.66 to 5.29. The mean sex-ratio for all colonies together was 1.24. In this sample, soldiers made up an average of 6.9% of a colony, with the small soldiers about three times more abundant than the large soldiers. The sex-ratio in both soldier castes is significantly weighted in favour of the males: for all 51 colonies the male–female ratios are $383/243 = 1.58$ for the small soldiers, and $116/83 = 1.40$ for the large soldiers. Both members of the royal pair were recovered in 41 of the colonies; in 31 of these, the king and queen were the primary reproductives, distinguishable from secondary (replacement) reproductives by their darker coloration and by the presence of wing-scars. In six of the remaining 10, both primaries had been replaced by secondaries, and in four the royal pair consisted of one primary and one secondary reproductive. Thus in 10 out of 41 (= 24%) of the colonies of *I. schwarzi* collected from nature, the king and queen are closely related—brother–sister, mother–son, and father–daughter—and would be expected to produce highly inbred offspring. In the other colonies, those headed by the primary reproductives, the degree of relatedness of the king and queen cannot be ascertained directly.

Colonies with alates can be found at almost any time of year; swarming may therefore be asynchronous, with no definite swarming season. This observation, along with the belief that alates are generally weak fliers and do not disperse long distances from the parent colony, might suggest that an alate's potential mates are usually other alates from the same colony—that is, siblings. However, the genetic data on *I. schwarzi* obtained so far do not lend much support to this idea. Preliminary data on an autosomal locus, *Pep-1*, in the termites that comprise the primary reproductives heading the colonies in the Oleta River Mangrove Preserve, an area of about 4 km^2 just north of Miami, indicate that the genotypes of these kings and queens are very close to what one would expect for a random mating population (Table 2.1). The low level of inbreeding calculated (F = 0.04) could be accounted for by the observed frequency of replacement reproductives in the natural population of kings and queens, and one might reasonably conclude that the *primary* reproductives are not significantly inbred at all. Unfortunately, the sample size is small, and one can say with 95% confidence only that something less than 60% of the royal pairs in the population are likely to be siblings (Spiess, 1977). More data will have to be collected to make the estimate of the amount of inbreeding in primary reproductives more precise.

TABLE 2.1. PEP-1 GENOTYPES OF PRIMARY REPRODUCTIVES IN *INCISITERMES SCHWARZI*, AS DETERMINED BY ELECTROPHORESIS OF THE KING AND QUEEN AND/OR THEIR OFFSPRING

	Genotypes		
	ss	sf	ff
Observed number	17	15	4
Number expected with random mating	16.7	15.6	3.7

Inbreeding coefficient F = 0.04 (standard error = 0.17).
s, slow allele; f, fast allele

The changes that occur in a colony when a primary reproductive is lost and replaced by one of its own offspring are well illustrated by colony PL69, which happened to have a combination of alleles favourable for reconstructing its history. When it was collected from the field and opened, the colony was found to have a primary male reproductive and a secondary (replacement) female reproductive. The results of analysis of the colony for EST-3 pheno-types (determined by a sex-linked gene—see Luykx, 1981) are given in Table 2.2. Workers, nymphs and alates comprised a different genetic population from the soldiers. The soldiers (about half of whom possessed a fast *Est-3* allele) could not in fact have been the offspring of the secondary queen present, but must have been the offspring of a heterozygous primary queen. The pedigree of this colony, as inferred from the distribution of EST-3

TABLE 2.2. EST-3 PHENOTYPES AND INFERRED GENOTYPES OF
INCISITERMES SCHWARZI COLONY PL69. SEE TEXT AND FIG. 2.2 FOR
EXPLANATION

	Slow	Heterozygous	Fast	Genotypes
Females				
Secondary queen	1	—	—	X^sX^s
Workers, nymphs, alates	27	3	1	Mostly X^sX^s
Soldiers	5	7	—	X^sX^s, X^sX^f
Males				
Primary king	—	*	—	(X^sY^f)*
Workers, nymphs, alates	—	20	1	Mostly X^sY^f
Soldiers	—	11	9	X^sY^f, X^fY^f

*The king was not analysed, but from the phenotypes of his offspring, he must have been an X^sY^f
heterozygote.

phenotypes, is shown in Fig. 2.2. Evidently the soldiers present were the
offspring of the original founders of the colony, the primary king and queen;
later the primary queen died and her place was taken by one of her daughters.
The workers, nymphs and alates—originally the offspring of the primary
royal pair, developmental stages that culminate in a swarming flight from the
colony—were then replaced over a period of several swarming seasons by the
offspring of the king and his daughter. After the turnover was complete, the
old soldiers were now left in the colony, not with their brothers and sisters, but
with their sister's offspring by their father (Fig. 2.2)!

Altered genetic relations between soldiers and other members of the colony,
for whom the soldiers are presumably giving up their own reproductive
output, would be expected to occur whenever a primary reproductive is
replaced by a secondary reproductive. Table 2.3 summarizes the genetic

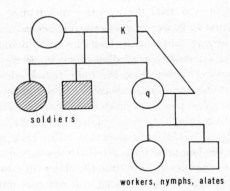

FIG. 2.2. Pedigree of *Incisitermes schwarzi* colony PL69, inferred from the data in Table 2.4.

TABLE 2.3. GENETIC RELATEDNESS OF SOLDIERS TO WORKERS IN
INCISITERMES SCHWARZI COLONIES HEADED BY DIFFERENT KINDS
OF REPRODUCTIVES, AS CALCULATED FROM OBSERVED PATTERNS
OF SEX-CHROMOSOMES, REPRODUCTIVE REPLACEMENT, AND
CASTE TURNOVER

Frequency	Royal pair	Calculated average genetic relatedness of soldiers and workers				
		ms:mw	*ms:fw*	*fs:mw*	*fs:fw*	*mean s:w**
75%	K, Q	0.625	0.375	0.375	0.625	0.501
5%	K, q	0.531	0.281	0.406	0.531	0.457
5%	*k*, Q	0.594	0.406	0.344	0.406	0.448
15%	k, q	0.531	0.406	0.375	0.500	0.455

*Assuming a sex-ratio of 1.24, the average value observed for all the non-reproductive castes together.

(m, male; f, female; s, soldier; w, worker; K, Q, primary reproductives; k, q, replacement reproductives)

relations expected between male and female soldiers and workers, for all the kinds of royal pairs that have been found in nature. The calculations follow the general approach of Michod and Anderson (1979), and are based on the particular findings in *I. schwarzi*, where half the genome is sex-linked, and where workers turn over in the colony much more rapidly than the soldiers. As the table illustrates, the genetic relations of workers and soldiers are affected by the sex of the individuals concerned, and by the kind of replacement and the kind of inbreeding that results. With changing reproductives, only the male soldier–male worker relatedness remains consistently higher than 0.5 (the parent–offspring relatedness). The reason for this is that the Y-chromosomes are passed, as a group, unchanged, from male parents to all male offspring, and thus are shared by all males—while X-chromosomes and autosomes are distributed to both sexes, and are subject to independent assortment at meiosis.

It is interesting to note that the average male:female sex-ratio is in fact significantly weighted in favour of males in this species: 1.53 for soldiers, and 1.22 for workers, nymphs and alates. The average relatedness of soldiers and workers within a typical colony, regardless of sex, is therefore affected more by the relatedness among males than by male–female or by female–female relatedness. Even so, the mean relatedness of soldiers and workers in a typical colony is greater than 0.5 only for colonies where the royal pair consists of the primary reproductives, and then only slightly (Table 2.3, last column).

It would seem that the shifting patterns of relatedness that occur between soldiers and workers when primary reproductives are replaced, would provide at best an unstable base for the evolution of soldier altruism by kin-selection. Most colonies of *I. schwarzi* in nature, however, are headed by primary reproductives, and the early evolution of sterile soldiers may have taken place in this kind of colony. The genetic relations between soldiers and workers may still be important in determining their interactive behaviour (e.g., see Greenberg, 1979); a good way to test this idea would be to look for altered behaviour patterns in colonies with replacement reproductives.

2.3 SUMMARY

Genetic relatedness among members of colonies of lower termites is influenced by the presence of multiple sex chromosomes, the sex of the individuals, the sex-ratio of the colony as a whole, the existence of replacement reproductives, and by the general level of inbreeding in the population. Studies on *I. schwarzi* show that about half the diploid set of 32 chromosomes behave like sex chromosomes, that the mean male–female sex ratio in natural populations is 1.24, and that the relatively low levels of inbreeding observed in natural populations can be accounted for by the presence of replacement reproductives in about 25% of the colonies. In such colonies, workers continue to mature into alates (potentially reproductive) and are replaced relatively rapidly by new offspring, while old soldiers, the offspring of the original royal pair, remain. Under these conditions the average relatedness of sterile soldiers and potentially reproductive workers is less than 0.5. Evolution of altruistic behaviour would not generally be favoured under such conditions, although since significantly more males than females become soldiers, and relatedness between male soldiers and male workers is higher than 0.5 in all kinds of colony, and because it is possible that interactions between colony members of the same sex are more frequent or more significant than between individuals of the opposite sex, the evolution of soldier altruism by kin-selection in termites remains a theoretical possibility.

2.4 ACKNOWLEDGEMENT

The work reported in this paper was supported by the National Science Foundation, grant no. DEB 79-02042.

2.5 REFERENCES

Bartz S. H. (1979) Evolution of eusociality in termites. *Proc. natl. Acad. Sci. USA* **76,** 5764–5768.
Darwin C. (1896) *The Origin of Species by Means of Natural Selection* 6th ed., Vol. I, pp. 358–359. D. Appleton and Co., New York.
Greenberg L. (1979) Genetic component of bee odor in kin recognition. *Science* **206,** 1095–1097.

Hamilton W. D. (1964) The genetical evolution of social behaviour, I, and II. *J. theor. Biol.* **7**, 1–52.

Hamilton W. D. (1972) Altruism and related phenomena, mainly in social insects. *Ann. Rev. Ecol. Syst.* **3**, 193–232.

Lacy R. C. (1980) The evolution of eusociality in termites: a haplo-diploid analogy? *Amer. Naturalist* **116**, 449–451.

Luykx P. (1981) A sex-linked esterase locus and translocation heterozygosity in a termite. *Heredity* **46**, 315–320.

Luykx P. and Syren R. M. (1979) The cytogenetics of *Incisitermes schwarzi* and other Florida termites. *Sociobiology* **4**, 191–209.

Luykx P. & Syren R. M. (1981) Multiple sex-linked reciprocal translocations in a termite from Jamaica. *Experientia* **37**, 819–820.

Michod R. E. & Anderson W. W. (1979) Measures of genetic relationship and the concept of inclusive fitness. *Amer. Naturalist* **114**, 637–647.

Spiess E. B. (1977) *Genes in Populations*, pp. 267–268. John Wiley & Sons, New York.

Syren R. M. & Luykx P. (1977) Permanent segmental interchange complex in the termite *Incisitermes schwarzi*. *Nature* **266**, 167–168.

Syren R. M. & Luykx P. (1981) Geographic variation of sex-linked translocation heterozygosity in the termite *Kalotermes approximatus* Snyder (Insecta: Isoptera). *Chromosoma* **82**, 65–88.

Vincke P. P. & Tilquin J. P. (1978) A sex-linked ring quadrivalent in Termitidae (Isoptera). *Chromosoma* **67**, 151–156.

White M. J. D. (1976) Blattodea, Mantodea, Isoptera, Grylloblattodea, Phasmatodea, Dermaptera and Embioptera. *Animal Cytogenetics*, Vol. 3, Insecta 2, Gebrüder Borntraeger, pp. 32–33. Berlin, Stuttgart.

CHAPTER 3

Caste Development in Mastotermes and Kalotermes:

Which is Primitive?

J. A. L. WATSON[1] and J. J. SEWELL[2]

[1] CSIRO, Division of Entomology, Canberra, Australia
[2] Education Department of Victoria, Melbourne, Australia

CONTENTS

3.1 INTRODUCTION

The philosophies advanced in this paper have emerged progressively during the last decade, as we have investigated caste development in a range of

Australian termites (and in *Hodotermes*), and have considered the ways in which division of labour, particularly among workers, is achieved in termites. We have come to believe that there is a basic uniformity in termite caste systems, and have gained a feeling for their flexibility, not their rigidity, and for the adaptive value of that flexibility. It is inevitable that much of what we have to say, and the background to it, has already appeared (Watson, 1971, 1973, 1974; McMahan & Watson, 1975; Cambell & Watson, 1975; Watson *et al.*, 1975; Watson & Abbey, 1977; Watson *et al.*, 1977a, b; Kriston *et al.*, 1977; Watson & McMahan, 1978; Watson *et al.*, 1978; Sewell, 1978; Watson & Sewell, 1981; Sewell & Watson, 1981). However, this paper emphasizes the adaptiveness of termite caste systems, rather than their formal structure, and complements other papers from our laboratory included in this volume (Watson & Abbey, Chapter 8; Lenz, Chapter 9; Lenz, Barrett & Williams, Chapter 10).

3.2   CLASSICAL MODELS OF TERMITE CASTE SYSTEMS

Watson & Sewell (1981) have discussed the two groups of developmental pathways that have served as classical models for the interpretation of caste development, and its evolution, in termites—the linear pathway of *Kalotermes flavicollis* (Fabricius), and the bifurcated pathways of the termitids—and we need emphasize only one point here. It is difficult to reconcile the idea that the caste system of *K. flavicollis* represents a primitive condition from the likes of which other conditions have evolved, for it depends on highly specialized endocrine mechanisms apparently unique to termites, the facultative reversal of metamorphosis and, almost as remarkable, the facultative recommissioning of metamorphosis after such a reversal. It is the kind of mechanism that Piepho (and his many successors) sought in vain when he implanted fragments of pupal and adult integuments into larvae, hoping that they would de-differentiate when the larvae moulted.

In *Kalotermes flavicollis*, such reversionary and conversionary moulting imparts an unparalleled flexibility to the development pathway, a flexibility which, were it primitive in termites, one might expect to be widespread among them. It is not. The most numerous termites, in terms of individuals as well as of species, are the termitids, in which, as Noirot (1955) showed so clearly, a common, relatively rigid, progressively differentiative pathway occurs, with the major developmental decision at the first moult, when the reproductive and non-reproductive lines diverge. In due course it became apparent that such bifurcated pathways are not necessarily the hallmark of the termitids, but occur in at least some hodotermitids and rhinotermitids (*cf*. Watson & Sewell, 1981). This led to two questions:

1. What is the developmental pathway in *Mastotermes darwiniensis* Froggatt, in morphological terms, arguably the most primitive surviving termite?
2. How widely can the model of *Kalotermes flavicollis* be applied to other lower termites?

This second question gained additional force from the realization that in at least some studies (*e.g.*, Watson, 1971), the classical model of development in *Kalotermes* imposed constraints on the approach to the problems, and on the interpretation of the answers. In many cases, the presentation of data was such that their reinterpretation was difficult, if not impossible (*cf.* Watson & Sewell, 1981).

3.3   DEVELOPMENT OF CASTES IN *MASTOTERMES*

Watson *et al.* (1977b) documented the development of *Mastotermes darwiniensis* in detail (Fig. 3.1):

1. In the present context, the most important finding was that the differentiative moult into worker and nymphal lines is the first, as in termitids, although wing buds do not develop until the fourth nymphal stage.
2. Reproductive potential is retained in the worker line, for neotenics develop from workers, rather than nymphs (*cf.* Watson & Abbey, Chapter 8).
3. *Mastotermes* appears to lack the capacity for reversionary moulting.
4. Although the number of nymphal stages is fixed at 11, there is an indefinitive number of worker stages, for the workers continue to moult, even if only in stationary fashion.

3.4   DEVELOPMENT OF CASTES IN AUSTRALIAN *KALOTERMES*

Sewell (1978), Watson & Sewell (1981) and Sewell & Watson (1981) described in detail the developmental pathways of four Australian forms of *Kalotermes*, *K. aemulus* Gay & Sewell, *K. banksiae* Hill and the montane and coastal forms of *K. rufinotum* Hill. It transpired that the pathways of all differ, and that none resembles the pathway of *K. flavicollis*.

All the pathways have substantial flexibility, conferred by reversionary moulting of nymphs, stationary moults, saltatorial moults (in which the termite moults to a stage two steps along the normal developmental path, omitting a stage that normally intervenes), and supplementary moults (which interpolate an extra, morphologically intermediate stage). These last two categories of moulting are also known to occur in *Hodotermes*, in the develop-

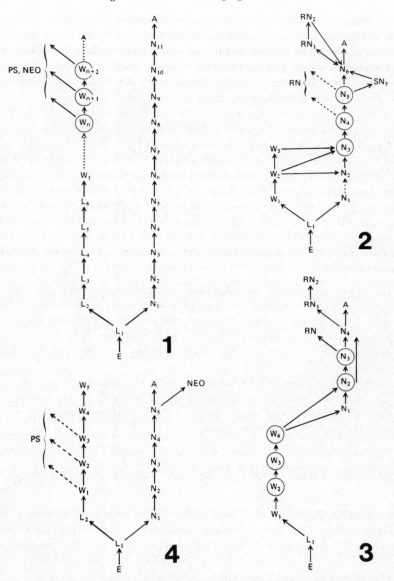

FIGS 3.1–3.4.   Developmental pathways of: *1, Mastotermes darwiniensis; 2,* montane *Kalotermes rufinotum; 3,* coastal *Kalotermes rufinotum; 4, Drepanotermes perniger.* Abbreviations: A = alate; E = egg; L = larva; N = nymph; NEO = neotenic; PS = presoldier; RN = reversionary nymph; SN = supplementary nymph; W = worker (i.e., primarily apterous individual on larva/worker line, with pigmented gut and mandibles). Subscript numbers indicate stage; circles indicate the occurrence of stationary moults; arrows formed of dashes indicate moults not documented in laboratory or field, and of dots, indefinite numbers of moults; and arrows parallel to the pathway indicate saltatorial moults. (Reprinted from Watson & Sewell, 1981, by kind permission of the publisher.)

ment of unpigmented workers into pigmented foragers (Watson, 1973; see Section 3.5.3). As with the reversion and conversion of nymphs, we have no physiological model to explain saltatorial and supplementary moulting, let alone the integration of a developmental pathway that incorporates them.

Two differences between caste development in the Australian *Kalotermes* and *K. flavicollis* are of major importance to our argument:

(a) *Kalotermes aemulus* and the montane form of *K. rufinotum* (Fig. 3.2) have a differentiative first moult leading to a short worker line and a long nymphal/alate line. In both species, the apterous, second instar individuals develop mandibular and gut pigmentation and, although we have no data on their behaviour, we assume that they perform at least some worker duties; certainly, the apterous, third stage of *K. banksiae* (W2) is a fully functional worker (see Section 3.5.2). We therefore regard them as first stage workers, rather than second stage larvae. First- (or, in *K. rufinotum*, later-) stage workers can moult to an appropriately advanced nymph, and there is no terminal worker stage. Nor is there one in *K. banksiae* or the coastal form of *K. rufinotum* (Fig. 3.3), in which a long worker line leads into a short nymphal/alate line. The transition from the worker line to the nymphal/alate line and, in coastal *Kalotermes rufinotum*, nymphal development itself, is beset with saltatorial and supplementary moulting.

(b) Nymphal reversion, commonly associated with damage done to wing buds by other members of the colony, occurs in all the Australian *Kalotermes* studied, and involves one or two moults, depending on the nymphal stage; but conversion back to the alate line was recorded only in montane *K. rufinotum*. The reversionary nymphs, whether produced by one or two moults, can readily be distinguished from primarily apterous workers of similar size. There is, in other words, no pool of "pseudergates"; there are primarily and secondarily apterous individuals of different appearance and, at least in those species where the position has been investigated, of different developmental potential (Sewell, 1978; Sewell & Watson, 1981).

3.5 THE WORKFORCE IN VARIOUS TAXA OF TERMITES

Having commented on the developmental pathways in *Mastotermes* and some Australian species of *Kalotermes*, we now look at the kinds of individuals that constitute the workforce in several termite taxa.

3.5.1 *Mastotermes darwiniensis*

The workforce in colonies of *Mastotermes* comprises apterous individuals, determined at their first moult; as mentioned above, they retain the capacity to develop into neotenics. Indeed, their natural end-point appears to be neotenic formation (Watson & Abbey, Chapter 8). Although we have some evidence to suggest that, in incipient colonies, behavioural transition from larvae to workers is progressive (Watson *et al.*, 1977b), we do not know if there is division of labour among workers of different ages. Nor do we know if the nymphal stages are part of the workforce.

3.5.2 *Kalotermes banksiae*

The potential composition of the workforce varies from one form of Australian *Kalotermes* to another. At one extreme is *Kalotermes aemulus*, in which nymphs and reversionary nymphs are virtually the only candidates, and at the other the montane form of *K. rufinotum*, with three worker stages, up to seven nymphal stages (including a supplementary nymph), and reversionary nymphs from three sources, N4, N5 and N6 (Fig. 3.2) (Sewell & Watson, 1981). However, we have experimental data on only one species, *K. banksiae*.

Sewell (1978) analysed the behaviour of groups of *Kalotermes banksiae* recorded on video. Each group consisted of three W2, N1, N2, N3 and RN (no distinction was made between reversionary nymphs of different origins), with or without one soldier or a pair of neotenic reproductives, 15–18 termites in all, and had been acclimatized for 14 days to the experimental conditions, at constant temperatures of 16 or 26°C. Ten activities were documented, of three principal kinds:

1. Alarm (oscillatory movements).
2. Construction (faecal plastering, pressing, carrying, and gnawing).
3. Trophallaxis (grooming, proctodaeal feeding, and soliciting). The two other activities followed protodaeal feeding: chewing and chasing (to "steal" proctodaeal food).

Sewell (1978) drew two conclusions of particular relevance to this paper:

(a) The occurrence of construction behaviour and trophallaxis in the stages investigated is influenced by temperature. At 16°C, all stages participate equally in the activities associated with construction, but N1 and RN are more active trophallactic donors than W2, N2 or N3. At 26°C, in contrast, all stages participate equally in trophallactic activities, but the most active stage in construction is N3.

(b) The reversionary nymphs are not more worker-like than the other stages. They take on no more of the construction activities, except in comparison with gnawing by N2 at 26°C. They participate equally in trophallaxis at 26°C although, in common with N1, they are more active than the other stages at 16°C. It follows that the reversionary nymphs do not serve as the principal food-donors; indeed, the reproductives receive trophallaxis equally from all stages at both temperatures.

We conclude that the primarily apterous workers, the brachypterous nymphs, and the secondarily apterous reversionary nymphs of *K. banksiae* all have the capacity to perform the essential worker tasks, and that their participation can be modified by temperature.

3.5.3   The family Hodotermitidae

Nel *et al.* (1969) showed that the pigmented "workers" and unpigmented "larvae" of the African harvester termite *Hodotermes mossambicus* (Hagen) have different jobs in the colony. Both stages are workers, in the functional sense. The unpigmented workers do the housework—they process the food, feed the dependent castes, and tend the eggs. The pigmented workers, which are dimorphic, are specialized for foraging; they gather grass in the open and, it transpired, are a dependent caste; they cannot feed themselves. Watson (1973) showed that the pigmented foragers develop from unpigmented workers, a process analogous to that of presoldier development and, as mentioned in Section 3.4, involving saltatorial and supplementary moulting. Dimorphism in the terminal worker stages (*sens.lat.*) also occurs in species of the behaviourally less specialized genus *Anacanthotermes*, in which the worker stages are unpigmented (Watson, 1973). Zhuzhikov *et al.* (1972) have shown that a differentiative moult into worker and nymphal lines occurs at the end of the second larval stage in *Anacanthotermes ahngerianus* Jacobson, and that neotenics develop from the nymphal rather than the worker line.

It therefore seems that polymorphism and polyethism are well developed in an independent worker line in the hodotermitids and, in the two behaviourally advanced genera *Hodotermes* and *Microhodotermes*, have been much elaborated (Watson, 1973).

3.5.4   The genus *Drepanotermes*

Drepanotermes includes the Australian harvester termites, ecologically a close equivalent to the hodotermitid harvesters, but derived from the cosmopolitan genus *Amitermes* (Watson & Perry, 1981). Watson (1974), Campbell and Watson (1975) and Watson and McMahan (1978) have dealt with the caste system and temporal polyethism in *Drepanotermes*. The caste system is a simple version of the typical termitid pattern, with a single worker line of five instars (Fig. 3.4). The first stage worker is unpigmented, but W4 and W5 are strongly pigmented, the colour and its intensity varying with species (Watson & Perry,

1981). As in the hodotermitids, the workers venture into the open, sometimes in sunlight, to gather grass, plant debris and seeds. It is the last two worker stages that do most of the foraging; the earlier the instar before the fifth, the lower its frequency in foraging parties. Likewise, W4 and W5 are the stages primarily involved in nest repair. Unlike the hodotermitid foragers, however, W4 and W5 are independent (Watson, unpubl. data).

This implies, but does not confirm, that the workers of earlier instars are more closely involved with housework. They do, however, appear to transport grass fragments through the peripheral galleries and stores back to the major storage region of the mound (Watson, unpubl. data; *cf.* Watson & Perry, 1981).

Watson (1974) showed that the mandibles of N4 of *Drepanotermes perniger* (Froggatt) become heavily worn before ecdysis to N5, implying that they are subject to heavy wear. Do N4 feed themselves? In other words, are the late nymphal stages to any degree independent? We return to this issue later.

3.5.5   The genus *Nasutitermes*

More is known of caste systems and polyethism in *Nasutitermes* than in any other termitid genus. Developmental or behavioural flexibility occurs in all castes, and many aspects impinge on worker development and functions.

3.5.5.1   *The Worker Stages*

Two points must be made over the worker stages in species of *Nasutitermes:*

(a) Although, as Noirot (1955) clearly showed, sexual dimorphism is common in the workers of *Nasutitermes* and its allies, it is now evident that the number of stages, particularly in the large worker line, varies considerably from species to species, and that the frequency of stages, *e.g.* SW2, also varies (*cf.* McMahan & Watson, 1975; McMahan, 1977; Watson & Abbey, unpubl. data). At least in *Nasutitermes exitiosus* (Hill), supernumerary large worker stages can develop in orphaned colonies (Watson & Abbey, unpubl. data; *cf.* McMahan & Watson, 1975), and Noirot (1969) reared supernumerary workers of *Nasutitermes arborum* (Smeathman) in the laboratory. We interpret these facts as indicating that the mechanisms regulating worker development, whatever they might be, are labile.

(b) Polyethism has long been recognized in workers of *Nasutitermes* (*cf.* McMahan, 1979; Jones, 1980). Although the pattern differs with species, depending, as it inevitably does, on the presence and frequencies of worker stages, there is a common tendency for later-stage workers to be associated with activities that impinge on the world outside the nest, *e.g.* the repair of nests, or the initiation of foraging trails. This pattern agrees closely with that found in *Drepanotermes* which shows more extreme specialization of W4 and W5 (see Section 3.5.4). Once the initial hazards of repair or trail-blazing have been coped with, workers of earlier instars become more heavily involved. Jones (1980) extended these observations and showed that, in *Nasutitermes costalis* (Holmgren), almost every type of behaviour studied (including 32 categories, involving aspects of investigation of surfaces, construction, grooming and locomotion) is exhibited during gallery repair by at least some individuals of each of the five worker stages (SW1, SW2, LW1–3; *cf.* McMahan, 1970). Worker polyethism in *N. costalis* is, then, primarily due to difference in emphasis, just as it is in *K. banksiae* (see Section 3.5.2). Unfortunately, we do not have comparable data on other species of *Nasutitermes*.

3.5.5.2 *The Reproductives*

Thorne & Noirot (1982) have commented on possible origins of replacement reproductives in *Nasutitermes corniger* (Motschulsky). In this species it seems that not only can alates be retained to replace lost primaries (Thorne, 1982) but, in addition, workers, of more than one instar, can differentiate *via* two moults into ergatoid reproductives. The ergatoids recorded in *N. corniger* were not functional, but functional ergatoids have been observed in the sympatric species *Nasutitermes columbicus* (Holmgren) (Thorne & Noirot, 1982) and in the South American species *Nasutitermes fulviceps* (Silvestri) (de Mosera, 1978). In contrast, *N. exitiosus*, perhaps the best known of the Australian termites (Watson & Gay, 1981), lacks ergatoid and nymphoid neotenics, but can replace lost primaries by retaining alates (Watson & Abbey, unpubl. data).

3.5.5.3 *Nymphs*

The reproductive nymphs of the higher termites are usually thought to be an entirely dependent caste, at least in their early stages (Noirot, 1969). Watson *et al.* (1978) have shown that late-stage nymphs of *N. exitiosus* are independent, in that they feed themselves. Whether, like the nymphs of the kalotermitids (see Section 3.5.2) and termopsids (*cf.* Howse, 1968), they participate in other work activities—particularly, for example, activities like outgoing trophallaxis, or faecal plastering—is unknown.

3.5.5.4 *Soldiers*

Sexually dimorphic soldiers have long been known in *Nasutitermes* and its allies—a large, generally female soldier and a small, male soldier (Noirot, 1955, 1969). As a rule, the two sexes are similarly armed, but in *N. exitiosus* and the remotely related *N. dixoni* (Hill) and *N. fumigatus* (Brauer), the large soldier usually has a short, downturned rostrum (McMahan & Watson, 1975). McMahan (1974) and Kriston *et al.* (1977) have shown that the large soldiers of *N. exitiosus* are not aggressive, but retreat from disturbance. They avoid sites contaminated with the spray from small soldiers, although the frontal glands of the two sexes contain the same terpenoid secretions (McMahan, 1974). It may be that the large soldiers are messengers of alarm, a worker-like task, recruiting workers and small soldiers when the colony is under attack.

It is also worth noting that the incidence of large soldiers in *N. exitiosus* can vary substantially from one locality to another (Watson & Abbey, unpubl. data), and that their frequency increases greatly after orphaning (Watson & Abbey, unpubl. data; *cf.* McMahan, 1974).

3.5.6 The Macrotermitinae

The Macrotermitinae, together with some genera on the *Subulitermes* branch of the Nasutitermitinae, are unique among termites in having only one worker instar; in the macrotermitines, the workers are sexually dimorphic, and follow three larval stages (Noirot, 1955; Okot-Kotber, 1981). The large, male workers are usually the food-gatherers, whereas the small, female workers appear to concentrate on intramural chores. However, a more intriguing polyethism may occur: the specialization of behaviour according to age within an instar. Noirot (1969) has suggested that it is the older workers of *Macrotermes bellicosus* (Smeathman) that participate in construction. The different spatial distribution of workers of different ages in nests of *Macrotermes michaelseni* (Sjöstedt) (J.P.E.C. Darlington, pers. comm.) also implies that there are age-dependent differences in the activities of workers. If this is true (and, unfortunately, experimental evidence is lacking), it would mean that polyethism in the worker stage of the macrotermitines resembles that found in the workers of social Hymenoptera (*cf.* McMahan, 1979).

3.6 DISCUSSION

These observations on the flexibility of caste systems in termites indicate a striking degree of adaptability, even in the termitids where, as Noirot (1969) has pointed out, "postembryonic development . . . is much more stereotyped than that in the other families" (p. 346). The lability of development and behaviour, sometimes within species and often within genera, raises many questions, none new, but all still challenging. What kinds of physiological mechanisms are involved? How, in physiological terms, are development and behaviour interrelated? How do selective forces operate to bring about changes in the caste systems, thereby producing the diversity that underlies the evolution of termites? And, particularly germane to this paper, what kind of system should be envisaged as primitive?

Watson & Sewell (1981) have examined this problem. Central to the argument is the fact that early differentiative moults have been found in all families of termites where search for them has been adequate. At least in *Mastotermes*, some *Kalotermes* and the termitids, it is the first moult. The fact that, in *Mastotermes*, wing buds do not develop until the fourth nymphal stage raises the intriguing possibility that in some of the lower termites where later differentiative moults have been recorded (*cf.* Miller, 1969; Watson & Sewell, 1981), the second (or later) "larval" stages may include cryptic nymphs, as in *Schedorhinotermes* (Renoux, 1976).

It has long been known that each developmental line can express at least some of the primary characteristics of the other. Thus the workers of *Mastotermes* retain reproductive potential, which may be irrepressible (Watson & Abbey, Chapter 8), and even in the termitids, workers of a few species can form ergatoid reproductives, *via* one or two differentiative moults (Noirot, 1969; Thorne & Noirot, 1982). Conversely, not only do the nymphs of at least some kalotermitids and termopsids constitute an important part of the workforce, but the late-stage nymphs of termitids can show some worker characteristics. The occurrence of presoldier/nymph or soldier/nymph and worker/nymph intercastes in termitids (*cf.* Noirot, 1969; Watson, 1974) also demonstrates that nymphs can express their latent worker/soldier potential.

We therefore argue that an early differentiative moult, perhaps the first, must have been a feature of the earliest caste systems in termites. It is not a feature that need be regarded as highly specialized, for analogous differentiation occurs in many other groups of insects (Watson & Sewell, 1981); it is the elaboration of the developmental lines arising from the differentiative moult that is exceptional in termites. The brachypterous nymphal line, leading to the formation of the winged adult, resembles in principle that found in other hemimetabolous insects. The apterous worker line, on the other hand, finds no counterpart elsewhere, unless it be in the unrelated polymorphism of the ants or dimorphism of the ptiliid beetles (Watson & Sewell, 1981); and its evolution into a terminal, virtually sterile caste, from which dependent soldier and forager castes are derived, has no parallel. We must, in addition, suppose that the potential for reproductive and worker behaviour was retained in latent form in both lines; however, concepts of this kind underlie the interpretation of postembryonic development and differentiation in all insects.

Two kinds of pattern could have emerged from such a system:

(a) A decrease in flexibility, with limitation on the independence of the nymphal line and, eventually, on the expression of reproductive potential in the worker line. Such relatively limited flexibility occurs in *Mastotermes*, the hodotermitids and termitids, and probably does in at least some rhinotermitids, such as *Coptotermes* (Watson & Sewell, 1981). The details of developmental pathways and caste systems differ greatly between (and within) these groups, particularly between *Mastotermes* and the others, but some generalizations emerge.

The colonies can be very large, exceeding a million individuals (Gay & Wetherly, 1970; Lee & Wood, 1971; Darlington, Chapter 15); indeed, tight social organization may be a requisite for large colony size. As a rule, the colonies live in relatively stable situations, each colony inhabiting a territory which produces the resources that the colony needs, and which the colony defends against other colonies. The temperature of the nest may be regulated, to a greater or lesser degree (*cf.* Holdaway & Gay, 1948; Lee & Wood, 1971). Under conditions as stable as this, regulation of colony size and structure can probably be achieved by modifying the output of the queen (*cf.* Watson & Abbey, Chapter 8), by culling, or, perhaps, by exporting surplus productivity in the form of increased numbers of alates. There may be no place for mechanisms that could capriciously alter the developmental fate of individuals.

Mastotermes (and, perhaps, species of *Reticulitermes* and *Heterotermes*; *cf.* Lenz, 1983) presents some substantial differences. The caste system of *Mastotermes* is rigid, as far as we can determine, and the colonies are large, up to several million strong (Hill, 1942). They are headed by numerous neotenics (Watson & Abbey, Chapter 8) and reproductive flexibility is well developed, for the neotenics that develop from ageing workers, under the influence of positive induction by the resident neotenics, provide an ever-present capacity for rapidly expanding the colony should circumstances be favourable (Watson & Abbey, Chapter 8). *Mastotermes* thus appears to be specialized as an opportunist, the opportunism being based on the multiplicity of neotenics, and the availability of a continuous supply of more (Watson & Abbey, Chapter 8).

(b) An increase in flexibility, with the elaboration of highly specialized (but as yet unknown) physiological mechanisms concerned with reversionary, supplementary and saltatorial moulting, and the conversion of workers to nymphs. Such flexibility is well developed in *Kalotermes*, and can lead to secondarily linear developmental pathways such as those found in *K. flavicollis*, *K. banksiae* and the coastal form of *K. rufinotum*, plus *K. atratus* Hill and *K. convexus* (Walker) (Sewell & Watson, 1981).

It is, perhaps, significant that the species in which these extremely flexible pathways have been found have small colonies, rarely more than a few thousand strong (Sewell, 1978), that live in relatively insecure habitats. The typical habitat of a kalotermitid is a circumscribed region of dead wood—scar tissue on a tree trunk, a branch stub, a piece of timber (or furniture). Nest temperature cannot be regulated (*cf.* Sewell, 1978). In other words, the habitat of a kalotermitid is inconstant and expendable, unlike the self-renewing, relatively stable habitats typical of most other termites. In these circumstances, mechanisms that enable the development of individuals to be altered, and rapidly, may confer on a colony a capacity for survival that a less flexible system would lack. The ability of kalotermitid colonies, in several genera, plus those of *Zootermopsis*, to divert almost all individuals into alates when circumstances become unfavourable can be seen as one example; the alates disperse, providing the chance for new colonies to be established (Watson & Sewell, 1981). The pathway of *K. flavicollis* can be viewed similarly; it involves mechanisms permitting individuals that would otherwise be committed to becoming alates, to return to the worker pool if, for example, climatic conditions become adverse. It must be remembered that *K. flavicollis* extends to latitudinal limits of termite distribution in Europe; and it may not be coincidental that the montane form of *K. rufinotum*, the only Australian species in which conversionary moulting has been recorded, extends to similar altitudinal limits in the high country of south-eastern Australia (Sewell & Watson, 1981).

To return to the question posed in the title of this paper—Caste Development in *Mastotermes* and *Kalotermes*: Which is Primitive? Neither is: each is highly specialized, to different ends, but each retains some primitive features. Linearity of the developmental pathway, we believe, is not one of them.

3.7 SUMMARY

The development and functions of castes in termites, particularly the castes that act as workers, are extremely variable and adaptable. Throughout the termites, however, there is a pattern of early differentiative moults, commonly the first, into apterous workers and brachypterous nymphs; such differentiation into two developmental lines, each retaining in latent form the characteristics of the other, is a primitive condition in termites. It is suggested that from such a system two divergent specializations developed, one towards lesser flexibility associated with large colonies and a relatively stable habitat, and the other towards extreme flexibility associated with small colonies inhabiting unstable situations, culminating in the secondarily linear pathways found in some species of *Kalotermes*.

3.8 REFERENCES

Campbell N. A. & Watson J. A. L. (1975) A multivariate study of mandibular characters in fifth instar workers and nymphs of *Drepanotermes perniger* (Froggatt) (Isoptera: Termitinae). *Insectes Sociaux* **22**, 293–306.

de Mosera S. L. (1978) Algunos aspectos del comportamiento grupal de reproductores de reemplazo de *Nasutitermes fulviceps* (Silvestri, 1901). (Isoptera, Termitidae, Nasutitermitinae). *Rev. Fac. Hum. Cienc. (Cienc. Biol.)* **1**, 1–7.

Gay F. J. & Wetherly A. H. (1970) The population of a large mound of *Nasutitermes exitiosus* (Hill) (Isoptera: Termitidae). *J. Aust. Ent. Soc.* **9**, 27–30.

Hill G. F. (1942) *Termites (Isoptera) from the Australian Region.* CSIRE, Melbourne.

Holdaway F. G. & Gay F. J. (1948) Temperature studies of the habitat of *Eutermes exitiosus* with special reference to the temperatures within the mound. *Aust. J. Sci. Res.* (B) **1**, 464–493.

Howse P. E. (1968) On the division of labour in the primitive termite *Zootermopsis nevadensis* (Hagen). *Insectes Sociaux* **15**, 45–50.

Jones R. J. (1980) Gallery construction by *Nasutitermes costalis*: polyethism and the behavior of individuals. *Insectes Sociaux* **27**, 5–28.

Kriston I., Watson J. A. L. & Eisner T. (1977) Non-combative behaviour of large soldiers of *Nasutitermes exitiosus* (Hill): an analytical study. *Insectes Sociaux* **24**, 103–111.

Lee K. E. & Wood T. G. (1971) *Termites and Soils*. Academic Press, London and New York.

McMahan E. A. (1970) Polyethism in workers of *Nasutitermes costalis* (Holmgren). *Insectes Sociaux* **17**, 113–120.

McMahan E. A. (1974) Non-aggressive behavior in the large soldier of *Nasutitermes, exitiosus* (Hill) (Isoptera: Termitidae). *Insectes Sociaux* **21**, 95–106.

McMahan E. A. (1977) Mound repair and foraging polyethism in workers of *Nasutitermes exitiosus* (Hill): (Isoptera: Termitidae). *Insectes Sociaux* **24**, 225–232.

McMahan E. A. (1979) Temporal polyethism in termites. *Sociobiology* **4**, 153–168.

McMahan E. A. & Watson J. A. L. (1975) Non-reproductive castes and their development in *Nasutitermes exitiosus* (Hill) (Isoptera). *Insectes Sociaux* **22**, 183–198.

Miller E. M. (1969) Caste differentiation in the lower termites. In *Biology of Termites* (K. Krishna & F. M. Weesner, eds), Vol. 1, pp. 283–310. Academic Press, New York and London.

Nel J. J. C., Hewitt P. H., Smith L. J. & Smit W. T. (1969) The behaviour of the harvester termite (*Hodotermes mossambicus* (Hagen)) in a laboratory colony. *J. Ent. Soc. Sth. Afr.* **32**, 9–24.

Noirot C. (1955) Recherches sur le polymorphisme des termites superieurs (Termitidae). *Ann. Sci. Nat., Zool.* **17**, 399–595.

Noirot C. (1969) Formation of castes in the higher termites. In *Biology of Termites* (K. Krishna & F. M. Weesner, eds), Vol. 1, pp. 311–350. Academic Press, New York and London.

Okot-Kotber B. M. (1981) Instars and polymorphism of castes in *Macrotermes michaelseni* (Isoptera, Macrotermitinae). *Insectes Sociaux* **28**, 233–246.

Renoux J. (1976) Le polymorphisme de *Schedohinotermes lamanianus* (Sjöstedt) (Isoptera— Rhinotermitidae). *Insectes Sociaux* **23**, 279–494.

Sewell J. J. (1978) *Developmental Pathways and Colony Organization in the Genus* Kalotermes Hagen *(Isoptera: Kalotermitidae)*. Thesis, Australian National University, Canberra.

Sewell J. J. & Watson J. A. L. (1981) Developmental pathways in Australian species of *Kalotermes* Hagen (Isoptera). *Sociobiology* **6**, 243–323.

Thorne B. L. (1982) Polygyny in termites: multiple primary queens in colonies of *Nasutitermes corniger* (Motschuls) (Isoptera: Termitidae). *Insectes Sociaux* **29**, 102–117.

Thorne B. L. & Noirot C. (1982) Ergatoid reproductives in *Nasutitermes corniger* (Motschulsky) (Isoptera: Termitidae). *Int. J. Insect Morph. Embryol.* **11**, 213–226.

Watson J. A. L. (1971) The development of "workers" and reproductives in *Mastotermes darwiniensis* Froggatt (Isoptera). *Insectes Sociaux* **18**, 173–176.

Watson J. A. L. (1973) The worker caste of the hodotermitid harvester termites. *Insectes Sociaux* **20**, 1–20.

Watson J. A. L. (1974) Caste development and its seasonal cycle in the Australian harvester termite, *Drepanotermes perniger* (Froggatt) (Isoptera: Termitinae). *Aust. J. Zool.* **24**, 471–487.

Watson J. A. L. & Abbey H. M. (1977) The development of reproductives in *Nasutitermes exitiosus* (Hill) (Isoptera: Termitidae). *J. Aust. Ent. Soc.* **16**, 161–164.

Watson J. A. L. & Gray F. J. (1981) *Eutermes exitiosus* Hill, 1925 (Insecta, Isoptera): proposed conservation by use of the plenary powers. *Bull. Zool. Nom.* **38**, 142–146.

Watson J. A. L. & McMahan E. A. (1978) Polyethism in the Australian harvester termite *Drepanotermes* (Isoptera, Termitinae). *Insectes Sociaux* **25**, 53–62.

Watson J. A. L. & Perry D. H. (1981) The Australian harvester termites of the genus *Drepanotermes* (Isoptera: Termitinae). *Aust. J. Zool., Suppl. Ser.* **78**, 1–153.

Watson J. A. L. & Sewell J. J. (1981) The origin and evolution of caste systems in termites. *Sociobiology* **6**, 101–118.

Watson J. A. L., Barrett R. A. & Abbey H. M. (1977a) Caste ratios in a long-established, neotenic-headed laboratory colony of *Mastotermes darwiniensis* Froggatt (Isoptera). *J. Aust. Ent. Soc.* **16**, 469–470.

Watson J. A. L., Metcalf E. C. & Sewell J. J. (1975) Preliminary studies on the control of neotenic formation in *Mastotermes darwiniensis* Froggatt (Isoptera). *Insectes Sociaux* **22**, 415–426.

Watson J. A. L., Metcalf E. C. & Sewell J. J. (1977b) A re-examination of the development of castes in *Mastotermes darwiniensis* Froggatt (Isoptera). *Aust. J. Zool.* **25**, 25–42.

Watson J. A. L., Ruyooka D. B. A. & Howick C. D. (1978) The effect of caste composition on wood consumption in cultures of *Nasutitermes exitiosus* (Hill) (Isoptera: Termitidae). *Bull. Ent. Res.* **68**, 687–694.

Zhuzhikov D. D., Zolotarev E.Kh. & Mednikova T. K. (1972) Postembryonic development of *Anacanthotermes ahngerianus* Jacobs. In *Termites (Collected Articles)* (E. Kh. Zolotarev, ed.), pp. 46–62. University Publishing House, Moscow.

CHAPTER 4

Pathways of Caste Development in the Lower Termites

Ch. NOIROT

Laboratory of Zoology, University of Dijon, Boulevard Gabriel, 21100 Dijon, France

CONTENTS

4.1 INTRODUCTION

The lower termites do not constitute a systematic unit. Each of the 5 or 6 families* represents a special evolutionary direction and they cannot be arranged in a linear phylogenetic order. The best definition of their heterogenous assemblage is by comparison with the higher termites, which form a unique well defined family. Their only common character is the symbiosis with flagellated Protozoa, which is correlated with a special type of trophallaxis, the exchange of proctodeal food.

Different families (and different genera in a given family) have reached different levels of evolution, in their morphology, social organization and

---

* I follow the classification of Grassé (1949), who considers Termopsidae and Hodotermitidae as separate families. The monospecific family Serritermitidae (Emerson & Krishna, 1975) seems close to the Rhinotermitidae, nothing is known about its caste system.

especially in polymorphism. The developmental pathways are much more varied than in the Termitidae (Noirot, Chapter 6), and it is tempting to search in the existing species the principal steps of the history of caste differentiation. In spite of the polyphyletic nature of the lower termites, this seems a reasonable assumption, because major trends of the caste system are very similar in lower and higher termites.

4.2 THE SOLDIER CASTE

The similarity between lower and higher termites is especially obvious in the soldier caste. This well defined caste is characteristic of the Isoptera, with no equivalent in other social insects. Their development occurs always through two successive moults in a very defined pattern: the first one gives rise to an intermediate stage named presoldier, soldier-larva or white soldier, which is unpigmented, unsclerotized and is not functional. On the contrary, it is entirely dependent on the active members of the society and thus behaves like a larva. This stage is of short duration (10–15 days), and by a second moult differentiates into the adult soldier. The transformation in two steps, with an intermediate non-functional stage, was accurately compared by Deligne (1970) with the metamorphosis of the holometabolous insects. This type of development is common in all the termites, and the absence of soldiers, clearly secondary, is only observed in some higher termites, subfamily Apicotermitinae (Sands, 1972). Thus, the soldier caste evolved very early and was, most probably, the first step towards polymorphism at the very origin of the Isoptera. This was recognized by Emerson as early as 1926. The soldier caste was, in my opinion, well established in the "Prototermite", the common ancestor of the Permian age (unfortunately unknown!), and from that time, maintained the same type of development, in spite of considerable diversification in morphology, physiology and behaviour.

There were many conflicting assumptions as regards the stages from which soldiers differentiate (summarized by Miller, 1969; Lüscher, 1974). It now seems clear that soldiers do not develop from a special developmental line, that no special type of larva (predetermined to become a presoldier) does exist in any lower termites, and that soldier differentiation is a truly epigenetic process. Precise origin of soldiers in the lower termites is a problem intricately related with that of the worker caste (see below). Suffice to say here that in all the species, soldiers may originate from *several* immature stages, and in many cases, every immature stage (beyond the third, even the second) is able to become a soldier. In incipient colonies, only the younger stages can express this potentiality (giving rise to "nanitic" soldiers). With the ageing of the society, soldiers develop from more and more advanced stages, but even in fully-grown colonies soldiers differentiate from different stages. In the more advanced species, soldier differentiation seems restricted to a limited number of immature stages, ending in the situation experienced in many higher termites where soldiers originate from one stage only (or, if two or more types of soldiers exist, each type is derived from one special stage (Noirot, 1969).

4.3 THE WORKER CASTE

The problem of evolution of the worker caste may be stated differently, because in the lower termites developmental possibilities may range from the absence of a worker caste to a well differentiated one. In my opinion, these intermediates can throw some light on the progressive emergence of the worker caste. Of course, the "primitive" species are not the direct ancestors of the "more evolved", and this arrangement in a phylogenetic order may be somewhat arbitrary. However, I consider that the workers, as the soldiers, are homologous throughout the entire order, that their emergence in the several evolutionary directions followed a similar pathway, but was arrested at different levels in different species or genera. This is probably an oversimplification of the situation, but possibly not too far from the real story.

A preliminary but central question must be asked: what is a worker? The definition cannot be the same in Isoptera as in social Hymenoptera. In the latter, workers are true imaginal insects, differentiating through a pupal stage, as in all the holometabolous insects. In the Isoptera, the situation is completely different, and a worker cannot be considered as an imago; even in the species where the workers appear as terminal instars, they retain their prothoracic glands. Many of their characters are shared with the larval instars, and in some species it is not easy to decide whether an individual is a worker or a larva. In my opinion, three criteria can be utilized for this distinction: functional, morphological and developmental (Noirot, 1982).

Functionally, in social insects, a worker is an insect which works. This is of course an essential condition, but not in itself sufficient. Owing to the hemimetabolous development, the immature stages are active insects, and can take part in the social tasks, even when obviously engaged in the imaginal differentiation. Morphologically, a worker is characterized by a simplified structural organization, by comparison with the imagines, evident in the structures associated with flight (wings, flight muscles), the sex organs, the eyes and optic lobes of the brain. All these characters appear mainly as larval and cannot establish a sharp distinction between a worker and an advanced larva. Others are positive adaptations for the working tasks namely more elaborate development of the head and the mandibular muscles, the gut and the salivary glands. However, these adaptations are mainly quantitative, not well marked in some species, and again cannot suffice to characterize a worker. Thus, the developmental criteria seem essential, in addition to the two others. A termite worker is not necessarily a terminal instar. It may retain several developmental potentials e.g. to become a soldier (indeed, in the higher termites, most of the soldiers have such an origin), or a replacement reproductive. However, a worker is never able to give rise to an imaginal (alate) reproductive.

In the termites, as in the social Hymenoptera, *the normal development is the imaginal line, ending in the fertile alates*. The other castes are the result of deviations from the normal pathway occurring at one or several steps of the development ("decision points" of Oster & Wilson, 1978). The earlier the deviation, the greater the differences (see Brian, Chapter 27, for the Hymenoptera). In termites, we can find all types of developmental steps between very *late* and *reversible* deviations giving rise to the *pseudergates*, as in the lower termites, and a true worker caste originating from an early and irreversible deviation, a situation well evidenced in the higher termites.

4.4   KALOTERMITIDAE AND TERMOPSIDAE

Kalotermes flavicollis is by far the best documented species and is considered as a good representation of the primitive conditions. It was the favourite material of Lüscher (1952a, b; 1974) inspired by the early work of Grassé & Noirot (1946–1947). Take again the three criteria for the definition of the worker caste: functionally, all the individuals beyond the third instar (except the soldiers and the reproductives) are able to perform all the social tasks. This is well demonstrated by the simple method of "homogeneous groups", or laboratory cultures composed of insects of the same stage. For example, a culture containing only fourth instar larvae is perfectly viable. Morphologically, the immature insects may be classified as *nymphs* or *larvae* by the presence or absence of wing buds. It is possible to recognize stages of nymphs, according to the size of the wing buds, but a noticeable variability exists, especially in the two first stages. Moreover, one finds, in field populations, a variable proportion of relatively large insects, but without wing buds or with greatly reduced ones. These are the *pseudergates* (Grassé & Noirot, 1947), a term which was sometimes misinterpreted. Indeed, the development follows a complicated pathway due to the regressive and stationary moults (Fig. 4.1). The normal development allows eight successive instars: four larval, three nymphal and the imaginal; the first five are easily distinguished by their size (best measured by head width), but beyond that there is a big overlap. This is classical developmental sequence of a hemimetabolous insect with the exception of late differentiation of the wing buds (at the fifth instar), whereas, in cockroaches, for example, they are already present in first instar larvae (Lefeuvre, 1969). Many deviations may occur from this fundamental pathway. Soldiers are produced (through the presoldier stage) by any instar from

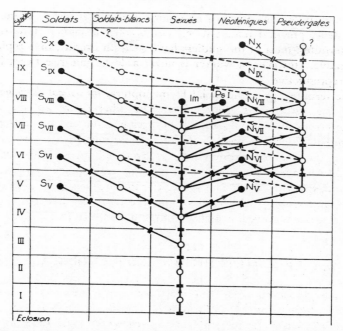

FIG. 4.1. Pathway of caste development in *Kalotermes flavicollis*, according to Grassé & Noirot (1947). From the *normal* developmental line, ending in imaginal alates (Im) through 7 larval and nymphal instars, many *deviations* may occur, either towards presoldiers and soldiers (S), or the neotenic reproductives (N), or the pseudergates. The pseudergates originate either from late larval instars (ascending way) or from nymphs (descending way, regressive moults). They can moult several times without change, or differentiate into soldiers or neotenics, or return to the imaginal line (not shown in the Fig.).

the fourth (the second in incipient colonies: Grassé & Noirot, 1957). The neotenic reproductives may originate (by special moult) from any instar after third. The last (fourth) instar larva may moult into a larger insect, but without wing buds. A nymph (any stage) may moult with a reduction or even a disappearance of the wing buds (regressive moult). These moults will lead to *pseudergates*, as defined by Grassé and Noirot (1947), either by an *ascending way* (growth of the larva without wing bud differentiation) or a *descending way* by the regressive moult. Except lack of wing buds, pseudergates do not differ from normal nymphs and retain the same developmental potentialities. In addition to the possible differentiation into soldiers or neotenic reproductives, they can revert to the nymphal and then imaginal stages.

This very flexible developmental pathway was summarized by Lüscher (1952a) in a classical scheme (Fig. 4.2), which seems sometimes misinterpreted: indeed, it suggests that one or several pseudergate instars are obligatory intermediates in the imaginal development (contrary to the scheme of

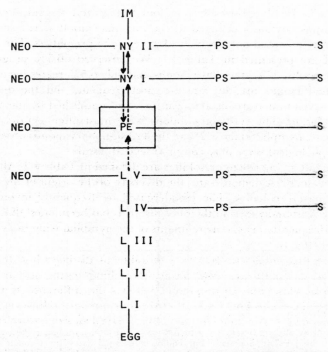

Fig. 4.2. Pathway of caste development in *Kalotermes flavicollis*, according to the data of Lüscher (1952a, 1974). The normal developmental line (L = larvae, NY = nymphs and IM = imagines) is usually interrupted by one or more pseudergate (PE) instars. The nymphs may also become pseudergates by regressive moults. The neotenics (NEO), presoldiers (PS) and soldiers (S) differentiate from any late larval, nymphal or pseudergate instar.

Grassé & Noirot, 1947). The question was not explicitly answered by Lüscher, as well as the real importance of the pseudergates in the colonies of *K. flavicollis*. Indeed, different types of pseudergates are easily obtained in laboratory cultures, and Lüscher (1952a) demonstrated well the importance of the number of insects: the regressive and stationary moults are much more frequent in small artificial colonies than in larger ones. Thus, what happens in natural colonies, where the population may be more than a thousand individuals? Available information remains scarce. Precise analysis of field populations, with the proportions of different stages, especially the pseudergates, and their possible variations in relation to the size of the colony, the season cycle is lacking.

In 1959 Noirot & Verron (unpubl. observ.) isolated from freshly collected field colonies, samples of *K. flavicollis* preparing to moult (identified by their whitish coloration). Each animal, carefully identified, was kept in a separate vial, and thus the type of moult occurring in subsequent days was easily determined. Only large-sized insects (fourth stage and beyond) were utilized. The nymphs obviously engaged in the imaginal moult were excluded; 467 moults were recorded out of which 14 gave rise to presoldiers. The 453 others recorded are presented in Table 4.1. We observed 66.5% progressive (or normal) moults, 27% stationary moults and only 6.5% regressive ones. Thus, the normal moults are, by far, the most frequent, and the development through seven immature instars seems to be accomplished by the majority of the population. The stationary moults were most often performed by the penultimate nymphal stage (72% of the 123 stationary moults observed), and this morphological stage may comprise several instars.

The moult giving rise to presoldiers are detailed in Table 4.2. Although the number is small, it demonstrates the diversity of the origin of the soldiers in normal mature colonies. The pseudergates are frequently involved, so do nymphs occasionally even in their last instar. It has been found that soldiers in the field frequently bear some remnants of the nymphal wing buds (Grassé & Noirot, 1946a, b).

To sum up, in *K. flavicollis* it is possible to distinguish a fundamental developmental pathway, very classical, resulting in the sexual alates. By comparison with other orthopteroid insects, the difference is in the late differentiation of the wing buds (after the fourth moult). However, numerous deviations may occur, and are actually observed under natural conditions. Besides the formation of soldiers and neotenics, the regressive and stationary moults produce the pseudergates, a not well defined category of insects,

TABLE 4.1. MOULTS OBSERVED IN FIELD COLONIES OF *KALOTERMES FLAVICOLLIS* (APRIL–AUGUST 1959)

Fourth stage and beyond—imaginal moults excluded

Total observed: 453 + 14 giving rise to presoldiers

Progressive: 301 = 66.5%

Stationary: 123 = 27%

Regressive: 29 = 6.5%

TABLE 4.2. *KALOTERMES FLAVICOLLIS*: ORIGIN OF THE 14 PRESOLDIERS OBSERVED IN FIELD COLONIES

Pseudergates:	8
Nymphs, penultimate stage (short wing buds):	5
Nymphs, last stage (long wing buds):	1

neither morphologically, nor functionally or developmentally. They are functionally workers, but no more than nymphs or old larvae, and they form only a limited part of the "worker force" of the society (the proportion of which may be variably adaptable, according to the conditions: they seem much more important in the young colonies!). Morphologically, they differ from nymph only by the absence or regression of the wing buds (neither the brain nor the sex organs seem regressed). Their development is slowed down, they remain longer in an immature stage, which in this case is also a working stage, but this is not irreversible. They are not real workers, and there is *no equivalent* in other insects; thus the word *pseudergate* was proposed. Conversely the nymphs, even in the last stage, with long wing buds, are *working insects*, and preserve all the developmental potentialities for differentiation into pseudergates, soldiers or neotenics, in addition to the normal, imaginal moult.

In several other species of Kalotermitidae, especially in the genus *Neotermes*, the developmental pathway seems similar (*N. tectonae* (Kalshoven, 1930); *N. jouteli* (Nagin, 1972); *N. connexus* (Myles, 1982)). There is no indication of a true worker caste, and the pseudergates are present, at least in *N. jouteli* and *N. connexus*. Pseudergates are reported too in the primitive species *Pterotermes occidentis* by Jones *et al.* (1981).

In the family Termopsidae, the developmental pathways are not so well known but seem not to be very different from *K. flavicollis*. According to the published data, no real worker caste does exist, and pseudergates are present in *Archotermopsis* (Imms, 1919), *Zootermopsis* (Castle, 1934), *Stolotermes* (Morgan, 1959) and *Porotermes* (Mensa-Bonsu, 1976), but neither their origin nor their potentialities are defined. So, until the past few years, *K. flavicollis* was considered as a good representative of polymorphism in the primitive lower termites, a useful landmark for the evolution of caste differentiation.

However, a recent publication of Sewell & Watson (1981) described the developmental pathways for three Australian species of *Kalotermes*, which, at first sight seem completely different from that of *K. flavicollis*, and inferred from their interpretations a new theory for the evolution of caste differentiation in termites (Watson & Sewell, 1981) contrary to current ideas on this problem.

They claim to have observed, in the three *Kalotermes* species, a true worker caste, differentiated (as a special line of development, or "worker line") after the first moult. In *K. aemulus* and the montane form of *K. rufinotum*, this first moult separates the "worker line" and the "nymphal or alate line", in *K. banksiae* and the coastal form of *K. rufinotum*, the "alate line" originates from a later stage of the "worker line". Although in all these species regressive and stationary moults regularly occur, they reject the concept of pseudergate, as meaningless because of the presence of a true worker caste. It is not possible, in this short review, to present a detailed discussion of these observations and interpretations (this will be done in a separate publication), the main criticism here may be summed as follows: the so-called "workers" are merely insects without wing buds, which finally develop into a nymphal stage, and ending in alates: they are exactly similar to the larvae of *K. flavicollis*; most of these "worker" instars are too small to work efficiently in the society. The "differentiative moult", believed to occur in some species at the end of the first instar and to produce distinct worker and alate lines, is inferred from very little evidence, and most probably does not exist at all. Thus in my opinion, the Australian *Kalotermes* studied by Sewell & Watson (1981) exhibit developmental pathways very similar to that of *K. flavicollis*, the main variations being in the time of appearance of the wing buds (sometimes from the second instar), and the degree of flexibility introduced by the regressive and stationary moults (with, in addition, saltatorial moults); the "reversionary line" evidenced by Sewell & Watson (1981) is strictly similar to the "pseudergates" of Grassé & Noirot (1947).

4.5 MASTOTERMITIDAE

Mastotermes darwiniensis is the only living representative of this family, and its polymorphism, recently re-examined by Watson *et al.* (1977) is reported by Watson in this volume. The essential point is the evidence of a differentiative moult, which is the first one and separate (irreversibly?) the worker and the alate lines. This separation is only evident by a difference in pilosity but the wing buds in the nymphal line are visible only at the fourth instar. Conversely, the workers bear protrusions at the lateral margins of the meso- and meta-notum, reminiscent of vestigial wing buds. Moreover, these workers are the exclusive origin of replacement reproductives. Thus, polymorphism of this species seems, by several characters, different from all the other termites so far studied.

M. darwiniensis is often considered to be a very primitive termite, on the basis of morphological characters, like wings and genital appendages of the alates. However, the social organization seems much more evolved than in the Kalotermitidae and Termopsidae. The soldiers evolved, in addition to the powerful mandibles, a chemical weapon, quinones (Moore, 1968) which are produced probably in the salivary glands. The recent observations of Baccetti and Dallai (1977, 1978) demonstrate in this species a type of spermatozoon unique in the animal kingdom since it bears about a hundred flagella. In the other termites examined (Baccetti *et al.*, 1981) the spermatozoa are very different: they are without flagella. From these observations, *Mastotermes* appears to follow a separate evolutionary line, isolated very early, and exhibiting a mixture of primitive and specialized characters. It is difficult to ascertain whether its polymorphism is primitive or not.

4.6 RHINOTERMITIDAE

By several characters (i.e. development of the frontal gland), this family is believed to be at a more advanced stage of evolution than the preceding ones. The few genera for which polymorphism is documented present very different developmental pathways.

In *Prorhinotermes simplex*, according to Miller (1942), the developmental pathway seems to be not very different from that of *K. flavicollis*, and is characterized by the very late differentiation of the nymphs (defined by the presence of wing buds). These nymphs may regress to a worker-like stage, comparable to the pseudergates. No indication exists about the differentiation of a worker line and a true worker caste. The genus *Prorhinotermes* appears as the most primitive in the family, and was recently included as a separate subfamily (Prorhinotermitinae) by Quennedey and Deligne (1975).

The genus *Reticulitermes* was the subject of numerous investigations, especially those of Buchli (1958) on two European species, *R. lucifugus* and *R. santonensis*. Exploring all the potentialities of each stage, he obtained a very complex developmental pathway, expressing a great flexibility. However, if the exceptional types of development (observed mostly in artificial situations) are omitted, then one obtains a simpler picture, summarized in Fig. 4.3. I did not for the sake of clarity represent the neotenic differentiation (the neotenics originate mainly from the penultimate nymphal stage, but also from several worker stages).

The most important is the separation, after the second moult, of two developmental lines, identified by the presence or absence of wing buds: the *sexual* or *nymphal line*, which gives rise to the alates through six nymphal instars, and the *worker line*. This separation was first demonstrated in several American species by Hare (1934). The workers here are morphologically differentiated, and are really functional by fourth instar, they undergo a series of moults, without modifications and only a very limited increase in size. However, they remain developmentally very flexible, differentiating into soldiers, or neotenic reproductives. It is important to emphasize that this last differentiation may be correlated with limited development of the wing buds (partial reversion towards nymphal morphology). Conversely, the nymphs, under laboratory conditions, may undergo regressive moults, to more or less worker-like individuals. But these pseudergates never attain complete worker morphology. Thus, the separation of the two developmental lines seems irreversible or, at most, only partially reversible.

The separation of the two developmental lines after the second moult occurs also in the genus *Coptotermes* (*C. intermedius*: Roy-Noël, 1968; *C. lacteus*: Watson & Sewell, 1981). A more detailed study of developmental pathways of this genus which is considered as one of the most primitive among the Rhinotermitinae (Emerson, 1971) is lacking.

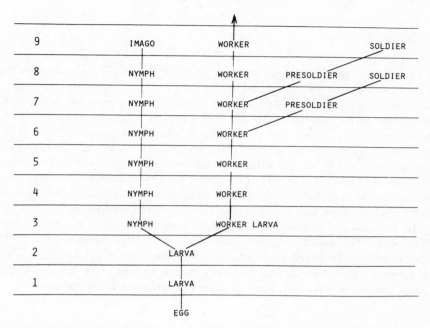

FIG. 4.3. Pathway of caste development in *Reticulitermes lucifugus* and *R. santonensis*, modified from Buchli (1958). In this simplified diagram, only the main developmental pathways, observed in normal situation, are shown. The formation of neotenic reproductives is not figured.

The genus *Psammotermes* is also considered as very primitive by many morphological characters (Emerson, 1971) but is ecologically very specialized, being the most desertic of all the termite genera. The only data on its polymorphism are those of Clement (1952) on *P. hybostoma*. Although developmental pathway was not established, a true worker caste seems to exist, with some unusual features: the size variation between workers is exceptionally large (successive instars or separate lines?) and the largest "workers" probably do not work and appear mainly as intermediate stages towards the large soldiers.

The subfamily Rhinotermitinae (*Prorhinotermes* excluded) appears as the most evolved (Krishna, 1970), especially by the differentiation of the soldier caste and its defensive behaviour (Quennedey & Deligne, 1975). The only species for which detailed information is available is *Schedorhinotermes lamanianus* (Renoux, 1976, Chapter 5). The differentiative moult occurs earlier, at the end of the first larval instar and, surprisingly, the worker line is composed of female insects only; thus, all the workers and soldiers are females. This represents a very specialized developmental pathway. As the genus *Schedorhinotermes* is considered to be relatively primitive among the *Rhinotermitinae*, the study of the more specialized genera is called for.

4.7 HODOTERMITIDAE

Formerly included in the Termopsidae, this family seems much more evolved, both in its biology and its polymorphism. The developmental pathway is known for two of the three living genera. *Hodotermes mossambicus* was recently re-examined by Luamba (1980a, b): a separation between a *worker line* and a *nymphal or alate line* is well evident after the second or third moult. However, in the worker line, a *sexual dimorphism* occurs, giving rise to two worker types, minor workers which are females, major which are males. In addition to this, soldiers originate only from the major worker line, thus they are all males (Fig. 4.4A). This sexual dimorphism of workers, and the specialization of one sex for the soldier formation, are frequently observed in the higher termites, and express a highly evolved polymorphism.

In the genus *Anacanthotermes*, a further step is achieved. In *A. ochraceus* (Clement, 1953) and *A. anhgerianus* (Zhuzikov *et al.*, 1972; Mednikova, 1977), all the neuters (workers and soldiers) are of the male sex. Compared with *Hodotermes* (Fig. 4.4B) this may be interpreted as a result of suppression of the small (female) worker line, however, the mechanisms remain obscure.

4.8 DISCUSSION AND CONCLUSION

Although a limited number of species are well documented, great diversity of polymorphism is evident among the lower termites. A reasonable assumption is to suppose that the most primitive species bears a more primitive developmental pathway.

A large group of primitive lower termites, namely the families Termopsidae and Kalotermitidae, have a developmental pathway similar or close to that evidenced in *K. flavicollis*. In my opinion, this type of caste formation is truly a primitive one, as was generally accepted (see reviews by Miller, 1969; Wilson, 1970; Lüscher, 1974; Grassé, 1982). On the contrary, recently Watson & Sewell (1981) challenged this view basing their argument on one hand, on the study of some Australian species of *Kalotermes* and on the other, on the case of *M. darwiniensis*. As regards the Australian *Kalotermes*, a careful examination of the data published by Sewell & Watson (1981) does not support their conclusions and discloses developmental pathways of the same type as for *K. flavicollis*. In *Mastotermes*, for which an early differentiation of a "worker line" seems best documented, I have emphasized the peculiarities of the caste system and the need for additional studies. This only living species of the family has many peculiarities rendering it unique in the phylogeny of termites, and even in its morphology appears, by several characters, more advanced than the primitive Termopsidae (Emerson, 1933, 1955; Krishna,

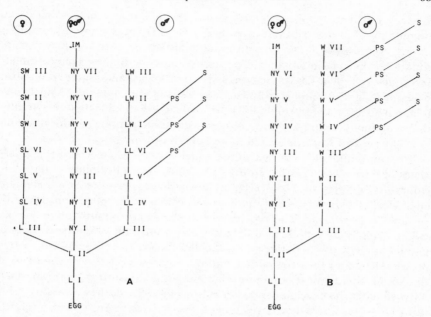

FIG. 4.4. Pathways of caste development in the family Hodotermitidae.
A. *Hodotermes mossambicus*, according to the observations of Luamba (1980a, b). In the normal (imaginal) line, the nymphs (NY) are recognized (wing buds) probably after the second moult, which separates the neuter line. In the latter, a sexual dimorphism occurs (the female larvae (SL) are smaller than the males (LL) giving rise to small female workers (SW) and large male workers (LW). Presoldiers (PS) and soldiers (S) differentiate from late large larvae, and earlier instars of large workers, and thus are of the male sex.
B. *Anacanthotermes ahngerianus*, from the data of Mednikova (1977). The imaginal line is very similar to that of *Hodotermes*. The neuter line however comprises of only male insects. Compared with *Hodotermes*, the small (female) workers and larvae are suppressed.

1970). Thus, the primitivity of caste development in *Mastotermes* may be questioned.

Social life in Isoptera probably appeared in an ancestral wood-eating cockroach associated with intestinal flagellates, and this association was of primary importance for the evolution of sociability as evidenced by Cleveland *et al.* since 1934. Larvae were obliged to remain with their parents for the acquisition of the symbiotic Protozoa (after hatching and after each moult). The burrowing xylophagous cockroach, *Cryptocercus punctulatus*, re-examined recently by Christine Nalepa (1982 and pers. comm.) is perhaps not too far from the social organization of the "Prototermite": association of a pair of adults with their offspring (which in *Cryptocercus* is maintained for 3 years at least), with proctodeal feeding and a common system of galleries in the wood.* A further step was attained with the differentiation of a soldier caste, originating from one or (most probably) several advanced larval (nymphal) instars. We do not know how this was realized, because no intermediate situation is known, in any living species. At the same time (geological time!) larval and nymphal life was lengthened by stationary and regressive moults, strengthening the parents–offspring association, and a better cooperation (communal burrowing, trophallaxis, care for the hatchlings and eventually the reproductive pair) was progressively established, ending in the situation now observed in *K. flavicollis* and many other lower termites.

It is more difficult to reconstitute further evolution, especially the emergence of a true worker caste. In my opinion, the large flexibility of the post-embryonic development observed in many lower termites is a primitive character, allowing the society to adapt its composition to the constraints of variable environment. The regressive and stationary moults, origin of the pseudergates, may well be modulated by these constraints (and more work is needed to verify this hypothesis). With better integration of the society, better protection against the external fluctuations (increase of the population and of the social communication, more elaborated nest insuring more constant microclimate) the developmental flexibility was reduced, the deviations (with regard to normal, imaginal development) restricted to more and more defined instars and becoming more and more irreversible. Especially the differentiation of a worker line (irreversibly separated from the imaginal line) was realized, the earlier the more advanced the species. Concurrently to the morphological differentiation, the division of labour became more and more pronounced, the successive instars of the imaginal line becoming completely dependent on the workers. In this perspective, the pseudergates of the lower termites appear really as an intermediate state in the differentiation of the worker caste. Of course, this remains only as an hypothesis but, I believe, the best fitted with the acquainted facts.

4.9 SUMMARY

Lower termites comprise several evolutionary lines, and the living species reached different degrees of evolution, especially in their caste development. By comparative studies, it seems possible to reconstitute the main steps of the evolution of the caste system in the Isoptera, especially the emergence of the worker caste.

In spite of recent contrary assertions, the developmental pathway well evidenced in *Kalotermes flavicollis* seems, in many ways, general for the Kalotermitidae and possibly for the Termopsidae. From the normal develop-

---

* In *Cryptocercus*, only one brood seems produced in the colony, which thus is typically composed of the imaginal pair and a group of nymphs of the same age (Nalepa, 1982).

mental line, ending in the sexual alates, many deviations can occur, giving rise to the soldiers, the neotenic reproductives and the pseudergates. The latter are not true workers, neither by their morphology nor by their developmental potentialities, but may be the first step towards the differentiation of a true worker caste. This caste appears as an irreversible deviation from the normal (imaginal) developmental line, realized at a definite larval instar, the earlier it appears the more evolved the species. Several steps of this evolution can be observed in the Rhinotermitidae. Hodotermitidae appear, as regards their polymorphism, as very advanced. Polymorphism of Mastotermitidae, where a worker line seems separated at the first moult, remains unexplained.

4.10 ACKNOWLEDGEMENTS

I would like to thank Prof. Henri Verron for the utilization of unpublished observations on *K. flavicollis*, and Dr Moses Okot-Kotber for the correction of the English manuscript.

4.11 REFERENCES

Bacetti B. & Dallai R. (1977) Sur le premier spermatozoïde multiflagellé du règne animal, découvert chez *Mastotermes darwiniensis*. *C.R. Acad. Sci.* **285** (D), 785–788.

Bacetti B. & Dallai R. (1978) The spermatozoon of Arthropoda. XXX. The multiflagellate spermatozoon in the termite *Mastotermes darwiniensis*. *J. Cell Biol.* **76**, 569–576.

Bacetti B., Dallai R. & Callaini G. (1981) The spermatozoon of Arthropoda: *Zootermopsis nevadensis* and isopteran sperm phylogeny. *Int. J. Invertebr. Reprod.* **3** (2), 87–99.

Buchli H. (1958) L'origine des castes et les potentialités ontogéniques des Termites européens du genre *Reticulitermes* Holmgren. *Ann. Sci. Nat., Zool.* (11) **20**, 261–429.

Castle G. B. (1934) The damp-wood termites of western United States, genus *Zootermopsis*. In *Termites and Termite Control*, 2nd ed., (ed. C. A. Kofoid), pp. 273–310. Univ. Calif. Press, Berkeley.

Clément G. (1952) Recherches sur le polymorphisme de *Psammotermes hybostoma* Desneux. *Ann. Sci. Nat., Zool.* (11) **14**, 95–116.

Clément G. (1953) Sur la différenciation d'ovocytes dans les testicules des "neutres" d'*Anacanthotermes ochraceus*. *C.R. Acad. Sci.* **236**, 1095–1096.

Cleveland L. R., Hall S. R., Sanders E. P. & Collier J. (1934) The wood-feeding roach *Cryptocercus*, its Protozoa, and the symbiosis between Protozoa and roach. *Mem. Amer. Acad. Arts Sci.* **17**, 185–342.

Deligne J. (1970) Recherches sur la transformation des jeunes en soldats dans la société de Termites (Insectes Isoptères). Thèse, Univ. Bruxelles.

Emerson A. E. (1926) Development of soldier Termites. *Zoologica* **7**, 69–100.

Emerson A. E. (1933) A revision of the genera of fossil and recent *Termopsinae* (Isoptera). *Univ. Calif. Publ. Entom.* **6**, 165–196.

Emerson A. E. (1955) Geographical origin and dispersion of termite genera. *Fieldiana, Zool.* **37**, 465–521.

Emerson A. E. (1971) Tertiary fossil species of the Rhinotermitidae (Isoptera), phylogeny of genera, and reciprocal phylogeny of associated Flagellata (Protozoa) and the Staphylinidae (Coleoptera). *Bull. Amer. Mus. Nat. Hist.* **146** (3), 245–303.

Emerson A. E. & Krishna K. (1975) The termite family Serritermitidae (Isoptera). *Amer. Mus. Nat. Hist.* **2570**, 1–31.

Grassé P.-P. (1949) Ordres des Isoptères ou Termites. *Traité de Zoologie, Anatomie, Systématique, Biologie,* Vol. 9 (ed. P.-P. Grassé), pp. 408–544. Masson, Paris.

Grassé P.-P. (1982) *Termitologia,* Vol. 1, 676 p. Masson, Paris.

Grassé P.-P. & Noirot Ch. (1946a) La production des sexués néoténiques chez le Termite à cou jaune (*Calotermes flavicollis* F.): inhibition germinale et inhibition somatique. *C.R. Acad. Sci.* **223**, 869–871.

Grassé P.-P. & Noirot Ch. (1946b) Le polymorphisme social du Termite à cou jaune (*Calotermes flavicollis* F.). La production des soldats. *C.R. Acad. Sci.* **223**, 929–931.

Grassé P.-P. & Noirot Ch. (1947) Le polymorphisme social du Termite à cou jaune (*Calotermes flavicollis* F.). Les faux-ouvriers ou pseudergates et les mues régressives. *C.R. Acad. Sci.* **224**, 219–221.

Grassé P.-P. & Noirot Ch. (1957) La société de *Calotermes flavicollis* (Insecte Isoptère), de sa fondation au premier essaimage. *C.R. Acad. Sci.* **246**, 1789–1795.

Hare L. (1934) Caste determination and differentiation with special reference to the genus *Reticulitermes* (Isoptera). *J. Morph.* **56**, 267–293.

Imms A. D. (1919) On the structure and biology of *Archotermopsis*, together with description of new species of intestinal Protozoa. *Phil. Trans. R. Soc. London* **209**, 75–180.

Jones S. C., La Fage J. P. & Wright V. L. (1981) Studies of dispersal, colony caste and sexual composition, and incipient colony development of *Pterotermes occidentis* (Walker) (Isoptera: Kalotermitidae). *Sociobiology* **6**, 221–242.

Kalshoven, L. G. E. (1930) De biologie van de Djatermiet (*Kalotermes tectonae* Damm) in verband met zijn bestridjding. *Meded. Inst. Plantzenz.* Wageningen **76**, 1–154.

Krishna K. (1970) Taxonomy, phylogeny, and distribution of termites. In *Biology of Termites* (eds K. Krishna & F. Weesner), Vol. 2, pp. 127–152. Academic Press, New York and London.

Lefeuvre J. C. (1969) Recherches sur les organes alaires des *Blattaria.* Thèse, Univ. Rennes.

Luamba J. L. N. (1980a) Recherches sur le polymorphisme et aperçu sur l'influence de l'analogue de l'hormone juvénile sur le développement d'un termite *Hodotermes mossambicus* (Isoptera, Hodotermitidae). *Biologie-Ecologie méditerranéenne* **7**, 169–171.

Luamba J. L. N. (1980b) Recherches sur le polymorphisme et aperçu sur l'influence de l'analogue de l'hormone juvénile sur le développement d'un termite, *Hodotermes mossambicus* (Isoptera, Hodotermitidae). Thèse, Univ. Berne.

Lüscher M. (1952a) Die Produktion und Elimination von Ersatzgeschlechtstieren bei der Termite *Kalotermes flavicollis* Fabr. *Zeitsch. Vergl. Physiol.* **34**, 123–141.

Lüscher M. (1952b) Untersuchungen über das individuelle Wachstum bei der Termite *Kalotermes flavicollis* Fabr. (Ein Beitrag zum Kastenbildungsproblem). *Biol. Zentralbl.* **71**, 529–543.

Lüscher M. (1974) Kasten und Kasten-differenzierung bei niederen Termiten. "*Sozialpolymorphismus bei Insekten*" (ed. G. H. Schmidt) pp. 694–739. Wiss. Verlagsges. Stuttgart.

Mednikova T. K. (1977) Caste differentiation in the termite *Anacanthotermes ahngerianus* Jacobson (Isoptera, Hodotermitidae). *Proceed. VIII Internat. Congress IUSSI,* Wageningen, pp. 118–120.

Mensa-Bonsu A. (1976) The biology and development of *Porotermes adamsoni* (Froggatt) (Isoptera, Hodotermitidae). *Insectes Sociaux* **23**, 155–165.

Miller E. M. (1942) The problem of castes and caste differentiation in *Prorhinotermes simplex* (Hagen). *Bull. Univ. Miami* **15**, 1–27.

Miller E. M. (1969) Caste differentiation in the lower termites. *Biology of Termites* (eds K. Krishna & F. M. Weesner), Vol. 1, pp. 283–310. Academic Press, New York.

Moore B. P. (1968) Studies on the chemical composition and function of the cephalic gland secretion in Australian Termites. *J. Insect Physiol.* **14**, 33–39.

Morgan F. D. (1959) The ecology and external morphology of *Stolotermes ruficeps* Brauer. *Trans. Roy. Soc. New Zealand* **86**, 155–195.

Myles T. G. (1982) Studies of the caste system and caste mechanisms of the Hawaiian forest tree termite, *Neotermes connexus* Snyder 1922. M.Sc. Thesis, Univ. Hawaii.

Nagin R. (1972) Caste determination in *Neotermes jouteli* (Banks). *Insectes Sociaux* **19**, 39–61.

Nalepa C. A. (1982) Colony composition of the wood-roach *Cryptocercus punctulatus.* The *Biology of Social Insects* (eds M. D. Breed, C. D. Michener, H. E. Evans), p. 181. Westview Press, Boulder.

Noirot Ch. (1969) Formation of castes in the higher termites. *Biology of Termites* (eds K. Krishna & F. M. Weesner), Vol. 1, pp. 311–350. Academic Press, New York.

Noirot Ch. (1982) La caste des ouvriers, élément majeur du succès évolutif des Termites. *Rivista di Biologia* 72, 157–195.

Oster G. F. & Wilson E. O. (1978) *Caste and ecology in the social insects (Monographs in population biology)*. Princeton University Press, 352 p.

Quennedey A. & Deligne J. (1975) L'arme frontale des soldats de Termites. I. Rhinotermitidae. *Insectes Sociaux* 22, 243–267.

Renoux J. (1976) Le polymorphism de *Schedorhinotermes lamanianus* (Sjöstedt) (Isoptera-Rhinotermitidae). Essai d'interprétation. *Insectes Sociaux* 23, 281–491.

Roy-Noel J. (1968) Etudes biométrique et morphologique du couvain de *Coptotermes intermedius*. *Insectes Sociaux* 15, 389–394.

Sands W. A. (1972) The soldierless termites of Africa. *Bull. British Mus. (Nat. Hist.) Entomol.* Suppl. 18, 244 p.

Sewell J. J. & Watson J. A. L. (1981) Developmental pathways in Australian species of *Kalotermes* Hagen (Isoptera). *Sociobiology* 6, 243–324.

Watson J. A. L., Metcalf E. C. & Sewell J. J. (1977) A re-examination of the development of castes in *Mastotermes darwiniensis* Froggatt (Isoptera). *Aust. J. Zool.* 25, 25–42.

Watson J. A. L. & Sewell J. J. (1981) The origin and evolution of caste systems in termites. *Sociobiology* 6, 101–118.

Wilson E. O. (1971) *The insect societies*. Harvard Univ. Press, Cambridge, 548 p.

Zhuzhikov D. P., Zolotarev E. Kh. & Mednikova T. K. (1972) (Postembryonic development of *Anacanthotermes ahngerianus* Jacobson). In Russian. *Termites (Collected articles)*. Transact. of Entomol. Div. n° 2, edit. by E. Kh. Zolotarev, Moscow Lomonosov State Univ.

CHAPTER 5

Dynamic Study of Polymorphism in Schedorhinotermes lamanianus (Rhinotermitidae)

JACQUES RENOUX

Laboratoire de Biologie des Populations, Université Paris val de Marne, Avenue du Général de Gaulle, 94 010 Creteil Cédex, France

CONTENTS

5.1 INTRODUCTION

In the family Rhinotermitidae larval development was studied in *Reticulitermes* (Lespes, 1856; Grassi & Sandias, 1893–4; Feytaud, 1912; Thompson, 1917; Snyder, 1925–6; Montalenti, 1927; Pickens, 1932; Hare, 1934; Bathellier, 1941; Buchli, 1958), *Coptotermes formosanus* (Oshima, 1919; King & Spink, 1974) and *Prorhinotermes simplex* (Banks & Snyder, 1920; Miller, 1942).

The development in *Schedorhinotermes lamanianus* is different from that found in other Rhinotermitidae (Renoux, 1976).

5.2   SEASONAL CYCLE

The cycle of development in *Schedorhinotermes lamanianus*, which takes months, culminates in two annual swarmings which coincide with maximum rainfall. During the swarming period only the female "neuters" are formed. The reappearance of reproductive larvae two months after swarming could be due to external influences or to the formation within the female reproductive system of specific oogonia (Fig. 5.1).

The rhythm of growth slows down during the cool dry season. The time of swarming is linked to the rains and takes place at night roughly 48 hr after a heavy fall, as is the case for *Macrotermes natalensis* (Ruelle, 1964).

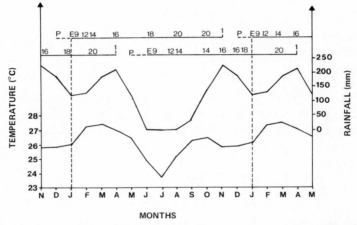

Fig. 5.1. Development cycle of reproductives in relation to the mean climatic conditions in Brazzaville during the years 1968 to 1973. E: hatching; 9–12–14–16–18–20: nymphal instars; I: imago (swarming); P: laying of eggs; Pr: rainfall in mm (right ordinates); T: temperature in Celsius degrees (left ordinates); thick line: mean monthly rainfalls; fine line: mean monthly temperature at 6.20 cm underground. One can note the slow development of the nymphs 12 and 14 in one series and 18 and 20 in the other during the dry and cool seasons. The predicted nymphal instars agree with the instars of individuals found in the nests.

5.3   LARVAE

The brood is distinguished from the rest of the population by certain morphological and physiological characteristics specific to itself. The larvae are divided into three instars, characterized by the number of antennal segments.

5.3.1   First instar larvae—9 antennal segments

They all appear morphologically identical and despite variations in measurements of the head and tibia, those of the antennae are characteristic ($p = 0.02$). The gonads present different characteristics during the reproductive formation and when reproductives are not being formed. In the former case only females exist, the size of ovaries is small and distributed normally around the mean ($p = 0.60$). This population, destined to produce neuters, is homogeneous. During the formation period of reproductives, two groups may be distinguished: one, with small ovaries, produces neuters and the other, with large ovaries, produces nymphs (Fig. 5.2).

These results lead us to examine the ovaries of embryos. The results

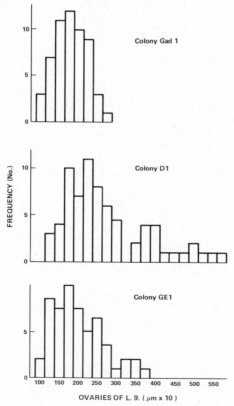

FIG. 5.2. The size of first instar larva ovaries during the seasonal cycle. In abscissas: size of ovaries; in ordinates: numbers of individuals; colony Gad-3: taken outside the formation period of reproductives; colony Di: taken during the formation period of reproductives; colony Ge-1: taken at the end of the formation period of reproductives.

indicated that two populations already exist at the period of the reproductive formation (χ^2, $p = 0.03$).

Thus, the separation into neuters and reproductives takes place at the latest in the course of the first larval instar, but possibly in the course of embryonic development or even during oogenesis.

5.3.2   Second instar larvae—12 antennal segments

The increase in number of segments takes place as a result of the division of the third segment.

The biometric study of larvae collected during the non-nymphal formation period reveals dimorphism in the sizes of the labra and the head, allowing the separation of individuals into narrow-headed larvae and broad-headed larvae (Fig. 5.3). Larvae collected during the period of nymphal formation, among the broad-headed larvae, formed a population with narrow thorax and

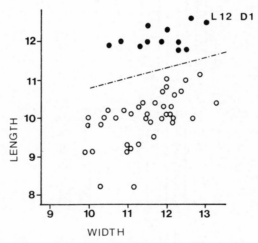

FIG. 5.3. Correlation between the length and width (μm) of the labrum of the second instar larvae from colony Di.

partially developed ovaries, and that with larger thorax and more developed ovaries could be distinguished. The latter group develops into nymphs, whereas the former will produce neuters. One also finds males with growing testes among the population with larger thorax. The individuals with more developed ovaries and testes represent the reproductive line which is morphologically distinct from the neuter line in the second instar.

5.3.3   Third instar larvae—14 antennal segments

The characteristics of nymphs in this instar will be outlined below in the paragraph on reproductives.

Regarding third instar larvae which develop into neuters, two categories can be drawn out, the large-headed larvae which will produce workers and the small-headed larvae whose labral formation and mandibles indicate that these individuals transform into soldiers (Fig. 5.4).

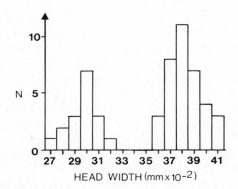

Fig. 5.4. Histogram of the head-width of the third instar larvae from colony Br-4.

The three larval instars depend on workers since they do not possess the symbiotic fauna which would allow them to digest cellulose. One notes, however, some exceptions among the third instar larvae of young colonies.

Just after the third moult a radical transformation brings about a sudden change from a larva into a worker, which is not typical in the lower termites.

5.4   WORKERS

The workers are distinguished from larvae as much by their behaviour as by their morphological characteristics. In this they differ from other Rhinotermitidae (Grassé *et al.*, 1950).

We can distinguish between workers with 16 (0.16) and 17 (0.17) antennal segments. Morphological study reveals specific worker characteristics: pigmentation, mandibular dentition, peculiarities of clypeus and labra. The gonads remain rudimentary, perhaps owing to the early separation from the line of reproductives. With rare exceptions, all workers are female.

Concerning the 0.16 workers, the measurements carried out in the course of biometric study yield complex results which have been interpreted with the aid of two correlations—length of antenna:length of tibia and length of antenna:size of head.

These data, coupled with rearing, experiments and observations of individuals in moult, show that the 0.16 workers can be divided into three populations: the 0.16–1 developed from large-headed larvae—14 are of the fourth instar; the 0.16–2, resulting from the moulting of the 0.16–1, are of the fifth instar as are workers 0.17–1 which have acquired an additional antennal segment; and the very rare 0.16–3, which seem to develop from workers 0.16–2 would thus be in the sixth instar.

The measurements carried out on the 0.17 also give very complex results. The population is heterogeneous, composed of groups of individuals which we will for convenience designate as 0.17–1, 0.17–2, 0.17–3 and 0.17–4. The 0.17–1 originate from the 0.16–2 by acquisition of one antennal segment. The 0.17–2 vary markedly in measurements and they are derived partly from the 0.16–2 and partly from the 0.17–1. The 0.17–3 comprise of two unequal subgroups. The smaller group composed of individuals with small third antennal segments are derived from the 0.16–2, whereas the larger group develops from the 0.17–2.

The 0.17–4 are rare and seem mostly to come from the 0.17–3. There are also certain rare individuals with 18 antennal segments.

Figure 5.5 sets out development pathways explaining polymorphism in workers and showing the five successive stages of development. The first is homogeneous, the succeeding instars each comprise of two categories characterized by the number of antennal segments. It would be interesting to know if these structural differences reflect physiological or ethological differences, or whether they merely represent chance factors of growth.

5.5 SOLDIERS

The general morphology of *S. lamanianus* soldiers described by Sjöstedt (1896, 1900, 1910, 1926a, b), Silvestri (1914, 1920), Wasmann (1911), Emerson (1928), Kemp (1955), Weidner (1956) and Harris (1968) separates them from the rest of the neuters. They are all females and clearly reveal visible secondary sexual characteristics. They depend for nourishment on the workers.

Casual examination enables us to distinguish between small soldiers "*sensu lato*" and large soldiers.

5.5.1 Small and medium-sized soldiers

A biometric study, based on variations in the measurements of head size of

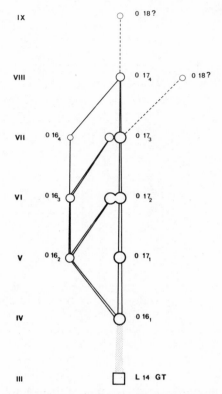

FIG. 5.5. Scheme of postembryonic development of workers.

the small soldiers "*sensu lato*" and to the relationship between head length and width, here called the "coefficient of narrowness", reveals two populations: the small soldiers (PS) with narrow heads and the other, less important, the broad-headed medium-sized soldiers (MS) (Fig. 5.6).

Among the PS, correlation between variations of head length and width shows heterogeneity which indicates a difference in origin.

Similarly, for the large soldiers (GS) a histogram of measurements of head width suggests that there are three or four categories each developed from a different worker stage.

The soldiers thus constitute a diverse group apparently developed from individuals at different stages and probably varied in their determinism.

These results are confirmed experimentally: the small-headed second instar larvae produce the PS and the workers the GS. The medium-sized soldiers develop from the third instar larvae.

The development of larvae, monitored systematically in the course of several experiments, has shown that the percentage of soldiers emerging

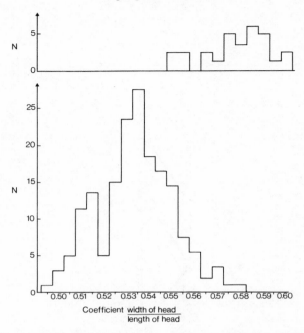

Fig. 5.6. Histograms representing the "coefficient of narrowness" of the head among the small and medium sized soldiers from the colony Br-4. Upper: medium-sized soldiers; lower: small soldiers.

varied with the number of soldiers existing in the colony, the presence of the latter tending to inhibit the formation of new soldiers.

The soldier line is probably determined in the course of the first instar and this leads to the development of special larvae from the second instar onwards. The determination is thus irreversible. The PS seem to inhibit the formation of new soldiers if they are already present before the period of determination.

Both PS and MS have characteristic morphology whose development is reinforced by moults in the course of the preceding larval stages: pear-shaped head, elongated labra and long sharp mandibles. The frontal gland is smaller than that of the GS: the gonads are also less developed.

5.5.2 Large soldiers (GS)

These are clearly larger than the PS, their labra less developed and their mandibles less pointed. The volume of the frontal gland which is more marked here is important as it secretes tetradecenone (Quennedey, 1973; Quennedey et al., 1973), a powerful insecticide.

Sexual development is more prominent than among the PS and MS and it is not uniform in the first four worker instars which occasionally transform into soldiers through two moults.

The defensive behaviour of the PS and GS is different, being of the mower type and biting type, respectively.

5.6 REPRODUCTIVES

The sexual line consists of five categories of nymphs bearing antennae with 12, 14, 16, 18 and 20 segments respectively.

From the morphological point of view, the first instar reproductives differ from neuters only by the presence of males and the size of the ovaries.

In the second instar (Ny 12) the larger paranota and the development of the ovaries, bearing oogonia and foreshadowing the ovarioles, clearly identifies the reproductives.

Third instar nymphs (Ny 14) have small wing-pads. The females display ventral valves and rudimentary dorsal valves which in later development disappear. In the males, the testes show numerous mitoses and attain their maximum size. The seminal vesicles are already recognizable.

In the fourth instar (Ny 16) the wing-pads are well-developed and the compound eyes appear. The seminal vesicles grow longer and the ejaculatory duct is already formed. The ovaries continue their growth and the accessory glands become quite prominent.

Fifth and sixth instars (Ny 18 and Ny 20) see these characteristics accentuated, and the external morphology undergoes modifications.

The imago which develops from sixth instar nymph attains its definitive form. The male is smaller than the female. It has a penis and possesses testes which are smaller than those of the ergatoid neotenic; the vasa deferentia contain no spermatozoa and the seminal vesicles conform to the type described for Rhinotermitidae (Weesner, 1956–69; Springhetti & Oddone, 1963a, b). The female gonads are similar to those of the ergatoid neotenics.

The sex ratio reveals an as yet unexplained imbalance, females being generally more numerous than males.

5.7 NEOTENICS

If the royal couple is last, this upsets the dynamic equilibrium between neuters and reproductives. Regulatory mechanisms permit certain immature individuals to develop sexual characteristics and become neotenics. We can distinguish ergatoid neotenic reproductives (NE) and nymphoid neotenic

(NN) as established in other Rhinotermitidae (Thompson & Snyder, 1920; John, 1925; Weyer, 1930; Ghidini, 1937; Miller, 1942; Buchli, 1958).

In the absence of the royal couple, from the fifth day onwards some individuals with 16 or 17 antennal segments and small wing-pads with more developed ovaries and gonads appear in the nurseries. These are the ergatoid preneotenics. Eight to 10 days afterwards these individuals moult into NE females which are different from the workers from which they originated.

The biometric study on the number of antennal segments, the length of the antenna, tibia, thorax and wing-pads, makes it possible to distinguish four populations, while the experimental study shows their origin (0.16–1:0.16–2 and 0.17–1:0.17–3) (Fig. 5.7).

The morphological study of the female genitalia shows similarities with workers as well as important differences from the imagos.

The very rare NE males are distinguished with difficulty from the workers, but easily from females. The testes are more developed than those of the male imago and the morphology of the ejaculatory duct suggests the presence of an aedeagus.

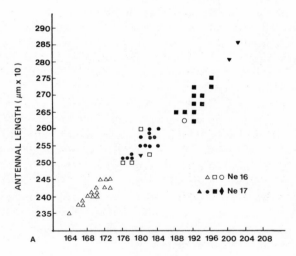

Fig. 5.7. Correlations among the NE from the colony Br-5: length of antenna and length of tibia (× 10).

△NE with 16 antennal segments ⎫
△NE with 17 antennal segments ⎭ originating in 1st instar workers

○NE with 16 antennal segments ⎫
○NE with 17 antennal segments ⎭ originating in 2nd instar workers

□NE with 16 antennal segments ⎫
□NE with 17 antennal segments ⎭ originating in 3rd instar workers

◇NE with 17 antennal segments   originating in 4th instar workers

Nymphoid neotenics are very rare in nature, but, in contrast, they develop readily in the nursery and the first eggs appear at the end of 40 days. The development of nymphs is normal until the fourth instar and from fifth instar onwards the nymphal characteristics are modified. Genital maturity is attained in the sixth instar and not in the seventh as in the imago.

Individual response to the removal of inhibition is quite possible either due to hereditary determination or to the existence of a variable threshold of receptivity during a period of "competence".

In natural colonies, the NE are extremely frequent, presumably due to the dilution of the inhibitory influence exercised by the royal couple in an extended nest comprising numerous secondary nests.

The transformation into a neotenic requires, therefore, a certain somatic development which takes place in the fourth instar. The fertility of young neotenics may be explained by the substantial development of the gonads. The females are always more numerous. The replacement of imagos by neotenics, which often occurs, is evidence of advance evolution in a society which by this means acquires potential immortality.

5.8   CONCLUSION

We have established that if from the morphological and physiological point of view *S. lamanianus* is a lower termite, the evolution of its post-embryonic development seems to be dissociated from its morphological and physiological evolution. This establishes a polymorphism comparable to that of higher termites, characterized by narrowly specialized castes the determination of which is rarely reversible and takes place at clearly determined stages. Some characteristics seem to be even more highly evolved than those of the Termitidae, in particular the specialization of a single sex in the formation of neuters and the replacement of the royal couple by neotenics which confers a potential immortality on a colony.

5.9   SUMMARY

The study of post-embryonic development in *Schedorhinotermes lamanianus* reveals numerous special characteristics. The neuters are all female right from the time of hatching onwards, and presumably from the time the eggs are laid. The determination of the neuter or reproductive line of development is made before hatching and the extent of growth of their gonads is determined from the first larval instar. The neuters are also formed during the period of reproductive formation.

Larvae go through three instars and depend on workers for food since they do not participate in any work. Workers moult from the third instar larvae, then acquire a symbiotic intestinal fauna. They may go through five successive moults without seeming to develop into adult form. Some workers may also develop from workers of preceding instar. No pseudergate has been observed.

The soldiers are divided into:

(1) Small soldiers, developing from specific larvae determined from the first instar onwards.
(2) Medium-sized soldiers are produced from third instar larvae which normally develop into workers.
(3) Large soldiers develop from different stages of workers.

All these soldiers develop through a white soldier intermediate stage and exerts an inhibitory action on the formation of new soldiers. This regulation seems to be through a pheromone.

The reproductive line consists of six instars and the development to imago extends over 11 months. Nymphs do not work and are fed by workers. Each year the same colony goes through two cycles of reproductive formation which swarm during the two long rainy seasons. The sex-ratio of swarming individuals is always in favour of females.

The royal couple found a colony and may be replaced by female ergatoid neotenics and by male and female nymphoid neotenics which generally pass through a preneotenic stage (Fig. 5.8).

Although *S. lamanianus* is classified from the anatomical and physiological points of view as a lower termite, its polymorphism and social organization are closer to those of the higher termites, which indicates a differential rate of evolution for different characteristics. This demonstrates the difficulty of adding new data to a general conception and theory of termite evolution.

5.10 REFERENCES

Banks N. & Snyder T. E. (1920) A revision of the neartic termites with notes on biology and geographic distribution. *Bull. Us. Nat. Mus.* **108**, 1–228.

Bathellier J. (1941) Sur le développement de *Leucotermes* (*Reticulitermes*) *lucifugus* Rossi. *C.r. hebd. Séanc. Acad. Sci. Paris* **213**, 663–665.

Buchli H. (1958) L'origine des castes et les potentialité ontogénétiques des Termites européens du genre *Reticulitermes* Holm. Masson éd., Paris 263–429.

Emerson A. E. (1928) Termites of the Belgian Congo and the Cameroun. *Bull. Am. Mus. nat. Hist.* (N.Y.) **7**, 401–574.

Feytaud J. (1912) Contribution à l'étude du Termite Lucifuge. *Archs. Anat. micros.* **13**, 481–607.

Ghidini G. M. (1937) I Reali di terza forma in *Reticulitermes lucifugus* Rossi. *Mem della Soc. Entom. Ital.* **16**, 25–36.

Grassé P. P., Noirot C., Clément G. & Buchli H. (1950) Sur la signification de la caste des ouvriers chez les Termites. *C.r. hebd. Séanc. Acad. Sci. Paris* **230**, 892–895.

Grassi B. & Sandias A. (1893–4) Costituzione e sviluppo della societa dei Termitidi. Atti. *Acad. Gioenia Sci. Nat. Catania* **6**, 1–75 et **7**, 1–76.

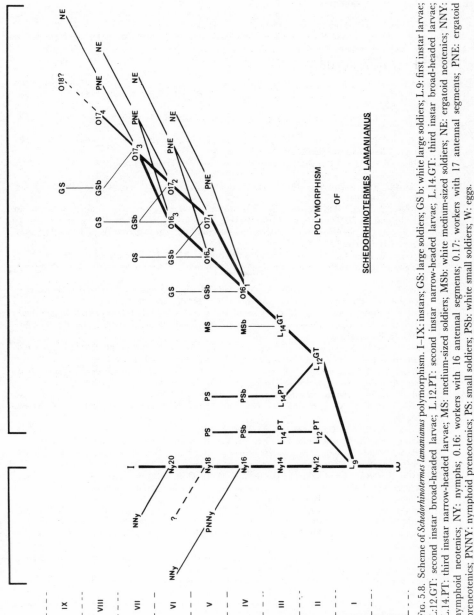

FIG. 5.8. Scheme of *Schedorhinotermes lamanianus* polymorphism. I–IX: instars; GS: large soldiers; GS b: white large soldiers; L.9: first instar larvae; L.12.GT: second instar broad-headed larvae; L.12.PT: second instar narrow-headed larvae; L.14.GT: third instar broad-headed larvae; L.14.PT: third instar narrow-headed larvae; MS: medium-sized soldiers; MSb: white medium-sized soldiers; NE: ergatoid neotenics; NNY: nymphoid neotenics; NY: nymphs; 0.16: workers with 16 antennal segments; 0.17: workers with 17 antennal segments; PNE: ergatoid preneotenics; PNNY: nymphoid preneotenics; PS: small soldiers; PSb: white small soldiers; W: eggs.

Hare L. (1934) Caste determination and differentiation with special reference to the genus *Reticulitermes* (Isoptera). *J. Morph* **56**, 267–293.

Harris W. V. (1968) African termites of the genus *Schedorhinotermes* (Isoptera: Rhinotermitidae) and associated termitophiles (Lepidoptera: Tineidae). *Proc. R. ent. Soc. Lond.* **37**, 103–113.

John O. (1925) Termiten von Ceylon, der malaiischen Halbinsel, Sumatra, Java und den Aruiseln. *Treubia* **6**, 360–419.

Kemp P. B. (1955) The Termites of North-Eastern Tanganyika: their distribution and biology. *Bull Ent. res.* **46**, 113–135.

King E. G. & Spink W. T. (1974) Laboratory studies on the biology of the Formosan subterranean termite with primary emphasis on young colony development. *Ann. Ent. Soc. Amer.* **67**, (6), 953–958.

Lespes C. (1856) Recherches sur l'organisation et les moeurs du Termite lucifuge. *Annls Sci. Nat. Zool.* **5**, 5–7, 227–282.

Miller E. M. (1942) The problem of castes and caste differentiation in *Prorhinotermes simplex* Hagen. *Bull. Univ. Miami* **15**, 1–27.

Montalenti G. (1927) Sul differenziamento delle caste nei *Termes lucifugus*. *Boll. Inst. Zoo. Univ. Roma* **7**, 1–23.

Oshima M. (1919) Formosan termites and methods for preventing their damage. *Philipp. J. Sci.* **15**, (4), 319–384.

Pickens A. L. (1932) Distribution and life history of the species of *Reticulitermes* Holm. in California. *Ph.D. Thesis*, Univ. Calif. Berkeley.

Quennedey A. (1973) Observations cytologiques et chimiques sur la glande frontale des Termites. *Proc. VII Congr. I.U.S.S.I.*, London.

Quennedey A., Brule G., Rigaud J., Dubois P. & Brossut R. (1973) La glande frontale des soldats de *Schedorhinotermes putorius* (Isoptera): Analyse chimique et fonctionnement. *Insect. Biochem.* **3**, 67–74.

Renoux J. (1976) Le Polymorphisme de *Schedorhinotermes lamanianus* (Sjöstedt) (Isoptera—Rhinotermitidae) Essai d'interprétation *Ins. Soc.* **23** (3b), 281–491.

Ruelle J. E. (1964) L'essaimage de *Macrotermes natalensis* Haviland dans la région de Léopoldville (Isoptera, Macrotermitinae). Coll. int. Termites Africans, Univ. Lovanium, A. Bouillen éd., Masson Paris, 213–245.

Silvestri F. (1914) Contribuzione alla conoscenza die Termitidi e Termitofili dell'Africa occidentale. *Boll. Lab. Zool. gen. agr. R. Scuola Agric. Portici, Termitidi* **9**, 1–146.

Silvestri F. (1920) Contribuzione alla conoscenza die Termitidi e Termitofili dell'Africa occidentale. *Boll. Lab. Zool. gen. agr. R. Scuola Agric. Portici, Termitofili* **14**, 265–318.

Sjöstedt Y. (1896) Termiten aus Kamerun. *Ent. Tidskr.* **17**, 297–298.

Sjöstedt Y. (1900–4) Monographie der Termiten Afrikas K. *Svenska. Vet. Akad. Handl.* **34–38**, 1–236.

Sjöstedt Y. (1910) Zur Termitenfauna Kongas. *Ent. Tidskr.* **32**, 137–170.

Sjöstedt Y. (1926a) Revision der Termiten Afrikas. K. *Svenska Vet. Akad. Handl.* **3**, 1–419.

Sjöstedt Y. (1926b) Kongo Termiten aus dem Ituri und Uelegebiet. *Revue Zool. afr.* **14**, 160–164.

Snyder T. E. (1925) The origin of castes in termites. *Proc. Biol. Soc. Wash.* **38**, 57–68.

Snyder T. E. (1926) The biology of the termite castes. *Quart. Rev. Biol.* 522–552.

Springhetti A. & Oddone P. (1963) Funzionalita dell'apparato genitale maschile in caste diverse di alcune termiti primitive. *Symp. Genet.* **11**, 311–334.

Springhetti A. (1963) Sugli organi genitali maschili delle Rhinotermitidae (Isoptera). *Insectes Soc.* **10**, (2), 143–152.

Thompson G. B. (1917) Origin of the castes of the common termite *Leucotermes flavipes*. *J. Morph.* **30**, 85–153.

Thompson G. B. & Snyder T. E. (1930) The "third form" the wingless reproductive type of termites in *Reticulitermes* and *Prorhinotermes*. *J. Morph.* **34**, 591–633.

Wasmann E. (1911) Zur Kenntnis det Termiten und Termitengäste von Belgischen Kongo. *Revue, Zool. Bot. afr.* **1**, 91–117 and 145–176.

Weesner F. M. (1956) The biology of colony foundation in *Reticulitermes hesperus* Banks. *Univ. Calif. Publ. Zool.* **61**, (5), 253–313.

Weesner F. M. (1969) The reproductive system. In: *Biology of Termites* (eds K. Krishna and F. M. Weesner), pp. 125–160. Academic Press, New York and London 1.

Weidner H. (1956) Beitrage zur Kenntnis der Termiten Angolas. *Publções cult. Co. Diam Angola* **19**, 55–106.

Weyer F. (1930) Sur Kenntnis des Keimdrusen bei Termiten-Arbeitern und Soldaten. *Zool. Anz.* **90**, 177–190.

CHAPTER 6

The Caste System in Higher Termites

Ch. NOIROT

Laboratory of Zoology, University of Dijon, Boulevard Gabriel, 21100 Dijon, France

CONTENTS

6.1 INTRODUCTION

Contrary to the lower termites, the higher termites form a well-defined systematic unit, the family Termitidae. It is subdivided into four subfamilies, recently redefined by Sands (1972): Termitinae, Apicotermitinae, Nasutitermitinae and Macrotermitinae. The characteristic digestive system (Grassé & Noirot, 1954), especially the hind-gut (with one or several paunches or "fermentation chambers") and its junction with the mid-gut is a very good parameter for defining these subfamilies. This is in contrast to the much more uniform structure of the digestive system encountered in the lower termites. This evolution may be related to the loss of symbiotic flagellates, the function of which is replaced (at least in part) by a complex of bacteria. Accordingly, the diet of higher termites is much more varied (sound or decayed wood, dead leaves, litter, humus etc.) each species specializing on a more or less defined kind of food, and most probably the bacterial complex differs adaptatively. Unfortunately, available information remains very limited, both on the types of bacteria and their role in the digestive process (see Breznak, 1982, and O'Brien & Slaytor, 1982, for recent reviews). The subfamily Macrotermitinae or the fungus-growing termites, reached a further step in the symbiotic utilization of ligno-cellulose material, by their association with the termitophilous fungi of the genus *Termitomyces*. By this character, and several others, including caste development, the Macrotermitinae appears somewhat isolated from the other subfamilies, probably separated early from the common trunk of the Termitidae.

6.2   DEVELOPMENTAL PATHWAYS

6.2.1   Adult colonies

The most characteristic pattern, observed in all the species so far studied, is the visible separation, at the first moult, of the sexual and the neuter lines (Noirot, 1969). The development of sexuals is related to a precise seasonal cycle, the young nymphs appearing during a limited period of the year, whereas the production of neuter larvae is continuous (Noirot, Chapter 12). The development of imaginal alates, through five nymphal instars after the undifferentiated first instar larva (Noirot, 1969), seems uniform throughout the family. The nymphs are completely dependent of the workers for their nourishment (except perhaps in some species, as *Amitermes evuncifer*, where the late nymphal instars are sometimes observed outside the nest). The first three nymphal instars receive only liquid food (saliva from workers), and this diet may be continued until the final instars, especially in humivorous species. The last two nymphal instars, in most species, bear a gut (especially the hindgut) full of wood or other plant material following stomodeal trophallaxis by workers (these nymphs never leave the nest) (Noirot, 1952).

The development of neuters (soldiers and workers) is much more variable, but follows for each species a very definite pathway (Noirot, 1955, 1969, 1974). The functional workers are preceded by two larval instars (including the first undifferentiated one) in all the subfamilies except the Macrotermitinae, where three larval instars exist.

There is an essential distinction between the larvae and the workers. The former are fragile insects, appearing white due to the absence of sclerotization (including the mandibles) and the gut appears optically empty and colourless. They remain in the nest and are completely dependent on the workers. The latter are, on the contrary, coloured insects to varying degrees as a result of some sclerotization and pigmentation of the cuticle on the one hand, and the gut content (solid food) on the other. The transformation of a larva into a worker occurs with very limited morphological modifications. However, the physiology and the behaviour are radically changed, as much as in true metamorphosis. This is in sharp contrast to the situation observed in most of the lower termites, where the transition between the larvae and the workers is progressive, and this difference can be related to the type of symbiosis: in the lower termites, where the brood is fed (at least in part) by proctodeal trophallaxis, the intestinal Protozoa may be acquired very early: in *Kalotermes flavicollis*, some flagellates are already present in first instar larvae, and the intestinal fauna is fully present in the second instar. In *Reticulitermes lucifugus*, the infestation begins in the second instar, and is fully achieved in the third (Grassé & Noirot, 1945).* With the proctodeal food, many wood particles are taken by the larvae, and thus a gradual transition from a dependent to an independent nourishment occurs. In the higher termites, proctodeal feeding never occurs. The brood is fed by purely liquid oral secretions (most probably from salivary glands) of the workers. After the moult which transforms the larva into a worker, an abrupt change occurs, both in the diet (crude food) and in the digestive process, although we have no information about the way by which the intestinal microflora is acquired.

Once differentiated, the workers, in many species, may moult again several times, usually without conspicuous growth (the genus *Trinervitermes* being the most noticeable exception), often with an increase in the degree of pigmentation and sclerotization. The number of worker instars is difficult to determine, because the later the instar, the more scarce the individuals become. For example, in *Nasutitermes arborum*, four successive instars are observed for the large (female) workers in field colonies, with very few insects in the fourth instar. In laboratory cultures, a few workers of the fifth instar were obtained, and it is not possible to ascertain whether or not it is a final instar (Noirot, 1955).

Another complication is introduced by a *sexual dimorphism* observed in the neuter line of many species. There is a difference in size between males and females evident in the second instar larvae (Noirot, 1955) and in an exceptional case this is observed in the first instar (*Trinervitermes*; Sands, 1965). Thus, two worker lines, males and females of different size are realized. Depending on the species, the larger workers are males (all the Macrotermitinae, some Termitinae, as *Microcerotermes*) or females (many Nasutitermitinae, but not in *Syntermes* where they are males). No relationship exists between the sexual dimorphism of the workers and that of the alates. In the latter, the sexual dimorphism, when present, is limited, and may be the opposite of what is found in the workers in the same species. By the combined effects of the successive instars and the sexual dimorphism, the worker caste may be

* In *Schedorhinotermes* however, no Protozoa are present in the two first instars, and very few in the third (Renoux, 1976). In this genus, where polymorphism is very evolved (see Renoux, Chapter 5), the larval–worker transition is sharper, tending to the higher termites type.

composed of a number of discrete categories, for example eight in *N. arborum* (three male workers and five large female workers). On the contrary, in the Apicotermitinae, and many humivorous Termitinae and Nasutitermitinae, sexual dimorphism is lacking (or evident only in the length of the antennae) and the workers cannot moult (except for the soldier production), and thus the worker caste appears monomorphic (Noirot, 1982).

Soldiers take their origin either from workers or from larvae. The worker origin is the most frequent, and seems general in the subfamilies Termitinae and Apicotermitinae (except of course the soldierless species!). In the Nasutitermitinae, the differentiation of workers into soldiers was first observed by Knower (1894) (*Nasutitermes*) and carefully described by Emerson (1926) in *Constrictotermes cavifrons*. Differentiation of soldiers from workers seem to be most frequent in this subfamily, although many genera (especially with a soldier polymorphism) were not studied. A larval origin was evidenced for the small soldiers of *Trinervitermes* (Noirot, 1955; Sands, 1965) and the monomorphic soldiers of *Tenuirostritermes* (Weesner, 1953). In these two genera, polymorphism appears to be very evolved (see below). Thus the worker may well be a primitive condition in the three subfamilies: Termitinae, Apicotermitinae and Nasutitermitinae. The subfamily Macrotermitinae seems different: in the species with only one type of soldiers, they originate from third instar larvae. When two types of soldiers occur, the smaller have the same origin, the larger differentiate either from true functional workers (*Ancistrotermes*), or from freshly moulted workers, which do not work during their short worker life (*Pseudacanthotermes*, *Macrotermes bellicosus*), or from a stage morphologically similar to the small workers, but slightly larger and larval-like (*Macrotermes michaelseni*; Okot-Kotber, 1981a, Chapter 7). Finally, in *Acanthotermes* (three types of soldiers) the large soldiers originate from workers, while the medium and small ones originate from larvae. It is difficult to decide what is the primitive condition (monomorphic or polymorphic soldiers) among the fungus-growing termites, because the phylogenetic relationship between the living genera are far from clear. Taken into account the difference in the number of larval instars (three in Macrotermitinae instead of two in other subfamilies), polymorphism of Macrotermitinae seems to have undergone a separate evolution.

Another important point is *the sex* of the soldiers. In the large majority of the species studied so far, the soldiers are of one sex. They are either males (most of the Nasutitermitinae) or females. (Macrotermitinae, except *Sphaerotermes*, many Termitinae and Apicotermitinae.) No clear relationship is evident between this phenomenon and the sexual dimorphism of the worker line. The unisexual status of the soldiers is found in the genera without worker polymorphism (Apicotermitinae, many Termitinae). When sexual dimorphism exists, the soldiers develop either from the larger worker line (female in *Microcerotermes*, male in *Sphaerotermes*) or from the small (female in the

Macrotermitinae except *Sphaerotermes*, male in the Nasutitermitinae). This specialization is pushed to the end in the genus *Trinervitermes*, where the small "workers" (males) do not work at all, and are only a transient stage towards the larger soldiers. Thus, all the functional workers are females and all the soldiers are males. The same situation possibly exists in *Tenuirostritermes* (Noirot, 1955).

6.2.2 Incipient colonies

During the lifetime of a termite colony, it is possible to recognize a *juvenile*, an *adult* and a *senile* period (Bodot, 1969; Noirot, 1969; Collins, 1981). During the juvenile period, only neuters (soldiers and workers) are produced; it is a time of exponential growth, extending through several years (documented for a few species only). In *Cubitermes sankurensis* (Bouillon and Lekie, 1964), where maximum size of the population is about 37,000 insects, the differentiation of nymphs and alates begins only with a population of 4500. In *C. severus*, the corresponding populations are 50,000 and 10,000 respectively, and for *C. subcrenulatus*, 35,000 and 4000 (Bodot, 1969). For these species, the absolute ages were not determined, but the duration of the juvenile period may be estimated as 3 or 4 years at least. For *Macrotermes bellicosus*, the juvenile period was estimated to be 5–6 years by Ruelle (quoted by Bodot, 1969) and 4–6 years by Collins (1981).

The development of incipient colonies was obtained in laboratory cultures (starting from a pair of alates collected in the nest or after the swarming) for several species, but the observations were limited to the very first steps. In these incipient colonies, soldiers and workers are constantly smaller than in adult societies (Light & Weesner, 1955; Noirot, 1955; Okot-Kotber, 1981; S. H. Han, in preparation). In most cases, these "nanitic" soldiers and workers underwent the same development pathways as in adult societies, especially for the differentiation of the soldiers. This was established for representatives of the subfamilies Termitinae (*Amitermes evuncifer*, Noirot, 1955; *Cubitermes fungifaber*, H. S. Han in preparation), Nasutitermitinae (*Tenuirostritermes tenuirostris*, Light & Weesner, 1955; five species of *Trinervitermes*, Sands, 1965), Macrotermitinae (*Macrotermes bellicosus*, Grassé & Noirot, 1955; *M. michaelseni*, Okot-Kotber, 1981; *Ancistrotermes guineensis*, Sands, 1960). The smaller size may be related to a conspicuous shortening of lifetime of the larval instars; this is evident, in *M. michaelseni*, by comparing the data of Okot-Kotber (1981b) for incipient colonies with those of Darlington (1982) for adult colonies. In two other cases, the first soldiers differentiate from an earlier instar than in adult colonies: *Pericapritermes urgens* (Termitinae, Noirot, 1955), *Nasutitermes ephratae* (Nasutitermitinae, Becker, 1961).

Some other differences between incipient and adult colonies were also observed: when two soldier types are present, only the smaller one appeared in the cultures (*M. bellicosus*, Noirot, 1955, Grassé & Noirot, 1955; *M. michaelseni*, Okot-Kotber, 1981; *Trinervitermes* spp., Sands, 1965). M. Lepage (personal communication) was able to follow the incipient colonies of *M. michaelseni* during a longer period (up to 20 months): he observed the large soldiers only after a long delay, one year at least (*vs.* 9–10 weeks for the small soldiers), but very variable from one colony to another. The minimal population was around 1000 individuals (including about 500 larvae). At the end of the observations, several colonies, well populated and in good condition, were still devoid of large soldiers. However, in *Pseudacanthotermes spiniger*, larger soldiers were observed, about 1 week after the first small soldier (Lüscher, 1951). When the workers follow several successive instars, they remain at the first (*Gnathamitermes perplexus*, Light & Weesner, 1947, *Amitermes evuncifer*, Noirot, 1955).

From these observations, particular conditions seem to exist in the incipient colonies, which influence, to a variable degree, caste differentiation. The nutritional status, most probably poorer at the beginning, may have some importance, but cannot explain the whole story, because the development is, in several well-documented instances, accelerated, either by a shorter duration of the larval instar or by a precocious differentiation of the soldiers, or both. It is even more difficult to explain the difference between the juvenile and adult periods, i.e. the differentiation of the first batch of nymphs.

6.3   DEVIATIONS FROM THE NORMAL PATHWAYS: THE INTERCASTES

The separation of the neuter and the sexual line, visible after the first moult, but possibly determined earlier (see Noirot, Chapter 12) seems irreversible, except in very exceptional cases, where intermediate individuals, or intercastes, may be observed, bearing a mixture of characters of both lines of development.

The most obvious examples are those of the *soldier-nymphs*, where the head is fully or partly of the soldier type, with often small compound eyes, but the thorax bears conspicuous wing buds (Noirot, 1969; Fontes & Terra, 1981 for further examples). These very rare insects are usually believed to originate from a late nymphal instar (last or penultimate), but this assumption is supported only by the morphological appearance. A more careful study was undertaken recently by Patrick Lefeuve (Dijon) and Barbara Thorne (Harvard) on two species of *Nasutitermes*. The detailed results will be published elsewhere, and only the main conclusions are presented here. In *N. columbicus*, the soldier-nymphs originate, without doubt, from an advanced nymphal instar (probably the penultimate). This is supported not only by the external morphology, but also by the anatomical study: the brain is of the nymphal type, with the optic lobes well developed (whereas these lobes are strongly reduced in the normal soldiers and workers). The sex organs too are nymphal, much more developed than in normal soldiers (all the intercastes examined were males, as the normal soldiers in this species). In *N. lujae* on the contrary, the soldier-nymphs take their origin in the small workers, like normal soldiers. The transformation was directly obtained, on two occasions, in laboratory cultures composed exclusively of minor workers. The anatomy is completely worker-like: the optic lobes of the brain are no more developed than in a normal soldier, although small compound eyes are well evident. The testes are as in normal soldiers.

The *soldier-worker* intercaste formation is, in the best documented cases, related to some internal parasite (dipteran larva, microsporidian ...) and their appearance may be easily explained by a modification of the hormonal equilibrium, especially the juvenile hormone level by this parasite (Noirot, 1969). As the soldiers originate from the worker line of development, what is surprising is not the observation of such intermediate individuals, but their rarity. More interesting cases are the *worker-nymph* intercastes, some of which were recently collected by Barbara Thorne in a single colony of *Nasutitermes columbicus*. Their study will be published elsewhere (Thorne & Noirot, in preparation). Briefly, these insects appear worker-like by their general appearance, the development of the gut (full of chewed wood), the paucity of the fat body. However, the thoratic nota bear more or less conspicuous wing buds, and the compound eyes are prominent. By their internal anatomy (sex organs, especially ovaries and optic lobes of the brain), they are entirely of nymphal type, and no sexual dimorphism in size is observed as in the nymphs but unlike in the workers. Most probably, they are individuals which started their development as nymphs, and reverted in part (perhaps at the third nymphal instar) towards a worker morphology. They are, in some respects, to be compared with the pseudergates of the lower termites, although they do not seem to work in the colony.

Thus, two general conclusions can be inferred from these results: first, the morphology alone cannot establish with certainty the origin of an intercaste. Second, in each developmental line some characters of the other line can be expressed, e.g. wing buds and compound eyes in intercastes derived from workers. In another report (Noirot, Chapter 12) the cases of ergatoid reproductives are also described, where the sexualization of the workers is often concomitant with the differentiation of somatic structures normally observed in the sexual line only (wing buds, eyes). This is strong evidence against genetic determination of castes in the higher termites. Of course, the characters of each caste have a genetic basis, but the best hypothesis is the presence, in every individual, of the complete set of genes determining the characters of all castes present in the species. Depending on the conditions experienced during the development, some genes are repressed, others expressed, resulting in the differentiation of the observed castes.

6.4 EVOLUTION OF THE SOLDIER CASTE

Comparing with the social Hymenoptera, termites appear as very vulnerable insects, and indeed several recent studies demonstrate the importance of predation in the dynamics of their societies (Bodot, 1961; Longhurst *et al.*, 1978, 1979; Collins, 1981; Lepage, 1981; Schaefer & Whitford, 1981). There is a strong selection pressure favouring the adaptations which minimize this predation, and the differentiation of a soldier caste is the most prominent, and a very primitive one in the termite society (see Noirot, Chapter 4). In the lower termites, the morphology of soldiers and their fighting behaviour is not very diversified, except in the Rhinotermitidae where the apparition of the frontal gland increases considerably the variations in defensive strategies (Quennedey & Deligne, 1975). It is to be noted that chemical defence appeared in *Mastotermes* (Moore, 1968), probably in the salivary glands and, in the Kalotermitidae, a "phragmotic head" differentiated in several evolutionary lines in the Kalotermitidae (Krishna, 1961). In the family Termitidae, the diversification of the soldier caste is much greater, by very varied combinations of the chemical weapons (frontal and/or salivary glands) and the mandibles. Accordingly, a tremendous diversity of fighting behaviour is observed (Deligne *et al.*, 1981). Another defensive adaptation is the building of an elaborate nest offering good protection against predators, and the building behaviour is exceptionally varied in the higher termites (review by Noirot, 1970). From recent observations of Deligne and Pasteels (1982 and personal communication), the nest structure on one hand and the proportion and fighting behaviour of soldiers on the other, seem closely interrelated, in a defensive strategy characteristic of each species. Thus, the evolution of the soldier caste cannot be understood without reference to the ecological adaptations of the species, especially the foraging and building behaviour.

6.5 EVOLUTION OF THE WORKER CASTE

In contrast to soldiers, workers are much less diversified. Their structure can be summarized as follows: it is the *simplified* organization of a generalized exopterygote *larva* with some *adaptations* for the social tasks (Noirot, 1982).

As stated above, the moult by which a larva becomes a worker is accompanied by very limited structural modifications and the morphology of the worker is essentially larval. Besides, during post-embryonic life, many structures undergo precocious developmental arrest and remain undifferentiated. These structures are those of no use for a termite worker, i.e. a non-reproductive caste with a cryptic life: sexual organs, wings, eyes and optic lobes of the brain.

The adaptations are mainly to maximize on the capacity for collection, digestion and transformation of food, and building of nests: powerful mandibles with strong mandibular muscles (although the structure of these mandibles remains of a generalized type: Ahmad, 1950); maximal development of the gut, especially the hindgut harbouring a complex symbiotic microflora: salivary glands elaborating the nutritive fluid which is the only food for the brood and the royal pair, but utilized too in the building behaviour. The most important adaptations of the workers are perhaps in their behaviour, a field which remains poorly documented. As a whole, workers appear as very efficient transformers of biomass, collected by various foraging strategies, digested by the combined action of their own enzymes and their intestinal symbionts, and converted into the salivary fluid for the nourishment of the brood and the royal pair (Noirot, 1982). On *Trinervitermes geminatus*, Josens (1982) worked out a ratio production:consumption and found it to be near 15%, which is exceptionally high for a herbivore.

The relative uniformity of the worker caste among the termites (by comparison with the ants) may be related to a much less diversified diet, which is, definitely, the plant cell walls, either sound or at different stages of degradation, ending with the humus feeders. However, the diet is more varied in the higher than in the lower termites, and a correlation between the diet and the worker morphology seems evident: the humivorous workers bear the smallest head (mandibular muscles less developed) and the largest gut (less nutritive food). On the other hand, in the fungus-growing termites, workers have larger heads (especially major workers, more involved in foraging) and less voluminous guts (food partly digested in the fungus comb). Similarly, the structure of the gut is much more varied in the Termitidae than in the lower termites (review in Noirot & Noirot-Timothée, 1969), and this is most probably in relation to different digestive physiological mechanisms and symbiotic associations which are unfortunately poorly known. As regards the *intraspecific* polymorphism of the worker caste, extensive possibilities exist as a result of various combinations of the sexual dimorphism and the succession of several instars (see above). However, the differences between the extreme worker types of the same species are not very important, far less than in many ants (Noirot, 1982). The division of labour, although evident, is never so well defined, and the "temporal polyethism" is very important (McMahan, 1979). Thus, one type of worker is always able to perform a variety of social tasks, hence is never strictly specialized for a defined activity. Although some specialization is evident (i.e. major workers in the harvester fungus-growing termites are the only ones collecting food, but are also involved in building behaviour) the workers appear essentially as multifunctional instruments adapting their activities to the needs of the society.

6.6 CONCLUSION

In the higher termites, caste system appears less flexible than in most of the lower termites. The precocious separation of the neuter (soldier-worker) and sexual lines is the expression of radical differences in behaviour and physiology, the nymphs being (with few exceptions) completely dependent and unable to perform any social tasks. It is probably a relationship between this phenomenon and the very marked seasonal cycle. According to the concept of Oster & Wilson (1978), the society of higher termites exhibits an alternation of *ergonomic stages*, where the budget is turned to increasing working efficiency (production of large numbers of soldiers and workers) and of *reproductive stages* where the investment is on the production of sexual alates. In my opinion, the more accentuated and precocious the differences between the two developmental lines, the more precise the seasonal cycle of nymph production. To test this hypothesis, a comparison between higher termites and the more evolved of the lower termites could be useful. As an example, in *Schedorhinotermes lamanianus*, where caste system is highly evolved, seasonal cycle appears as well determined as in the higher termites (Renoux, 1976).

6.7 SUMMARY

In the higher termites, two developmental lines are evident after the first moult. The neuter line produces workers and soldiers all through the year; the sexual line appears at a definite season.

After three (Macrotermitinae) or two (other subfamilies) instars, larvae become workers, with limited morphological changes but radical transformation in physiology and behaviour. Polymorphism may occur in the worker caste, either by sexual dimorphism or by occurrence of successive worker stages, or both.

Soldiers differentiate either from larvae or from workers, their origin being well defined for each species. In most cases, they are all of the same sex, male or female depending on the species.

In young colonies, caste formation bears special character. The most important is the differentiation of the neuter line alone during the first years. The observations done on incipient colonies in laboratory cultures are reviewed.

Intercastes are rarely observed in the higher termites. A brief account is given on different types, their origin and their significance.

The soldier caste is much more diversified in the higher than in the lower termites, but this evolution is integrated in various defensive strategies, in relation with foraging and building behaviour.

The worker caste, much more uniform than the soldiers, and with a simplified organization, is mainly adapted to the collection and transformation of the biomass. Its polymorphism is discussed in relation to division of labour.

6.8 ACKNOWLEDGEMENTS

My thanks to H. S. Han, Patrick Lefeuve, Michel Lepage and Barbara Thorne for permission to quote their unpublished observations. B. M. Okot-Kotber kindly revised the English text.

6.9 REFERENCES

Ahmad M. (1950) The phylogeny of Termite genera based on imago-worker mandibles. *Bull. Amer. Mus. Nat. Hist.* **95**, 37–86.

Becker G. (1961) Beobachtungen und Versuche über den Beginn der Kolonie-Entwicklung von *Nasutitermes ephratae* (Holmgren) (Isoptera). *Z. ang. Entomol.* **49**, 78–96.

Bodot P. (1961) La destruction des termitières de *Bellicositermes natalensis* par une fourmi: *Dorylus (Typhlopone) dentifrons* Wasm. *C.R. Acad. Sci.* **253**, 3053–3054.

Bodot P. (1969) Composition des colonies de Termites: ses fluctuations au cours du temps. *Insectes Sociaux* **16**, 39–54.

Bouillon A. & Lekie R. (1964) Populations, rythme d'activité diurne et cycle de croissance du nid de *Cubitermes sankurensis* Wasmann in *"Etudes sur les Termites africains"* (ed. A. Bouillon) pp. 197–213. Édit de l'université, Leopoldville.

Breznak J. A. (1982) Intestinal microbiota of termites and other xylophagous insects. *Ann. Rev. Microbiol.* **36**, 323–343.

Collins N. M. (1981) Populations, age structure and survivorship of colonies of *Macrotermes bellicosus* (Isoptera: Macrotermitinae). *J. Anim. Ecol.* **50**, 293–311.

Darlington, J. P. E. C. (1982) Population dynamics in an African fungus-growing termite. *The Biology of Social Insects* (eds M. C. Breed, C. D. Michener, H. E. Evans), pp. 54–58. Westview Press, Boulder.

Deligne J. & Pasteels J. M. (1982) Nest structure and soldier defense: an integrated strategy in termites. *The Biology of Social Insects* (eds M. D. Breed, C. D. Michener, H. E. Evans), pp. 288–289. Westview Press, Boulder.

Deligne J., Quennedey A. & Blum M. S. (1981) The enemies and defense mechanisms of termites. *Social Insects*, Vol. II (ed. H. R. Hermann), pp. 1–76. Academic Press, New York.

Emerson A. E. (1926). Development of soldier termites. *Zoologica* **7**, 69–100.

Fontes L. R. & Terra P. S. (1981) A study on the taxonomy and biology of the neotropical termites *Nasutitermes aquilinus* (Isoptera, Termitidae, Nasutitermitinae). *Rev. bras. Ent.* **25**, 171–183.

Grassé P. P. & Noirot Ch. (1945) La transmission des Flagélles symbiotiques et les aliments des Termites. *Bull. Biol. France Belgique* **79**, 273–292.

Grassé P. P. & Noirot Ch. (1954) *Apicotermes arquieri* n.sp. ses constructions et sa biologie. Considerations generales sur les Apicotermitinae. *Ann. Sc. Nat., Zool.* (11) **16**, 345–388.

Grassé P. P. & Noirot Ch. (1955) La fondation de nouvelles societes par *Bellicositermes natalensis* Hav. *Insectes Sociaux* **2**, 213–220.

Josens G. (1982) Le bilan énergétique de *Trinervitermes geminatus* (Wasmann) (Termitidae, Nasutitermitinae). 2. Mesures de consommation en laboratoire. *Insectes Sociaux* **29**, 511–523.

Knower H. (1894) Origin of the "Nasutus" of *Eutermes*. *Johns Hopkins Univ. Circ.* **13**, 58–59.

Krishna K. (1961) A generic revision and phylogenetic study of the family Kalotermitidae (Isoptera). *Bull. Amer. Mus. Nat. Hist.* **122**, 307–408.

Lepage M. G. (1981) Etude de la prédation de *Megaponera foetens* (F.) sur les populations récoltantes de Macrotermitinae dans un écosystème semi-aride (Kajiado-Kenya). *Insectes Sociaux* **28**, 247–262.

Light S. F. & Weesner F. M. (1947) Development of castes in higher termites. *Science* **106**, 244–245.

Light S. F. & Weesner F. H. (1955) The incipient colony of *Tenuirostritermes tenuirostris* (Desneux). *Insectes Sociaux* **2**, 135–146.

Longhurst C., Johnson R. A. & Wood T. G. (1978) Predation by *Megaponera foetens* (F.) (Hymenoptera: Formicidae) on termites in the Nigerian southern Guinea savanna. *Oecologia* **32**, 101–107.

Longhurst C., Johnson R. A. & Wood T. G. (1979) Foraging, recruitment and predation by *Decamorium uelense* (Santschi) (Formicidae Myrmicinae) on termites in southern Guinea savanna, Nigeria. *Oecologia* **38**, 83–91.

Lüscher M. (1951) Beobachtungen über die Kolonie-grundung bei verschiedenen afrikanischen Termitenarten. *Acta tropica* **8**, 36–43.

McMahan E. A. (1979) Temporal polyethism in termites. *Sociobiology* **4**, 153–168.

Moore B. P. (1968) Studies on the chemical composition and function of the cephalic gland secretion in Australian termites. *J. Insect Physiol.* **14**, 33–39.

Noirot Ch. (1952) Les soins et l'alimentation des jeunes chez les Termites. *Ann. Sci. Nat., Zool* (11) **14**, 405–414.

Noirot Ch. (1955) Recherches sur le polymorphisme des Termites supérieurs (Termitidae). *Ann. Sci. Nat., Zool.* (11), **17**, 399–595.

Noirot Ch. (1969) Formation of castes in the higher termites. *Biology of Termites*, Vol. I (eds K. Krishna & F. M. Weesner), pp. 311–350. Academic Press, New York.

Noirot Ch. (1970) The nests of Termites. *Biology of Termites*, Vol. II (eds K. Krishna & F. M. Weesner), pp. 73–125. Academic Press, New York.

Noirot Ch. (1974) Polymorphismus bei Höheren Termiten. *Sozial-polymorphismus bei Insekten* (ed. G. A. Schmidt), pp. 740–765. Wiss. Verlagsges, Stuttgart.

Noirot Ch. (1982) La caste des ouvriers, élément majeur du succes évolutif des Termites. *Rivista di Biologia* **72**, 157–195.

Noirot Ch. & Noirot-Timothée, C. (1969) The digestive system. *Biology of Termites*, Vol. I (eds K. Krishna & F. M. Weesner), pp. 49–88. Academic Press, New York.

O'Brien R. W. & Slaytor M. (1982) Role of Microorganisms in the Metabolism of Termites. *Aust. J. Biol. Sci.* **35**, 239–262.

Okot-Kotber B. M. (1981a) Instars and polymorphism of castes in *Macrotermes michaelseni* (Isoptera, Macrotermitinae). *Insectes Sociaux* **28**, 234–246.

Okot-Kotber B. M. (1981b) Polymorphism and the development of the first progeny in incipient colonies of *Macrotermes michaelseni* (Isoptera, Macrotermitinae) *Insect Sci. Application* **1**, 147–150.

Oster G. F. & Wilson E. O. (1978) *Caste and ecology in the social insects* (Monographs in population biology). Princeton University Press, 352 p.

Quennedey A. & Deligne J. (1975) L'arme frontale des soldats de Termites. I Rhinotermitidae. *Insectes Sociaux* **22**, 243–267.

Renoux J. (1976) Le polymorphisme de *Schedorhinotermes lamanianus* (Sjöstedt) (Isoptera-Rhinotermitidae). Essai d'interprétation. *Insectes Sociaux* **23**, 281–491.

Sands W. A. (1965) Alate development and colony foundation in five species of *Trinervitermes* (Isoptera, Nasutitermitinae) in Nigeria, West Africa. *Insectes Sociaux* **12**, 117–130.

Sands W. A (1972) The soldierless termites of Africa. *Bull. British Mus. (Nat. Hist.) Entomol. Suppl.* **18**, 244 p.

Schaefer D. A. & Whitford W. G. (1981) Nutrient cycling by the subterranean termite *Gnathamitermes tubiformans* in a Chihuahuan desert ecosystem. *Oecologia* **48**, 277–283.

Weesner F. M. (1953) Biology of *Tenuirostritermes tenuirostris* (Desneux) with emphasis on caste development. *Univ. Calif. Publ. Zool.* **57**, 251–302.

CHAPTER 7

Caste Polymorphism in a Higher Termite, Macrotermes michaelseni (Termitidae, Macrotermitinae)

B. M. OKOT-KOTBER

International Centre of Insect Physiology and Ecology, P.O. Box 30772, Nairobi, Kenya

CONTENTS

7.1 INTRODUCTION

The ability of an animal species to exist in two or more morphological forms is often referred to as polymorphism. Termites are known to display this phenomenon in the form of castes. The details of polymorphism of castes in both lower and higher termites will be dealt with in other chapters of this book. We shall present some detailed data of polymorphism of a fungus-growing species of a higher termite, *Macrotermes michaelseni*; and it may suffice here only to state that there is more plasticity in the development of lower termites than in the higher.

Intensive work by Noirot (1955) examined polymorphism in representative species of the whole family of higher termites, Termitidae. An elaborate scheme of development was established for *Macrotermes bellicosus* (*"Bellicosit-*

ermes natalensis") as a representative species of the genus *Macrotermes* (Noirot, 1955, 1969) and was later slightly modified by Lüscher (1976). The scheme basically shows an early differentiation between male and female larvae occurring at the moult to second instar. The smaller larvae, which are females, undergo three successive moults to become minor workers, minor presoldiers, or through another moult of unpigmented minor workers into major presoldiers; whereas the larger male larvae also go through three moults before becoming exclusively major workers. The presoldiers subsequently moult into soldier; workers and soldiers are terminal sterile castes. The reproductive caste (sexuals) also differentiate from first instar larvae and the nymphs go through five moults to become sexually mature reproductives (alates).

Studies on polymorphism of termites are important in the light of investigations into their biology. It is imperative first to establish the developmental patterns in a colony under controlled conditions. There have been reports on this which documented studies on all families covering a wide range of genera. Grassé & Noirot (1946, 1958) and Lüscher (1952) reared *Kalotermes flavicollis* and established developmental pathways in this species. Buchli (1950, 1956, 1958) carried out similar studies on several species of rhinotermitid, which enabled him to determine polymorphism in *Reticulitermes lucifugus* and *R. L. santonensis*, to mention but a few. On the higher termites, however, this has not been so comprehensive, probably due to handling difficulties involved in rearing. Nevertheless, there are some notable reports, especially those of Light & Weesner (1947) on the development of neuter castes in *Tenuirostritermes tenuirostris* and *Gnathamitermes perplexus*, Noirot (1949) on the development of *Nasutitermes arborum*, which enabled him to establish a developmental scheme for this species; and Grassé & Noirot (1955) on *Macrotermes bellicosus*.

Recently we reported on similar studies on *M. michaelseni* (Okot-Kotber, 1981a, b). Here we will draw comparisons between the developmental schemes of a laboratory colony and field materials, and also focus our attention on major differences between the scheme of development in *M. michaelseni* and what was reported earlier for other species of *Macrotermes*.

7.2   POLYMORPHISM IN FIELD COLONIES

7.2.1   Larval instars and polymorphism in adult neuter castes

Biometric analysis of fixed characters such as head capsule, posterior tibia, and antenna of termites enables one to distinguish between different castes or developmental groups. Noirot (1955) applied this technique to establish polymorphism in different species of Termitidae. We recently (Okot-Kotber, 1981a) employed the same technique for determination of the nature of polymorphism in *M. michaelseni*. Specimens were collected from Kajiado, Kenya. Head capsule width, posterior tibia length and antennal length measurements revealed that *M. michaelseni* larvae from a mature colony can be separated into six groups as shown by histograms in Figs 7.1, 7.2 and 7.3. The head capsule measurements give the most obvious separation between groups, particularly the earlier stages, but this may vary from species to species. Workers and soldiers could also be distinguished into majors and minors using the same technique (Table 7.1). Measurements of tibia and antennal lengths may form broad distributions; but in this case, they make better separation of more advanced larval groups. It is, therefore, necessary to use more than one parameter in combination in order to achieve the best possible distinction between groups.

In a situation like this one, where a complex pattern of polymorphism prevails, transformations of biometric data may be necessary to distinguish between individuals belonging to the same instar, but to different developmental pathways. We used a logarithmic plot of head capsule width against posterior tibia length measured on the same individuals. An almost linear relationship was found (Fig. 7.4). The first, second, fourth and sixth larval groups and minor workers fall within one curve, while the first, third, fifth larval groups and major workers fall within another. This suggested that group 1 larvae, which are homogeneous in size and morphology, are a mixture of the two sexes, and that during their first moult, some of these larvae grow larger than others, thus separating into groups 2 and 3. Subsequently, group 2 larvae moult into group 4 and group 3 into group 5. Finally, group 4 larvae moult into minor workers or into group 6 individuals while those of group 5 moult exclusively into major workers.

This interpretation was supported by the results of studies of the rudimentary sex organs of larvae belonging to the six groups (Fig. 7.5). Group 1 includes both sexes, whereas larvae of groups 2, 4 and 6 are all females and those of groups 3 and 5 are all males. Minor workers, minor and major presoldiers were also shown to be females. This means that these individuals develop through the same pathway. Major workers, on the other hand, were found to be males; thus the groups of larger larvae (3, 5) develop only into major workers.

The sixth group of larvae deserves special consideration here, for it represents a major difference between developmental scheme of *M. michaelseni* (Okot-Kotber, 1981a) and those of the other species of *Macrotermes* described by Noirot (1955, 1969). These larvae are characterized by morphological features which may be summarized as follows: They are larger, much less

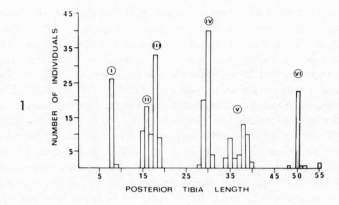

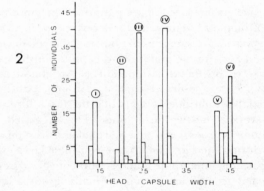

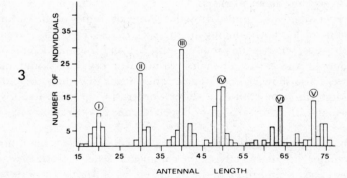

FIGS 7.1, 7.2, 7.3. Distributions of posterior tibia length (1), head capsule width (2) and antennal length (3) of larvae. Measurements are in arbitrary units (1 unit = 0.04 mm). Roman numerals indicate larval groups.

TABLE 7.1. MEAN VALUES OF MEASUREMENTS OF HEAD CAPSULE
WIDTH, POSTERIOR TIBIA LENGTH, ANTENNAL LENGTH AND THE
NUMBER OF ANTENNAL SEGMENTS OF NEUTER CASTES

Development stage	Sample size	Head capsule width (mm) ($\bar{x} \pm$ S.D.)	Posterior tibia length (mm) ($\bar{x} \pm$ S.D.)	Tibia Length/ head width	Antennal length (mm) ($\bar{x} \pm$ S.D.)	No. of antennal segments
Minor workers	38	1.64 ± 0.08	1.70 ± 0.09	1.04	2.33 ± 0.43	17
Major workers	29	2.66 ± 0.13	2.33 ± 0.09	0.88	3.83 ± 0.15	18
Minor presoldiers	23	1.75 ± 0.10	1.99 ± 0.05	1.14	3.63 ± 0.09	17
Major presoldiers	45	3.11 ± 0.36	2.79 ± 0.16	0.90	3.86 ± 0.23	17
Minor soldiers	30	2.78 ± 0.11	2.94 ± 0.05	1.06	4.61 ± 0.17	17
Major soldiers	30	4.55 ± 0.17	3.77 ± 0.11	0.83	5.37 ± 0.16	17

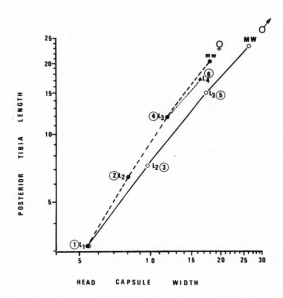

FIG. 7.4. Logarithmic plot of head capsule width versus posterior tibia length of larvae and workers (1–6—larval groups, L_1–L_4—larval instars, mw—minor workers and MW—major workers). Each point represents a mean of 25 measurements or more.

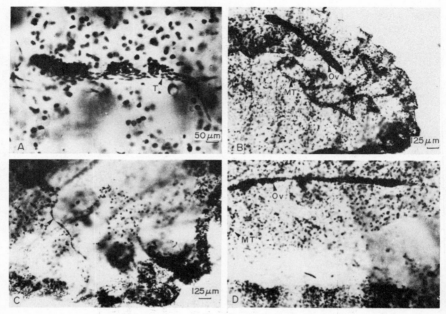

Fig. 7.5. Dissected abdomens of larvae showing rudimentary sex organs. a: first instar male (testis); b: first instar female (ovary); c: second instar male (testis); d: second instar female (ovary). T—testis, OV—ovary, MT—Malpighian tubule.

pigmented and less sclerotized than minor workers. The legs and antennae are larger, the abdomens in older individuals are much more distended and the posterior tibiae grow relatively more rapidly compared with their head capsules (unlike those of minor workers) (Table 7.2).

The developmental fate of this interesting group of larvae was investigated in two ways. First, a brief examination of their mandibles was made after 70% ethanol fixation overnight. Pharate presoldier mandibles were clearly visible in them; the mandibles of teneral workers did not show these structures (Fig. 7.6). Second, one-year-old incipient laboratory colonies were used to adopt some of the larvae. A couple of days prior to this, the existing soldiers and/or presoldiers were removed from the colonies so as to remove any inhibition that they may have exerted on the development or survival of the larvae. The individuals to be studied were singly introduced into each of the recipient colonies, and were thereafter checked daily. After an average of about three days all the adopted larvae had moulted into major presoldiers.

TABLE 7.2. MAJOR DIFFERENCES BETWEEN MINOR WORKERS AND FOURTH INSTAR LARVAE

Stage	n	Head capsule width (mm) Mean ± S.D.	Posterior tibia length (mm) Mean ± S.D.	Antennal length (mm) Mean ± S.D.	Mandible	Pigmentation	Type of moult	Capacity to work
Minor workers	38	1.64 ± 0.08*	1.70 ± 0.0**	2.33 ± 0.13***	Worker mandible without future presoldier mandible	Darkly pigmented	Do not moult	Functional
Fourth instar larvae	28	1.80 ± 0.0Ĩ	2.02 ± 0.06**	2.51 ± 0.11***	Worker mandible enclosing future presoldier mandible	Lightly pigmented	Moult into major presoldiers	Non-functional

Students' Test: *P < 0.001, **P < 0.001, ***P < 0.001.

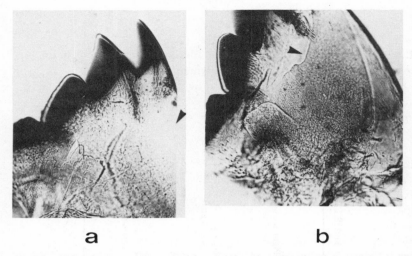

a   b

Fig. 7.6. Mandibles of: (a) a newly moulted functional worker, (b) a fourth instar larva before a major presoldier moult. Note that the mandible of a minor worker does not show any sign of a future presoldier mandible while the fourth instar mandible does (see arrows).

This gave conclusive evidence that the fourth instar female larvae that exist in established field colonies develop exclusively into major presoldiers.

The finding that these larvae are larger than female third instars, and even larger than minor workers and have presoldier mandibles within the old worker-like ones, suggests that the onset of a chain of developmental events that leads to major presoldier differentiation may be prompted before the female third instar moult. In *M. bellicosus* it was reported (Noirot, 1955, 1969) that major presoldiers develop from minor workers which are morphologically similar to the others, but incompletely sclerotized and non-functional, suggesting that in this species major soldier differentiation occurs after third moult or during the moult itself. While studying development in another genus of Macrotermitinae, *Ancistrotermes*, they found that major soldiers are derived from normal functional minor workers (Noirot, 1955, 1969); suggesting a later determination than even in *M. bellicosus*.

The development of minor presoldiers from third instars is a common phenomenon in Macrotermitinae (Noirot, 1955, 1969); and the results obtained from casual observations of field materials (Okot-Kotber, 1981a) and from laboratory incipient colonies where only minor presoldiers are produced (besides workers) (Okot-Kotber, 1981b), show that *M. michaelseni* is not an exception.

7.2.2 Polymorphism in nymphs and reproductives

Biometric studies of *M. michaelseni* obtained from the field facilitated recognition of nymphal instars. Measurements of head capsule width, posterior tibia length, and wing-pad length provided clear separation of the instars and are summarized in Table 7.3. It is clear from this Table that there are five nymphal instars before the moult to the alate. The ratio, tibia length: head capsule width, remains almost constant throughout the development into reproductives suggesting uniformity in the growth rates of tibia and head capsules, whereas the wing-pads grow progressively faster during the successive moults with a peak being attained during the last moult.

No sexual dimorphism was detected in the nymphal stages; however, a slight sexual dimorphism was found in the imagos, males being a little larger than females.

Five nymphal instars are a common occurrence during the development of reproductives in Termitidae. Bathellier (1927) found five nymphal stages in several species from Indo-China, Noirot (1952) in a number of species of Termitidae, Weesner (1953) in *Tenuirostritermes tenuirostris*, Bouillon & Mathot (1964) in *Cubitermes exiguus*, Hecker (1966) in *M. bellicosus* and, more recently, N'Diaye (1977) quoting Noirot and Bodot and his own findings on *Cubitermes fungifaber*. However, Kaiser (1956) and Sands (1965) found only four nymphal instars in *Anoplotermes pacificus* and species of *Trinervitermes* respectively. Noirot (1969), on the other hand, reported five nymphal instars in other species of these two genera, which makes them not unique in this repect.

TABLE 7.3. MEAN VALUES OF HEAD CAPSULE WIDTH, POSTERIOR TIBIA LENGTH, WING-PAD LENGTH AND THE NUMBER OF ANTENNAL SEGMENTS OF NYMPHS AND ALATES

	Sample size (n)	Head capsule width (mm) ($\bar{x} \pm$ S.D.)	Posterior tibia length (mm) ($\bar{x} \pm$ S.D.)	Tibia length/ head capsule width	Wing-pad length (mm) ($\bar{x} \pm$ S.D.)	No. of antennal segments
1st	10	0.77 ± 0.02	$0.6 = 0.04$	0.83	$0.20 \pm <0.01$	14
2nd	36	1.21 ± 0.06	$1.19 = 0.02$	0.98	0.46 ± 0.09	16
3rd	30	1.66 ± 0.12	$2.03 = 0.12$	1.22	1.43 ± 0.08	18
4th	48	2.26 ± 0.14	$2.88 = 0.16$	1.27	3.11 ± 0.27	19
5th	18	3.03 ± 0.12	$3.57 = 0.17$	1.18	6.68 ± 0.41	19
Adult	35	3.54 ± 0.06	$4.41 = 0.12$	1.25	37.90 ± 0.06	19

The results of these biometrical and developmental studies led us to propose a scheme of post-embryonic development in *M. michaelseni* (Fig. 7.7) (Okot-Kotber, 1981a). The proposed scheme is not unique, for Noirot (1955, 1969) described a similar scheme in other species of *Macrotermes*, which was later slightly modified by Lüscher (1976). However, whereas Noirot suggested that a teneral, non-functional minor worker moults into the major presoldier, we have shown that a specific fourth instar larva is the precursor of the major presoldier.

7.3 POLYMORPHISM IN INCIPIENT COLONIES

Let us now turn to the developmental pattern of *M. michaelseni* in a laboratory situation. It is a prerequisite to establish precisely the pathways of development and instar duration in a given species of termites, if meaningful work on mechanisms of caste determination has to be undertaken.

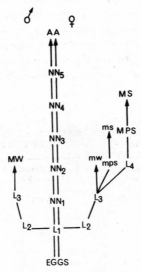

FIG. 7.7. A scheme of post-embryonic development in a mature colony of *Macrotermes michaelseni*. L₁–L₄—larval instars, MW—major workers, mw—minor workers, mps—minor presoldiers, ms—minor soldiers, mps—major presoldiers, MS—major soldiers, NN₁–NN₅—nymphal instars and AA—imagos (adult reproductives).

Such studies are often carried out with material collected from mature field colonies. However, in *M. michaelseni* (and perhaps in all the fungus growers) it is difficult to maintain field-collected groups in the laboratory for long enough to allow experimentation. However, it is possible to start a viable colony with a pair of reproductives collected from the field, preferably during swarming (Okot-Kotber, 1981b). Reproductives of *M. michaelseni* were collected from the Kajiado area, Kenya and pairs were established in plastic Petri dishes containing moistened mound soil. These were examined daily to determine when the eggs were laid, their incubation period, and the duration of the larval instars. The results are summarized in Table 7.4.

The data on development of the first progeny in *M. michaelseni* are similar to those reported earlier for *M. bellicosus* by Noirot (1955) and Grassé & Noirot (1955). The number of larval instars in both cases is the same. However, there are differences in some details which might reflect species characteristics. Thus in *M. michaelseni* the mean incubation period of eggs is slightly shorter, although the time taken between hatching and the emergence of minor presoldiers or minor workers is about the same. Grassé & Noirot reported much longer intervals for development into major workers and minor soldiers than was the case for *M. michaelseni*.

Biometric studies of individuals from these incipient colonies were conducted as for field materials mentioned above. It proved to be more difficult to differentiate between groups of larvae on the basis of distributions of head capsule width, posterior tibia length or antennal length alone. It was necessary, therefore, to transform the data into ratios. A plot of head capsule width versus the ratio of antennal length to head capsule width suggested that

TABLE 7.4. INSTAR DURATION OF LARVAE COLLECTED FROM THE FIRST PROGENY OF INCIPIENT COLONIES

Instars	No. of colonies observed	Instar duration (Mean ± S.E.)	Range (days)	Instar duration (Mean ± S.E.)	Range (days)
First	24	5.5 ± 0.2	4– 7	5.6 ± 0.2	4– 7
Second	20	5.2 ± 0.4	3–11	8.0 ± 0.5	5–12
Third before presoldier moult	54	10.2 ± 0.3*	7–18	—	—
Third before worker moult	54	14.5 ± 0.3†	7–19	13.9 ± 0.4	9–17
Minor presoldiers	63	11.7 ± 0.2	9–16	—	—
Total developmental period after hatching		25.2mw 32.6ms		27.5MW	

*Duration of a female 3rd instar developing into a minor presoldier.
†Duration of a female 3rd instar developing into a minor worker.
mw—minor worker; MW—major worker; ms—minor soldier.

five groups were present (Fig. 7.8) which was confirmed by the examination of their sexes. The results showed that even by this computation it is not possible to segregate between male and female larvae in the first group as was also the case in the field-collected materials (Okot-Kotber, 1981a). Morphological studies showed that groups 2 and 4 larvae were females, whereas those in groups 3 and 5 were males. This strongly suggested that, as in mature colonies, the developmental pathway of larvae in the incipient colonies is forked.

The workers are dimorphic, but not the soldiers, as shown by measurements of head capsule width, posterior tibia length and antennal length (Figs 7.9, 7.10, 7.11 for workers and Figs 7.12, 7.13, 7.14 for presoldiers).

The relative smallness in the size of individuals from incipient colonies as compared with the size of those from mature field colonies is not limited to *M. michaelseni*. The same was found for *M. bellicosus* (Noirot, 1955) and even in some lower termites species as reported by Pickens (1932) and Buchli (1950) on species of *Reticulitermes*, and in the most primitive of all, *Mastotermes darwiniensis* (Watson, 1974). This phenomenon is a well-known feature in termite colony development.

The proposed scheme of post-embryonic development in incipient colonies of *M. michaelseni* (Fig. 7.15) is similar to that for individuals from mature colonies except that it lacks fourth instar larvae and, consequently, major soldiers, and there is no reproductive line since reproductives are not produced in incipient colonies.

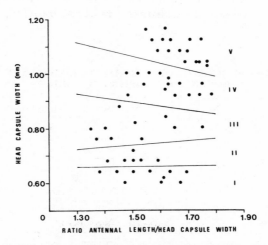

Fig. 7.8. A plot of head capsule width versus the ratio of antennal length to head capsule width of larvae from incipient colonies. I–V—larval groups.

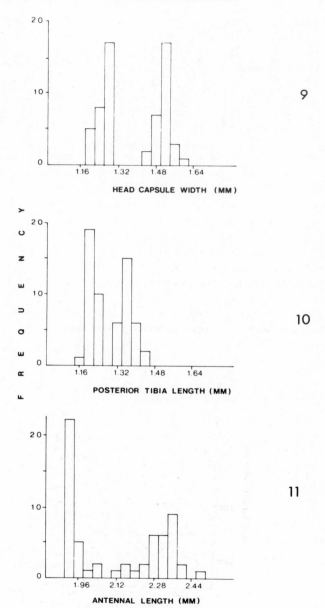

FIGS 7.9, 7.10, 7.11. Bimodal distribution of: (9) head capsule width, (10) posterior tibia length and (11) antennal length of workers from incipient colonies.

B. M. Okot-Kotber

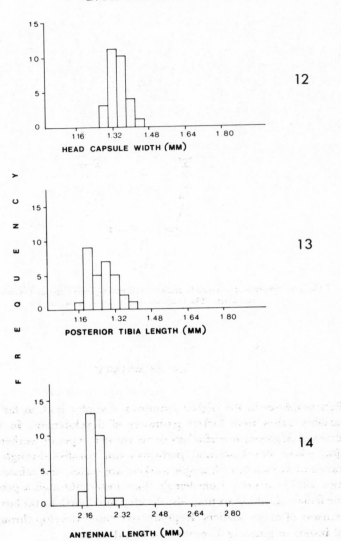

FIGS 7.12, 7.13, 7.14. Monomodal distribution of (12) head capsule width, (13) posterior tibia length and (14) antennal length of presoldiers from incipient colonies.

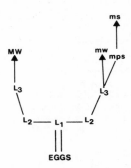

FIG. 7.15. The scheme of post-embryonic development in incipient colonies of *Macrotermes michaelseni*. The symbols are the same as in Fig. 7.7.

7.4 SUMMARY

Polymorphism in the higher termites is complex and, as far as is known, invariably arises from forked pathways of development. In mature, field colonies of *Macrotermes michaelseni* there are two types of workers, minor and major, whose developmental pathways run parallel through three larval instars and are sex linked; major workers are males, and minors are females. Minor soldiers develop from female third instars through a presoldier stage. Some female third instars may also develop into fourth instar larvae which are precursors of major soldiers. Reproductive castes develop through five nymphal instars originating from the first larval instar.

In incipient colonies, developmental pathways are basically the same as in the mature nests, except that major soldiers and reproductives are not produced and individuals are much smaller than those of the same stages in mature colonies.

7.5 REFERENCES

Bathellier J. (1927) Contribution à l'étude systématique et biologique des termites de l'Indo-Chine. *Fauna colonies France* **1**, 125–265.

Bouillon A. & Mathot G. (1964) Observations sur l'écologie et le nid de *Cubitermes exiguus*, Mathot. Description des nymphes-soldats et d'un pseudimago. In *Etudes sur les Termites Africains* (ed. Bouillon A.), pp. 215–230. Masson, Paris.

Buchli H. (1950) Recherche sur la fondation et le développement des nouvelles colonies chez le Termite lucifuge (*Reticulitermes lucifugus* Rossi). *Physiol. Comparata Oecol.* **2**, 145–160.

Buchli H. (1956) Le cycle de développement de castes chez *Reticulitermes*. *Insectes Sociaux* **3**, 395–401.

Buchli H. (1958) L'origine des castes et les potentialites ontogéniques des termites européens du genre *Reticulitermes*. *Ann. Sci. Nat. Zool. Biol. Animale.* **20**, 263–429.

Grassé P. P. & Noirot C. (1946) Le polymorphisme social du Termite à cou jaune (*C. flavicollis* Fabr.). La production des soldats. *Compt. Rend. Acad. Sci., Paris* **223**, 929–931.

Grassé P. P. & Noirot C. (1955) Le fondation de nouvelles societes par *Bellicositermes natalensis* Hav. *Insectes Sociaux* **3**, 213–220.

Grassé P. P. & Noirot C. (1958) La société de *Calotermes flavicollis* (Insecte, Isoptere), de sa fondation au premier essaimage. *Compt. Rend. Acad. Sci. Paris* **246**, 1789–1795.

Hecker H. (1966) Das Zentralnervensystem des Kopfes und seine postembryonale Entwicklung bei *Bellicositermes bellicosus* (Smeath.) (Isoptera). *Acta Trop.* **23**, 297–352.

Kaiser P. (1956) Die Hormonalorgane der Termiten mit der Entstehung ihrer Kasten. *Mitt. Hamburgischen Zool. Museum Inst.* **54**, 129–178.

Light S. F. & Weesner F. M. (1947) Development of the castes in higher termites. *Science* **106**, 244–245.

Lüscher M. (1952). Untersuchungen über das individuelle Wachstum bei der Termite *Kalotermes flavicollis* Fabr. (Ein Beitrag zum Kastenbildungsproblem). *Biol. Zentr.* **71**, 529–543.

Lüscher M. (1976) Evidence for an endocrine control of caste determination in higher termites. In *Phase and Caste Determination in Insects. Endocrine Aspects* (ed. Lüscher M.), pp. 91–103. Pergamon Press, Oxford and New York.

N'Diaye M. S. (1977) Le développement post-embryonnaire de l'appareil génital chez les sexes de *Cubitermes fungifaber* Sjöstedt (Termitidae. Termitinae). *Insectes Sociaux* **24**, 37–60.

Noirot C. (1949) Le développement des neutres chez les Termites superieurs (Termitidae). II. Nasutitermitinae. *Compt. Rend. Acad. Sci. Paris* **228**, 2053–2054.

Noirot C. (1952) Le polymorphisme social chez les Termites et son déterminisme. In *Structure et Physiologie des Sociétés Animales* (ed. CNRS), pp. 103–116. Imprimerie Nationale, Paris.

Noirot C. (1955) Recherches sur le polymorphisme des Termites supérieurs (Termitidae). *Ann. Sci. Nat. Zool. Biol. Animale.* **17**, 399–595.

Noirot C. (1969) Formation of castes in higher termites. In *Biology of termites* (eds Krishna K. & Weesner F. M.), pp. 311–350. Academic Press, New York and London.

Okot-Kotber B. M. (1981a) Instars and polymorphism of castes in *Macrotermes michaelseni* (Isoptera, Macrotermitinae). *Insectes Sociaux* **28**, 233–246.

Okot-Kotber B. M. (1981b) Polymorphism and the development of the first progeny in incipient colonies of *Macrotermes michaelseni* (Isoptera-Macrotermitinae). *Insect Sci. Application* **1**, 147–150.

Pickens A. L. (1932) Observations on the genus *Reticulitermes* Holmgren. *Pan-Pacific Entomologist* **8**, 178–180.

Sands W. A. (1965) Alate development and colony foundation in five species of *Trinervitermes* (Isoptera, Nasutitermitinae) in Nigeria, W. Africa. *Insectes Sociaux* **12**, 117–130.

Watson J. A. L. (1974) The development of soldiers in incipient colonies of *Mastotermes darwiniensis* Froggatt (Isoptera). *Insectes Sociaux* **21**, 181–190.

Weesner F. M. (1953) Biology of *Tenuirostritermes tenuirostris* Desneux with emphasis on caste development. *Univ. Calif.* (Berkeley) *Publ. Zool.* **57**, 251–302.

Section C

Environment and Caste Composition Regulation

CHAPTER 8

Development of Neotenics in Mastotermes darwiniensis Froggatt: An Alternative Strategy

J. A. L. WATSON and HILDA M. ABBEY

CSIRO, Division of Entomology, Canberra, A.C.T. 2601, Australia

CONTENTS

8.1 INTRODUCTION

It has long been recognized that *Mastotermes darwiniensis* Froggatt is an unusual termite morphologically, but its biological uniqueness has only recently begun to emerge. In terms of its reproductive biology, perhaps the most unusual feature is the fact that in field colonies, numerous neotenics are the rule; primary reproductives have not yet been found in them, although experiments in the laboratory have shown that primaries can survive for at least 10 years after establishment, and neotenics can be produced while both primaries are present (Watson, unpubl. data).

The caste system of *Mastotermes* is a rigid one, with externally visible separation of worker and nymphal lines at the first larval ecdysis (Watson *et al.*, 1977b; Watson & Sewell, Chapter 3). Soldiers and neotenics develop from the worker line, and the neotenics do not become highly physogastric. The workers continue to moult indefinitely and, having reached mature size perhaps some 18 months after hatching, grow little; counts of instars, or attempts at ageing based on size or morphology, are not feasible (*cf.* Watson *et al.*, 1977b).

Rather more than a decade ago, we began a range of laboratory studies on *Mastotermes* from northern Queensland, primarily to develop techniques for using it in studies of materials; it is Australia's most destructive termite. We soon noticed that workers collected from the field rarely develop into neotenics, although orphaned or half-orphaned incipient colonies produce them readily, albeit with some delay (Watson *et al.*, 1975). It also transpired, most unexpectedly, that the addition of a neotenic to an orphaned field group can stimulate the production of further neotenics, in some groups within 15 days (Watson *et al.*, 1975). Female neotenics are more powerful inducers than males or a pair; in all cases, male and female neotenics are induced in equal numbers (Watson *et al.*, 1975).

These findings led to experiments in which workers were exposed to extracts of female neotenics, but this project foundered on the failure of our bioassay: control groups, to which a female neotenic was added, responded erratically, if at all. Since then, our investigations have centred on the factors that influence the response of workers to an inducer neotenic. It is now clear that positive induction of neotenics is the main element in a reproductive strategy that differs from any known elsewhere among the termites. In this paper, we present a summary of the findings and discuss the way in which, we believe, this alternative strategy works in the field.

8.2 MATERIALS AND GENERAL METHODS

Workers of *Mastotermes darwiniensis* were obtained near Townsville (Queensland) and Darwin (Northern Territory), both in northern Australia, in quantities sometimes exceeding 10 kg (approximately 250,000 termites); most were collected from infested tree trunks or posts (*cf.* Watson & Howick, 1975; Howick *et al.*, 1975) or from perforated 200-l steel drums filled with pieces of timber scantling as bait (L. R. Miller, unpubl. data). Groups of 200–250 g were maintained in the laboratory for up to 30 months at 31–32°C in 10 l or larger, vented, perspex or glass containers, in a matrix of 50:50 w/w mixture of *Pinus radiata* D. Don. sawdust and grade IV vermiculite (a heat-expanded mica, particle size 2–6 mm, water-holding capacity about 350% w/w) to which 300% v/w of water had been added. Cubes of *P. radiata* wood, 5 cm wide, were provided as food. The cultures were watered whenever the surface of the matrix appeared dry, and were reset with fresh wood whenever food supplies dwindled. Under these conditions, workers from Townsville did not develop into neotenics (Watson *et al.*, 1975); those from Darwin did so, and established breeding colonies (see Section 8.3.1). However, even after 12 months and more, the original workers were clearly recognizable because of their greater size.

Experiments on the production of neotenics were usually carried out in closed rectangular plastic boxes 18.0 × 11.5 × 6.0 cm high. The floor of each box was covered with 5 g of the sawdust/vermiculite mixture, moistened with 15 ml of water, and over it a piece of damp *P. radiata* veneer was placed, slightly smaller than the floor of the box and supported on one or more damp *P. radiata* blocks approximately 1 cm high. It was found necessary to add 4–6% (by number) of soldiers to each group of workers, to prevent presoldier production competing with the formation of neotenics (Watson & Abbey, unpubl. data); this figure was based on the percentage of soldiers found in small primary- and secondary-headed colonies (Watson *et al.*, 1977a). All experiments were carried out at 32°C over a period of 35 days, and all were inspected daily, any neotenics that had formed being removed. The temperature chosen is close to the optimal temperature for the establishment of incipient colonies of *Mastotermes* (Watson, E. C. Metcalf & Abbey, unpubl. data). The period of 35 days is the longest an experiment can be run before the induction of spurious neotenics becomes possible. We know that neotenics can induce a response in 12 hr, and that newly-moulted neotenics appear to have inductive capacity (see Section 8.3.5.2). The first few neotenics induced in an experiment, undergoing ecdysis some 15–16 days after its establishment, could induce further neotenics, which would appear a similar time later, i.e., after rather more than 30 days.

Two problems have affected the design of our experiments. First, the maintenance of large numbers of neotenics in the laboratory has been difficult; second, as will be shown, responses adequate for assay purposes occur only in workers that have been kept in the laboratory for approximately 12 months. As a result, it has often been the case that the supply of inducer neotenics, or of sensitive workers, has been insufficient to include all desirable treatments in an experiment.

Specific details of experimental techniques accompany the accounts of the individual experiments. The abbreviations for castes and stages are as follows: NEO = neotenic; S = soldier; W = worker. In the Tables, $\bar{X}$ = the average over groups, and N = the number of groups.

8.3   FACTORS AFFECTING NEOTENIC INDUCTION

Many factors might affect the response of workers to an inducer neotenic. In this paper we concentrate on three sets of factors which, we have shown, are of major importance:

(a) the age of the workers;
(b) the size, and density of housing, of the assay groups; and
(c) the condition of the inducer neotenic.

However, it is necessary to discuss first a relatively late finding that appeared to cast doubt on the general applicability of our model, namely, the difference in response to orphaning between *Mastotermes* from Townsville and those from Darwin.

8.3.1   Provenance of the workers

During 1980, circumstances forced us to move the centre of our field studies on *Mastotermes* from Townsville to Darwin, more than 1800 km distant. As a result, our source of laboratory stocks changed. It was soon apparent that orphaned groups of *Mastotermes* workers from Darwin behave differently from those collected in Townsville: as mentioned above, neotenics can develop readily in them, often within a month or so of collection, and reproductively active laboratory colonies are easy to establish. The question immediately arose: is there a basic difference in the mechanisms controlling neotenic development at the two localities? More specifically, can added neotenics induce neotenic development in *Mastotermes* from Darwin?

Groups of 300W + 12S of *Mastotermes* collected in Darwin in June 1980 were set up in standard boxes in November 1980, seven without and seven with a young female neotenic produced 2–3 days beforehand in an experiment with Townsville workers. Older neotenics from the same source had been rapidly attacked when added to groups of Darwin workers, and some of the younger neotenics were also attacked; when injured, they were replaced. The results are summarized in Table 8.1 and Fig. 8.1.

From the start, both the experimental and control groups produced a steady trickle of neotenics (8 female, 5 male in experimental groups and 12 female, 2 male in control groups by day 14) (Fig. 8.1). As the period between induction of a neotenic moult and ecdysis is at least 13, and commonly 14–16 days (Watson *et al.*, 1975; and see later sections), these neotenics must have commenced their metamorphosis before the experiment was set up. The last neotenic to appear in a control group did so on day 16 (Fig. 8.1); thereafter, the controls behaved just as Townsville controls routinely do throughout an experiment. The experimental groups, on the other hand, continued to produce neotenics, and at an enhanced rate (Fig. 8.1).

TABLE 8.1. NEOTENIC PRODUCTION OVER A PERIOD OF 35 DAYS IN
GROUPS OF *MASTOTERMES* FROM DARWIN

| Group composition | Number of neotenics produced | | | | | |
| | Days 1–14 | | | Overall | | |
	X̄	Range	N	X̄	Range	N
300W + 12S + ♀NEO	2.14	0–6	7	11.14	1–23	7
300W + 12S	2.14	0–6	7	2.43	0– 6	7

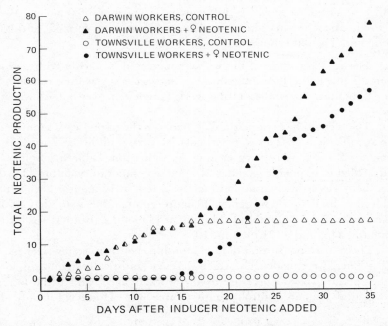

Fig. 8.1. Time-course of neotenic production in groups of *Mastotermes* workers from Darwin and Townsville, held for 35 days with or without a female neotenic.

We conclude that, whatever the mechanism may be that results in the initial development of neotenics in groups of orphaned *Mastotermes* workers from Darwin, subsequent neotenics are induced, just as they are in *Mastotermes* from Townsville.

8.3.2 The age of the workers

Examination of the data from the earlier experiments (Watson *et al.*, 1975) suggested that the responsiveness of workers to an inducer neotenic might vary with the time that they had been maintained in the laboratory prior to the experiment. Groups of workers were, therefore, assayed for responsiveness at intervals of 3–6 months, for more than 2 years after they had collected in the field.

The experiments involved workers collected in Townsville in June–July 1976, 1977 and 1978. In each assay, groups of 100W + 5S (100W only in the first 11 months of experiments on the 1976 material) each received a female neotenic, other groups without neotenics acting as controls. The results are summarized in Tables 8.2 and 8.3. It should be noted that in Table 8.3, the number of survivors includes the neotenics, which were removed as they appeared, and the surviving presoldiers and soldiers formed during the experiment. The data show that:

(a) The responsiveness of the workers increased markedly with period of culture (Table 8.2). During the first 12 months there was little response but, after 18 months, up to 40% of the workers moulted to neotenics within 35 days.

(b) There could be great variability between the responses of groups of the same age (Table 8.2). This was particularly marked in the 1977 workers, the responses of which were very erratic. As shown on Table 8.2, some 1977 groups failed to respond even after 21 months in laboratory culture. Furthermore, there was erratic variation from test to test: at 12 months, seven groups produced a total of 57 neotenics, a figure comparable with that of 1978 workers assayed as 12 months (Table 8.2); at 15 months, the total was three; at 18 months, 115; and at 21 months, 10.

(c) There was no substantial relationship between responsiveness and vitality. There were tendencies, which were not statistically significant, for the number of survivors to decrease as the workers aged, and to be lower in experimental than in control groups (Table 8.3). However, if only those

TABLE 8.2. NEOTENIC PRODUCTION IN GROUPS OF 100
MASTOTERMES WORKERS FROM TOWNSVILLE WHEN EXPOSED TO
A FEMALE NEOTENIC FOR 35 DAYS FOLLOWING DIFFERENT
PERIODS OF LABORATORY CULTURE

Month after collection	Number of neotenics produced by workers collected in											
	1976				1977				1978			
	Experimental			Control		Experimental			Control		Experimental			Control	
	$\bar{X}$	Range	N	$\bar{X}$	N	$\bar{X}$	Range	N	$\bar{X}$	N	$\bar{X}$	Range	N	$\bar{X}$	N
0–< 6	0.2	0– 2	23	—	0	<0.1	0– 1	21	0	21	0.8	0– 2	5	0	5
6–<12	5.3	2–10	7	—	0	1.7	0– 9	27	0	29	0.1	0– 1	7	0	7
12–<18	17.3	9–27	7	0	7	4.3	0–12	14	0	14	8.7	1–15	7	0	7
18–<24	30.1	24–39	7	0	7	8.4	0–25	14	0	14	24.2	19–30	6	0	8
≥24	30.1	25–40	7	0	7	—	—	0	—	0	—	—	0	—	0

TABLE 8.3. SURVIVAL AFTER 35 DAYS OF EXPOSURE TO A FEMALE
NEOTENIC IN GROUPS OF 100 *MASTOTERMES* WORKERS FROM
TOWNSVILLE, FOLLOWING DIFFERENT PERIODS OF LABORATORY
CULTURE

Month after collection	Treatment	Number of survivors of workers collected in								
		1976			1977			1978		
		X̄	Range	N	X̄	Range	N	X̄	Range	N
0–< 6	Experimental	81.9	70– 91	23	93.7	84–100	21	92.6	89–96	5
	Control	—	—	0	92.9	84–106	21	91.2	86–96	5
6–<12	Experimental	83.3	79– 91	7	88.8	76– 96	26	74.0	66–80	7
	Control	—	—	0	89.7	80– 96	29	78.6	68–89	7
12–<18	Experimental	84.3	75– 91	7	87.4	78– 94	14	78.0	63–89	7
	Control	96.6	85–101	7	91.6	86– 96	14	84.0	72–89	7
18–<24	Experimental	84.1	73– 94	7	86.3	64– 95	14	71.0	45–80	6
	Control	89.6	82– 96	7	89.5	83– 95	14	83.9	75–92	8
≥24	Experimental	78.0	68– 83	7	—	—	0	—	—	0
	Control	81.3	58– 92	7	—	—	0	—	—	0

experiments were considered in which there could be substantial response (i.e. with workers that had been kept in the laboratory for 12 months or more), there was significantly lower survival in the experimental groups ($P = 0.039$, sign test). Although significant, the difference in viability was minor compared with the difference in responsiveness.

It is evident that age is a major component in the variability of worker responsiveness, but it is not the only important component.

8.3.3 Preliminary study of worker stocks and neotenics

The highly erratic responses of the 1977 workers gave the opportunity for a preliminary check on other possible sources of variability. The worker termites examined included new groups (of 100W + 5S) taken from the residues of stocks from which the 15- and 18-month assays had been set up, and the 21-month controls (averaging 91.0 workers, range 87–94, plus 5S); and the inducers included the neotenics used in the 21-month assays, new neotenics less than a week old at commencement, and mature females 8 months old. When the experiment was carried out, all the workers had been maintained in the laboratory for 23 months. Although the limited availability of material precluded a satisfactory experimental design, the results, summarized in Table 8.4, provided useful leads.

8.3.3.1 *Variation between worker stocks*

Three comparisons call for comment:

(a) The workers from the residues of the 15-month and 18-month stocks gave a similar response at 23 months ($P > 0.20$, U-test). Data from the two residual stocks were, therefore, pooled for other comparisons.

(b) The response of 15-month stock was much greater at 23 months than it had been at 15 ($P < 0.002$, U-test), but that of 18-month stock was significantly diminished at 23 months ($P < 0.05$, U-test).

(c) The 21-month control workers showed a greater response at 23 months than the experimental workers had done in the 21-month assay ($P < 0.01$, U-test).

The facts that the 15-month and 18-month residual stock responded similarly, and quite unlike the previous responses of workers from the same cultures, and that the 21-month controls produced substantially more neotecnics at 23 months than had developed in the 21-month assay, suggested that some aspect of culture conditions might be involved. Unfortunately, we do not have any data on this point. However, culture conditions could not have been responsible for the variability within treatments such as, for example, the 21-month controls, whose maintenance was uniform. This suggested that the assay might have been operating close to some kind of threshold, so that secondary factors could cause major changes in the expression of the basic, age-dependent sensitivity. This suggestion led to experiments on the effects of group size and density of termites.

8.3.3.2   *Variation between neotenics*

Two points emerged from the data on the inductive performance of the various neotenics (Table 8.4):

(a) The neotenic inducers from the 21-month assay evoked a greater response in the 23-month test than they had in the 21-month assay ($P = 0.002$, U-test). However, there was no correlation between the performance of

TABLE 8.4. NEOTENIC PRODUCTION IN GROUPS OF 100 23-MONTH OLD *MASTOTERMES* WORKERS FROM TOWNSVILLE, EXPOSED FOR 35 DAYS TO FEMALE NEOTENICS FROM VARIOUS SOURCES, COMPARED WITH RESULTS OF EARLIER ASSAYS OF WORKERS FROM THE SAME STOCK

| Age or source of | | Number of neotenics produced | | | | | |
| | | Previous assay | | | 23-month assay | | |
Neotenics	Workers	X̄	Range	N	X̄	Range	N
Mature	15-month stock	0.6	0– 2	7	8.1	5–12	8
< 7 days	15-month stock	—	—	—	2.0	2	2
Mature	18-month stock	16.4	4–31	7	8.2	4–16	6
< 7 days	18-month stock	—	—	—	2.0	2	2
8 months	21-month assay	1.4	0– 4	7	9.3	0–15	7
8 months	15 + 18-month stock	—	—	—	7.7	4–12	7
< 7 days	15 + 18-month stock	—	—	—	2.0	2	4
21-month assay	15 + 18-month stock	1.4	0– 4	7	8.6	3–16	7

individual neotenic inducers in the two assays (Spearman $r = 0.4732$, $P > 0.10$).

(b) The 8-month old neotenics were more powerful inducers than those only a week old at the beginning of the assay ($P = 0.002$, U-test).

Thus the age of the neotenic can influence the response of the workers, but other factors exert a greater influence.

8.3.4   Group size and density

8.3.4.1   *Group size*

The effect of altering the size of the worker group was studied in *Mastotermes* collected in Townsville in February 1979. Groups of 50, 100, 200 and 300 workers were set up in June 1980, in standard containers with 6% soldiers and a laboratory-reared, mature female neotenic; there were four or five replicates at each group size. The results are summarized in Tables 8.5 and 8.6 and Fig. 8.2).

TABLE 8.5. NEOTENIC PRODUCTION AND THE TIME TO THE APPEARANCE OF THE FIRST NEOTENIC IN VARIOUS-SIZED GROUPS OF *MASTOTERMES* WORKERS FROM TOWNSVILLE, EXPOSED TO A FEMALE NEOTENIC FOR 35 DAYS

Group size	Number of neotenics produced per 100 initial workers			Number of days to first neotenic		
	$\bar{X}$	Range	N	$\bar{X}$	Range	N
50W + 3S	8.8	0–16	5	>26.6	23–>35	5
100W + 6S	7.3	1–16	4	23.5	19– 26	4
200W + 12S	19.0	12.5–36.5	5	17.8	16– 19	5
300W + 18S	20.4	13.3–30.7	5	16.6	16– 17	5

TABLE 8.6. RATES OF NEOTENIC PRODUCTION IN VARIOUS-SIZED GROUPS OF *MASTOTERMES* WORKERS FROM TOWNSVILLE, EXPOSED TO A FEMALE NEOTENIC FOR 35 DAYS

Days after inducer added	Average number of neotenics produced per day over 5-day period per 100W initially in group sizes of							
	50W + 3S(N = 5)		100W + 6S(N = 4)		200W + 12S(N = 5)		300W + 18S(N = 5)	
	$\bar{X}$	Range	$\bar{X}$	Range	$\bar{X}$	Range	$\bar{X}$	Range
11–15	0.0	0	0.0	0	0.0	0	0.0	0
16–20	0.0	0	0.05	0–0.2	0.56	0.3–0.9	1.20	0.6–1.8
21–25	0.32	0–0.8	0.30	0–1.8	1.44	0.8–2.7	1.36	0.7–2.5
26–30	0.80	0–1.2	0.65	0–1.8	1.18	0.4–2.6	0.96	0.5–1.5
31–35	0.84	0–1.6	0.50	0–1.4	0.62	0.3–1.1	0.54	0.2–1.1

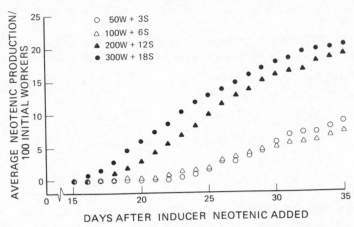

FIG. 8.2. Time-course of neotenic production in various-sized groups of *Mastotermes* workers from Townsville, exposed to a female neotenic for 35 days.

(a) Analysis of variance showed that the number of neotenics produced per hundred workers (Table 8.5, Fig. 8.2) differed significantly between treatments ($P < 0.05 > 0.01$); there was no significant heterogeneity in variance (maximum F-ratio 2.497). Although no average differed significantly from any other ($P > 0.05$, Tukey's w-procedure), the major divergence lay between the two smaller groups on the one hand and the two larger groups on the other (Fig. 8.2).

(b) The time to the appearance to the first neotenic (Table 8.5) was also significantly heterogeneous, being least in the largest group ($P < 0.01 > 0.001$, Kruskal-Wallis ANOVA). As variability is relatively limited within group size, it is unlikely that these differences arose from the lesser chance that, on any given day, a worker would moult in the smaller groups.

(c) The rates of neotenic production, expressed as the number of neotenics produced per hundred (initial) workers per day over 5-day intervals, reached a peak earlier in the two large groups (days 21–25) than in the groups of 100 (26–30) or 50 (31–35) (Table 8.6). This difference is reflected in the significant heterogeneity of rates between the different group sizes in days 16–20 ($P < 0.01 > 0.001$) and 21–25 ($P < 0.05 > 0.02$) (Kruskal-Wallis ANOVA).

(d) The unaccounted loss of workers (i.e. the percentage discrepancy between the initial number of workers and the number of surviving workers plus the neotenics and presoldiers formed) did not differ significantly between group sizes ($P < 0.70 > 0.50$, Kruskal-Wallis ANOVA).

8.3.4.2 *Group density*

As the experiment on group size was carried out in standard boxes, the differences observed might have arisen not from group size itself, but from differences in the density of workers, i.e. the number of workers per unit area of floor space. Sets of modular boxes, of similar construction and height to the standard boxes, were therefore used in an experiment to dissociate the two factors.

The standard boxes have a floor area of approximately 207 cm². The modular boxes were 17.0 cm square (floor area approximately 290 cm²), 16.9 × 8.0 cm (approximately 135 cm²) or 8.1 cm square (approximately 66 cm²), sizes appropriate for groups straddling the major divergence of group size (100W and 200W) and density (approximately 1 or 2 cm²/termite) found in the group-size experiment.

The experimental layout was as shown on Table 8.7; other details were as usual.

The workers had been collected in Townsville in February 1979, and the experiment commenced in October 1980; a single, laboratory-reared female neotenic more than one month old was added to each group. The results are summarized in Table 8.8 and Fig. 8.3.

Kruskal-Wallis analysis of variance showed that the number of neotenics produced per hundred initial workers differed significantly between treatments ($P < 0.02 > 0.01$). Comparison of treatments in which the densities were similar also showed significant differences ($P < 0.05 > 0.02$ for 75W/small box, 150W/medium box, 300W/large box, Kruskal-Wallis ANOVA; $P = 0.013$ for 75W/medium box and 150W/large box, U-test). However, comparisons

TABLE 8.7. LAYOUT FOR AN EXPERIMENT ON THE EFFECT OF GROUP DENSITY ON THE RESPONSE OF *MASTOTERMES* WORKERS TO A FEMALE NEOTENIC

Box size	Group size	cm²/termite	Wood blocks	Matrix (g)	Replicates
Small	75W + 2S	0.88	1	2.5	6
Medium	75W + 2S	1.80	2	5.0	6
	150W + 4S	0.90	2	5.0	6
Large	150W + 4S	1.93	4	10.0	6
	300W + 8S	0.97	4	10.0	2

TABLE 8.8. NEOTENIC PRODUCTION IN VARIOUS-SIZED GROUPS OF *MASTOTERMES* WORKERS FROM TOWNSVILLE, EXPOSED FOR 35 DAYS TO A FEMALE NEOTENIC IN BOXES OF VARIOUS SIZES

| Container size | Number of neotenics produced per 100 initial workers in groups of | | | | | | | | |
| | 75W + 2S | | | 150W + 4S | | | 300W + 8S | | |
	X̄	Range	N	X̄	Range	N	X̄	Range	N
Small (X)	20.7	12–28	6	—	—	—	—	—	—
Medium (2X)	20.2	16–25	6	30.1	21–46	6	—	—	—
Large (4X)	—	—	—	34.2	19–45	6	53.0	49–57	2

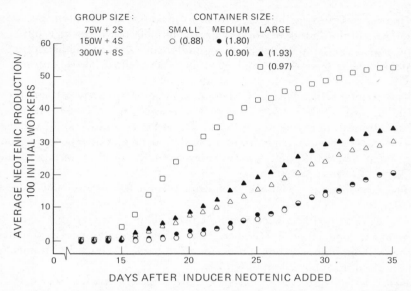

Fig. 8.3.   Time-course of neotenic production in various-sized groups of *Mastotermes* workers from Townsville, exposed to a female neotenic in containers of various sizes (worker density shown, in parentheses, as cm²/termite).

within group size showed no significant differences (P = 0.531 for 75W, 0.294 for 150W, *U*-test).

We conclude that the responsiveness of a group of workers to an inducer neotenic is strongly influenced by the size of the group, but not by the density at which the termites are housed. There appears to be a threshold between 100 and 200 workers, above which the response is heightened. In later experiments, therefore, each group contained at least 150 workers.

8.3.5   The condition of the inducer neotenic

Watson *et al.* (1975) showed that female neotenics are more powerful inducers than males or pairs, and the 23-month experiment with 1977 workers indicated that newly moulted female neotenics are less powerful than mature females. We have re-examined the inductive performance of the two sexes; have compared neotenics collected in the field with those reared in the laboratory, and laboratory-reared female neotenics of different ages; and have tested the effect of two neotenics of like sex on groups of workers.

8.3.5.1   *Provenance and sex of the inducer neotenic*

Ten slightly physogastric female neotenics (*cf.* Fig. 8.4) collected from a field colony near Darwin in April 1981 were each set up 10 days later with 150 workers collected in Darwin in June 1980, plus six soldiers. Ten neotenics of unknown age, developed in a laboratory culture of Darwin workers from the same 1980 colony, were similarly treated; 10 groups without neotenics served as controls. The results are summarized in Table 8.9.

The field neotenics produced a greater response than those reared in the laboratory ($P < 0.02 > 0.002$, U-test). The difference in response was not due to differences in survival of workers, which averaged 71.7 (range 17–91) in the groups with field neotenics, and 68.4 (range 41–95) in those with laboratory-reared neotenics.

TABLE 8.9. NEOTENIC PRODUCTION IN GROUPS OF 150
MASTOTERMES WORKERS FROM DARWIN, EXPOSED FOR 35 DAYS
TO FEMALE NEOTENICS FROM VARIOUS SOURCES

Origin of inducer neotenic	Number of neotenics produced		
	$\bar{X}$	Range	N
Field colony	5.4	0–9	10
Laboratory group	2.1	0–7	10
Control	0.0	0	10

A similar experiment was set up to compare field- and laboratory-reared male neotenics with females. Each of seven male and seven female neotenics collected from a field colony near Darwin in August 1982 was placed two weeks later with 150W + 6S originally gathered in Darwin in April 1981. Seven males and seven females of unknown age that had developed in the worker stocks were similarly set up; there were seven control groups without neotenics. The results appear in Table 8.10.

The responsiveness of the workers was much greater than in the preceding experiment, presumably because they were older, and the difference between the effects of field- and laboratory-reared female neotenics was not significant ($P > 0.05$, Wilcoxon matched-pairs signed-ranks test). The response to female

TABLE 8.10. NEOTENIC PRODUCTION IN GROUPS OF 150
MASTOTERMES WORKERS FROM DARWIN, EXPOSED FOR 35 DAYS
TO MALE OR FEMALE NEOTENICS FROM VARIOUS SOURCES

Sex and origin of inducer neotenics	Number of neotenics produced					
	Days 1–14			Overall		
	$\bar{X}$	Range	N	$\bar{X}$	Range	N
Female, field colony	1.6	0–3	7	38.4	23–50	7
Female, laboratory group	0.7	0–2	7	35.3	25–46	7
Male, field colony	0.3	0–2	7	1.0	0– 3	7
Male, laboratory group	0.1	0–1	7	1.0	0– 2	7
Control	0.1	0–1	7	0.1	0– 1	7

neotenics of either kind, however, far outweighed the response to males ($P < 0.001$, U-test), which was meagre, whatever their origin (Table 8.10). It is worth noting that the sex ratio of the neotenics formed was similar for the male inducers as for either group of females ($P > 0.05$, X^2).

8.3.5.2 *Age of the inducer neotenic*

It is evident from the preceding experiments that:

(a) Mature female neotenics from the field may induce neotenic formation more powerfully than laboratory-reared females;

(b) Mature, laboratory-reared female neotenics are more powerful inducers than newly moulted females; and

(c) Newly moulted females have at least some inductive capacity within a few days after moulting. This point is confirmed by the occasional induction of neotenic formation in control groups in which a neotenic develops 'spontaneously' (*cf.* Watson *et al.*, 1975); we know that exposure to a female neotenic for 12 hours is sufficient to trigger a response in sensitive workers (Watson & E. C. Metcalf, unpubl. data).

The question arises, how short-lived is the limited capacity of newly metamorphosed neotenics? As the young female neotenics used in the 23-month experiment with the 1977 workers were less than a week old at commencement and, hence, less than 4 weeks old when the last neotenics recorded in the experiment were induced, a further experiment was carried out in which laboratory-reared female neotenics 3–6 weeks old at commencement were compared with laboratory-reared females 6 months or more old. The target groups of 150W + 4S were set up in August 1980 from cultures collected in Townsville in February 1979; unfortunately, stocks were insufficient to set up groups with newly moulted neotenics, or controls. The results are summarized in Table 8.11. There was no significant difference in neotenic production in the two treatments; as inducers, laboratory-reared, female neotenics 3–6 weeks old are the equals of females 6 months old.

Taken together, these results on field and laboratory neotenics suggest that there is an increase in the inductive capacity of neotenic females during their first few weeks after ecdysis, and further increase as they become slightly physogastric, which our laboratory-reared females have not done (Fig. 8.5). Such changes might be linked to reproductive activity—sexual maturation in

TABLE 8.11. NEOTENIC PRODUCTION IN GROUPS OF 150
MASTOTERMES WORKERS FROM TOWNSVILLE, EXPOSED FOR 35
DAYS TO FEMALE NEOTENICS OF DIFFERENT AGES

Age of inducer neotenic	Number of neotenics produced		
	X̄	Range	N
20–40 days	38.4	32–43	5
More than 6 months	37.8	34–41	6

FIG. 8.4. Neotenic pair of *Mastotermes darwiniensis* collected in the field.

FIG. 8.5. Worker and neotenic female of *Mastotermes darwiniensis* reared in the laboratory.

the first instance, and ovarian hypertrophy in the second—but we have no relevant experimental data.

8.3.5.3 *The numbers of inducer neotenics*

Watson *et al.* (1975) showed that pairs of neotenics induce less response from workers than do single females. Although this suggests that a neotenic pair, like a pair of primaries, can inhibit the normal inductive process, the question arises, is such inhibition demonstrated by more than one neotenic female? Unfortunately, it is difficult to carry out an experiment involving more than two inducer neotenics, for destruction of the surplus inducers is then commonplace (Watson & E. C. Metcalf, unpubl. data).

Ten groups of 150 workers collected in Darwin in June 1981, were each set up in March 1982 with one or two laboratory-reared, female neotenics, or with none, and with six soldiers; insufficient material was available to set up groups with neotenic pairs. The results of the experiment appear in Table 8.12. A few neotenics appeared in all three treatments up to day 18; beyond day 18, no neotenics developed in the controls whereas many developed in the experimental groups. Although the average number of neotenics produced after day 18 in response to two female inducers was greater than when only one was present, the difference was only marginally significant ($P = 0.05$, 1-

TABLE 8.12. NEOTENIC PRODUCTION IN GROUPS OF 150
MASTOTERMES WORKERS FROM DARWIN, EXPOSED FOR 35 DAYS
TO VARIOUS NUMBERS OF FEMALE NEOTENICS

| Number of inducer neotenics | Number of neotenics produced | | | | | |
| | Days 1–35 | | | Days 19–35 | | |
	$\bar{X}$	Range	N	$\bar{X}$	Range	N
0	1.3	0–5	10	0.0	0	10
1	21.4	10–28	10	18.8	7–26	10
2	28.7	14–41	10	25.3	12–36	10

tailed U-test); however, significantly more neotenics were produced each day after day 18 in the groups with two inducers than in groups with one ($P < 0.001$, sign test).

We conclude that, unlike the situation with a neotenic pair, the inductive effect of two female neotenics is greater than that of a single female.

8.4 DISCUSSION

In interpreting the results of these experiments, and attempting to extrapolate from them to the situation in the field, the starting point must be the unusual, positive response of *Mastotermes* workers to an inducer neotenic.

To summarize the findings:

(a) Orphaned groups of *Mastotermes* workers from Darwin readily form neotenics, whereas groups from Townsville, once orphaned, remain so. However, workers from the two populations react similarly to an inducer neotenic.

(b) The most important factor influencing the response of a worker to an inducer neotenic is age; the older the worker is, the more responsive.

(c) The response of an orphaned worker group to an inducer depends critically on the size of the group. In small groups, the responsiveness is low, and there appears to be a threshold between 100 and 200 workers, above which substantial response can be obtained in the laboratory.

(d) Neotenics vary in their capacity to induce. The most powerful are mature, field-caught neotenic females, but these need not differ from laboratory-reared neotenics, and even newly moulted neotenics have inductive capacity. So, too, do pairs. Although the effects of two females together are not strictly additive, they are certainly greater at the same group size than the effect of a single female.

What, then, of the situation in the field?

There seems little reason to doubt that an established field colony of *Mastotermes* is normally headed by several to many neotenic reproductives. We have collected more than 100 neotenics from fragments of field colonies

(Watson, unpubl. data). We know that in the laboratory, the loss of a primary from a small colony is followed by the development of a neotenic (even if only after a long delay, presumably enabling a worker to develop competence), and that small colonies need not lose their primaries in order to develop neotenics (Watson *et al.*, 1975; Watson, unpubl. data). Although Howick *et al.* (1975) and Watson *et al.* (1977a) reported a surplus of male neotenics in field and laboratory colonies from Townsville, collections of neotenics from field colonies in Darwin in 1981 and 1982 have shown almost exactly equal numbers of the two sexes in samples of 40–160 neotenics (Watson, unpubl. data). Although most neotenics collected in the field are very dark brown in colour, and the females are often slightly physogastric (Fig. 8.4), some are pale, not unlike young, laboratory-reared neotenics, and are not physogastric (Fig. 8.5) (Watson, unpubl. data).

It is also clear that *Mastotermes* is an opportunistic termite and, should the carrying capacity of a colony's environment increase, the colony can rapidly increase its population to take advantage of the new resources (Watson *et al.*, 1975).

We interpret these field observations, and our laboratory data, as indicating that, in a static field colony of *Mastotermes*, most larvae develop into workers, although an annual batch enters the first nymphal stage at the first ecdysis (*cf.* Watson *et al.*, 1977b), becoming alates approximately 12 months later (Watson, unpubl. data). Some of the workers, in turn, develop into presoldiers then soldiers, the regulatory mechanism being similar to that in other termites: presoldiers develop when the proportion of soldiers is depressed below, perhaps, 5%, to judge from the data of Watson *et al.* (1977a) (Watson, unpubl. data). The remainder continue to moult (Watson *et al.*, 1977b) and, as they age, they become competent to respond to the inductive influence of the resident neotenics. The point at which they will do so will, presumably, depend on the number, sex and age of these neotenics, and the size of the colony. However, they will eventually respond; this metamorphosis is, we believe, the natural end-point of worker development.

Those neotenics that are surplus to requirements will be destroyed by the remaining workers, as happens in the laboratory. We can, however, envisage a situation where a field colony is faced by an expanded environment: a woodland devastated by fire or cyclone, an unprotected wooden building, a railway line supported on susceptible timber sleepers. Such a colony is in a position to take rapid advantage of this opportunity for, unlike most other termite colonies, it can increase its reproductive capacity by increasing the number of reproductives; the general rule in termites is that increase has to be achieved by modifying the reproductive capacity of a single, highly physogastric female, occasionally a few. Even in those other termites where multiple neotenics occur (as, e.g., species of *Porotermes*, *Coptotermes* and *Reticulitermes*), a rapid response to a favourable environmental change may be limited by the inhibitory effect that the resident neotenics exert on further neotenic development (*cf.* Lenz, Chapter 9).

The essence of this opportunistic strategy in *Mastotermes* is the possession of multiple neotenics, coupled with the continuous generation of many more. In such a situation, there is little call for the kind of inhibitory regulation which predominates in other termites; only during the establishment of an incipient colony of *Mastotermes* will the death of a reproductive imperil the survival of the group. At that time, as we have shown, the loss of a primary results in the formation of a neotenic replacement.

8.5 SUMMARY

The addition of a neotenic to an orphaned group of *Mastotermes* workers induces the formation of further neotenics. The response becomes greater as the workers age, increasing rapidly between 12 and 24 months after collection from the field, and as group size increases above a threshold between 100 and 200 workers. Female neotenics are more powerful inducers than males, and two females are more powerful than one; mature, field-collected females are probably the strongest inducers, but some inductive capacity is present in laboratory-reared neotenics on the day after ecdysis. The neotenic stage appears to be the natural end-point of worker development, and the abundant neotenics produced give the colony extreme flexibility in its reproductive capacity, and the ability to increase its population opportunistically.

8.6 REFERENCES

Howick C. D., Creffield J. W. & Lenz M. (1975) Field collection and laboratory maintenance of *Mastotermes darwiniensis* Froggatt (Isoptera: Mastotermitidae) for biological assessment studies. *J. Aust. Ent. Soc.* **14**, 155–160.

Watson J. A. L. & Howick C. D. (1975) The rediscovery of *Mastopsenius australis* Seevers (Coleoptera: Staphylinidae). *J. Aust. Ent. Soc.* **14**, 19–21.

Watson J. A. L., Barrett R. A. & Abbey H. M. (1977a) Caste ratios in a long-established, neotenic-headed laboratory colony of *Mastotermes darwiniensis* Froggatt (Isoptera). *J. Aust. Ent. Soc.* **16**, 469–470.

Watson J. A. L., Metcalf E. C. & Sewell J. J. (1975) Preliminary studies on the control of neotenic formation in *Mastotermes darwiniensis* Froggatt (Isoptera). *Insectes Sociaux* **22**, 415–426.

Watson J. A. L., Metcalf E. C. & Sewell J. J. (1977b) A re-examination of the development of castes in *Mastotermes darwiniensis* Froggatt (Isoptera). *Aust. J. Zool.* **25**, 25–42.

CHAPTER 9

Is Inter- and Intraspecific Variability of Lower Termite Neotenic Numbers due to Adaptive Thresholds for Neotenic Elimination?—Considerations from Studies on Porotermes adamsoni (Froggatt) (Isoptera: Termopsidae)

M. LENZ

CSIRO, Division of Entomology, Canberra, A.C.T. 2601, Australia

CONTENTS

9.1 INTRODUCTION

The number of functional neotenics that can be found in field colonies and laboratory cultures of lower termites varies both between species and between colonies of a given species. This number ranges widely, from a pair to well over 100 neotenics in species belonging to the Mastotermitidae, Termopsidae and Rhinotermitidae (Beal, 1967; Becker, 1962, 1979; Bess, 1970; Esenther, 1969; Howard & Haverty, 1980; Lenz & Barrett, 1982; Mensa-Bonsu, 1976a, b; Watson *et al.*, 1975).

As a rule only one pair of neotenics is found in colonies of the Kalotermitidae (Lüscher, 1952; Nagin, 1970; Ruppli, 1969; Sewell, 1978). This situation is the result of a complex regulative process. In colonies which lose their primary reproductives, termites in excess of the required one male and one female replacement moult into neotenics. The surplus is eliminated through the combined activity of dominant neotenics and other castes, leaving only one pair to become functional reproductives (Lenz *et al.*, 1982b; Lenz, Barrett & Williams, Chapter 10; Lüscher, 1952; Nagin, 1972; Ruppli, 1969; Ruppli & Lüscher, 1964).

A view commonly held is that the reproductive strategies of all species that can maintain more than a single pair of neotenics in each colony do not involve any control over the number of reproductives. However, the possibility should be considered that a colony with several neotenics might have contained even more reproductives at an earlier stage, and their number has been brought down to a lower level by elimination. In other words, the difference between Kalotermitidae and the other families of the lower termites might be one of threshold only. For a given colony, the threshold level at which elimination of reproductives starts could vary with time as the colony grows, or vary according to other circumstances; be higher under conditions of food surplus, but lower when the colony is faced with a food shortage. Neotenic numbers in a colony might be dynamic rather than static.

The "no regulation" view is supported mainly by the results of laboratory experiments with *Zootermopsis* spp. (Termopsidae) in which the elimination of neotenics could not be recorded (Lüscher, 1974), at least not in small experimental groups (Stuart, 1979). Yet, in experiments with the Australian termopsid *Porotermes adamsoni* more neotenics were always produced than were finally permitted to live (Mensa-Bonsu, 1976a). Observations on *Mastotermes darwiniensis* (Mastotermitidae) (Watson *et al.*, 1975) and *Reticulitermes lucifugus* (Rhinotermitidae) (Buchli, 1956, 1958) indicate that the extent to which laboratory colonies eliminate neotenics bears some relation to the colony's food supply and available space. These cases clearly give support to the idea that "regulation" might be more common than previously envisaged.

Experiments with *Cryptotermes brevis* (Kalotermitidae) have shown that the process of neotenic production in orphaned groups can be modified by experimental conditions (Lenz *et al.*, 1982b). Further, the use of small numbers of termites in experiments can distort the normal pattern of neotenic production and elimination, as recorded for *Kalotermes flavicollis* (Kalotermitidae) (Lüscher, 1952); the same is implied by Stuart (1979) in his work with *Zootermopsis*.

It is therefore difficult to extrapolate from laboratory results to the field situation, unless the laboratory experiments are run under conditions more closely resembling those in the field. In the present study, instead of using small groups of termites fed only on filter paper in a petri-dish, we have used populous groups of *Porotermes adamsoni*—a species in which several neotenics are involved in colony propagation—and maintained them under conditions in which orphaned groups could re-establish themselves as functional colonies.

9.2 MATERIALS AND METHODS

Data on neotenic production in *P. adamsoni* were obtained from two sources:

(1) experiments on colony re-establishment in orphaned groups, described in detail here, and kept for periods of 0.5–12 months; and
(2) experiments on effects of constant temperatures and diets on survival and wood consumption over an 8-week period. Details will be given elsewhere (Lenz *et al.*, unpubl. data). Only the results on neotenic numbers are reported here.

9.2.1 Changes in neotenic numbers with time in orphaned groups of termites

The work was carried out in two consecutive stages, the principal difference between the two being the amount of food supplied: termites in the second stage received twice as much food as those in the first. Termites from separate colonies (colony I + II) were used for the two stages of the experiment. The termites were collected in April 1980 and September 1981, from the Brinda-bella Range near Canberra, A.C.T. The colonies inhabited standing mature trees of snow gum (*Eucalyptus pauciflora*). The trees were cut near the base; several metres of bole were then split and the termites extracted.

Orphaned termites were set up in groups each weighing 4 g (287 ± 14 termites for colony I and 382 ± 21 for colony II; the latter colony contained more of the smaller termites). Other groups of 10 g were established from colony I. The caste composition of the groups was that of the samples taken from the trees, except that the soldiers were removed. Uniform distribution of soldiers between replicates could not be guaranteed when weighing out the termite groups, and soldiers from field colonies display great variation in size. On both grounds, it was thought best to exclude soldiers from the groups. Some additional groups were given one or two functional neotenics from their corresponding nests.

Groups were maintained in glass jars with a volume of 540 ml (colony I, 4 g) or plastic jars with a volume of 1200 ml (colony II, 10 g groups of colony I). The jars were filled with 30 g (small jars) or 50 g (large jars) of grade IV vermiculite (a heat-expanded mica of aluminium–iron–magnesium, particle size 2–6 mm, water-holding capacity *ca.* 350% v/m). The matrix was mois-tened to 300% v/m with distilled water. Lumps of wood were stacked in the remaining jar space and partly buried in the vermiculite. The timber originated from a log of *E.* ?*viminalis*, from the Brindabellas, well decayed by brown rot fungi. The log had once housed a colony of *P. adamsoni*. The larger jars (colony II) received twice as much wood as the small jars (colony I). The jars were closed with screw top lids, first screwed on tightly, then unscrewed about a quarter turn to allow ventilation. Jars were held at 21°C.

The vermiculite was re-moistened after 6 months in cultures which were kept for longer periods. Apart from this, the cultures required no additional maintenance.

Diet, temperature and general maintenance conditions were chosen from experience as being very suitable for long-term laboratory experiments with this termite species (Lenz *et al.*, 1982a).

Types and numbers of groups set up, and the sampling and recording schedule, were as follows:

colony I (small amount of food)

140 groups of 4 g   10 groups each, randomly selected,
                                    examined after 0.5, 0.75, 1, 2 and
                                    then at monthly intervals up to
                                    12 months

4 groups of 4 g + 1 functional male neotenic from nest	all groups examined after 3 months
15 groups of 4 g + 1 functional female neotenic from nest	10 groups examined after 3 months, 5 after 12 months
10 groups of 10 g	5 examined after 3 months, 5 after 12 months

colony II (large amount of food)

72 groups of 4 g	6 groups each, randomly selected, examined after 1, 2 and then at monthly intervals up to 12 months
4 groups of 4 g + 1 pair of functional neotenics from nest	examined after 3 months and again after 11 months

At the final inspection, all termites were separated from the wood and matrix, weighed and preserved in 80% ethanol. Since it can be difficult to distinguish freshly formed neotenics from other freshly moulted termites with the naked eye, all material was examined under the microscope. Even freshly moulted neotenics, without the characteristic brownish coloration, could readily be differentiated from precursor stages, having fewer hairs on the pronotum and legs; female neotenics also had fewer hairs on the terminal sternites, which were shorter than those of the males. Females as a rule lose their styli when they differentiate into neotenics; those styli that remain after the moult are reduced in size.

9.2.2 Influence of constant temperatures and diets on neotenic production

These experiments yielded data on neotenic numbers in termite groups of 2 g, held at various temperatures and/or in different timbers. The termites originated from colony II. General maintenance conditions were comparable to those described earlier (small jars; amount of matrix and its moisture content as in colony I). In the experiment evaluating temperature effects, termites were kept on the same kind of timber, decayed *E. ?viminalis*, as in the study on colony re-establishment, but received blocks of known mass with the dimensions 5 × 2.5 × 1.5 cm. In the other experiment, groups were offered timber from their own nest tree (*E. pauciflora*). They received two blocks of known mass and of the same size as given above, of either outer heartwood, with no or only slight signs of decay, or well-decayed inner heartwood or one of each type (Lenz *et al.*, unpubl. data).

9.2.3   Analysis of results

Separate analyses of variance were carried out on neotenic numbers from the two colonies using the statistical package GENSTAT (Alvey *et al.*, 1977). For each colony, single classification analyses of variance were used to compare neotenic production over the periods up to 12 months. Other single classification analyses of variance provided a comparison of the various termite groups at 3 and 12 months for colony I, and 3 and 11 months for colony II. As the numbers of neotenics produced were usually low, the data were not transformed, except that $x + 1$ values were used for the analysis of the male to female neotenic ratios to overcome the problem of occasional zero values.

9.3   RESULTS

9.3.1   Change in neotenic numbers with time in 4 g orphaned groups of termites

Surplus food was available to all groups, including those with the smaller amount of wood (colony I). The amount of food was doubled for the groups of colony II with the idea that over-abundant food might stimulate reproduction, and lead to the production of larger numbers of neotenics. However, in this situation termites did not feed on all lumps of wood at the same time, but rather moved in sequence from one block to the next. In those pieces of wood left unattacked for some time, decay increased considerably, thus reducing the amount of food available to the termites. In consequence, differences between the two sets of groups, based on the variation in the food supply, were negligible.

9.3.1.1   *Colony survival*

At no time during the year did the live mass of the groups from either colony fall below 80% of the initial mass (Fig. 9.1), a clear indication that maintenance conditions were satisfactory for the species. From 4 months

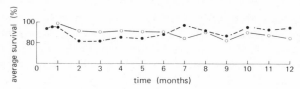

FIG. 9.1. Survival (%) in 4-g groups of *Porotermes adamsoni* over a 12-month period: (●) colony I; (○) colony II.

onwards, all groups contained eggs and larvae, but the level of recruitment was such that there was generally no change in the mass of the groups.

9.3.1.2 *Losses in terminal castes: alates, soldiers, neotenics*

The decrease in number (and in mass) will (apart from natural mortality of group members) be due largely to the production, and subsequent loss, of terminal castes in the experimental groups.

Alates, by their very nature, are a loss to the colony, except in those few species which can retain one or more of them to replace lost reproductives. Alates were found 3–6 months after starting the experiment with termites from colony I (July to October) and after 2–4 months in those from colony II (November to January) (Fig. 9.2). Alates have been recorded in the Canberra region from late December to early February (Hill, 1942). Thus development of alates was accelerated in both colonies under laboratory conditions. However, the total number of alates was lower in colony I, since only 50% of the groups produced alates despite the presence of large nymphs in all of them (maximum average 1.8 ± 1.8 in the fourth month). In contrast, all replicates from colony II produced alates (maximum average 13.3 ± 3.2) in the second month (Fig. 9.2).

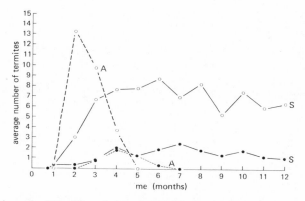

Fɪɢ. 9.2. Numbers of soldiers (S) and alates (A) in 4-g groups of *Porotermes adamsoni* over a 12-month period: (●) colony I; (○) colony II.

We have no data on production of surplus neotenics. However, Mensa-Bonsu's studies (1976a) indicated that more neotenics were produced than finally survived. None of the relatively common neotenic/worker intercastes (see below) attained full pigmentation; they were, apparently, not tolerated for long by the other termites in the groups.

Numbers of soldiers built up during the first half of the year, reaching a peak at 6–7 months in groups from both colonies (Fig. 9.2), but fell thereafter, indicating adjustment of numbers to colony needs. The number of soldiers remained surprisingly low in groups from colony I, but was much higher, and closer to normal for *P. adamsoni*, in colony II.

9.3.1.3   Neotenics

It should be stressed that the numbers of neotenics (totals, males, females) shown in Figs 9.3 and 9.4 represent only those neotenics found at the time of inspection, and may not necessarily be the total numbers of neotenics produced during those periods. The total numbers could not be established from experiments of this design.

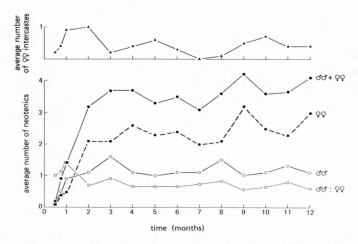

Fig. 9.3. Numbers of neotenics and worker/neotenic intercastes in 4-g groups of orphaned *Porotermes adamsoni* over a 12-month period (colony I).

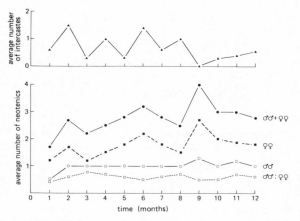

Fig. 9.4. Numbers of neotenics and worker/neotenic intercastes in 4-g groups of orphaned *Porotermes adamsoni* over a 12-month period (colony II).

Observed numbers of neotenics reached an initial maximum after 3 months in colony I and 2 months in colony II, with further peaks at 6 and 9 months in both cases, and 12 months in colony I. Highest numbers were present after 9 months in both series (4.2 and 4.0 neotenics respectively).

A more pronounced pattern emerged when variations in the number of the sexes were considered. The number of females fluctuated more than the number of males, especially in colony II (Figs 9.3 and 9.4). From 2 months onwards, when all groups contained neotenics, 1–2 males and 1–5 females were found in each colony. The male:female ratio was therefore almost invariably shifted in favour of the females. The only exception was during the first 4 weeks of the experiment, when groups from colony I had equal or significantly more ($p < 0.001$) males than females, at 2 weeks and 3–4 weeks respectively. Subsequent increase in female numbers reversed the trend. (Groups from colony II were not examined earlier than 1 month after establishment, at which time females already outnumbered males.)

9.3.1.4 *Neotenic/worker intercastes*

All functional neotenics of *P. adamsoni* we have so far found in field colonies and in the course of laboratory experiments were, apart from their coloration when mature, readily distinguished from other castes by a reduction in the number of hairs on various parts of the body, especially on the pronotum and the terminal sternites (see above). Nevertheless, many groups from both colonies contained individuals with final sternites of similar structure to those of neotenics, but bearing hairs on the pronotum as found in the precursor stages (workers, nymphs). All had recently moulted, and none were found with the brown to pink pigmentation of neotenics, or the light-brown to yellow colour of workers and nymphs. The ovaries of these termites were enlarged to the same extent as in newly moulted, true neotenics, whereas workers and nymphs did not show any sign of gonadal development. These individuals must be classified as intercastes. In colony I, we could find only females: colony II also contained a few males. The number of intercastes per group ranged from 0–3, with some individuals being found during most of the monthly checks (Figs 9.3 and 9.4). Because of the apparent brief survival period of the intercastes and the relative infrequency of sampling, these numbers were probably underestimates of the total.

9.3.2 Change in neotenic numbers with time in 10 g orphaned groups of termites

The numbers of neotenics in the two group sizes (4 and 10 g) did not differ significantly after 3 months. However, after one year the larger groups contained significantly more females ($p < 0.001$), although the number of males remained similar to those in the small groups (Table 9.1).

TABLE 9.1. AVERAGE NUMBERS, AFTER 3 AND 12 MONTHS, OF
NEOTENICS AND SOLDIERS IN 4-G AND 10-G GROUPS OF ORPHANED
POROTERMES ADAMSONI (COLONY I)

| Caste | 3 months | | 12 months | | LSD |
	4 g	10 g	4 g	10 g	(5% level)
♂♂	1.6	1.6	1.1	1.4	0.84
♀♀	2.1	2.4	3.0	4.6	1.50
Both sexes	3.7	4.0	4.1	6.0	1.87
♂♂:♀♀	0.8	0.7	0.4	0.3	—
Soldiers	0.8	3.2	1.1	2.0	2.64

9.3.3 Change in neotenic numbers with time in groups with one or two mature neotenics

Some of the neotenic reproductives found in the nest-trees of colony I and II were added to 4 g groups to determine whether they stimulated or inhibited neotenic production.

Addition of one mature male to groups from colony I resulted in significantly more neotenics after 3 months than was achieved by adding one mature female ($p < 0.001$) (Table 9.2). The difference was due mainly to increased production of females in groups that started off with a mature male. After 3 months, orphaned groups contained neotenic numbers intermediate between those of groups in which one of the sexes was present from the beginning (Table 9.2).

After 12 months, orphaned groups were headed by significantly more female neotenics than were groups which were given one mature female ($p < 0.001$) (Table 9.2). In fact, all the latter groups still contained their original mature neotenics, which were darker and more physogastric than those produced in orphaned groups and probably equalled two or three of the

TABLE 9.2. AVERAGE NUMBERS, AFTER 3 AND 12 MONTHS, OF
NEOTENICS AND SOLDIERS IN 4-G GROUPS OF *POROTERMES
ADAMSONI*, ORPHANED OR PARTIALLY ORPHANED WITH EITHER
ONE MATURE MALE OR ONE MATURE FEMALE NEOTENIC ADDED
(COLONY I)

| Caste | 3 months | | | 12 months | | LSD |
	orphaned + 1 mature ♂	+ 1 mature ♀	orphaned	+ 1 mature ♀		(5% level)
♂♂	1.6	2.0	1.2	1.1	1.0	0.84
♀♀	2.1	2.8	1.6	3.0	1.0	1.50
Both sexes	3.7	4.8	2.8	4.1	2.0	1.87
♂♂:♀♀	0.8	0.7	0.8	0.4	1.0	—
Soldiers	0.8	1.3	2.9	1.1	5.0	2.64

new females in reproductive output (see also below). The average live masses of both types of groups were similar after 12 months: 3.85 ± 0.30 g for orphaned groups and 3.91 ± 0.41 g for those with a mature female.

More soldiers developed in groups with mature neotenics than in orphaned groups. The difference was already evident after 3 months ($p < 0.01$), but became more pronounced after 12 months ($p < 0.001$) in the case of colony I (Table 9.2); it was highly significant ($p < 0.001$) at 3 and 11 months in groups from colony II (Table 9.3).

The mature neotenic pairs added to four groups of colony II were still alive after 3 months, except for one male which was replaced. No additional neotenics were present. The originally orphaned groups were headed by a similarly low number of neotenics. After 11 months, neotenic numbers had increased by one in both cases, with the rise mainly due to new females (Table 9.3). The four groups with the mature pair revealed an interesting plasticity in reproductive strategy (Table 9.4). In one case the old female became significantly more physogastric between 3 and 11 months. In two cases the mass of the mature female had not increased, but two new females had been added, raising neotenic biomass to the level equal to or above that of the

TABLE 9.3. AVERAGE NUMBERS, AFTER 3 AND 12 MONTHS, OF NEOTENICS AND SOLDIERS IN 4-G GROUPS OF *POROTERMES ADAMSONI*, ORPHANED OR WITH ONE PAIR OF MATURE NEOTENICS ADDED (COLONY II)

Caste	3 months orphaned	+ 1 mature pair	12 months orphaned	+ 1 mature pair	LSD (5% level)
♂♂	1.0	1.0	1.2	1.0	0.28
♀♀	1.2	1.0	1.8	2.0	0.76
Both sexes	2.2	2.0	3.0	3.0	0.96
♂♂:♀♀	0.8	1.0	0.7	0.5	—
Soldiers	6.7	15.5	6.0	15.3	5.72

TABLE 9.4. NUMBERS, AGES AND MASSES (MG) OF NEOTENICS IN 4-G GROUPS OF *POROTERMES ADAMSONI*, TO WHICH ONE PAIR OF MATURE NEOTENICS WAS ADDED (COLONY II)

♂♂ numbers, age and mass at months			♀♀ numbers, age and mass at months					Total after
0	3	11	0	3	11			11 months
1m*:29	1m:28	1m:28	1m:56	1m:45	1m:46	1nf†:27		2:73
1m:28	1m:26	1m:30	1m:57	1m:39		1nf:31	1nf:23	2:54
1m:28	1nf:17	1nf:21	1m:61	1m:46	1m:46	1nf:28		3:99
1m:29	1m:26	1nf:32	1m:56	1m:37	1m:74			1:74

*mature; †nf: newly formed.

group with a single mature female. In the fourth case the group lost the old female some time after 3 months; two new females were produced with a combined mass after 11 months still below that of the neotenics in the other groups.

9.3.4 Influence of constant temperatures on neotenic production

Within the 8-week period of the experiment, neotenics developed from 17°C upwards with the highest and similar numbers between 21 and 27°C (Fig. 9.5). A temperature of 29°C was lethal to most of the termites after several weeks (see also Lenz *et al.*, 1982a). As to the question of whether or not

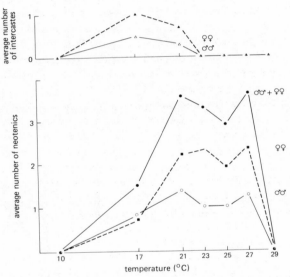

FIG. 9.5. Effect of constant temperatures on the numbers of neotenics and worker/neotenic intercastes in 2-g groups of orphaned *Porotermes adamsoni* after 8 weeks.

neotenic numbers are regulated, the most important result is that intercastes were recorded only for the two lower temperatures, 17 and 21°C, above that temperature, either none were produced or none survived long enough to be detected.

9.3.5 Influences of diets and constant temperatures on neotenic production

This study confirmed the previous results on the effects of temperature (Fig.

9.6). It indicated that 15°C is close to the lower threshold of the critical temperature range, in which neotenics would be expected to appear within 8 weeks. Neotenic numbers were again comparable at 21 and 27°C. When groups were fed decayed wood only, more females were present at 27°C, but the difference was not significant. There was no indication that diet influenced the number of males (Fig. 9.6).

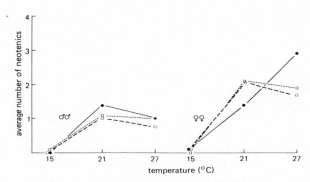

Fig. 9.6. Effects of constant temperatures and three diets (outer heartwood (○) or inner heartwood (●) of nest tree, or a choice of both (□)) on the number of neotenics in 2-g groups of orphaned *Porotermes adamsoni* after 8 weeks.

9.4   DISCUSSION

9.4.1   Evidence for regulation of neotenic numbers and for adaptive thresholds for neotenic elimination in *Porotermes adamsoni*

The results given here, together with those by Mensa-Bonsu (1976a, b), clearly demonstrate that colonies of *P. adamsoni* regulate the number of neotenic reproductives. However, the "norm" is not one pair, but a particular but small number of neotenics in a sex ratio favouring females. Evidence for regulation of neotenic numbers includes the following:

(1)   Apart from an initial phase, the number of males never exceeds that of females. This is supported by laboratory results and records of the number of neotenic reproductives in field colonies (Table 9.5 for our observations; Mensa-Bonsu, 1976b for data from the Adelaide region). Orphaned groups initially produce more males than females [experiments with groups of larvae in equal sex ratios (Mensa-Bonsu, 1976a)] or at least males develop earlier than females (Fig. 9.3); but surplus males are eliminated preferentially (Mensa-Bonsu, 1976a).

(2)   The fluctuations in neotenic numbers over the 12-month period in our experiments (Figs 9.3 and 9.4) may also indicate that there is an

TABLE 9.5. NUMBERS, SEXES AND MASSES (G) OF REPRODUCTIVES
IN FIELD COLONIES OF *POROTERMES ADAMSONI* FROM THE
BRINDABELLA RANGE NEAR CANBERRA, A.C.T.

Collected	Season	♂♂		♀♀		♂♂:♀♀	No. of termites extracted from the nest tree*
		No.	Mass	No.	Mass		
Feb 78	summer	30n†	0.8	92n	3.7	0.33	20 000
March 80	autumn	1pr‡	0.029	1pr	0.076	1.0	30 000
April 80	autumn	4n	0.099	16n	0.69	0.25	55 000
May 79	autumn	1pr	0.042				
		1n	0.034	4n	0.19	0.5	29 000
Sept 79	spring	1pr	0.031	29n	0.96	0.03	11 000
Sept 81	spring	7n	0.21	8n	0.45	0.9	62 000

*We have no estimate what proportion of the total population this number represents.
† n: neotenic.
‡ pr: primary.

optimum number of reproductives at any given time, depending on the condition of the colony. The overall pattern after 2–3 months involved an average of approximately one male and two females in each 4 g group. The changes in neotenic numbers imply that neotenics were being produced throughout the experiments; additional neotenics were at times tolerated, and at other times eliminated.

(3) The number of neotenics maintained in a group is related to the size of that group (Table 9.1; Mensa-Bonsu, 1976a). It can take over 3 months under experimental conditions for differences between group sizes to manifest themselves.

(4) Environmental factors, such as temperature (season) (Figs 9.5 and 9.6; Mensa-Bonsu, 1976b) and the quality and quantity of food (Fig. 9.6; Mensa-Bonsu, 1976a) influence neotenic numbers. *Porotermes laticeps* from southern Africa has only limited food resources available over most of its range. Colonies are therefore fairly small and relatively short-lived. Once the primaries die, most colonies probably perish. Food restrictions at individual nesting sites make colony re-establishment a rare event, even though the species has a well-developed capacity to form neotenics (Coaton & Sheasby, 1976).

(5) Colonies can pursue various reproductive strategies to ensure growth at the appropriate rate. Evidence for this appears in the results from groups with an added pair of mature neotenics (Table 9.4). Colonies may support a small number of reproductives with enhanced ovarian development in females, or maintain a larger number of neotenics with less physogastric females. The same reproductive output (measured indirectly by the biomass of the females) can be achieved in both situations as, indeed, in any variation between the two extremes. The final state in each case will have resulted from an interaction between

variation in the ability of functional neotenics to inhibit development of further neotenics, and the degree of support (rate of feeding and "maintenance") each neotenic received from other colony members. As a consequence, colonies with a few neotenics (more or less controlled number of neotenics) are directly comparable with others, containing more (obviously not controlled).

9.4.2 Evidence for regulation of neotenic numbers and for adaptive thresholds for neotenic elimination in other lower termites

Factors which influence neotenic numbers in *P. adamsoni* are likely to operate in other species of lower termites (data on higher termites are too fragmentary to be included in this discussion). The literature provides several examples demonstrating that the number of neotenics is not a matter of chance, but a reflection of both colony condition and species characteristics. Inter- and intraspecific variation in neotenic numbers can be explained by a combination of factors operating at two levels, the species or population (Springhetti, 1967, 1968) and the colony. Factors which affect the colony are, e.g., food, season, colony size, caste composition and characteristics of the individual functional reproductives. At the species or population level, differences in reproductive strategy are of major significance, with modifications imposed by colony circumstances.

9.4.2.1 *Colony specific factors*

The numbers of dependent termites (final nymphal stages, alates, presoldiers, soldiers, larvae) generally bear some relation to the number of termites available to maintain them and to the environment of the colony (Becker, 1948; Buchli, 1958; Dhanarajan, 1978; Haverty, 1977, 1979; Haverty & Howard, 1981; Howard & Haverty, 1981; Lenz, 1976; Lenz et al., 1980; Lüscher, 1973; Miller, 1942; Ratcliffe et al., 1952; Watson et al., 1978). Certainly, this social homeostasis has also to include the number of neotenic reproductives; unlike primary reproductives, neotenics are highly dependent on other colony members for the maturation of their gonads (e.g. Greenberg & Stuart, 1979; Light & Illig, 1945).

Laboratory cultures of *Mastotermes darwiniensis*, headed by a neotenic pair and restricted in space and/or food, continuously produce and eliminate new neotenics. The same mechanism probably operates in field colonies with food and space restrictions, but neotenic numbers can be built up rapidly once the environment permits colony propagation, as during clearing of land or laying of railway lines with susceptible timber sleepers (Watson et al., 1975; Watson & Abbey, Chapter 8). In cultures of *R. lucifugus*, Buchli (1956, 1958) noted the occasional formation of new neotenics in the presence of functional reproductives; the surplus was, as a rule, eliminated rapidly, but could be tolerated if the groups were provided with more space.

Direct relationships between an improvement in nutrition and a rise in the number of neotenics are reported for *Heterotermes indicola*, when this species is offered wood decayed by brown rot fungi rather than sound wood (Lenz & Becker, 1975), and for *Zootermopsis angusticollis* fed filter paper, treated with faeces of the same species, rather than filter paper alone (Greenberg & Stuart, 1980).

9.4.2.2 *Species specific factors*

Particular sex ratios of neotenics are recorded for a number of species. Field colonies of *Reticulitermes flavipes* contained neotenics in varying numbers, yet in the approximate ratio of one male:two females (Howard & Haverty, 1980). A surplus of females is also reported for natural colonies of *Reticulitermes speratus* (Shimizu, 1970) and *Coptotermes* spp. (Chiuh & Shen, 1960; King, 1971; Lenz & Barrett, 1982). On the other hand, some established field and laboratory colonies of *M. darwiniensis* are characterized by a surplus of neotenic males (Howick *et al.*, 1975; Watson *et al.*, 1977), whereas others have a balanced sex ratio (Watson & Abbey, Chapter 8); the two sexes are produced in equal numbers in laboratory experiments (Watson *et al.*, 1975).

Suggested mechanisms leading to unequal sex ratios involve differences in the sex ratio of the precursor stages for neotenics, and stimuli of different strength for male or female termites to develop into neotenics (Howard & Haverty, 1980).

Mechanisms so far observed involve different rates of production of the two sexes (own data and Mensa-Bonsu, 1976a for *P. adamsoni*; Greenberg & Stuart, 1982 for *Zootermopsis*); and differences between the rates at which the surpluses of the two sexes are eliminated (Mensa-Bonsu, 1976a for *P. adamsoni*).

The reproductive strategies of some species are based on continuous production of neotenics, with tolerance towards the new neotenics when colony circumstances allow for increased reproduction and propagation, but elimination of them under less favourable conditions. This strategy ensures rapid response to changes in the environment. Examples are provided by *M. darwiniensis* (Watson & Abbey, Chapter 8), *R. flavipes* (Esenther, 1969), *R. lucifugus* (Buchli, 1958) and, from the study described here, *P. adamsoni*.

Some particular reproductive strategies are associated with differences between species in colony size and nesting habit. Small colonies of several hundred to a few thousand termites, inhabiting limited food sources or restricted areas within larger masses of wood, are typical of the Kalotermitidae. One pair of reproductives, whether primary or neotenic, is sufficient to ensure appropriate colony growth. The threshold for elimination of surplus reproductives is, as a rule, just above one pair. But even this strictly regulated system has its exceptions. The presence of more than one pair of reproductives (primaries, primaries and neotenics, or neotenics only) has been recorded in some colonies of Australian *Kalotermes* spp. (Sewell, 1978), *Cryptotermes queenslandis* (Lenz *et al.*, unpubl. data), *Neotermes larseni*, *Marginitermes hubbardi* (Nutting, 1970), and *Pterotermes occidentis* (Nutting, 1970; Jones *et al.*, 1981) from North America, as well as in laboratory cultures of *Cryptotermes brevis* (Lenz, unpubl. data). These examples demonstrate that, even in the Kalotermitidae, circumstances may permit a rise in tolerance levels for reproductives, suggesting that differences between the Kalotermitidae and other lower termites in terms of the regulation of the numbers of reproductives, are relative rather than absolute.

Colonies of species belonging to the other families of the lower termites are usually substantially larger than those of the Kalotermitidae, ranging from several thousand (*Zootermopsis*) to one million or more individuals (*Mastotermes*, *Coptotermes*). Colonies can occupy large trees (*Porotermes*, *Coptotermes*) or, as in the case of subterranean species, ground areas of up to 0.6 ha or more (Ratcliffe & Greaves, 1940; Spragg & Paton, 1980). At least some species with diffuse nest systems, such as *Mastotermes*, *Reticulitermes* and *Heterotermes*, have numerous neotenics (Becker, 1962; Esenther, 1969; Howard & Haverty, 1980; Watson *et al.*, 1975; Watson & Abbey, Chapter 8; Weidner, 1978). Neotenics and fractions of the population can "bud off" from the main nest, thus spreading the species over wider areas.

Species which construct a well defined nest, such as representatives of the genus *Coptotermes* have colonies normally headed by one pair of primary reproductives. Queens are very physogastric and have oviposition rates of many tens of thousands of eggs per year (Nutting, 1969). If a primary queen dies, no single neotenic can attain the same degree of ovarian development, and therefore several neotenic females are needed to replace the queen if the colony is to maintain its growth rate. A larger number of neotenics would be required to exceed this growth rate (Lenz & Barrett, 1982).

Several *Coptotermes* species can establish satellite nests when rich food sources are available. Neotenics can develop under these circumstances in the presence of primary reproductives; the neotenics are then usually found in the satellite nest (Lenz & Barrett, 1982).

Mature field colonies of *M. darwiniensis* continuously produce neotenics which, as mentioned above, are tolerated when the circumstances of the colony improve. Thus, the fate of newly formed neotenics is not controlled by the existing functional reproductives, but by colony circumstances (Watson & Abbey, Chapter 8).

Species of *Coptotermes* and *Reticulitermes* which rely primarily on alates to establish new colonies in their natural range will switch to the use of neotenics (in varying numbers) when introduced to other areas (Esenther, 1969; Lenz & Barrett, 1982; Weidner, 1978).

In summary, in the Mastotermitidae, Termopsidae and Rhinotermitidae, a single pair of neotenic reproductives is apparently insufficient to meet species- and colony-specific needs for reproductive output. The threshold for either elimination, or tolerance and support, of more than one pair of neotenics is, apparently, higher than in the Kalotermitidae, but remains flexible.

The number of neotenics observed in the field or in the course of an experiment will reflect the response of the colony or group to a range of stimulatory and inhibitory influences. Alterations in any one, or in several, of these variables will lead to adjustments in the number of reproductives. The speed with which colonies or groups respond to changes in environmental factors which call for changes in the number of reproductives will vary, but can often be, at least under laboratory conditions, lower than anticipated (see Table 9.1). Experiments on species other than *P. adamsoni* have often been designed to achieve a rapid reponse. If this were not so, the experiments might never have provided the combination of factors which evoked regulation.

Further, these experiments might not have taken into account the degree of plasticity colonies and species can display. We still lack the information needed to express, in quantitative terms, the relationship between the number of neotenic reproductives maintained in a colony on the one hand, and factors such as food supply, season and colony size on the other.

There is the further possible complication that there might be additive or synergistic effects, or interactions, between these factors and the likely modification of the reproductive strategy of the species or population. The variability in the number of neotenics we observe in the field is, then, the result of a balance between many influences. The principal distinctions made between the Kalotermitidae, which are considered to exhibit full control of neotenic reproductives, and the other families of the lower termites which, apparently, do not possess such regulative capacities (Lüscher, 1974; Stuart, 1979), no longer appear to be valid. Many factors may determine where a species, population, colony or experimental group will be ranked in terms of the expression of its regulative capacity.

9.5 SUMMARY

There is evidence of continuous neotenic production and elimination or tolerance of surplus neotenics in *Porotermes adamsoni*, depending on conditions. The number of neotenics in populous groups (4 g, 10 g) maintained over a period of up to 12 months may fluctuate and can be influenced by group size, food and temperature. Most groups are headed by more than a single pair of neotenics. As a rule, females outnumber males. Colonies can achieve similar reproductive output by supporting either fewer females with enhanced ovarian development, or larger numbers of less physogastric females. Addition of mature neotenics (male, female or both) to groups of workers and nymphs influences the number of newly produced neotenics and leads to an increase in the number of soldiers. At lower temperatures (17–21°C) worker/neotenic intercastes are produced. They are eliminated shortly after their moult.

The great variation in neotenic numbers in field colonies of representatives of the lower termites can be explained in terms of factors operating at the colony level (food, temperature, colony size) and the species or population level (reproductive strategies). Differences between the Kalotermitidae which, as a rule maintain only one pair of reproductives, and the Mastotermitidae, Termopsidae and Rhinotermitidae with several or many reproductives, are not absolute, but reflect differences of thresholds for the elimination of surplus neotenics. The threshold is adaptive, even in the Kalotermitidae, where, in several species, colonies with more than one pair of reproductives have now been found. It is influenced by the particular circumstances of a colony, or a laboratory group, and the reproductive strategy of the species.

9.6 ACKNOWLEDGEMENTS

I am grateful to Mr R. A. Barrett for his skilled assistance in the field and the laboratory, to Mrs H. M. Abbey for her help at various times during the experiments and to Dr E. R. Williams (CSIRO Division of Mathematics and Statistics) for the statistical analysis of the data. The manuscript benefited from comments made by Mr P. Ferrar and Dr J. A. L. Watson.

9.7 REFERENCES

Alvey N. G. *et al.* (1977) GENSTAT. A general statistical program. Harpenden, Herts., Rothamsted Expt. Stn.

Beal R. H. (1967) Formosan invader. *Pest Control* **35**, 13–17.

Becker G. (1948) Über Kastenbildung und Umwelteinfluss bei Termiten. *Biol. Zbl.* **67**, 407–444.

Becker G. (1962) Laboratoriumsprüfung von Holz und Holzschutzmitteln mit der süd-asiatischen Termite *Heterotermes indicola* Wasmann. *Holz als Roh- u. Werkstoff* **20**, 476–486.

Becker G. (1979). Testing and research results with an Indian termite species in Berlin-Dahlem. *J. Timb. Dev. Assoc. (India)* **25**, 16–23.

Bess H. A. (1970) Termites of Hawaii and the Oceanic Islands. In *Biology of Termites*, Vol. 2 (Krishna K. & Weesner F. M., eds), pp. 449–476. Academic Press, New York.

Buchli H. (1956) Die Neotenie bei *Reticulitermes*. *Insectes Sociaux* **3**, 132–143.

Buchli H. (1958) L'origine des castes et les potentialités ontogéniques des termites européens du genre *Reticulitermes* Holmgren. *Ann. Sci. Nat. Zool. Biol. Animale* **20**, 263–429.

Chiuh T. & Shen L. (1960) Notes on the types of the reproductive castes of subterranean termites, *Coptotermes formosanus* Shiraki and *Reticulitermes flaviceps* Oshima (Isoptera, Rhinotermitidae). *Acta ent. Sinica* **10**, 302–306.

Coaton W. G. H. & Sheasby J. L. (1976) National survey of the Isoptera of southern Africa. 12. The genus *Porotermes* Hagen (Termopsidae: Porotermitinae). *Cimbebasia (A)* **3**, 173–181.

Dhanarajan G. (1978) Cannibalism and necrophagy in a subterranean termite (*Reticulitermes lucifugus* var. *santonensis*). *Malay. Nat. J.* **31**, 237–251.

Esenther G. R. (1969) Termites in Wisconsin. *Ann. ent. Soc. Amer.* **62**, 1274–1284.

Greenberg S. L. W. & Stuart A. M. (1979) The influence of group size on ovarian development in adult and neotenic reproductives of the termite *Zootermopsis angusticollis* (Hagen) (Hodotermitidae). *Int. J. Invertebr. Reprod.* **1**, 99–108.

Greenberg S. L. W. & Stuart A. M. (1980) Control of neotenic development in a primitive termite (Isoptera: Hodotermitidae). *J. N.Y. entomol. Soc.* **88**, 49–50.

Greenberg S. L. W. & Stuart A. M. (1982) Precocious reproductive development (neoteny) by larvae of a primitive termite *Zootermopsis angusticollis* (Hagen). *Insectes Sociaux* **29**, 535–547.

Haverty M. I. (1977) The proportion of soldiers in termite colonies: a list and a bibliography. *Sociobiol.* **2**, 199–216.

Haverty M. I. (1979) Soldier production and maintenance of soldier proportions in laboratory experimental groups of *Coptotermes formosanus* Shiraki. *Insectes Sociaux* **26**, 69–84.

Haverty M. I. & Howard R. W. (1981) Production of soldiers and maintenance of soldier proportions by laboratory experimental groups of *Reticulitermes flavipes* (Kollar) and *Reticulitermes virginicus* (Banks) (Isoptera: Rhinotermitidae). *Insectes Sociaux* **28**, 32–39.

Hill G. F. (1942) *Termites (Isoptera) from the Australian Region*. Council Sci. Ind. Res., Melbourne.

Howard R. W. & Haverty M. I. (1980) Reproductives in mature colonies of *Reticulitermes flavipes*: abundance, sex-ratio and association with soldiers. *Environ. Entomol.* **9**, 458–460.

Howard R. W. & Haverty M. I. (1981) Seasonal variation in caste proportions of field colonies of *Reticulitermes flavipes* (Kollar). *Environ. Entomol.* **10**, 546–549.

Howick C. D., Creffield J. W. & Lenz M. (1975) Field collection and laboratory maintenance of *Mastotermes darwiniensis* Froggatt (Isoptera: Mastotermitidae) for biological assessment studies. *J. Aust. ent. Soc.* **14**, 155–160.

Jones S. C., La Fage J. P. & Wright V. L. (1981) Studies of dispersal, colony caste and sexual composition, and incipient colony development of *Pterotermes occidentis* (Walker) (Isoptera: Kalotermitidae). *Sociobiol.* **6**, 221–242.

King E. G. (1971) Biology of the Formosan subterranean termite, *Coptotermes formosanus* Shiraki, with primary emphasis on young colony development. Thesis, Louisiana State University.

Lenz M. (1976) The dependence of hormone effects in termite caste determination on external factor. In *Phase and Caste Determination in Insects. Endocrine Aspects* (Lüscher M., ed.), pp. 73–89. Pergamon Press, Oxford.

Lenz M. & Barrett R. A. (1982) Neotenic formation in field colonies of *Coptotermes lacteus* (Froggatt) in Australia, with comments on the roles of neotenics in the genus *Coptotermes*. *Sociobiol.* **7**, 47–60.

Lenz M. & Becker G. (1975) Einfluss von Basidiomyceten auf die Entwicklung von Ersatzgeschlechtstieren bei *Heterotermes indicola* (Isoptera). *Mater. u. Org.* **10**, 223–237.

Lenz M., Barrett R. A. & Williams E. R. (1982a) Influence of diet on the survival and wood consumption of *Porotermes adamsoni* (Froggatt) (Isoptera: Termosidae) at different temperatures. *Bull ent. Res.* **72**, 423–435.

Lenz M., McMahan E. A. & Williams E. R. (1982b) Neotenic production in *Cryptotermes brevis* (Walker): influence of geographical origin, group composition, and maintenance conditions (Isoptera: Kalotermitidae). *Insectes Sociaux* **29**, 148–163.

Lenz M., Ruyooka D. B. A. & Howick C. D. (1980) The effect of brown and white rot fungi on wood consumption and survival of *Coptotermes lacteus* (Froggatt) (Isoptera: Rhinotermitidae) in a laboratory bioassay. *Z. angew. Ent.* **89**, 244–362.

Light S. F. & Illig P. I. (1945) Rate and extent of development of neotenic reproductives in groups of nymphs of the termite genus *Zootermopsis*. *Univ. Calif. Publ. Zool.* **53**, 1–40.

Lüscher M. (1952) Die Produktion und Elimination von Ersatzgeschlechtstieren bei der Termite *Kalotermes flavicollis* Fabr. *Z. vergl. Physiol.* **34**, 123–141.

Lüscher M. (1973) The influence of the composition of experimental groups on caste development in *Zootermopsis* (Isoptera). *Proc. VII Congr. IUSSI, London*, 253–256.

Lüscher M. (1974) Kasten und Kastendifferenzierung bei niederen Termiten. In *Sozialpolymorphismus bei Insekten. Probleme der Kastenbildung im Tierreich* (Schmidt G. H., ed.), pp. 694–739. Wissenschaftl. Verlagsges., Stuttgart.

Mensa-Bonsu A. (1976a) The production and elimination of supplementary reproductives in *Porotermes adamsoni* (Froggatt) (Isoptera, Hodotermitidae). *Insectes Sociaux* **23**, 133–154.

Mensa-Bonsu A. (1976b) The biology and development of *Porotermes adamsoni* (Froggatt) (Isoptera, Hodotermitidae). *Insectes Sociaux* **23**, 155–166.

Miller E. M. (1942) The problem of castes and caste differentiation in *Prorhinotermes simplex* (Hagen). *Bull. Univ. Miami* **15**, 3–27.

Nagin R. D. (1970) Caste regulation in the termite, *Neotermes jouteli* (Banks). Thesis, Rockefeller University, New York.

Nagin R. D. (1972) Caste determination in *Neotermes jouteli* (Banks). *Insectes Sociaux* **19**, 39–61.

Nutting W. L. (1969) Flight and colony foundation. In *Biology of Termites*, Vol. 1 (Krishna K. & Weesner F. M., eds), pp. 233–282. Academic Press, New York.

Nutting W. L. (1970) Composition and size of some termite colonies in Arizona and Mexico. *Ann. ent. Soc. Amer.* **63**, 1105–1110.

Ratcliffe F. N. & Greaves T. (1940) The subterranean foraging galleries of *Coptotermes lacteus* (Frogg.). *J. Counc. Sci. Industr. Res. Aust.* **13**, 150–161.

Ratcliffe F. N., Gay F. J. & Greaves T. (1952) *Australian Termites. The biology, recognition, and economic importance of the common species.* Commonw. Sci. Ind. Res. Org., Melbourne.

Ruppli E. (1969) Die Elimination überzähliger Ersatzgeschlechtstiere bei der Termite *Kalotermes flavicollis* (Fabr.). *Insectes Sociaux* **16**, 235–248.

Ruppli E. & Lüscher M. (1964) Die Elimination überzähliger Ersatzgeschlechtstiere bei der Termite *Kalotermes flavicollis* (Fabr.). *Rev. suisse Zool.* **71**, 626–632.

Sewell J. J. (1978) Developmental pathways and colony organization in the genus *Kalotermes* Hagen (Isoptera: Kalotermitidae). Thesis, Australian National University, Canberra.

Shimizu K. (1970) Studies on the caste differentiation of the supplementary reproductives of the Japanese termite, *Reticulitermes speratus* (Kolbe). *Bull Fac. Agric. Univ. Miyazaki* **17**, 1–46.

Spragg W. T. & Paton R. (1980) Tracing, trophallaxis and population measurement of colonies of subterranean termites (Isoptera) using a radioactive tracer. *Ann. entomol. Soc. Amer.* **73**, 708–714.

Springhetti A. (1967) Incroci tra reali di alcune popolazioni italiane di *Kalotermes flavicollis* Fabr. *Ann. Univ. Ferrara (N.S.) Biol. anim.* **3**, 11–17.

Springhetti A. (1968) Produzione di reali di sostituzione in popolazioni di differenti regioni italiane di *Kalotermes flavicollis* Fabr. *Archiv. Zool. Ital.* **53**, 1–10.

Stuart A. (1979) The determination and regulation of the neotenic reproductive caste in the lower termites (Isoptera): with special reference to the genus *Zootermopsis* (Hagen). *Sociobiol.* **4**, 223–237.

Watson J. A. L., Barrett R. A. & Abbey H. M. (1977) Caste ratios in a long-established, neotenic-headed laboratory colony of *Mastotermes darwiniensis* Froggatt (Isoptera). *J. Aust. ent. Soc.* **16**, 469–470.

Watson J. A. L., Metcalf E. C & Sewell J. J. (1975) Preliminary studies on the control of neotenic formation in *Mastotermes darwiniensis* Froggatt (Isoptera). *Insectes Sociaux* **22**, 415–426.

Watson J. A. L., Ruyooka D. B. A. and Howick C. D. (1978) The effect of caste composition on wood consumption in cultures of *Nasutitermes exitiosus* (Hill) (Isoptera: Termitidae). *Bull ent. Res.* **68**, 687–694.

Weidner H. (1978) Die gelbfüssige Bodentermite *Reticulitermes flavipes* (Kollar, 1837) in Hamburg (Isoptera). *Entomol. Mitt. Zool. Mus. Hamburg* **6**, 49–100.

CHAPTER 10

Reproductive Strategies in Cryptotermes: Neotenic Production in Indigenous and "Tramp" Species in Australia (Isoptera: Kalotermitidae)

M. LENZ,[1] R. A. BARRETT[1] and E. R. WILLIAMS[2]

[1] CSIRO, Division of Entomology, Canberra, A.C.T. 2601, Australia
[2] CSIRO, Division of Mathematics and Statistics, Canberra, A.C.T. 2601, Australia

CONTENTS

10.1   INTRODUCTION

Species of *Cryptotermes* are among the most destructive of termites attacking seasoned timber in buildings (Williams, 1976, 1977). The association between *Cryptotermes brevis* and structural timber has become particularly close; this species has not yet been found in natural habitats. Most of the pest species have been accidentally introduced, by trade, to many areas outside their natural range (Gay, 1967, 1969; Williams, 1977).

The climatic tolerances of a species will largely determine whether it could become established in alien areas. The most widely distributed "tramp" species, *C. brevis* and, to a lesser extent, *Cryptotermes dudleyi*, readily tolerate a wide range of temperatures and relative humidities (Steward, 1981, 1982, 1983). Other species, especially those of limited distribution, thrive only within a comparatively narrow range of temperature/humidity regimes (Steward, 1983).

Termites can be introduced to areas outside their natural range either as intact colonies or as isolated fragments of a colony. Given that the local climate and food supply are adequate, only those orphaned groups that can produce a pair of reproductives will survive. It is characteristic of "tramp" species such as the rhinotermitids *Coptotermes formosanus* and *Reticulitermes flavipes* that, when introduced to a new region, they achieve colony establishment and growth, and spread mainly through neotenics rather than primary reproductives. However, alates are the chief means of propagation of these two species in their natural range, as they are of other species of the two genera (Lenz & Barrett, 1982).

Differences in reproductive strategies between indigenous and "tramp" species of *Cryptotermes* have not yet been described. Since all species of Kalotermitidae have the potential to produce neotenics, it might be thought that in *Cryptotermes* the deciding factor as to which species can become "colonizers" and which cannot might be the ability to adapt to new climates rather than the possession of a particular reproductive strategy (in contrast, for example, to *Coptotermes*, in which the readiness of a species to produce neotenics is linked to its ability to colonize new environments). However, there appear to be differences between species of Kalotermitidae in two important aspects of colony re-establishment after orphaning: the time it takes to obtain a functional pair of neotenics, and the number of surplus neotenics produced and eliminated, *i.e.*, the cost in terms of group members being lost. The only data available come from laboratory studies with *Kalotermes flavicollis* (Lüscher, 1956), *Neotermes jouteli* (Nagin, 1972) and *C. brevis* (Lenz *et al.*, 1982). Unfortunately, the results of these studies are difficult to compare, because of differences in experimental design.

For *C. brevis*, it has been shown that the pattern of neotenic production can be influenced by the way the termites are housed and by the type of wood on which they are fed (Lenz *et al.*, 1982). The recorded losses of termites in the course of neotenic elimination are greatest in *C. brevis*, up to 65%, in individual cases even 100% of the termites may convert into neotenics (Lenz *et al.*, 1982; Williams, 1977). The figures for losses are 25% in *K. flavicollis* (Lüscher, 1956) and 40% in *N. jouteli* (Nagin, 1972).

The production of multiple neotenics in *C. brevis* has been interpreted as an "incompetent" pattern of neotenic formation (Williams, 1977), or as an indication that, under laboratory conditions, factors that would normally prevent such an overshoot in neotenic development, are not fully effective (Lenz *et al.*, 1982). However, it has become increasingly evident that there are substantial differences between the patterns of neotenic production in *C. brevis* and those in some of the endemic Australian species of *Cryptotermes*, suggesting that there may be pronounced differences in reproductive strategies.

In this paper we describe comparative studies involving two indigenous Australian species, *Cryptotermes primus* and *Cryptotermes queenslandis*, and two "tramp" species, *C. brevis* and *Cryptotermes domesticus*. The biology and Australian distribution of these species are described in Gay & Watson (1982). They present a wide spectrum: *C. queenslandis* known only from a relatively restricted area in south-eastern Queensland, and there only in trees; *C. primus*, widely distributed in coastal eastern Australia, occurring in natural habitats as well as in structures, and accidentally established on Lord Howe Island; *C. domesticus*, widely distributed in the Pacific region, in natural and man-made habitats; and *C. brevis*, unknown in the wild. We have compared their patterns of neotenic production in orphaned groups and, in addition, have looked at some of the ways in which colony regeneration is affected by the size of the groups, the amount of timber provided, and the way the experimental groups are housed.

10.2 MATERIALS AND METHODS

10.2.1 Effects of volume of food timber and group size on neotenic production in *Cryptotermes domesticus* and *C. primus*

10.2.1.1 *Termites*
Stocks of *C. primus* were obtained in July 1980 from Cape Cleveland, near Townsville, Queensland. The termites were extracted from dead branches of

eucalypt trees and set up in groups of 200 in $5 \times 5 \times 2$ cm blocks of *Eucalyptus regnans* within a central hole 3 cm in diameter and 1.5 cm deep. The cells were sealed with glass plates taped to the wood. Each group originated from only one field colony.

C. *domesticus* was collected in October 1980 from a shed in Cooktown, Queensland. Sub-colonies, each of 200 termites, were established in coachwood *Ceratopetalum apetalum* in the same way as described for C. *primus*.

Experiments were set up within a few days after the stock cultures arrived in Canberra. By that time the termites had scarcely started to tunnel into the wood and could be shaken gently from the cells. Brachypterous nymphs of medium size (average weight: C. *primus* 40 mg; C. *domesticus* 37 mg) were selected, pooled from all sub-colonies and kept as one group for 24 hr on blocks of the appropriate timbers, stored in sealed containers at 27°C and 80% r.h. This procedure helped to ensure that the termites used to set up the experiment on the following day were healthy; losses were, however, negligible. Termites were assembled into groups of 10 and 20, the individuals being picked at random from the bulk supply.

10.2.1.2 *Maintenance conditions*

Termites were housed in cells, 2.0 cm wide and *ca* 0.6 cm deep, drilled into blocks of *Eucalyptus regnans* (C. *primus*) or *Ceratopetalum apetalum* (C. *domesticus*). The blocks were of three lengths in the proportion 1:2:4 ($2.5 \times 2.5 \times 1.5$ cm; $5.0 \times 2.5 \times 1.5$ cm; $10.0 \times 2.5 \times 1.5$ cm) (Fig. 10.1). The cells were positioned in the centre of the widest surface of each block. Microscope cover slides taped

Fig. 10.1 Arrangement for housing groups of *Cryptotermes domesticus* and C. *primus* in cells within wooden blocks of 3 lengths in the ratio 1:2:4.

to the wood, sealed the cells. Each block was placed singly in a clear, closed plastic box (10.5 × 8.0 × 2.5 cm). These boxes were arranged at random into piles of 10 in a room at 27°C and 80% r.h. Groups were checked at two- or three-day intervals for 41 days (*C. domesticus*) or 55 days (*C. primus*). All neotenics that developed were left in their group, but dead termites were removed.

10.2.1.3 *Replication*
Ten replicates of each block size × group size were established with *C. domesticus* and 30 of each with *C. primus*.

10.2.2 Effects of the area of living space and of group size on neotenic production in *Cryptotermes brevis* and *C. queenslandis*

10.2.2.1 *Termites*
C. brevis was collected on two occasions in 1977, from furniture and floor boards in Brisbane, Queensland. Colonies were cultured on *Pinus radiata* timber at 27°C and 80% r.h. Termites were extracted from the stock cultures in April–May 1982.

C. queenslandis was collected from trees in Yarraman State Forest, Queensland, during late March–early April 1982. The termites were maintained on *Pinus radiata* until the experiments were started in mid-April, as described for the other species. As detailed earlier, we selected brachypterous nymphs of medium size, but a few smaller nymphs of *C. brevis* had to be included to make up the required numbers (average weight: *C. queenslandis* 57 mg; *C. brevis* 37 mg). All selected termites of each species were held as one group for 24 hr as described earlier, and individuals were then randomly assigned to the different test groups. The groups of *C. brevis* contained 30 termites, whereas those of *C. queenslandis* comprised 20, 30 or 40.

10.2.2.2 *Maintenance conditions*
Each group was housed in a cell in the upper layer of a 2-layer sandwich of *Pinus radiata* veneer, 16 × 15 × 0.2 cm; the layers were stuck together with non-toxic glue and placed between two glass plates. The whole system was held together with strips of sticky tape. The cells were circular with diameters of 2, 3, 4, 5, 6 or 8 cm for *C. queenslandis* and of 2 and 4 cm for *C. brevis*. This configuration of cells formed part of a wider comparison on the effect of the structure of living space on neotenic production in *C. brevis* and *C. queenslandis*, which will be published elsewhere.

Groups of *C. brevis* were inspected daily until about day 30, then every 1–3 days until day 61, the frequency of inspection depending on the course of events in the experiment. Groups of *C. queenslandis* were checked every day until day 23, and thereafter at 2–3 day intervals until day 62, with a final inspection at 76 days.

10.2.2.3 *Replication*
All variations in housing and group size were set up with 10 replicates in *C. queenslandis* and seven in *C. brevis*. A total of 240 sandwiches (including 180

from the experiment described here) were randomized into 12 piles of 20 each, according to an experimental layout designed to assess a possible influence of position of a group (either between or within piles) on its performance. The sandwiches containing *C. brevis* were completely randomized into four piles of seven (including 14 from the experiment described here). The experiments were carried out in a room at 27°C and 80% r.h. As in the other experiments, neotenics produced were left with their group, but dead termites were removed at each inspection.

10.2.3   Analysis of results

Analyses of variance were carried out using the statistical package GEN-STAT (Alvey *et al.*, 1977). For the *C. domesticus* and *C. primus* data, variables V(1...14) were established following the methods used by Lenz *et al.* (1982), thereby permitting a comparison with earlier results for *C. brevis*. The rate of neotenic production in the early stages was measured by fitting linear regressions to the data from the first two or three weeks of each set.

For the *C. brevis* and *C. queenslandis* data, separate analyses of variance were performed on the accumulated neotenic production at regular intervals up to the termination of the experiments. For *C. queenslandis*, the number of last stage nymphs produced up to day 62 was also analysed.

10.3   RESULTS

10.3.1   Effects of volume of food timber and group size on neotenic production in *Cryptotermes domesticus* and *C. primus*

There were substantial differences between the two species in neotenic production and the regulation of neotenic numbers. In addition, these processes were strongly influenced by the size of the experimental groups, but not by timber volume. Results are summarized in Table 10.1 and Figs 10.2 and 10.3. The information on the pattern of neotenic production and elimination (Table 10.1) also allows a comparison with corresponding data for *C. brevis* (Lenz *et al.*, 1982).

The main differences between the two species were in the speed with which neotenics are produced (Table 10.1; Variable 1) and the number of termites which moult into neotenics (Variable 8). All other variables, given in Table 10.1, are derived from these two and most of them do not warrant further detailed discussion here.

In *C. domesticus* the first neotenics appeared on average 8.6–9.6 days after the start of the experiment (*i.e.*, 9.6–10.6 days after orphaning, see Materials and Methods), whereas in *C. primus* 23.9–37.6 days elapsed. The response in replicates of *C. primus* varied from 8 to more than 55 days; indeed, 46 out of 180 groups had not produced a neotenic by the end of the experiment. In both species, groups of 20 responded faster than groups of 10 (*C. domesticus* P < 0.05; *C. primus* P < 0.01).

In *C. domesticus* an average of between 4.6 and 10.8 neotenics developed, depending on group size, but in *C. primus* only 0.9–1.7; thus after 55 days, groups of *C. domesticus* had produced reproductives well in excess of one pair, whereas in none of the *C. primus* experiments did the average production of neotenics replace the lost reproductives.

In groups of 20 termites, a smaller proportion developed into neotenics than in groups of 10 (*C. domesticus* P < 0.01; *C. primus* P < 0.05) (Table 10.1). However, to judge from the regression coefficients for the initial linear part of the neotenic production curves, neotenics were produced more rapidly in the larger groups of *C. domesticus* (Table 10.2, Fig. 10.2). The slopes were similar for all timber volumes within a group size, but significantly different between group sizes (P < 0.001). In *C. primus* the slopes differed between timber sizes, but were in general not different for groups of 10 or 20 termites (Table 10.2, Fig. 10.3).

Neotenics began to be eliminated in groups of *C. domesticus* 5 days after they first appeared (Table 10.1, Fig. 10.2). As with neotenic production, elimination of excess neotenics proceeded significantly faster in groups of 20 termites than in groups of 10 (P < 0.001) (Table 10.2, Fig. 10.2). In *C. primus*, where neotenic production was low, few neotenics were killed, but elimination sometimes occurred when only one neotenic had been produced and was not followed closely by further differentiation of termites into neotenics.

In neither species did timber volume exert a significant influence on colony re-establishment when termites were housed in cells of uniform size (Tables 10.1 and 10.2, Figs 10.2 and 10.3). Nevertheless, to judge from the behaviour of the groups, *C. primus* responded to timber dimensions. When the cells were drilled, the tip of the drill bit left a small hole in the centre, approximately 1 mm deeper than the cell floor (Fig. 10.1). The majority of termite groups in the larger blocks widened the hole, but those in small blocks tunnelled from this depression deeper into the wood (Table 10.3). In blocks of medium size, widening or tunnelling was observed in a similar number of cases when 20 termites were housed in the cells, but widening was the dominant activity with groups of 10 termites (Table 10.3). The differences in the incidence of these activities in different block sizes were highly significant (P < 0.001). No such pattern was observed in *C. domesticus*.

10.3.2 Effects of the area of living space and of group size on neotenic production in *Cryptotermes brevis* and *C. queenslandis*

The position of a sandwich in the stacks had no apparent effect on the production of neotenics in it.

TABLE 10.1. RESULTS (AVERAGES) FOR VARIABLES DESCRIBING THE PATTERN OF NEOTENIC PRODUCTION IN GROUPS OF 10 OR 20 NYMPHS OF *CRYPTOTERMES DOMESTICUS* AND *C. PRIMUS*, HOUSED IN CELLS IN WOODEN BLOCKS OF THREE SIZES

Variables		*Cryptotermes domesticus* group size							*Cryptotermes primus* group size						
		10			20			Significance for group size†	10			20			Significance for group size†
		block size			block size				block size			block size			
		small	medium	large	small	medium	large		small	medium	large	small	medium	large	
(1) No. days to 1st neotenic		9.0	8.9	9.6	8.6	8.6	8.7	*	37.6	36.9	34.5	23.9	24.0	31.2	**
(2) No. days to 1st death of neotenic		14.6	14.1	15.0	13.4	13.1	12.7	***	96.4	113.7	92.2	88.8	85.0	96.4	*
(3) Max. no. neotenics alive at any one time	total	3.4	3.4	3.8	4.6	4.4	4.5	***	1.1	0.8	0.9	1.4	1.6	1.1	***
	per 10 ter.	3.4	3.4	3.8	2.3	2.2	2.3	***	1.1	0.8	0.9	0.7	0.8	0.6	*
(4) Total no. dead neotenics	total	2.6	3.1	3.6	7.0	6.9	6.6	***	0.2	0.2	0.3	0.4	0.4	0.2	ns
	per 10 ter.	2.6	3.1	3.6	3.5	3.5	3.3	ns	0.2	0.2	0.3	0.2	0.2	0.1	ns
(5) No. dead nymphs before 1st neotenic	total	0.0	0.0	0.5	0.2	0.3	0.2	ns	0.1	0.03	0.1	0.0	0.07	0.03	ns
	per 10 ter.	0.0	0.0	0.5	0.1	0.15	0.1	ns	0.1	0.03	0.1	0.0	0.04	0.02	ns
(6) No. dead nymphs after 1st neotenic	total	1.3	0.6	0.7	1.7	1.4	1.6	**	0.5	0.4	0.3	0.6	1.0	0.7	**
	per 10 ter.	1.3	0.6	0.7	0.8	0.7	0.8	ns	0.5	0.4	0.3	0.3	0.5	0.4	ns

		1	2	3	4	5	6		7	8	9	10	11	12	
(7) Total no. dead nymphs	total	1.3	0.6	1.2	1.8	1.7	1.8	**	0.6	0.4	0.4	0.6	1.0	0.7	**
	per 10 ter.	1.3	0.6	1.2	0.9	0.9	0.9	ns	0.6	0.4	0.4	0.3	0.5	0.4	ns
(8) Total no. neotenics produced	total	4.6	5.4	5.5	9.1	8.8	8.7	***	1.1	0.9	1.0	1.7	1.7	1.2	***
	per 10 ter.	4.6	5.4	5.5	4.6	4.4	4.4	**	1.1	0.9	1.0	1.7	0.8	0.6	*
(9) Total no. neotenics + no. dead nymphs after 1st neotenic	total	5.9	6.0	6.2	10.8	10.2	10.3	***	1.6	1.2	1.3	2.2	2.6	1.9	***
	per 10 ter.	5.9	6.0	6.2	5.4	5.1	5.2	**	1.6	1.2	1.3	1.1	1.3	1.0	ns
(10) Difference (days) between 1st neotenic and 1st death of a neotenic		5.6	5.2	5.4	4.8	4.5	4.1	*	58.9	76.7	57.7	64.9	61.0	65.2	ns
(11) Time (days) to 1st occurrence of max. no. neotenics alive		14.2	13.4	13.5	13.2	12.4	12.0	*	46.5	43.4	41.2	29.9	30.3	36.4	**
(12) Difference (days) between 1st neotenic and 1st max. no. neot. alive		5.2	4.5	3.9	4.7	3.8	3.3	ns	9.0	6.5	6.7	6.0	6.3	5.2	ns
(13) No. neotenics in % adjusted for losses of nymphs		46.1	52.3	58.1	46.7	45.1	44.2	*	11.1	8.7	9.4	8.3	8.4	6.2	ns
(14) Total no. dead termites	total	3.9	3.7	4.8	8.8	8.6	8.4	***	0.8	0.6	0.7	0.5	0.7	0.5	ns
	per 10 ter.	3.9	3.7	4.8	4.4	4.3	4.2	ns	0.8	0.6	0.7	0.3	0.4	0.3	*

DSI-F*

† Results for block size were not significantly different from each other. ns: not significant; *: $P<0.05$; **: $P<0.01$; ***: $P<0.001$

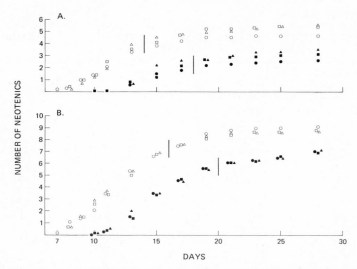

Fig. 10.2. Average number of neotenics produced (open symbols) and eliminated (closed symbols) in groups of 10 (A) or 20 (B) nymphs of *Cryptotermes domesticus*, housed in wooden blocks of 3 lengths. The vertical bars indicate the linear part of the curves. Block size: (○) small; (□) medium; (△) large.

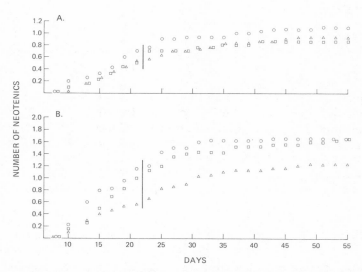

Fig. 10.3. Average number of neotenics produced in groups of 10 (A) or 20 (B) nymphs of *Cryptotermes primus*, housed in wooden blocks of 3 lengths. The vertical bars indicate the linear part of the curves. Block size: (○) small; (□) medium; (△) large.

TABLE 10.2.   REGRESSION COEFFICIENTS (±SE) FOR THE INITIAL
LINEAR PART OF THE NEOTENIC PRODUCTION AND ELIMINATION
CURVES FOR GROUPS OF 10 OR 20 NYMPHS OF *CRYPTOTERMES
DOMESTICUS* (FIG. 10.2) AND *C. PRIMUS* (FIG. 10.3)

Group size	Block size ratio	*C. domesticus* neotenics produced	neotenics eliminated	*C. primus* neotenics produced
10	1	0.593 (0.021)	0.300 (0.087)	0.084 (0.007)
	2	0.583 (0.050)	0.305 (0.030)	0.036 (0.002)
	4	0.738 (0.075)	0.475 (0.159)	0.045 (0.001)
	av	0.582 (0.054)	0.326 (0.033)	0.054 (0.001)
20	1	0.871 (0.073)	0.690 (0.049)	0.048 (0.004)
	2	0.830 (0.033)	0.676 (0.065)	0.076 (0.005)
	4	0.917 (0.038)	0.641 (0.028)	0.043 (0.004)
	av.	0.873 (0.032)	0.669 (0.043)	0.056 (0.001)

TABLE 10.3.   NUMBER OF REPLICATE GROUPS OF *CRYPTOTERMES
PRIMUS* (OUT OF 30) SHOWING THREE ACTIVITIES (WIDENING,
TUNNELLING OR BOTH) AT A SMALL HOLE IN THE CENTRE OF A
CELL, LOCATED WITHIN WOODEN BLOCKS OF THREE LENGTHS

Block size ratio	Group size 10			Group size 20		
	widening	widening + tunnelling	tunnelling	widening	widening + tunnelling	tunnelling
1	8	1	21	3	1	26
2	20	3	7	14	3	13
4	25	2	3	25	4	1

10.3.2.1 *Cryptotermes brevis*

Orphaned groups of the West Indian drywood termite rapidly produced neotenics, the first being noted 5–6 days after the experiment was set up (*i.e.*, 6–7 days after orphaning). Moults to neotenics had ceased by day 15. By that time, an average of 9–10 neotenics had developed, most of which were quickly eliminated, and after 16–20 days most groups contained only one pair. The groups remained stable for a further 3 weeks, and some females began to lay eggs. The pattern was very similar in both sizes of cell, and no significant differences were apparent (Fig. 10.4).

It is worth noting that from day 47 onwards a second crop of neotenics appeared in many groups, even in those with fully functional neotenics and eggs (Fig. 10.4). This second crop raised average neotenic production to approximately 16 (*i.e.*, more than 50%) by day 61. At this stage, we do not know how the production of the second crop is initiated, nor what its significance might be.

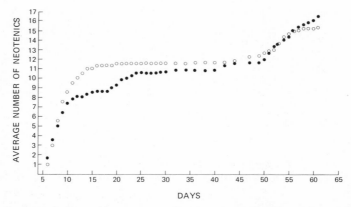

FIG. 10.4. Average number of neotenics produced in groups of 30 *Cryptotermes brevis* nymphs, housed in pine veneer sandwiches with a single cell of 2 cm (●) or 4 cm (○) diameter as living space.

Marked variation of neotenic numbers between replicates was a characteristic feature of the results with *C. brevis*. The lowest number of neotenics recorded from a group after 61 days was six, and the highest was 26.

10.3.2.2   *Cryptotermes queenslandis*

Like *C. primus*, *C. queenslandis* responded to orphaning in a markedly different way to the "tramp" species, *C. brevis*. *C. queenslandis* produced few neotenics, and at a slow rate. On average, taking elimination into account, none of the treatments resulted in the establishment of a pair of reproductives within 76 days (Fig. 10.5). In some cases single neotenics were killed, well before further neotenics appeared.

The number of days that elapsed before the first neotenic appeared varied greatly, from 6 to more than 76 days; thus the overall response was not unlike that of *C. primus*.

In contrast to *C. brevis*, *C. queenslandis* responded to its pattern of housing. The diameter of the cells in the sandwiches exerted some control over neotenic output, the effect being similar for all group sizes. The largest cell (θ 8 cm) and the smaller cells (θ 2–3 cm) gave the highest neotenic counts, and diameters between 4 and 6 cm produced lower numbers (Fig. 10.5).

The opposite pattern was observed for occurrence of last stage nymphs (count at day 62). Progressive nymphal differentiation was maximum in the medium-sized cells and least in the largest and the smallest cells ($P < 0.001$) (Fig. 10.6).

10.4   DISCUSSION

Two of the major issues emerging from these studies require more detailed

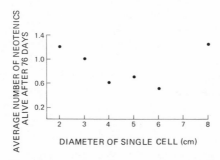

Fɪɢ. 10.5. Average number of neotenics alive after 76 days in groups of nymphs of *Cryptotermes queenslandis*, housed in pine veneer sandwiches with a single cell of various diameters as living space.

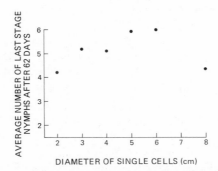

Fɪɢ. 10.6. Average number of last stage nymphs produced after 62 days in groups of *Cryptotermes queenslandis*, housed in pine veneer sandwiches with a single cell of various diameters as living space.

discussion: the substantial differences between indigenous and "tramp" species in the intensity of neotenic production; and the extent to which an external factor such as the area of living space can influence the development of reproductives in a group of termites.

Both the Australian native species, *C. primus* and *C. queenslandis* take a long time to produce even a few neotenics. On average 55 days (*C. primus*) and 76 days (*C. queenslandis*) were insufficient to replace a lost reproductive pair and, hence, to re-establish groups as functional colonies. In contrast, both "tramp" species, *C. domesticus* and *C. brevis*, exhibit a distinctly different reproductive strategy, *i.e.*, a very rapid production of neotenics well in excess of requirements for a short period soon after orphaning, and then a rapid elimination of the excess neotenics.

Two conflicting advantages can readily be perceived in these two strategies. (A) In the two native species, few surplus neotenics were produced, and the cost, in terms of nymphs lost, was low. Thus a pair of replacement reproductives was left with a strong group to support it. In the two "tramp" species, on the other hand, the production of surplus neotenics was high, averaging 32–35% in *C. domesticus* and 31–49% in *C. brevis* (in the latter with variation between replicates from 13 to 80%). This means that the new reproductives headed much smaller colonies. They could, therefore, be at a disadvantage in terms of reproductive output (*cf.* Greenberg & Stuart, 1979).

(B) As the neotenics are produced from non-identical offspring of the original reproductives, genetic recombination will have occurred and selection for the fittest neotenic is possible. In *C. primus* and *C. queenslandis*, the range of candidates is very limited. In *C. brevis* and *C. domesticus*, on the other hand, the multiplicity of neotenics and the fact that earlier-formed neotenics can be replaced by those formed later, may favour the retention of the pair best suited to the circumstances in which the group finds itself.

The strategy of the two indigenous species may be termed "conservative". They have to replace lost reproductives only within their natural range, *i.e.* within the environment to which they are already well adapted. In contrast, the position of the "tramp" species may be seen as "experimental". Their strategy has enabled establishment over a wider range of climatic regimes in the course of passive transportation, with *C. brevis* as the most outstanding example; it has been found in all major faunistic zones of the world (Becker & Kny, 1977; Gay, 1967, 1969; Williams, 1977).

In a situation where an orphaned group, or colony, of termites is placed in an alien environment, there is strong selective pressure for the production of neotenics, rather than alates (Lenz & Barrett, 1982). We believe that in such a situation, the advantages of limited neotenic production with its corollary of greater support, could be outweighed by the wider options of climatic or other tolerances that might be offered by the development of many neotenics, and the operation of selective pressures among them.

It might be argued that because we mixed termites from different colonies, the production and elimination of surplus neotenics was an artefact. However, as surplus neotenics were produced on a significant scale in both "tramp" species, but only in very low numbers in either of the indigenous, and their elimination followed, despite the fact that colonies were combined in both, this argument has little force. Furthermore, we know that in laboratory cultures of *C. brevis* established from single colonies, intensive neotenic production takes place, as reported with stocks from Africa (Williams, 1977) and Australia (Lenz *et al.*, 1982). Substantial intragroup competition for the place of reproductives (West-Eberhard, 1981) in the "colonizer" species as a result of stronger selection pressure than in "residents" could explain the observed differences in the pattern of colony re-establishment.

Little comparative information is available to suggest that external factors, such as area of the living space, have a strong bearing on caste development (Lenz, 1976, unpubl. data; Lenz *et al.*, 1982) as has been demonstrated for *C. queenslandis*. In this species, the area of the space provided determined the reproductive strategies on which the orphaned groups placed emphasis: in large and small cells relatively rapid establishment of a neotenic pair occurred, and only limited progressive differentiation of nymphs towards alates, but in medium-sized cells, a higher percentage of nymphs moulting into last stage nymphs and retardation of neotenic development.

It seems probable that the area of the living space (nest) affects caste development by influencing the behaviour of the termites (Lenz *et al.*, unpubl. data) or, more specifically, by varying the number of contacts between individuals of a group and thus the rate of trophallactic exchange. Trophallaxis serves a number of important functions for social integration of a colony. McMahan (1969) lists them as follows: efficient use of nutrients, recognition of colony mates, communication between individuals and distribution of pheromones involved in caste differentiation and in caste elimination. Thus, transmission of pheromones related to caste differentiation could vary due to changes in behaviour patterns, that are indirectly induced by the area of the nest system.

Our work on reproductive strategies, complements the studies by Williams (1976, 1977) and Steward (1981, 1982, 1983) on climatic tolerances in species of *Cryptotermes*; all were aimed at a better understanding of the way in which a few species of *Cryptotermes* have become successful invaders of man-made habitats. The results also highlight the importance of apparently trivial factors in experimental design, such as the diameter of a circular living space, in shaping the course of caste differentiation in a group of termites and, thus, our perception of its reproductive strategy.

So far, we have examined only two of the native Australian species of *Cryptotermes*. The Australian *Cryptotermes* fauna comprises at least 19 species (Gay & Watson, 1982, unpubl. data), including three "tramp" species. It provides a wealth of material with which to investigate the question as to whether or not native and "tramp" species differ in the way they re-establish colonies after orphaning. Some of the characteristics of reproductive biology in the "tramp" species, such as speed and extent of neotenic production, may not necessarily be restricted to that group of species, but could well be found within the complex *Cryptotermes* fauna of Australia. The indigenous species of the genus occur in a range of habitats, some with more predictable, others with more erratic climates. Selective pressures might therefore vary in intensity and direction, even between populations in the case of widely distributed species. Comparisons of the reproductive biology within the Australian species of *Cryptotermes* could, therefore, greatly aid our understanding of the biology of "tramp" species.

10.5 SUMMARY

Orphaned groups of the two indigenous Australian species, *Cryptotermes primus* and *C. queenslandis*, produced few neotenics, and at a slow rate; groups of *C. primus* and *C. queenslandis* required at least 55 and 77 days, respectively, to re-establish themselves as functional colonies. The "tramp" species *C. domesticus* and *C. brevis*, however, produced numerous neotenics within a few days of orphaning, and all but one pair were soon eliminated, markedly reducing the strength of the groups (in some groups of *C. brevis* by 80%). The extent of neotenic production in *C. brevis* was highly variable. When termites were housed in cells within wooden blocks, the size of the block had no influence on neotenic development (*C. domesticus, C. primus*). Smaller groups produced relatively more neotenics (*C. domesticus, C. primus, C. queenslandis*), whereas larger groups produced neotenics more rapidly (*C. domesticus, C. primus*). The area of living space (single cells of different diameter) influenced caste differentiation, probably *via* a change in behaviour which affected trophallaxis, and hence, a pheromone transfer. It prompted stronger or weaker differentiation of termites into neotenics or last stage nymphs (*C. queenslandis*). We suggest that the production of multiple neotenics and intragroup competition for the position of reproductives in "tramp" species is adaptive, increasing the probability that the ensuing pair of reproductives will be the individuals best suited to the situation in which the colony finds itself. This would facilitate the establishment and growth of colonies in alien environments where, for other reasons, reliance on neotenics rather than alates appears to offer the best chance for survival.

10.6 ACKNOWLEDGEMENTS

We thank the Queensland Department of Forestry for granting permission to obtain stocks of *Cryptotermes brevis* and *C. queenslandis*, the New South Wales Forestry Commission for providing coachwood and Mr J. W. Creffield (CSIRO, Division of Chemical and Wood Technology, Melbourne) for supplying pine veneers. We also greatly appreciated the assistance given by Messrs P. J. Hart, L. R. Miller and Dr J. A. L. Watson. The paper has greatly benefited from comments made by Mr P. Ferrar and Dr J. A. L. Watson.

10.7 REFERENCES

Alvey N. G. *et al.* (1977) GENSTAT. A general statistical program. Harpenden, Herts., Rothamsted Exp. Stn.

Becker G. & Kny U. (1977) Überleben und Entwicklung der Trockenholz-Termite *Cryptotermes brevis* (Walker) in Berlin. *Anz. Schädlingskde., Pflanzenschutz, Umweltschutz* **50**, 177–179.

Gay F. J. (1967) A world review of introduced species of termites. *Bull. Commonwealth Sci. Ind. Res. Organ.* **286**, 1–88.

Gay F. J. (1969) Species introduced by man. In *Biology of Termites* (ed. Krishna K. & Weesner F. M.), Vol. 1, pp. 459–494. Academic Press, New York.

Gay F. J. & Watson J. A. L. (1982) The genus *Cryptotermes* in Australia (Isoptera: Kalotermitidae). *Aust. J. Zool., Suppl. Ser.* No. 88, pp. 1–64.

Greenberg S. L. W. & Stuart A. M. (1979) The influence of group size on ovarian development in adult and neotenic reproductives of the termite *Zootermopsis angusticollis* (Hagen) (Hodotermitidae). *Int. J. Invertebr. Reprod.* **1**, 99–108.

Lenz M. (1976) The dependence of hormone effects in termite caste determination on external factors. In *Phase and Caste Determination in Insects. Endocrine Aspects* (ed. Lüscher M.), pp. 73–89. Pergamon Press, Oxford.

Lenz M. & Barrett R. A. (1982). Neotenic formation in field colonies of *Coptotermes lacteus* (Froggatt) in Australia, with comments on the roles of neotenics in the genus *Coptotermes*. *Sociobiol.* **7**, 47–60.

Lenz M., McMahan E. & Williams E. R. (1982) Neotenic production in *Cryptotermes brevis* (Walker): Influence of geographical origin, group composition, and maintenance conditions (Isoptera: Kalotermitidae). *Insectes Sociaux* **29**, 148–163.

Lüscher M. (1956) Die Entstehung von Ersatzgeschlechtstieren bei der Termite *Kalotermes flavicollis* Fabr. *Insectes Sociaux* **3**, 119–128.

McMahan E. A. (1969) Feeding relationships and radioisotope techniques. In *Biology of Termites*. (ed. Krishna K. & Weesner F. M.), Vol. 1, pp. 387–406. Academic Press, New York.

Nagin R. D. (1972) Caste determination in *Neotermes jouteli* (Banks). *Insectes Sociaux* **19**, 39–61.

Steward R. C. (1981) The temperature preferences and climatic adaptation of building-damaging dry-wood termites (*Cryptotermes;* Isoptera). *J. therm. Biol.* **6**, 153–160.

Steward R. C. (1982) Comparison of the behavioural and physiological responses to humidity of five species of dry-wood termites, *Cryptotermes* species. *Physiol. Entomol.* **7**, 71–82.

Steward R. C. (1983) The effects of humidity, temperature and acclimation on the feeding, water balance and reproduction of dry-wood termites (*Cryptotermes*). *Ent. exp. & appl.* **33**, 135–144.

West-Eberhard M. J. (1981) Intragroup selection and the evolution of insect societies. In *Natural Selection and Social Behaviour. Recent Research and New Theory* (ed. Alexander R. D. & Tinkle D. W.), pp. 1–17. Blackwell Sci. Publ., New York.

Williams R. M. C. (1976) Factors limiting the distribution of building-damaging dry-wood termites (Isoptera, *Cryptotermes* spp.) in Africa. *Mater. Organismen, Beih.* **3**, 393–406.

Williams R. M. C. (1977) The ecology and physiology of structural wood destroying Isoptera. *Mater. Organismen* **12**, 111–140.

CHAPTER 11

The Function of the Royal Pair in the Society of Kalotermes flavicollis (Fabr.) (Isoptera: Kalotermitidae)

A. SPRINGHETTI

Institute of Zoology, University of Ferrara, Via Borsari 46, 44100 Ferrara, Italy

CONTENTS

11.1 INTRODUCTION

For many years, even subsequent to Grassi and Sandias's classic studies (1893), the royal pair of *Kalotermes flavicollis* continued to be considered of importance only for its function in reproduction and conservation of the species. Although the earliest experiments done to demonstrate the royal pair's control over the differentiation of supplementary reproductives (neotenics) were carried out on other species of Isoptera (Pickens, 1932; Castle, 1934; Light, 1944), it was with *K. flavicollis* that such research provided the first clear experimental results. Grassé & Noirot (1946a, b; 1947; 1960a, b) and Lüscher's (1952; 1956a, b; 1958; 1960; 1961; 1963; 1964) studies on the differentiation of neotenics served as a stimulus for further research on the role of a royal pair within a society of *K. flavicollis*, including studies on trophallaxis (Alibert, 1965, 1968; Alibert-Bertho, 1969), on the control of differentiation of alates (Springhetti, 1969a, 1971, 1972a; Lebrun, 1963, 1967a, b, 1969, 1972) and that of soldiers (Springhetti, 1969b, 1970, 1972b, 1973a, b, 1975, 1976; Lebrun, 1967a, b, c, 1969, 1970, 1973, 1978) as well as on the stimulation of aggressiveness in pseudergates (Springhetti, unpub. data).

11.2   CONTROL OVER THE DIFFERENTIATION OF SUPPLEMENTARY REPRODUCTIVES

Lüscher (1960, 1961, 1974) lucidly summarized the findings on this subject.

When the colony lacks one or both reproductives, supplementary reproductives (neotenics) differentiate. The functioning royal pair prevents the differentiation of neotenics by means of inhibitory pheromones. The king and queen produce different pheromones with complementary action, and neither's pheromones alone are totally effective. Pseudergates and larvae receive the royal pheromones with the anal food or through grooming, distribute them to all other members of the colony by trophallaxis, and perhaps function as "amplifiers".

The action of the king differs from that of the queen. To a certain extent, the queen is capable on her own of inhibiting the differentiation of queens. The king by himself, on the other hand, lacks the capacity to inhibit the differentiation of kings, but stimulates the differentiation of queens. Two kings (with no queen) seem instead to stimulate each other to inhibit to a certain degree the differentiation of supplementary kings. Grassé & Noirot (1960a) however, demonstrated that even a single primary king can inhibit the differentiation of supplementary kings.

It seems likely in addition, that there is reciprocal stimulation between king and queen to produce inhibitory pheromones, and this may be the reason why they usually stay near each other in the nest (Springhetti, 1980).

The mechanism by which functioning royals control the differentiation of neotenics appears to be very complex, exercised by means of both inhibitory and stimulatory pheromones (Fig. 11.1). It is, however, an extremely efficient mechanism, in that it ensures the prompt substitution of the missing reproductive (or royal pair), yet prevents the differentiation of too many superfluous neotenics which would be killed in any case.

11.3   CONTROL OVER THE DIFFERENTIATION OF SOLDIERS

Studying *K. flavicollis*, Springhetti (1969b, 1970, 1972b, 1973a, b, 1975,

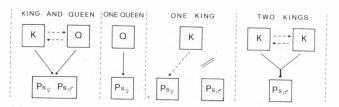

FIG. 11.1. The royals' control over the differentiation of supplementary reproductives (according to Lüscher, 1960, 1961). (Solid arrow = inhibitory effect; broken arrow = stimulatory effect.)

1976), prompted by Lüscher's results and research methods, conducted a number of experiments, the results of which can be summarized as follows:

The functioning king and queen produce pheromones that stimulate the differentiation of soldiers. The queen's stimulatory capacity is roughly twice that of the king. The stimulatory effect of a king and a queen together, or that of two kings, is equal to the sum of their separate effects. The influence of two queens however is not different from that of one queen, probably because the second queen is "rejected" by the group of pseudergates and is thus rendered "inactive", like the "achrestogonimes" described by Grassé & Bonneville (1935).

The soldiers on the other hand produce pheromones that inhibit the differentiation of more soldiers.

For the royals' stimulatory influence and the soldiers' inhibitory influence to be exerted, both royals and soldiers must be in direct contact with the pseudergates. Their influence is not felt if they are separated from the pseudergates by a screen through which only the antennae and odours can pass. It is therefore likely that the pseudergate receive the pheromones by mouth (through trophallactic exchanges or grooming) and then transmit them to all the members of the colony.

It is thus the equilibrium between the two types of pheromones that keeps the percentage of soldiers in the population constant—Miller (1942) demonstrated this in *Prorhinotermes simplex*—by determining whether other soldiers can differentiate and (possibly) whether the extra ones are killed (Fig. 11.2).

In addition to the two main types of influence of the royal pair and the soldiers, there are also secondary types of influence. Very few soldiers differentiate in groups of orphan pseudergates (when there are no soldiers), possibly due to the influence of the pseudergates themselves. Furthermore, a "group effect" has been observed in colonies with a royal pair but without soldiers: if the soldiers are removed as soon as they emerge, higher percentages of soldiers are formed in the more numerous colonies, perhaps because their royal pairs are better cared for and more efficient in producing the pheromones.

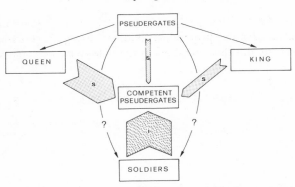

Fig. 11.2. Control over the differentiation of soldiers. (The thickness of the arrows indicates the intensity of the stimuli.)

11.4   CONTROL OVER THE DIFFERENTIATION OF ALATES

In small groups of last-stage nymphs isolated with the royal pair, fewer alates differentiate than in groups of orphan nymphs. Although frequency of metamorphosis varies depending on the season of the year, the royal pair's inhibitory influence is exerted in all seasons. The differentiation of alates is therefore to some extent controlled by the pheromones of the royals (Fig. 11.3; Springhetti, 1969a, 1971, 1972a).

Maximum inhibitory effect is obtained when both king and queen are present. The queen by herself has a greater inhibitory influence than the king alone. The inhibitory effect of a king and a queen together, or that of two kings, is equal to the sum of their separate effects. On the other hand, the effect of the presence of two queens is not different from that of only one, as if the second had lost all, or nearly all of her inhibitory capacity.

The royals exert their inhibitory effect only when they have direct contact with the nymphs, and not when they are separated from the nymphs by a screen which permits the passage of only the antennae and odours. It is

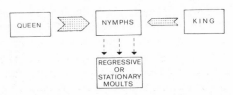

Fig. 11.3. Inhibitory influence of the royals on the metamorphosis of last-stage nymphs. (The thickness of the arrows indicates the intensity of the stimuli.)

therefore likely that the nymphs receive the pheromone by mouth either with the stomodeal and/or the proctodeal food, or through grooming, and they may transmit it to all other members of the colony by trophallaxis.

11.5 COMPETENCE FOR DIFFERENTIATION

Each caste differentiation is accomplished by means of a moult. There are different periods (of specific competence) during which the pseudergates (*sensu* Grassé & Noirot, 1947) of *K. flavicollis* are sensitive to social stimuli which determine their differentiation into the various castes.

For the differentiation into supplementary reproductives, maximum competence is generally restricted to the beginning of intermoult period; 50% of pseudergates lose this competence by 20 days after the moult (Lüscher, 1956a). Differentiation occurs within a much shorter moult interval than the interval between two stationary moults (Lüscher, 1952) (in Italian populations it may last as short as 8 days). However, not all orphan pseudergates isolated just after the stationary moult immediately become supplementary reproductives; some undergo another stationary or nymphal moult and only after that they differentiate into neotenics. This suggests that individual competence may vary, and that it may be genetically controlled. In any case, populations of *K. flavicollis* from different Italian regions differ in their tendency to produce supplementary reproductives (Springhetti, 1968).

The intermoult period preceding the differentiation into soldiers is only slightly shorter than the one preceding the stationary moult, and competence for the differentiation into soldiers falls in the second half of each intermoult. Prior to this period of competence a pseudergate does not respond to the stimuli arising from the concurrent absence of soldiers and presence of a royal pair (Springhetti, 1972b). However, if orphan pseudergates which are isolated immediately following the moult are treated with juvenile hormone (JH), they moult into white soldier intercastes after an interval as long as the one preceding the moult into supplementary reproductives (Springhetti, 1975). The competence for differentiation into soldiers thus seems to depend on the capacity of the corpora allata (CA) to become active, rather than on the insensitivity of the tissues to the action of the hormone of the CA.

Thus the periods of competence for differentiation into supplementary reproductives and into soldiers do not coincide: the insect only acquires the latter when it has already lost the former. Indeed, the two types of competence seem to be mutually exclusive, since the former corresponds to a period of inactivity of the CA (Lüscher, 1963), whereas the latter requires that these glands be active. This fact prevents the formation of intercastes, which are of little use to the society.

Almost nothing is known about the period of competence for metamorphosis into alates. However, it probably occurs at the end of a rather long moult interval and comes at the moment when the CA are inactive. In fact, when last-stage orphan nymphs are isolated, the moults into alates take place slightly later than stationary and regressive moults, on average; and if the nymphs are treated with juvenile hormone analogues (JHA), both adultoids and alate–soldier intercastes are obtained (Lebrun, 1978).

11.6 STIMULATION OF THE PSEUDERGATES' AGGRESSIVENESS

It is known that workers and pseudergates collaborate with soldiers in killing insects of other species placed in the nest.

When foreign insects are placed in *K. flavicollis* nests, they are killed more promptly if the royal pair is present. Fig. 11.4 illustrates the phenomenon, summarizing 10 experiments in which six larvae of *Attagenus* were placed in artificial nests containing 20 pseudergates of *K. flavicollis* with or without the royal pair. When the royal pair was present, the *Attagenus* larvae were killed more rapidly. Similar experiments with larvae and adults of the dermestid beetle *Anthrenus* and with larvae of the mealworm *Tenebrio* produced comparable results.

It seems improbable that the royal pair participates in any active way in the killing of the intruders, but no experiments have yet been done to clarify whether they actually do influence the aggressiveness of the pseudergates. In this regard, Stuart (1969) observes that workers (and pseudergates) contribute to the defence of the nest with behaviour which they normally adopt in other activities. Bruinsma and Leuthold (1977) have demonstrated that the odour

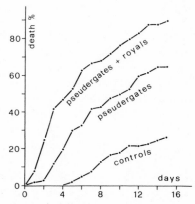

FIG. 11.4. Mortality of the larvae of *Attagenus* sp. placed in artificial nests of *K. flavicollis* and in control nests (with no *K. flavicollis*).

of the queen influences the work of reconstructing the royal cell in *Macrotermes subhyalinus*. It may therefore be that what the royal pair stimulates is not so much the pseudergates' aggressiveness but their activity in general, which in this case takes the form of more prompt killing of insects coming from outside the nest.

11.7 THE PHEROMONES

With the exception of cis-3-exan-1-ol (Verron, 1963), no pheromones of *K. flavicollis* have yet been isolated. Those produced by the royals and the soldiers to control caste differentiation, all seem to be non-volatile or only slightly volatile substances which are transmitted by trophallaxis to all members of a colony.

In view of the multiple nature of influence exerted by the royals, it might seem that they produce a large number of different pheromones, although this is not necessarily so. Jucci (1961) advanced the hypothesis that a hormone emitted in the original or a slightly modified form might function as a pheromone. Springhetti (1969b) has suggested that the same pheromone might, by activating the CA, both favour the differentiation of soldiers and prevent the metamorphosis of nymphs. Grafting of CA (Lüscher, 1958; Lüscher & Springhetti, 1960; Lebrun, 1967c) or treatment with JH (Lüscher, 1969; Springhetti, 1974) does indeed induce the transformation of pseudergates into soldiers, whereas in last-stage nymphs this may induce stationary and regressive moults and the formation of adultoids (Lüscher, 1974; Lebrun, 1969).

Lüscher (1963) found that the administration of JH to orphan pseudergates decreases the differentiation of supplementary reproductives, and also that the administration of bee "queen substance" prevents the CA of orphan pseudergates from enlarging and favours their differentiation into supplementary reproductives. Putting these two facts together with those mentioned above, Lüscher (1972) came to the conclusion that the royal pheromone is indeed the JH, which directly inhibits the differentiation of supplementary reproductives and alates and at the same time stimulates the differentiation of soldiers. According to this hypothesis, the queen produces enough JH to prevent the differentiation of neotenic females, whereas preventing the differentiation of neotenic males requires more JH, or a different JH, which the king produces only when stimulated by the queen. When the queen is missing, the king produces a JH-inhibitor which favours the differentiation of neotenic females. Lüscher (1972) further suggested that the soldiers' pheromone must be an anti-JH which, in addition to inhibiting the differentiation of the soldiers, favours the differentiation of supplementary reproductives and the metamorphosis to alates.

Springhetti (1976) found that, when pseudergates are treated with small doses of JHA in the presence of soldiers, fewer soldier intercastes are formed. Furthermore, Lüscher (1972) reprocessed Springhetti's data (1969a, b) to demonstrate the soldiers' stimulatory influence on the differentiation of supplementary reproductives. (Nevertheless, the experiments providing the data may not have been entirely suitable for this purpose, and however attractive the hypothesis may be it awaits confirmation.)

Lüscher's theory, suggesting that the royal control over the differentiation of all *K. flavicollis* castes is governed by their ability to regulate JH circulation in the colony, seems perhaps over simplified in spite of evidence supporting it and lack of solid proof to the contrary. The following points may be raised:

(1)   To control even a medium-sized colony, the amount of JH secreted by the reproductives would have to be very large, if the hormone is to be distributed to all members of the colony.

(2)   When newly moulted pseudergates are treated with JHA, many of them, after a brief instar, become neotenic/soldier intercastes with the genital plates and/or pigmented eyes of the neotenic and the mandibles and head of the soldier (Lebrun, 1970; Springhetti, 1975). The JH, therefore, prevents neither the development of the features of the neotenic nor the brevity of the instar which precedes such a moult. If the reproductives do release large amounts of JH in the colony, intercastes of this sort, instead of being very rare, should be frequent.

(3)   The administration of bee "queen substance" to *K. flavicollis* reduces the queen's fecundity (Springhetti & Pinamonti, 1977). The soldier phero-mone should also have this negative effect, if it is an anti-JH with a non-specific action.

It therefore appears more likely that the reproductives produce at least two types of pheromones, one designed to control the differentiation of supple-mentary reproductives, the other to control the differentiation of alates and soldiers. The second pheromone must not be the JH itself, but must activate the CA of the pseudergates and the nymphs in some way. The soldier pheromone might be antagonistic to the action of the hormone of the CA by acting on the tissues from which the soldier-specific structures develop. Another possibility is that the JH produced by the royals and the anti-JH produced by the soldiers might interact during trophallactic exchanges, each one losing its effectiveness.

11.8   CONCLUSIONS

In spite of the fact that numerous studies have been carried out on the differentiation of castes of *K. flavicollis*—more than on any other species of termite—many questions remain to be answered or at least clarified. The more deeply the investigations probe into the problems, the clearer it becomes that the royal pair performs functions that are by no means limited to reproduction, as was once thought, and that it has a dominant role in the society (Lüscher, 1977). Indeed, to use Emerson's words (1950), it seems to be a "centre of a behaviour gradient".

To be sure, the conclusions reached in *K. flavicollis* cannot be extended to all species of termites. As Sewell and Watson (1981) observe, *K. flavicollis* has particular characteristics, which explains why the results obtained are sometimes very different from those obtained with other species.

11.9   SUMMARY

Within a society of *Kalotermes flavicollis* Fabr., the royal pair plays a very complex part, many aspects of which are still relatively unexplored. So far, their only role to have been investigated in depth is the one they perform in the differentiation of castes: supplementary reproductives, alates and soldiers.

In all three of these cases, control is exerted through the production of pheromones which influence in some way the activity of the corpora allata of the pseudergates and/or the nymphs which are "competent" for metamorphosis. Although the king and queen differ in their capability for controlling differentiation of all castes, their influence is concurrent: *i.e.*, both inhibit the differentiation of supplementary reproductives and alates, but stimulate the differentiation of soldiers. The reproductives produce at least two types of pheromones, one which controls the differentiation of supplementary reproductives, the other which controls the differentiation of alates and soldiers.

The differentiation of new soldiers is inhibited by pheromones produced by the soldiers already present.

Some other aspects of the reproductives' activity, such as their influence on pseudergate aggressiveness, have only recently been identified.

11.10   REFERENCES

Alibert J. (1965) La trophallaxie proctodéale chez *Calotermes flavicollis*. C.R. Ve Congr. UIEIS Toulouse, 79–92.
Alibert J. (1968) Influence de la société et de l'individu sur la trophallaxie chez *Calotermes flavicollis* Fabr. et *Cubitermes fungifaber* (Isoptera). Coll. Intern. CNRS no. 173: "L'effet de Groupe chez les Animaux", 237–288.
Alibert-Bertho J. (1969) La trophallaxie chez le termite à cou jaune, *Calotermes flavicollis* Fabr., étudiée à l'aide de radio-elements. *Ann. Sc. Nat. Zool.* **11**, 235–325.
Bruinsma O. & Leuthold R. H. (1977) Pheromones involved in the building behaviour of *Macrotermes subhyalinus* (Rambur). Proc. 8th Intern. Congr. IUSSI Wageningen, 257–258.
Castle G. B. (1934) The damp-wood termites of western United States, genus *Zootermopsis*

(formerly, *Termopsis*). In *Termites and Termite Control* (ed. Kofoid C. A.), pp. 273–310. Univ. Calif. Press, Berkeley.

Emerson A. E. (1950) The organization of insect societies. In *Principles of Animal Ecology* (eds Allee W. C., Park O., Emerson A. E., Park T. & Schmidt K. P.), pp. 419–435. Saunders Co., Philadelphia.

Grassé P. P. & Bonneville P. (1935) Les sexués inutilisés ou achrestogonimes des Protermitides. *Bull. Biol. Fr. Belg.* **69,** 474–491.

Grassé P. P. & Noirot C. (1946a) La production des sexués néoténiques chez le termite à cou jaune (*Calotermes flavicollis* F.) Inhibition germinale et inhibition somatique. *C.R. Acad. Sci. Paris* **223,** 869–871.

Grassé P. P. & Noirot C. (1946b) Le polymorphisme social du termite à cou jaune (*Calotermes flavicollis* F.). La production des soldats. *C.R. Acad. Sci. Paris* **223,** 929–931.

Grassé P. P. & Noirot C. (1947) Le polymorphisme social du termite a cou jaune (*Calotermes flavicollis* F.). Les faux ouvriers ou pseudergates et les mues régressives. *C.R. Acad. Sci. Paris* **224,** 219–221.

Grassé P. P. & Noirot C. (1960a) Rôle respectif des mâles et des femelles dans las formation des sexués néoténiques chez *Calotermes flavicollis*. *Insectes Sociaux* **7,** 109–123.

Grassé P. P. & Noirot C. (1960b) L'isolement chez le termite à cou jaune (*Calotermes flavicollis* Fab.) et ses conséquences. *Insectes Sociaux* **7,** 323–331.

Grassi B. & Sandias A. (1893/94) Cosittuzione e sviluppo delle società dei termitidi. Atti Accad, Gioen. Sc. Nat. Catania, 6/7.

Jucci C. (1961) Recenti ricerche sulla biologia delle termiti. *Symp. Gen. Biol. Ital.* **7,** 16–28.

Lebrun D. (1963) Implantation de glandes de mue de *Periplaneta americana* dans les sexués néoténiques de *Calotermes flavicollis* Fabr. *C.R. Acad. Sci.* **257,** 2181–2182.

Lebrun D. (1967a) La détermination des castes du termite à cou jaune *Calotermes flavicollis* Fabr. *Bull. Biol. Fr. Belg.* **101,** 139–217.

Lebrun D. (1967b) Nouvelles recherches sur le déterminisme endocrinien du polymorphisme de *Calotermes flavicollis*. *Ann. Soc. ent. Fr.* **3,** 867–871.

Lebrun D. (1967c) Hormone juvénile et formation des soldats chez le termite à cou jaune *Calotermes flavicollis* Fabr. *C.R. Acad. Sc. Paris* **265,** 996–997.

Lebrun D. (1969) Glandes endocrines et biologie de *Calotermes flavicollis* Proc. *VI Congr. IUSSI Bern*, pp. 131–136.

Lebrun D. (1970) Intercastes expérimentaux de *Calotermes flavicollis* Fabr. *Insectes Sociaux* **17,** 159–175.

Lebrun D. (1972) Effets de l'implantation de glandes mandibulaires sur la différenciation imaginale de *Calotermes flavicollis*. *C.R. Acad. Sc. Paris* **274,** 2077–2079.

Lebrun D. (1973) Pheromones et déterminisme des castes de *Calotermes flavicollis* Fabr. *Proc. 7th Congr. IUSSI, London*, pp. 220–224.

Lebrun D. (1978) Implications hormonales dans la morphogenèse des castes du termite *Kalotermes flavicollis* Fabr. *Bull. Soc. Zool. Fr.* **103,** 351–358.

Light S. F. (1944) Experimental studies on ectohormonal control of the development of supplementary reproductives in the termite genus *Zootermopsis* (formerly *Termopsis*). *Univ. Calif. Publ. Zool.* **43,** 413–454.

Lüscher M. (1952) Die Produktion und Elimination von Ersatzgeschlechstieren bei der Termite *Kalotermes flavicollis* (Fabr.). *Z. vergl. Physiol.* **34,** 123–141.

Lüscher M. (1956a) Die Entstehung von Ersatzgeschlechstieren bei der Termite *Kalotermes flavicollis* (Fabr.). *Insectes Sociaux* **3,** 119–128.

Lüscher M. (1956b) Hemmende und förndernde Faktoren bei der Entstehung der Ersatzgeschlechtstiere bei der Termite *Kalotermes flavicollis* (Fabr.). *Rev. suisse Zool.* **63,** 261–267.

Lüscher M. (1958) Über die Entstehung der soldaten bei Termiten. *Rev. suisse Zool.* **65,** 372–377.

Lüscher M. (1960) Hormonal control of caste differentiation in termites. *Ann. N.Y. Acad. Sci.* **89,** 549–563.

Lüscher M. (1961) Social control of polymorphism in termites. In *Insect Polymorphism* (ed. Kennedy J. S.), *Symp. R. Entomol. Soc. London*, 57–67.

Lüscher M. (1963) Functions of the corpora allata in the development of termites. *Proc. 16th Int. Congr. Zool. Washington*, **4,** 244–250.

Lüscher M. (1964) Die spezifische Wirkung männlicher und weiblicher Ersatzgeschlechstiere auf die Entstehung von Ersatzgeschlechtstieren bei der Termite *Kalotermes flavicollis* (Fabr.). *Insectes Sociaux* 11, 79–90.

Lüscher M. (1969) Die Bedeutung des Juvenilhormones für die Differenzierung der Soldaten bei der Termite *Kalotermes flavicollis*. *Proc. VI Congr. IUSSI, Bern*, pp. 165–170.

Lüscher M. (1972) Environmental control of juvenile hormone (JH) secretion and the caste differentiation in termites. *Gen. Comp. Endocrinol., suppl.* 3, 509–514.

Lüscher M. (1974) Kasten und Kastedifferenzierung bei niederen Termiten. In "*Socialpolymorphismus bei Inseckten*" (ed. Schmidt G. H.), pp. 694–740. Wiss. Verlagsges. MBH, Stuttgart.

Lüscher M. (1977) Queen dominance in termites. *Proc. 8th Intern. Congr. IUSSI Wageningen*, pp. 238–242.

Lüscher M. & Springhetti A. (1960) Untersuchungen über die Bedeutung der Corpora allata für die Differenzierung der Kasten bei der Termite *Kalotermes flavicollis*. *F.J. Insect Physiol.* 5, 190–212.

Miller E. M. (1942) The problem of castes and caste differentiation in *Prorhinotermes simplex* (Hagen). *Bull. Univ. Miami* 15, 3–27.

Pickens A. L. (1932) Distribution and life histories of the species of *Reticulitermes* Holmgr. in California. Dissertation. Univ. Calif., Berkeley.

Sewell J. J. & Watson J. A. L. (1981) Developmental pathways in Australian species of *Kalotermes* Hagen (Isoptera). *Sociobiology* 6, 243–323.

Springhetti A. (1968) Produzione di reali di sostituzione in popolazioni di differenti regioni italiane di *Kalotermes flavicollis* Fabr. *Arch. Zool. Ital.* 53, 1–10.

Springhetti A. (1969a) Il controllo sociale della differenziazione degli alati in *Kalotermes flavicollis* Fabr. (Isoptera). *Ann. Univ. Ferrara, Sez. Biol. anim.* 3, 73–96.

Springhetti A. (1969b) Influenza dei reali sulla differenziazione dei soldati in *Kalotermes flavicollis* Fabr. *Proc. VI Congr. IUSSI Bern*, pp. 267–273.

Springhetti A. (1970) Influence of the king and queen on the differentiation of soldiers in *Kalotermes flavicollis* Fabr. *Monitore Zool. Ital.* (n.s.), 4, 99–105.

Springhetti A. (1971) Il controllo dei reali sulla differenziazione degli alati in *Kalotermes flavicollis* Fabr. *Boll. Zool.* 38, 101–110.

Springhetti A. (1972a) I feromoni nella differenziazione delle caste in *Kalotermes flavicollis* Fabr. *Boll. Zool.*, 39, 83–87.

Springhetti A. (1972b) The competence of *Kalotermes flavicollis* Fabr. pseudergates to differentiate into soldiers. *Monitore Zool. Ital.* (an.s.) 6, 97–111.

Springhetti A. (1973a) Il ruolo delle pseudergati nella differenziazione dei soldati di *Kalotermes flavicollis* Fabr. *Atti Acc. Sc. Ferrara*, 50, 1–15.

Springhetti A. (1973b) Groups effects in the differentiation of the soldiers of *Kalotermes flavicollis* Fabr. *Insectes Sociaux* 20, 333–342.

Springhetti A. (1974) The influence of farnesenic acid ethyl ester on the differentiation of *Kalotermes flavicollis* Fabr. soldiers. *Experientia* 30, 541–542.

Springhetti A. (1975) Pseudergates' responsiveness and the differentiation of soldiers in *Kalotermes flavicollis* Fabr. (Isoptera). *Monitore Zool. Ital.* (n.s.) 9, 11–23.

Springhetti A. (1976) The influence of soldiers on the action of farnesenic acid ethyl ester in *Kalotermes flavicollis* Fabr. (Isoptera). *Monitore Zool. Ital.* (n.s.) 10, 413–420.

Springhetti A. (1980) A "Royal area" in the nest of *Kalotermes flavicollis* Fabr. (Isoptera). *Monitore Zool. Ital.* 14, 53–61.

Springhetti A. & Pinamonti S. (1977) Some effects of queen bee extracts (*Apis mellifera* L.) (Hymenoptera) on *Kalotermes flavicollis* Fabr. (Isoptera). *Insectes Sociaux* 24, 61–70.

Stuart A. M. (1969) Social behavior and communication. In *Biology of Termites* (ed. Krishna K. & Weesner F. M.), Vol. 1, pp. 193–232. Academic Press, N.Y.

Verron H. (1963) Rôle des stimuli chimiques dans l'attraction sociale chez *Calotermes flavicollis* Fabr. *Insectes Sociaux* 10, 167–336.

CHAPTER 12

Differentiation of Reproductives in Higher Termites

Ch. NOIROT

Laboratory of Zoology, University of Dijon, Boulevard Gabriel, 21100 Dijon, France

CONTENTS

12.1 INTRODUCTION

As in lower termites, the colony of the higher termites (family Termitidae) is normally headed by a pair of dealated imagines (the king and the queen), which have founded the society after swarming. The replacement of the imaginal (or primary) pair, so frequently observed in most of the lower termites, seems much less easy in the higher termites, and very variable according to the species.

12.2 PRIMARY OR IMAGINAL REPRODUCTIVES

As mentioned in my preceding paper, the alates of the higher termites

177

develop through five nymphal instars (defined as such by the presence of wing buds) and this "imaginal line" is morphologically individualized at the moult of the first instar (undifferentiated) larva. In other words, the separation of the "imaginal line" and the "neuter line" is morphologically visible at the moult of the first instar larva (presence or absence of wing buds). In tropical regions, the neuter line is produced all over the year, and the young nymphs only appear during a short period (usually several weeks) at a given season (Noirot, 1969). Examples are given by Darlington (Chapter 15), and Mensa-Bonsu (unpubl. data). Thus, the differentiation of young nymphs, and then the alates, is a *discontinuous* process, whereas the production of neuters is *continuous*, except in some non-tropical species where the development is arrested in winter (i.e. *Tenuirostritermes tenuirostris* in N. America, Weesner, 1953; *Drepanotermes perniger* in Australia, Watson, 1974). The seasonal cycle is evidently determined (or at least synchronized) by the climatic factors, but we have no idea on the mechanisms involved. Similarly we do not know why nymphs are not produced during the first years in the incipient colonies (see for example Okot-Kotber, Chapter 7).

12.2.1   Time of determination

During the formation of young nymphs, the differentiation of the neuter line is not arrested, and it is never possible to observe a pure nymphal brood. Even at the peak of nymph production, the second instar larvae are more numerous than the first instar nymphs. These peculiarities explain the difficulties in solving the important questions of time and mechanism of determination. Indeed, the first (differentiative) moult is the expression of a process determined earlier, but when and how? The determination is realized, *at the least*, during the first larval instar, but possibly earlier, either during the embryonic development or oogenesis in the queen ovaries (a genetic mechanism seems unlikely, from the analysis of intercastes, especially the soldier-nymphs (Noirot, 1955, 1969, Chapter 6)). At the present time, the problem remains far from clear. The observations of Mensa-Bonsu (unpubl. data) show, in *Amitermes evuncifer*, that the differentiation (development of the gonads) of the future nymphs is evident in young first instar larvae, but cannot decide whether the determination occurs early in this instar or is already realized at the hatching from the egg.

12.2.2   Mechanisms

The endocrinological studies on the physogastric queens were the origin of another type of approach. Large amounts of ecdysteroid hormones were discovered in these queens, especially in the ovaries, passing into the eggs (Bordereau *et al.*, 1976; Delbecque *et al.*, 1978; Lanzrein *et al.*, 1977). Besides, high concentration of juvenile hormone (JH) was found in the haemolymph of the queen of *Macrotermes* and then in the eggs (Meyer *et al.*, 1976; Lanzrein *et al.*, 1977). These observations prompted Lüscher (1976) to put forward the hypothesis of a blastogenic caste determination, related to the JH content of the eggs: a higher titre would determine a bias toward the neuter line, a lower titre toward the imaginal line. The JH titre of the eggs could be controlled by the JH titre in the haemolymph of the queen, and its seasonal variations. This hypothesis is discussed at length by Lanzrein, Gentinetta & Fehr (Chapter 22), and the conclusion remains uncertain, due to the variability between the different queens and nests, and the impossibility to have a pure batch of nymph-producing eggs. Thus, a blastogenic determination remains an attractive hypothesis, awaiting definitive evidence. However, such a determination (if proved) could not be irreversible, as stated by Lüscher himself (1976). The experiments of Bordereau (1975) point in this direction, as he observed in *Macrotermes bellicosus* the appearance of an unseasonal batch of nymphs after the removal of the royal pair in most (but not all) of the experimental nests. However, in *M. michaelseni*, similar experiments gave negative results (Sieber & Darlington, 1982).

Whatever the moment of determination may be, the morphogenesis of neuter *vs.* nymphal development is controlled by the endocrine system. However, our information remains very limited, based only on the relative development of the corpora allata (CA) and the prothoracic glands (PG). The histological study by Okot-Kotber (1980) on *M. michaelseni* does not suggest a major role of CA and JH in this differentiation (whereas their importance in soldier formation is well evidenced). A differential role of the PG and their ecdysteroid hormones remains a possibility (Noirot, 1977), which ought to be studied by a more direct approach. Thus, the old controversy of a blastogenic or an epigenic caste determination is not yet resolved in higher termites (except for the differentiation of the soldiers, which is clearly epigenic). In the lower termites, the blastogenic hypothesis must be excluded (except perhaps in *Mastotermes*, see Watson, Chapter 3). However, as discussed by Noirot (Chapter 6) the more evolved the termite species, the earlier the determination. More observations are needed to confirm whether or not this process has pulled the time of determination back to the oogenesis.

12.3 REPLACEMENT REPRODUCTIVES

The replacement of the royal pair by secondary reproductives seems not so easy in the higher termites as in most of the lower termites, and was observed only in a limited number of species. Three categories of replacement reproductives may be observed: the imaginal or adultoids, clearly coming from alates matured in the nest, the brachypterous or nymphoids, more or less similar to advanced nymphal instars, their supposed origin, and ergatoids, worker-like in morphology and believed to originate from workers. In several species, more than one type of replacement reproductives were observed, but never in the same colony (Noirot, 1956). Our knowledge on these reproductives is based, in most of the species, on casual observations in the field colonies. In a limited number of species, they were observed after the experimental elimination of the royal pair in entire nests; very rarely, they were obtained in laboratory cultures of known composition.

12.3.1 Adultoids

The occurrence of this type of replacement reproductives was never reported in any lower termites. These reproductives are morphologically indistinguishable from the primaries (except sometimes they have lighter pigmentation). When several imaginal reproductives are found in the field colony, it is sometimes difficult to decide whether they are replacement adultoids (alates matured in their nest) or resulted from the foundation of the colony by association of several swarming insects (multiple primaries). Indeed, multiple foundations seem possible in some species (Thorne, 1982a, b). However, they involve a very limited number of individuals, and when numerous imaginal reproductives are found in the same colony, they are surely replacement adultoids. Conversely, if the primary pair is replaced by only one male and one female imagines, the new pair becomes completely similar to the preceding one, and cannot be identified as replacement reproductives, unless the suppression of the primaries was previously established. Fortunately, the apparition of adultoid reproductives was observed several times after the elimination of the founding pair (Noirot, 1956), now well documented in *M. michaelseni* (Sieber & Darlington, 1982) and discussed at length by Sieber (Chapter 14). I would like only to discuss the problem of the *maturation* of some alates in their own nest. This maturation never occurs in normal conditions. Some time after the imaginal moult, the alates remain tightly clustered in peripheral chambers until swarming, do not present any sexual behaviour nor sexual maturation. From the observations of Hewitt *et al.* (1972), in *Hodotermes mossambicus*, this inhibition is mainly behavioural, triggered by reciprocal antennal stimulation. However, before their gathering in peripheral chambers, the newly moulted alates maintain, most probably, many more relationships with the other members of the society, and so, may be "informed" of the absence of the royal pair. As a working hypothesis, this period could be the one in which the inhibition (perhaps of pheromonal origin) may be removed. Indeed, the adultoid reproductives are reported, in several instances, as incompletely pigmented (Noirot, 1956), which points to a sexual maturation occurring just after the imaginal moult, or even a precocious metamorphosis.

The only case where adultoids were obtained in laboratory cultures was that of *Astalotermes quietus* (Noirot, 1956, formerly identified as *Anoplotermes* near *sanctus* and named here according to Sands, 1972). This species, a subterranean humus-feeder, builds occasionally, on small trees, very fragile constructions named by Grassé (1938) "pseudoécies", the significance of which remains obscure. They contain a variable population of workers (several hundred at most), with sometimes some larvae or nymphs, and more frequently a limited number of fully pigmented alates. When the population of a pseudoecie is isolated and cultured in the laboratory, the alates quickly shed their wings, and some eggs are observed after an interval of between 8 and 36 days. This was obtained in the four cultures realized, and in one which survived long enough, about 20 larvae were observed. In a fifth experiment, 100 workers were isolated with 10 nymphs from the penultimate instar: 74 days later, three adultoids were present with several eggs and four larvae. Thus, in this species, the sexual maturation of the alates is quickly and easily realized in the absence of the royal pair, and this species could be a good system for the analysis of the phenomenon.

12.3.2 Nymphoids

Although frequently collected in field nests (Noirot, 1956), they remain poorly documented. In the few instances where the description was accurate, they appear to differ from normal nymphal stages. The nymphoids described by Silvestri (1914) in *A. evuncifer* possess very short wing buds (much shorter than the nymphs of the same size, i.e. last or penultimate instar). In *Amitermes hastatus*, studied as *A. atlanticus* by Skaife (1955), the "secondary reproductives" originate from short wing-padded nymphs which are most probably from the penultimate instar. The small morphological differences between the nymphs and the secondary reproductives (especially in the shape of the wing pads) are clear indication of a differentiative moult. In *Microcerotermes amboinensis*, Weyer (1930) collected nymphoid reproductives in several field colonies, and obtained experimentally their differentiation in 18 out of 55 nests, 6–8 weeks after the removal of the queens. Both in natural and experimental nests, the nymphoids are of very variable morphology as regards the development of the wings, from insects with very short tips at the posterior margins of the meso- and metanotum to wing pads longer than in last-instar nymphs. From the drawings of Weyer (1930) the size of the different types seems very similar (not in proportion of the wing development), but the eyes seem larger in individuals with long wing buds. In *Microcerotermes parvus*, I observed (Noirot, 1956) the apparition of several nymphoids in a laboratory culture composed of about 700 workers and several dozens of nymphs from the two last instars. At the first examination (after 53 days) no nymphoids had differentiated, but several were evidently formed at the second (after 108 days); thus they appeared most probably between 8 and 15 weeks after the initiation of the culture. These nymphoids bear long wing buds, of about the same length as in last-instar nymphs, but conspicuously narrower. They are much more pigmented than the nymphs, a little less than the normal imagos.

From these observations, one moult at least is necessary for the transformation of a nymph into a replacement reproductive. In most cases, however, it is difficult to decide from what nymphal instar a given type of nymphoid originated. The insects with long wing pads developed certainly from nymphs of the last or penultimate instar, but those with short or very short wing pads may come either from an earlier instar (after several moults without any growth of the wing buds) or from a late instar, after one or several regressive moults. More experimental evidence, especially with laboratory colonies, is needed to clarify the precise steps of the differentiation.

12.3.3 Ergatoids

Although less frequent, the ergatoid reproductives are better known for, in several instances, the stages of their differentiation were observed in natural populations where the processes were in progress. In such cases, a detailed analysis of the population, especially the insects near a moult (recognized by their whitish opaque colour), discloses the sequences of the phenomenon. This was experienced in *Termes hospes* (Noirot, 1955) in three separate colonies and *Nasutitermes corniger* (Thorne & Noirot, 1982) in one colony. In these two species, the workers belong to several (at least three) successive instars, and are also precursors of soldiers (female workers for *T. hospes*, male workers for *N. corniger*). In the four societies analysed, the workers were found to be perfectly normal (by comparison with colonies without ergatoids). However, the study of the workers fixed just before a moult shows two types of insects. In the first one, no development of the sex organs can be detected (as in the normal moults of the workers). In the second, a conspicuous development of the gonads and accessory structures is observed. This development is especially evident in the females, where, besides the ovaries and oviducts, anlages of the spermatheca and the colleterial glands are well visible. The moult of these workers give rise to a first instar ergatoid, or E1, which is a transient stage, where the growth of the sex organs takes place again, ending, after a second moult, into the second instar ergatoids, or E2, which cannot moult again. In *T. hospes*, the E2 were fully mature and functional (numerous eggs and young larvae in the nests, spermatheca of the female E2 full of spermatozoa), with about an equal number of each sex. In *N. corniger*, none of the female E2 (much more numerous than the males) were fully mature and their ovaries disorganized, with frequently some degree of degeneration. The few males however seemed more like normal reproductives. From these observations, on two unrelated species of Termitidae, and some more limited results on *M. amboinensis* (Noirot, 1955) and *Cubitermes severus* (Mme P. Bodot, unpubl. obs.), a general developmental pathway may be proposed, with two successive moults: [worker (any instar)→E1→E2].

It is worth noting that the same scheme was evidenced by Buchli (1956) in *Reticulitermes* and by Renoux (1976) in *Schedorhinotermes* (family Rhinotermitidae). In this sequence, the morphology of the transformed workers may be more or less modified. In *T. hospes*, the modifications are very limited, and the ergatoids appear completely worker-like without eyes or wing buds. In *N. corniger*, an enlargement of the meso- and metanotum, with small lateral expansions reminiscent of wing buds, appears in E1 and becomes more prominent in E2. Very small compound eyes are evident in E2. However, in histological sections, the brain remains essentially worker-like, with very limited development of the optic lobes (nearly absent in the workers). The ergatoids of *N. corniger*, although differing little from the workers, develop, to a limited extent, some imaginal characters, in addition to those related to the sexualization. Recently, Barbara Thorne (pers. comm.), discovered in Panama a colony of another species of *Nasutitermes*: *N. columbicus*, containing more than 300 functional ergatoids (about 1 male for 6 females), the morphology of which looks very similar to those of *N. corniger*, although the eyes and the wing buds are a little more evident. These studies are in progress (Thorne and Noirot, in preparation) and will be published elsewhere. Although, in this colony, no intermediate stages were found (only functional ergatoids), the similarity with E2 of *N. corniger* (not only in morphology, but also in the anatomy, especially the brain) points to the same developmental pathway.

Unfortunately, in none of the above examples were the precise conditions for the differentiation determined. The elimination of the royal pair is most probably an essential factor, although in *N. columbicus* the imaginal king was still present (this last observation may be an indication of the prevalent action of the queen, see also Sieber, Chapter 14). An inhibitory pheromone may be involved, but this remains hypothetical and *a fortiori*, its way of action is unknown. The nutritional factors are certainly important: in *N. corniger*, the workers to be transformed are fed by normal workers; in the workers engaged in a normal moult, the mandibles are conspicuously eroded. On the contrary, if the moult is giving rise to an ergatoid (as judged by the development of the sex organs) the cutting edge and the molar plates of the mandibles remain very sharp. The same unworn conditions are also observed in the mandibles of

E1 and E2. Thus, it seems likely that the transformed workers and the ergatoids do not work in the colony and are fed by the normal workers, with chewed wood and saliva. The transformation is concomitant with a change of feeding behaviour, both in the maturing workers and ergatoids, which are fed, and the normal workers, nourishing them. It is not possible to ascertain whether or not this change is the *primum movens* of the maturation.

The regulation of the number of ergatoids seems variable according to the species. In *T. hospes*, no regulation was apparent. The functional ergatoids seem short-living insects, with very limited reserves (fat-body). Most probably, they are quickly exhausted and continuously replaced by new ones. In *N. columbicus*, a different situation may occur. In the only colony observed, the differentiation of new ergatoids was completely arrested. The functional ergatoids, with well-developed sex organs, nutriment similar to that of normal reproductives (worker saliva), conspicuous fat body (of the "royal" type in the females) seemed long-living individuals, which may probably exert (as the primary reproductives) sexual inhibition on the workers.

12.4   CONCLUSION

The social control of sexual maturation is a common feature of eusocial insects, but is particularly rigorous in termites. In the higher termites, the separation of the "neuter line" *vs.* the "sexual line" occurs very early during the development, and the insects of the former undergo a more or less complete arrest of differentiation for many imaginal characters, especially the sex organs, the wing apparatus and the eyes. The mechanisms by which this arrest of differentiation is realized, as well as the seasonal cycle which so strongly affect the differentiation, remain poorly understood. The replacement of the royal pair was observed in many species, although it seems not so easy as in many lower termites. In several instances, and especially in fungus-growing termites, the replacement reproductives are imaginal alates, maturing in the nest. It is worth noting that this phenomenon was never observed in any lower termite, perhaps because other types are more easily and more quickly obtained. The nymphoid reproductives, frequently observed in field colonies but poorly documented, are true neotenics by their morphology and their origin. One moult at least seems necessary for their differentiation from a nymphal stage. The ergatoids too must be considered as neotenics. Their morphology bears numerous larval characters, as the workers from which they originate, and this is a consequence of the arrest of development observed at the origin of the "neuter line". The differentiation of these ergatoids necessitates two successive moults in the few analysed cases, and this may be of general occurrence. Thus, the possibility of moulting is a prerequisite for a worker to become an ergatoid. During these moults, the sex organs resume their development, and some other imaginal characters may sometimes undergo initial stages of differentiation (small wing buds and compound eyes).

In contrast with the foundation of new colonies, which very rarely depart from the classical scheme (pairing of dealated imagines), the replacement of the primary reproductives may occur, in the higher termites, with very different strategies. In some species, post-embryonic development retains sufficient strategies for the differentiation of neotenic reproductives (nymphoids or ergatoids). In others, the maturation *in situ* of imaginal alates seems the only way by which the founding pair may be replaced. And for many species nothing is known!

12.5 SUMMARY

The development of imaginal alates (which after the flight become primary reproductives of the new society), is very uniform among the higher termites. During the major part of the year, the larvae develop only into soldiers and workers, but at a definite season, the first larvae (apparently undifferentiated) differentiate at the first moult, either into nymphs or neuter larvae. However, the determination may occur earlier, and the mechanisms involved remain poorly understood.

Replacement of the primary pair seems less frequent and more difficult than in most of the lower termites, and very variable according to the species, especially for the type of replacement reproductives. They may be adultoids (imaginal alates maturing into their nest of origin), a condition which was never observed in any lower termites. The nymphoid replacement reproductives differentiate from some late instar nymphs, and one moult at least seems necessary. The ergatoids proceed from true workers, through two successive moults. On the whole, our information on the formation of replacement reproductives in higher termites appears very fragmentary, particularly for the mechanisms acting either on the individuals (neuroendocrinological factors) or in the society (pheromones, nutrition . . .).

12.6 ACKNOWLEDGEMENTS

Many thanks to Barbara Thorne for fruitful cooperation, and the permission to quote unpublished observations. Dr B. M. Okot-Kotber kindly revised the English manuscript.

12.7 REFERENCES

Bordereau C. (1975) Déterminisme des castes chez les Termites Supérieurs: mise en évidence d'un contrôle royal dans la formation de la caste sexuée chez *Macrotermes bellicosus* Smeathman (Isoptera, Termitidae). *Insectes Sociaux* 22, 363–374.

Bordereau C., Hirn M., Delbecque J. P. & De Reggi M. (1976) Présence d'ecdysone chez un Insecte adulte: la reine de Termite. *C.R. Acad. Sci.* 282 (D), 885–887.

Buchli H. (1956) Die Neotenic bei *Reticulitermes*. *Insectes Sociaux* 3, 131–143.

Delbecque J. P., Lanzrein B., Bordereau C., Imboden H., Hirn M., O'Connor J. D., Noirot C. & Lüscher M. (1978) Ecdysone and ecdysterone in physogastric termite queens and eggs of *Macrotermes bellicosus* and *Macrotermes subhyalinus*. *Gen. Comp. Endocrinol.* 36, 40–47.

Grassé P. P. (1938) Les faux nids ou pseudoécies, constructions probables des *Anoplotermes*. *Bull. Soc. entomol. France* 43, 195–196.

Hewitt P. H., Watson J. A. L., Nel J. J. C. & Schoeman I. (1972) Control of the change from group to pair behaviour by *Hodotermes mossambicus* reproductives. *J. Insect Physiol.* 18, 143–150.

Lanzrein B., Gentinetta V. & Lüscher M. (1977) *In vivo* and *in vitro* studies on the endocrinology of the reproductives of the termite *Macrotermes subhyalinus*. Proc. 8th Congress IUSSI, Wageningen, pp. 265–268.

Lüscher M. (1976) Evidence for an endocrine control of caste determination in higher termites. In *Phase and caste determination in insects. Endocrine aspects* (Lüscher M., ed.), pp. 91–103. Pergamon Press, Oxford.

Meyer D. R., Lanzrein B., Lüscher M. & Nakanishi K. (1976) Isolation and identification of a juvenile hormone (J.H.) in termites. *Experientia* 32, 773.

Noirot C. (1955) Recherches sur le polymorphisme de Termites supérieurs (Termitidae). *Ann. Sci. nat., Zool.* 17, 399–595.

Noirot C. (1956) Les sexes de remplacement chez les Termites supérieurs (Termitidae). *Insectes Sociaux* 3, 145–158.

Noirot C. (1969) Formation of castes in the higher termites. In *Biology of Termites*, Vol. 1 (Krishna K. & Weesner F. M., eds), pp. 311–350. Academic Press, New York.

Noirot C. (1977) Various aspects of hormone action in social insects. Proc. 8th Internat. Congress IUSSI, Wageningen, pp. 12–16.

Okot-Kotber B. M. (1980) Histological and size changes in corpora allata and prothoracic glands during development of *Macrotermes michaelseni* (Isoptera). *Insectes Sociaux* 27, 361–376.

Renoux J. (1976) Le polymorphisme de *Schedorhinotermes lamanianus* (Sjöstedt) (Isoptera-Rhinotermitidae). Essai d'interprétation. *Insectes Sociaux* 23, 281–491.

Sands W. A. (1972) The soldierless termites of Africa. *Bull. British Mus. (Nat. Hist.) Entomol. Suppl.* 18, 244 p.

Sieber R. & Darlington J. P. E. C. (1982) Replacement of the royal pair in *Macrotermes michaelseni*. *Insect. Sci. Application* 3, 39–42.

Silvestri F. (1914) Contribuzione alla conoscenza dei Termitidi e Termitofili dell' Africa Occidentale. I-Termitidi. *Bull. Lab. Zool. Gen. Agr. R. Scuol. Sup. Agr. Portici* 9, 1–146.

Skaife S. H. (1955) *Dwellers in Darkness. An Introduction to the study of Termites*. Longmans, London, 134 p.

Thorne B. L. (1982a) Polygyny in termites: Multiple primary queens in colonies of *Nasutitermes corniger* (Motschulsky) (Isoptera: Termitidae). *Insectes Sociaux* 29, 102–177.

Thorne B. L. (1982b) Multiple primary queens in Termites: phyletic distribution, ecological context, and comparison to polygyny in Hymenoptera. *The Biology of Social Insects* (Breed M. D., Michener C. D., Evans H. E., eds), pp. 206–211. Westview Press, Boulder.

Thorne B. L. & Noirot C. (1982) Ergatoid reproductives in *Nasutitermes corniger* (Motschulsky) (Isoptera: Termitidae). *Int. J. Insect Morphol. Embryol.* 11, 213–226.

Watson J. A. L. (1974) Caste development and its seasonal cycle in the Australian harvester termite, *Drepanotermes perniger* (Froggatt) (Isoptera: Termitidae). *Austr. J. Zool.* 22, 471–487.

Weesner F. M. (1953) Biology of *Tenuirostritermes tenuirostris* (Desneux) with emphasis on caste development. *Univ. Calif. Publ. Zool.* 57, 251–302.

Weyer F. (1930) Uber Ersatzgeschlechstiere bei Termiten. *Zeitschr. Morph. Okol. Tiere* 19, 364–380.

CHAPTER 13

Multiple Primary Reproductives in the Termite Macrotermes michaelseni (Sjöstedt)

J. P. E. C. DARLINGTON*

International Centre of Insect Physiology and Ecology, P.O. Box 30772, Nairobi, Kenya

CONTENTS

13.1 INTRODUCTION

Some termite nests contain more than a single pair of reproductives (king and queen). This may be as a result of the production of neotenic or secondary reproductives to augment or replace the founders (Noirot, 1956). In the Macrotermitinae neotenic reproductives are not known (Noirot, 1956), but multiple adultoid primary reproductives are sometimes found in the nests (summarized in Thorne, 1982a). There are four possible mechanisms for the production of these.

Firstly, a nest may be founded by a group of de-alates instead of a pair. Instances (both experimental and observational) have been recorded in

---

*Present address: Section of Entomology, National Museums of Kenya, P.O. Box 40658, Nairobi.

DSI-G*   *187*

several termite genera, but usually these rapidly resulted in the elimination of all but a single pair of reproductives (Nutting, 1969).

Secondly, a nest may lose its founders and replace them with a group of new primary reproductives. Occasional instances of this in the Macrotermitinae have been reported in the literature (summarized in Thorne, 1982a).

Thirdly, the number of primary reproductives may be increased by the addition of new, young reproductives to a functional pair or group. Occasional instances have been interpreted thus (e.g. Coaton, 1949; Roonwal & Gupta, 1952; Sieber & Darlington, 1982).

Fourthly, a colony may bud off a subsidiary colony which then develops its own primary reproductives from alates initially present. This has been reported for *Nasutitermes* (Thorne, 1982a) and suggested for *Anoplotermes* and *Trinervitermes* (Grassé & Noirot, 1951) but is not known for any member of the Macrotermitinae.

In the course of a study on the termite *Macrotermes michaelseni* (Sjöstedt) in semi-arid grassland at Kajiado, Kenya, a large amount of data was recorded about the reproductives. Using this information it is now possible to examine the properties, origin and function of multiple reproductives in this species.

13.2   METHODS

About 500 nests of *Macrotermes michaelseni* have been excavated, some in connection with population sampling and surveys, and many others to provide material for physiological and behavioural work by colleagues at the ICIPE. The opportunity was taken to accumulate a substantial body of data on numbers, weight, size and condition of the reproductives.

Best results were obtained by taking the intact royal cell within a solid block of defensive building to the laboratory. It was usually inverted, since the cell often lies near the bottom of the block, and its floor tends to be better isolated and more accessible than its roof. This has the advantage that the queen or queens, resting in the curve of the roof, are less likely to roll out and suffer damage when the cell is opened. The reproductives were weighed and measured immediately after removal from the royal cell, and as soon as possible after removal from the nest. If weighing was delayed for more than 2–3 hr after removal from the nest the results were not used, because live queens lose weight rapidly in the form of eggs laid and anal fluid eliminated. Fumigated queens, however, probably do not lose weight as long as they are in the humid atmosphere of the nest, and so weights measured on the day after fumigation are considered acceptable.

Some difficulty in interpretation arises from the fact that the nests were not randomly selected. There was a tendency to choose nests of moderate size which could be dug out quickly, especially for behavioural work. This introduced a bias, the effects of which cannot be evaluated.

13.3 RESULTS

13.3.1 Multiple reproductives in mature nests

Multiple primary reproductives occurred in about a quarter of all nests sampled. They were always (with one exception, see below) found together in the same royal cell. Queens occurring together as multiples seemed always (with two exceptions, see below) to be of the same age, to judge from their colour and degree of physogastry. (The colour of the inter-segmental membranes of the abdomen is pale cream in young physogastric queens, and darkens gradually through buff to brown or putty-colour in old ones.) The weights of queens occurring together as multiples are usually similar, unless one or more of them is defective (see below).

Young, middle-aged and senile physogastric queens have been found as multiples, in apparently stable associations. There is thus no indication that multiple queens are normally a transition stage to single queens except as a statistical accident.

The overall frequency of occurrence of multiple primary reproductives in mature nests is presented in Table 13.1. Multiple queens occur in 23.3% of the nests, and are thus four to five times as frequent as multiple kings, which are present only in 5.3% of the nests.

TABLE 13.1 FREQUENCY OF OCCURRENCE OF SINGLE AND MULTIPLE KINGS AND QUEENS IN MATURE NESTS OF *MACROTERMES MICHAELSENI* (361 OBSERVATIONS)

Number of kings	Number of queens						
	1	2	3	4	5	6	7
1	274	49	9	7	1	1	1
	75.9%	13.6%	2.5%	1.9%	0.3%	0.3%	0.3%
2	3	9	4				
	0.8%	2.5%	1.1%				
3		1					
		0.3%					
4			2				
			0.6%				

Multiple kings were present in 5.3% of nests.
Multiple queens were present in 23.3% of nests.

13.3.2   Multiple reproductives in immature nests

Mature nests are those that are large enough to produce broods of alates. This stage is reached when the queen's fresh weight exceeds 8 g (J. P. E. C. Darlington, unpubl. obs.). Data from nests used in population sampling show that there is a roughly linear relationship between total nest population and the queen's fresh weight, and that multiple queens are equivalent to a single queen of weight equal to their combined weight (J. P. E. C. Darlington, unpubl. obs.). Thus an immature nest can be defined as one in which the queen's weight, or the summed weight of all the queens present, is less than 8 g.

Using this criterion, the observed number of immature nests with pairs of primary reproductives is 21 (77.8%); with multiple queens only is four; and with multiple kings and queens is two. Thus, the overall frequency of multiple queens in immature nests is 22.2% and of multiple kings is 7.4%. This is similar to the frequency distribution in mature nests. However, these figures cannot be relied upon because bias may arise from the fact that very young single-queen nests are smaller and less likely to be found than nests with multiple queens of the same size.

13.3.3   Multiple reproductives in newly-settled groups of de-alates

Multiple reproductives may arise as co-founders of the nest. After the nuptial flight in *Macrotermes michaelseni*, de-alates have often been observed running in multiple tandems and starting to dig in as a group. It is also possible that several pairs might independently choose to dig in at the same favoured spot.

Attempts to dig up de-alates after settlement were usually unsuccessful since the de-alates dug in quite deeply and left little trace on the surface. However, on 14 February 1982 a flight occurred when the soil had been moistened only to a depth of a few cm. The dry soil below was brick hard and prevented the de-alates from digging any deeper. Thus on the morning after this flight it was relatively easy to locate the newly-settled de-alates. The sample is rather small (only 41 observations) but no other information is available. The frequency of occurrence of multiple males and females in these settled groups is presented in Table 13.2. About half the groups contained multiples, and multiple males occurred as often (48.8%) as multiple females (46.3%). There is a very highly significant association between multiple kings and multiple queens.

Experience in rearing de-alates in the laboratory suggests that about half the flown alates of both sexes will soon die, despite favourable conditions for settlement and complete protection from predators. If this mortality occurs at

TABLE 13.2. FREQUENCY OF OCCURRENCE OF SINGLE AND
MULTIPLE MALE AND FEMALE DE-ALATES OF *MACROTERMES
MICHAELSENI* AFTER SETTLEMENT (41 OBSERVATIONS)

| Number of males | Number of females | | | | | |
	1	2	3	4	5	6
1	20 48.8%	1 2.4%				
2	2 4.9%	2 4.9%	2 4.9%		2 4.9%	
3		4 9.8%	1 2.4%	2 4.9%		
4		1 2.4%	1 2.4%			
5		1 2.4%			1 2.4%	
6						
7						1 2.4%

Multiple males were present in 48.8% of settled groups.
Multiple females were present in 46.3% of settled groups.

random it may alter the ratio of multiple to single reproductives. To take a very simple model, let us suppose that the initial number of settlements (X) consisted of half single queens $(X/2)$ and half double queens $(X/2)$ and that the intrinsic mortality of the queens was 50%, distributed at random. Half of the single-queen settlements would die, leaving $X/4$ survivors. Of the double-queen settlements, one quarter would die $(X/8)$, one quarter would survive as double-queen settlements $(X/8)$ and half would survive as single-queen settlements, having lost one of their queens $(X/4)$. Thus the total number of surviving single-queen settlements would be $X/4 + X/4 = X/2$, whereas there would only be $X/8$ double-queen settlements left (20% of the total survivors, compared with 50% initially). This model also illustrates the advantage of multiple founders, since the initial double-queen settlements gave rise to 50% more surviving settlements $(3X/8)$ than did the single-queen settlements $(X/4)$.

If the intrinsic mortality is equally distributed between the sexes in the field, as it is in the laboratory, then a mechanism such as that proposed in the model cannot explain both the reduction from 46.3% to 23.3% in the multiple queens, and the much greater reduction from 48.8% to 5.3% in the multiple kings. The simplest explanation for the sexual difference might be that young females are mutually tolerant but young males are antagonistic.

It is not known what level of intrinsic mortality may occur in the field, nor whether it might be affected favourably or unfavourably by living in groups. The strong association between multiple males and multiple females shown in Table 13.2 would probably increase the survival rate of multiple groups compared with pairs. However, it is also possible that multiple groups may be more vulnerable to predation, being larger and perhaps easier to find.

It is not clear why multiple tandems form. Male alates are attracted to females by a pheromone, so multiple-male groups would be easily explicable. However, Table 13.2 shows that multiple-female groups are equally common. It seems possible that nest-odour may contribute to the formation of multiple-female groups, in which case the associated females are probably sisters, which could explain their mutual tolerance. If the multiple-male groups are composed of individuals flown from different nests attracted to the same female(s), a higher degree of intolerance might be expected. However, nothing is known at present about the frequency of cross-mating between nests, so this speculation is offered merely as a possible topic for future study.

13.3.4 Multiple reproductives as replacements

The replacement of primary reproductives which die in the nest is not rare. Long-term observations of intact nests show that from time to time they pass through phases of inactivity which may represent replacement, during which the population declines. The duration and severity of these inactive phases varies greatly and it is not possible to make a confident estimate of how often replacement occurs in nature. Replacement reproductives do not differ morphologically from founders.

Where the primary reproductives had been removed and the nests became active again within a year or two we can be confident that replacement reproductives had been produced. The frequency of replacement under these conditions is variable; in the drought years (1975–1976) very few nests were observed to replace their reproductives, whereas in wet years of high grass biomass (e.g. 1978, Lepage 1981) when the termite population was expanding, the rate of replacement was probably of the order of 25%. Some nests replaced their reproductives three or four times in succession, having been dug out at intervals of 1.5 to 2 years.

One of the first examples of replacement recorded was in a nest containing a large, healthy population including many nymphs in early instars, from which a large king and a queen weighing 21.6 g (fresh weight) were removed in May 1976. In May 1977 rebuilding was observed on the remains of the old mound. In July 1977 the rejuvenated nest was found to contain a king of average size, a queen of 22.4 g (fresh weight), a sterile population of over 2m and about 9000 nymphs in their final instar. For a nest to achieve this size, starting from de-alates only would take about 5 years (J. P. E. C. Darlington, unpubl. obs.).

In most of the cases recorded, a pair was replaced by a new pair. In one case, two queens and a king were replaced by a pair. In another case a pair was replaced by three queens and a king (see also Sieber & Darlington, 1982). One nest produced a long series of multiples; two queens and a king were removed initially, and replaced by two queens and a king, which were replaced by two kings and a queen, which in turn were replaced by three queens and two kings. The probability that this was chance is about one in 100. Thus multiple primary reproductives need not be founders, but can also arise as replacements for dead reproductives.

Of 22 nests that are known to have replaced their reproductives, 16 (72.2%) produced a pair, 5 (21.7%) produced multiple queens and 2 (8.7%) produced multiple kings (one of these nests produced both multiple queens and multiple kings). These frequencies are similar to those observed in mature nests, whose reproductives are of unknown origin (Table 13.1).

The phenomenon of replacement of the reproductives raises some very interesting points. It only occurs when there are nymphs or alates in the nest at the time the primary reproductives are removed (Sieber & Darlington, 1982; Sieber, Chapter 14). The replacements are offspring of the founders, and therefore carry many of the same genes. Alates which become replacement reproductives have a far greater chance (by several orders of magnitude) to survive and to reproduce than do alates which fly in the normal way. Thus the replacement mechanisms clearly confers a selective advantage on a genetic constitution which has it. The behaviour involved is presumably innate in the sterile castes, since the founders are already dead when it comes into operation. The occurrence of small, unseasonal broods of nymphs (Sieber & Darlington, 1982; Darlington, Chapter 15) may also be part of this system, since it increases by several months in the year the period during which the nest is capable of replacing its primary reproductives. Thus the production of unseasonal nymphs is an insurance for the nest against the death of their primary reproductives. Since serial replacement of the primary reproductives demonstrably can occur, a nest once established is potentially immortal.

Perhaps the most difficult question that arises from these observations is how, out of a brood of thousands of young reproductives, just one pair or a very few individuals are chosen to be reared as replacements.

13.3.5 Comparison of the weights of single and multiple reproductives

The distributions of fresh weights of monogynous, polygynous and polyandrous kings from all nests, and of a sample of male alates, are presented as histograms in Figure 13.1. The overlap between kings' weights and alates' weights occurred mostly because of the inclusion of data from immature nests in the former (blocked in). The mean weights of monogynous, polygynous and polyandrous kings from mature nests were not significantly different (tested using one-way analysis of variance, $F(2,316) = 1.26$, $p > 0.05$). Thus it

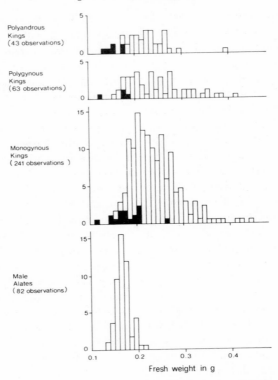

Fig. 13.1. Histograms of the fresh weights of male reproductives of *Macrotermes michaelseni* (interval of 0.1 g) (solid squares are kings from immature nests).

appears that the weight of a mature king is not affected by his conjugal status.

Polyandrous kings were overall significantly closer in weight to other members of their group than would be expected by chance (tested by model II analysis of variance, F (18,24) = 5.70** *p* < 0.01). However, there were a few double kings that differed from one another in weight. In one case the lighter king, which was close to the median weight (0.2054 g fresh weight) was in a very good condition, with one leg slightly damaged. The heavier king (0.2768 g) was in a very bad state, with every leg damaged, four of them amputated at the femoro-coxal joint and one half way down the femur. He also had large scars on the thorax near the alar scales. Though still alive he was so mutilated that he was unable to stand. In this case there can be little doubt that the old king was being replaced by a younger one, and his injuries may have resulted from the attacks of his rival (which was presumably his own offspring). In a second case, the lighter king (0.2668 g) had slight damage to one leg, while the heavier king (0.3980 g), which appeared to be fat and feeble, had superficial damage to five of his legs. In a third case, two kings were rather different in weight (0.2293 g and 0.2665 g) and both were moderately damaged. In both these latter cases it is possible, but far from certain, that one king was supplanting the other. Mutilation of the legs and antennae of primary reproductives is quite common in pairs as well as multiple groups, and so is difficult to interpret here.

The distributions of the fresh weights of single, double and multiple queens are presented as histograms in Figure 13.2. There are significant differences between the mean weights of single, double and multiple queens, and the mean of the summed weights of all double and multiple queens (tested using

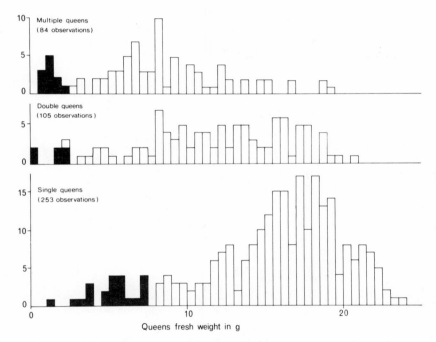

FIG. 13.2. Histograms of the fresh weights of queens of *Macrotermes michaelseni* (interval of 0.5 g) (solid squares are queens from immature nests).

one-way analysis of variance, F (3,461) = 162.7** $p < 0.01$; and t-test comparisons of the means). There is an inverse geometric relationship between the mean weights of individual queens and the number of queens present in a mature nest, but a positive linear relationship between the summed weight of queens and the numbers of queens present (Fig. 13.3).

The positive relationship between queen's weight and total nest population indicates that multiple queens are functionally equivalent to a single queen of

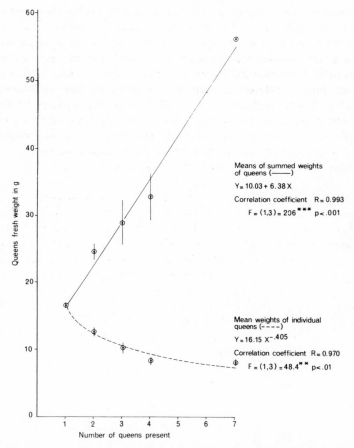

Fig. 13.3. Graph of means of summed weights of queens and mean weights of individual queens plotted against the number of queens present (vertical bars are standard errors).

weight equal to the sum of their weights (J. P. E. C. Darlington, unpubl. obs.). Thus, two 10 g queens are equivalent to one of 20 g. The group of seven queens (Table 13.1) had a combined weight of 55.9 g, far more than any single queen could attain. Thus a nest with multiple queens can grow larger than a nest with only one queen. Large nest populations are presumably advantageous, since this species has many adaptations that enable it to maintain populous nests. Thus, even if the queens are unrelated, it could be of advantage to each of them (in terms of maximizing their reproductive potential) to collaborate in maintaining a successful large colony. If the queens are sisters (see above) they also have a genetic stake in each other's progeny.

The members of a group of multiple queens are usually alike in colour and size. They are significantly closer in weight to other members of their group than would be expected by chance (tested by model II analysis of variance, which for double queens has F $(48,49) = 11.74**$ $p \ll 0.01$ and for multiple queens has F $(22,56) = 29.26**$ $p \ll 0.01$). The weights of double queens from all nests are linearly related, with the weight of the smaller queen averaging 82% of the weight of the larger queen, with 95% confidence limits of 81–83% (Fig. 13.4). The relationships between the weights of queens in multiple groups are shown schematically in Figure 13.5. In cases where one member is much lighter, she is sometimes clearly defective in some way, being shrunken or deformed.

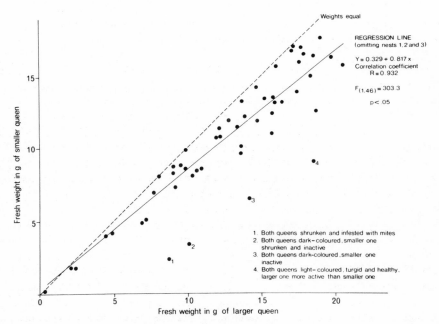

FIG. 13.4. Graph of fresh weight of smaller queen against fresh weight of larger queen, from nests with two queens.

On only two occasions were multiple queens ever found which appeared to differ in age. In one case, a young partially physogastric queen was found sharing the royal cell with a shrivelled, dark-coloured, moribund old queen (R. Sieber, pers. comm.). The second case is discussed in the next paragraph.

One single case has been observed which may represent a stage in the complete replacement of functional primary reproductives. A king and two fully physogastric queens (16.0 g and 13.2 g fresh weight) were together in a

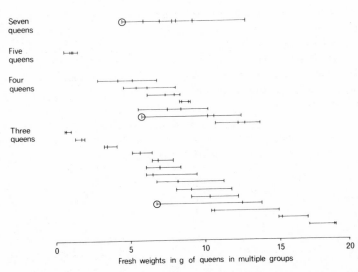

Fig. 13.5. Variations in fresh weight between queens in multiple groups. Vertical bars represent fresh weight of one queen, ringed if queen is obviously defective; horizontal lines connect members of a group.

large, well-built royal cell. Below the floor, but in the same massive block of soil, was a second, tiny but recognizable royal cell containing a young king and queen (2.0 g fresh weight). The primary reproductives were in good condition and the nest healthy, so an attempt to rear replacements seems premature.

The paucity of these observations (a mere three cases of probable replacement out of about 90 observations of multiple reproductives) indicates that the production of replacement reproductives while the primary reproductives are still alive is a rare event. Co-habitation of the old and new reproductives is also transient, and only a very small proportion of the observed cases of multiple reproductives can confidently be explained in this way. There is no evidence for the production of stable multiple associations by the addition of young reproductives to existing ones, though in the case of kings this might be difficult to detect.

13.4 DISCUSSION

The observations detailed above indicate that in *Macrotermes michaelseni* multiple reproductives may cohabit in stable and prolonged associations. These associations commonly arise as founder groups or as replacements for dead founders. Occasionally multiple groups are formed by transient additions of young to older reproductives.

The only previous systematic observations on multiple reproductives are those of Thorne (1982a, b) on *Nasutitermes* spp. in Panama. She found that 34.3% of the nests of *N. corniger* had multiple queens (between 2 and 22 per nest) and that these queens were usually very similar in weight. Multiple queens usually occurred in young colonies and were never found in very large nests, although some associations of queens were thought to have persisted for years. The eventual transition to monogyny in this species differs from the apparently stable polygyny observed in *M. michaelseni*.

Thorne (1982a, b) deduced that in *Nasutitermes*, multiple queens commonly arose as founders, as replacements, or during colony budding. She also observed a phase of "king replacement" in which a number of functional "king candidates" were temporarily present. This could be analogous to the occasional replacement of kings suggested for *M. michaelseni*.

Thorne and Noirot (1982) also reported the appearance of non-functional ergatoid reproductives in one nest of *Nasutitermes corniger* from which the primary reproductives had been removed. This has never been observed in any of the many orphaned nest of *M. michaelseni* that have been studied.

Thorne (1982a, b) suggested that polygynous nests of *N. corniger* may (1) grow faster in their vulnerable early stages, and (2) have a lower age of first reproduction, than do monogynous conspecific nests. In *M. michaelseni* the first suggestion is dubious, since it is apparently not the queen's ability to increase in size and in egg-laying rate that regulates population growth, as is shown by the extremely rapid growth of replacement queens (above, and also Sieber & Darlington, 1982). Population growth may be governed by a feedback from the workers' success in provisioning, which in turn might be affected by the availability of food, among other external factors. Thus a polygynous nest may grow no faster than a monogynous one in its early stages. For the same reason, the second suggestion is also dubious.

The main advantage to *M. michaelseni* of having multiple reproductives would appear to be as insurance against the death of the reproductives (as in *Nasutitermes*) and as a means of increasing the population of the mature nest (unlike *Nasutitermes*).

13.5 SUMMARY

Multiple primary reproductives occur in about a quarter of all nests. Multiple queens are four to five times as common as multiple kings.

Multiple reproductives may arise as nest founders, or as replacement reproductives reared from nymphs or alates in the nest after the death of the founders. Occasionally replacements are reared while the primary reproductives are still alive.

The weight of a king is not related to his conjugal status. Queens occurring together as multiples appear to be of the same age and are usually similar in weight. The weight of an individual queen is inversely related to the number of queens present but the summed weight of multiple queens is positively related to the number of queens present.

13.6 ACKNOWLEDGEMENTS

The observations presented here were made in the course of a project on the ecological role of termites in semi-arid grassland, sponsored by the United Nations Development Programme and the United Nations Environment Programme.

For collaboration in field work I am most grateful to Dr O. H. Bruinsma and Dr R. Sieber. Dr R. D. Dransfield has very kindly advised and assisted me with statistical analyses.

13.7 REFERENCES

Coaton W. G. H. (1949) Queen removal in termite control. *Fmg. S. Afr.* **24**, 335–338.

Grassé P. P. & Noirot C. (1951) La sociotomie: Migration et fragmentation de la termitiere chez les *Anoplotermes* et les *Trinervitermes*. *Behaviour* **3**, 146–166.

Lepage M. G. (1981) L'impact des populations récoltantes de *Macrotermes michaelseni* (Sjöstedt) (Isoptera, Macrotermitinae) dans un écosystème semi-arid (Kajiado, Kenya). 2. La nourriture récoltée, comparaison avec les grands herbivores. *Insectes Sociaux* **28**, 309–319.

Noirot C. (1956) Les sexués de remplacement chez les termites supérieurs (Termitidae). *Insectes Sociaux* **3**, 154–158.

Nutting W. L. (1969) Flight and colony foundation. In *Biology of Termites*, Vol. 1 (Krishna K. & Weesner F. M., eds), pp. 233–282. Academic Press, London and New York.

Roonwal M. L. & Gupta S. D. (1952) An unusual royal chamber with two kings and two queens in the Indian mound-building termite, *Odontotermes obesus* (Rambur) (Isoptera: Family Termitidae). *J. Bombay nat. Hist. Soc.* **51**, 293–294.

Sieber R. & Darlington J. P. E. C. (1982) Replacement of the royal pair in *Macrotermes michaelseni*. *Insect Sci. Application* **3**, 39–42.

Thorne B. L. (1982a) Polygyny in termites; multiple primary queens in colonies of *Nasutitermes corniger* (Motschulsky) (Isoptera: Termitidae). *Insectes Sociaux* **29**, 102–117.

Thorne B. L. (1982b) Multiple primary queens in termites: phyletic distribution, ecological context, and comparison to polygyny in Hymenoptera. In *The Biology of Social Insects* (Breed M. D., Michener C. D. & Evans H. E., eds). *Proc. 9th Int. Congr. I.U.S.S.I., Boulder, Colorado*, 206–211.

Thorne B. L. & Noirot C. (1982) Ergatoid reproductives in *Nasutitermes corniger* (Motschulsky) (Isoptera: Termitidae). *Int. J. Insect Morphol. and Embryol.* **11**, 213–226.

CHAPTER 14

Replacement of Reproductives in Macrotermitinae (Isoptera, Termitidae)

R. SIEBER*

The International Centre of Insect Physiology and Ecology, P.O. Box 30772, Nairobi, Kenya

CONTENTS

14.1 INTRODUCTION

14.1.1 Replacement reproductives in the family Termitidae

After the death of one or both primary reproductives, a termite colony can only survive if replacement reproductives develop to undertake production

* Present address: Sandoz Ltd, Pharmaceutical Research, CH-4002 Basle, Switzerland.

and fertilization of eggs. In the higher termites of the family Termitidae, three different types of replacement reproductives have been found. Due to their origin they were classified as adultoids, derived from alates which reached sexual maturity in the parental nest; nymphoids, derived from nymphs which had not yet developed to alates; and ergatoids, derived from workers after additional moults (Noirot, 1956, 1969).

14.1.2 Replacement reproductives in the sub-family Macrotermitinae

In the sub-family of the fungus-growing Macrotermitinae only adultoid replacement reproductives have been found. Harms (1927), and Mukerji & Mitra (1949) described one pair of replacement reproductives in *Macrotermes gilvus* (Hagen) and in *Odontotermes redemanni* (Wasmann). Coaton (1949) found most of the removed reproductives of *Macrotermes natalensis* (Haviland), *Odontotermes badius* (Haviland) and *Odontotermes latericius* (Haviland) replaced after a period of 3–5 years and Roy-Noël (1974) found replacement reproductives in *Macrotermes bellicosus* (Smeathman) between 7 months and 7 years after the removal of the primary reproductives.

Although Coaton (1949) stated that replacement of the reproductives was only possible when nymphs or alates were present in the mound at the time of the removal, there was previously no experimental confirmation. On the contrary, Bordereau (1975) found unseasonal development of nymphs after the removal of the primary reproductives of *M. bellicosus*. He concluded that the development of the nymphs was induced by the removal of royal inhibition and that those nymphs could give rise to replacement reproductives.

Replacement reproductives of the adultoid type have also been found in *Macrotermes michaelseni* (Sjöstedt) (Sieber & Darlington, 1982). However, in this species replaced reproductives were only found if nymphs or alates were present in the nest at the time the primary reproductives were removed. Unseasonal broods of nymphs were not observed after the removal of king and queen. Even if this had happened, it is unlikely that the colony could have survived. Development of nymphs takes about 7 months, whereas a nest without reproductives declines after 3 months and collapses before the final moult of the nymphs (Sieber & Darlington, 1982). In any species in which the developmental time of the alates is longer than the period of survival of the colony after the death of the reproductives, replacement is probably only possible if nymphs or alates are present in this colony at the time the primary reproductives die.

14.1.3 Replacement of king or queen

All experiments performed so far have involved removal of both reproductives to determine the replacement rate. However, in a few colonies a young queen not yet fully physogastric was found beside a weak queen in *M. natalensis*, *O. badius* and *O. latericius* (Coaton, 1949) and in *M. michaelseni* (Sieber & Darlington, 1982). It was therefore assumed that only the queen but not the king was replaced. However, since the replacement of corresponding kings has never been investigated up to now it is not known whether they may also be replaced. Sieber and Leuthold (1982) found that a physogastric queen could only lay fertile eggs for a short period of about 13 days after the removal of the king. A colony would therefore not survive the death of the king unless a new king from an alate would replace the old one. Experiments were devised to test whether a removed king would be replaced in the cases where alates were in the mound at the time the primary king was removed.

The results presented in this paper compare the replacement rate of a removed royal pair in *M. michaelseni* with the results of experiments where only the king was removed. In addition, possible regulation mechanisms which act during replacement of the reproductives are discussed.

14.2 MATERIALS AND METHODS

All experiments were performed on medium-sized mature mounds of *M. michaelseni* at Kajiado, 50 km south of Nairobi. Mounds were opened with pick and shovel and the royal cell located and removed. It was either put back in the same place as a control; opened carefully with a knife to remove the king and subsequently put back; or not put back. Mounds were then carefully closed to prevent predation. Experimental mounds were reopened after different periods and the instars found were recorded.

14.3 RESULTS

14.3.1 Replacement of the royal couple after removing the royal cell

Whenever a royal cell was removed, opened and subsequently put back into the nest, the reproductives survived. This shows that interference with the mound did not influence the results.

Out of 64 nests from which the royal cell was removed at various times of year, five had produced replacement reproductives after 218–350 days (Table

14.1). Only 54 of these nests had nymphs or alates at the time the royal cell was removed and thus had the potential to replace their primary reproductives. The actual replacement rate observed was therefore 9.2% (Sieber & Darlington, 1982). Nests which did not produce replacements continued to rear the eggs and juveniles that were in the nest. After about 100 days without primary reproductives no larvae were left, although workers and soldiers were still numerous. After about 170 days there were no live termites left.

TABLE 14.1. REPLACEMENT OF THE ROYAL COUPLE IN *M. MICHAELSENI* AFTER REMOVING THE ROYAL CELL AT DIFFERENT TIMES OF THE YEAR

Time of removal	Number of nests from which royal cells were removed	Number of these nests with:		Number of nests with replacement reproductives
		nymphs	alates	
November	24	—	4*	2
January	8	1	4**	—
March	8	1	—	1
May	8	8	—	—
July	8	8	—	2
September	8	1	—*	—
Total	64	19		5

* Alates were probably present in all mounds.
**Alates were not seen, but flight holes after a slight shower indicated their presence.

In two cases, however, dead alates were found in the ventilation system of the mound. Possibly these alates, having been reared to maturity by the last surviving workers, were unable to leave the mounds when the rains started, because the workers which normally build the flight holes had already died.

In three cases the replaced royal cell contained one king and queen and in two cases, two queens and one king were found. These were not the same number of queens and kings which had originally been removed from the particular nests and no statistical difference could be found between the total number of reproductives removed and the number of replacement reproductives.

14.3.2 Removal of the king

Because of the results obtained by removing both primary reproductives, kings were only removed in November and December before the rains, when alates were expected to be in the mound. Although alates were seen in five of the 18 mounds only, it is probable that in the other nests alates had fled into passages outside the hive when the mounds were opened (Sieber & Darlington, 1982).

Groups of four or five mounds were re-opened between 50 and 84 days after the removal of the king. In no case was a replacement king found with the queen. Table 14.2 shows that between 50 and 77 days after the removal of the king the queens became weak and finally died. In cases where queens were found to be weak, distinctly fewer workers were found in the royal cell than in a cell were the queen still looked healthy, or in a control colony with a healthy royal pair.

TABLE 14.2. INFLUENCE OF EXPERIMENTAL REMOVAL OF THE KING
ON THE REMAINING QUEEN

Number of colonies from which the king was removed	Interval up to control (days after removal)	Condition of the queen (number)	Condition of the royal cell (number)
5	50	healthy (5)	intact (5)
4	62	healthy (1) weak, shrivelled (2), dead (1)	intact (1) with big holes (2) partially destroyed (1)
5	77	not found	not found
4	84	not found	not found

14.4 DISCUSSION

14.4.1 Immortality of a Macrotermitinae colony

As a result of the findings that removed primary reproductives of *M. natalensis*, *O. badius* and *O. latericius* may be replaced, Coaton (1949) suggested that termite colonies of the sub-family Macrotermitinae are potentially immortal. Roy-Noël (1974) concluded that the seven out of 12 dead colonies of *M. bellicosus* found at different times after the removal of the primary reproductives had died because of drought or as a consequence of damage to the mound, rather than lack of replacement reproductives. However, mature colonies found after 7 years could also be new foundations in old mounds because Collins (1981) found in this species maximum populations in 4–6-year-old colonies.

Observations of *M. michaelseni* colonies after removing the reproductives show that replacement of the reproductives is not universal. The presence of nymphs or alates at the time the reproductives die seems to be a prerequisite for the replacement of the reproductives in this species. Even when this prerequisite is fulfilled, a replacement rate of less than 10% is distinctly lower than the replacement rates found in other species of the same sub-family. A higher rate of 31.2% was found when the primary reproductives died in the mound instead of being removed (Sieber & Darlington, 1982). Probably the replacement rate will be affected by climatic fluctuations and other factors. However, these results clearly show that not all the colonies of *M. michaelseni* which have the potential to replace dead or removed reproductives actually do so.

14.4.2 Replacement of the king

In this experiment kings were not replaced despite the presence of alates in the colonies at the time the primary kings were removed. The remaining queen laid fertile eggs for only a short period of about 13 days (Sieber & Leuthold, 1982). Subsequently, the physogastric queen was progressively abandoned by the workers and all these queens died between 50 and 77 days after the removal of the king. Although the limited number of 18 experimental colonies does not exclude the possibility of the replacement of the male, it seems that in *M. michaelseni* a dead male induces death of the queen and by that, either death of the colony or the development of a replacement royal pair.

14.4.3 Regulation mechanisms during replacement

It is generally assumed that a healthy queen releases an inhibitory pheromone which prevents the acceptance of new reproductives, as has been demonstrated in lower termites (Lüscher, 1974). In *M. bellicosus* such a pheromone was even postulated to suppress unseasonal nymph production, because Bordereau (1975) found unseasonal nymphs after removal of the reproductives. This would also imply that a large number of replacement reproductives would be produced under such conditions and in fact Coaton (1949) found a higher number of replacement reproductives than the original primary reproductives. However, in *M. michaelseni* removal of the primary reproductives did not induce unseasonal nymph production and the number of replaced reproductives was not higher than of the primary ones. The present results might even point to another regulation mechanism in *M. michaelseni*. The incubation period of an egg of *M. michaelseni* is about 28 days (Darlington, 1982) and a physogastric queen is able to lay fertile eggs in the absence of the male for about 13 days (Sieber & Leuthold, 1982). Thus after about 41 days since the removal of the king no more first instar larvae hatch. At this time the queens without kings still looked healthy, but subsequently they were abandoned by the workers, became weak and died. Perhaps the workers abandon the queen although she is still laying eggs, once they detect that larvae are no longer hatching. This does not, however, rule out possible pheromone release by the queen, but points to some possible role of the workers.

14.5 SUMMARY

After removing the primary reproductives of *Macrotermes michaelseni* only about 10% of the colonies which had nymphs or alates at the time of the removal produced replacement reproductives. Thus although replacement can occur, it does not do so in all possible cases. When only the king was removed from a nest, he was not replaced even when alates were present at the time. The remaining queen continued laying eggs, but she was only maintained by workers until the fertilized eggs had hatched. A possible role of the workers in the replacement process is discussed.

14.6 REFERENCES

Bordereau C. (1975) Déterminisme des castes chez les termites supérieurs: mise en évidence d'un contrôle royal dans la formation de la caste sexuée chez *Macrotermes bellicosus* (Smeathman) (Isoptera, Termitidae). *Insectes Sociaux* **22**, 363–374.
Coaton W. G. H. (1949) Queen removal in termite control. *Farming S. Afr.* **24**, 335–338.
Collins N. M. (1981) Populations, age structure and survivorship of colonies of *Macrotermes bellicosus*.(Isoptera: Macrotermitinae). *J. Anim. Ecol.* **50**, 293–311.
Darlington J. P. E. C. (1982) Population dynamics in an African fungus-growing termite. *Proc. IXth Congr. IUSSI, Boulder*, pp. 54–58.
Harms J. W. (1927) Koloniengründung bei *Macrotermes gilvus* Hag. *Zool. Anz.* **74**, 221–236.
Lüscher M. (1974) Kasten und Kastendifferenzierung bei niederen Termiten. In *Sozialpolymorphismus bei Insekten* (ed. Schmidt G. H.), pp. 694–739. Wissenschaftliche Verlagsgesellschaft, Stuttgart.
Mukerji D. & Mitra K. (1949) Ecology of the mound building termite, *Odontotermes redemanni* (Wasmann) in relation to measures of control. *Proc. Zool. Soc. Bengal.* **2**, 9–27.
Noirot C. (1956) Les sexués de replacement chez les termites supérieurs (Termitidae). *Insectes Sociaux* **3**, 145–158.
Noirot C. (1969) Formation of castes in the higher termites. In *Biology of Termites* (eds Krishna K. & Weesner F.), Vol. 1, pp. 311–350. Academic Press, New York.
Roy-Noël J. (1974) Contribution à la connaissance des reproducteurs de remplacement chez les Termites supérieurs: observations sur *Bellicositermes natalensis* (Macrotermitinae). *C.r. hebd. Séanc. Acad. Sci. Paris* **278**, 481–483.
Sieber R. & Darlington J. P. E. C. (1982) Replacement of the royal pair in *Macrotermes michaelseni*. *Insect Sci. Applications* **3**, 39–42.
Sieber R. & Leuthold R. H. (1982) Repeated copulation and testes enlargement in *Macrotermes michaelseni*. *Physiol. Entomol.* **7**, 457–465.

CHAPTER 15

Some Observations on the Initiation and Regulation of Castes in Nests of the Termite Macrotermes michaelseni in the Field

J. P. E. C. DARLINGTON*

International Centre of Insect Physiology and Ecology, P.O. Box 30772, Nairobi, Kenya

CONTENTS

15.1 INTRODUCTION

A detailed study has been made of the population dynamics of the termite *Macrotermes michaelseni* (Sjöstedt) in semi-arid grassland at Kajiado, Kenya (Darlington, 1982a). From the large body of observations and data obtained, some deductions can be made about the regulation of caste frequencies and the initiation of alate production in intact or damaged nests in the field. These findings were generally incidental to other measurements and are therefore not very systematic. They do however enable some comparisons to be made with the results of laboratory studies on the same species carried out by the Termite Physiology Section at the International Centre of Insect Physiology and Ecology (ICIPE) (e.g. Okot-Kotber, Chapter 7; Sieber, Chapter 14).

*Present address: Section of Entomology, National Museums of Kenya, P.O. Box 40658, Nairobi.

15.2 METHODS

Nests were sampled by initial fumigation with methyl bromide gas. After de-gassing overnight, the whole nest contents were removed. The termites were separated out by floatation in water to give an aqueous sludge. Total numbers were estimated from replicated counts of small sub-samples of the sludge. Fumigation was found to be essential in this species. For nests dug alive, the total populations were underestimated by as much as an order of magnitude, and caste and instar ratios were grossly disturbed in ways that depended mainly on the time taken to dig out the nest, which means that they were affected by nest size (Darlington, 1984).

For intact nests, the results obtained by this standard sampling technique are extremely consistent. However, the method does not sample the whole nest population, but only that part of it which is inside the nest at the time of fumigation. A large number of adult termites is always outside the nest, in the network of underground passages which connects the nest to its foraging territory (Darlington, 1982b). The effect of this on the observed nest population will be discussed below.

15.3 RESULTS

15.3.1 Composition of the sterile population

The development sequence of worker castes consists of three larval instars in both sexes. All male sterile larvae develop into major workers. Most female sterile larvae develop into minor workers, but a small proportion undergo one extra moult to a minor presoldier and then to a minor soldier, or two extra moults to a fourth instar larva, then a major presoldier, then a major soldier (Okot-Kotber, 1981).

The mean percentage composition of the larval population in a mature nest is shown in Figure 15.1A. First and second instar larvae of the two sexes are counted together, but third instar larvae are separated. Mortality during larval life is extremely low (Darlington, 1982a). Development to the worker takes longer in male than in female larvae, but the last instar is of approximately the same duration. Thus the nearly equal numbers of male and female third instar larvae indicate that steriles are produced with a sex ratio of male:female = 1:1.

The mean percentage composition of sterile adults in a mature nest is shown in Figure 15.1B. The apparent sex ratio in adults is approximately male:female = 1:2. The difference between this and the 1:1 sex ratio produced is mainly caused by the presence of large numbers of major workers (the

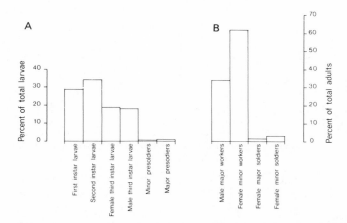

FIG. 15.1. Composition of the sterile population of a mature nest of *Macrotermes michaelseni*: A. Percentage of each larval instar in the total larval population; B. Percentage of each adult caste in the total adult population.

foraging caste) outside the nest. There is also mortality from predation on the foragers, but the work of Lepage (1981) and G. H. N. Nyamasyo (pers. comm.) indicates that this is quite small. Offtake by the dominant predator, the ant *Megaponera foetens* (F.), is equal to approximately 2% of total termite production.

The percentages of the first three larval instars vary little with nest size or with season, indicating a steady throughput from eggs to adult workers. For soldier production, however, the situation is different. The counts of presoldier are always relatively low, and the confidence limits on estimates of their total numbers are therefore relatively wide. Nevertheless, there does seem to be a very large variation in the numbers of presoldiers. The coefficients of variation for major and minor presoldiers are 54.9% and 58.9%, compared with 24.1% and 28.9% for the third instar male and female larvae that precede the two worker castes. Thus it seems that new soldiers are produced in bursts, not at a steady rate, as the workers are. Bursts in the production of minor presoldiers do not necessarily correspond with bursts in the production of major presoldiers (Fig. 15.2). This may indicate that different mechanisms are involved in determining the two types of soldiers, but it could also result from the time lag introduced by the extra moult and the much greater size increase involved in producing the major presoldier. There is no synchrony between nests in the occurrence of presoldier bursts, indicating that the mechanism of determination is endogenous.

The percentage of major presoldiers in the larval population is shown plotted against total larval population in Figure 15.3 and similarly the

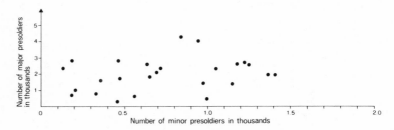

Fig. 15.2.   Graph of numbers of major presoldiers against numbers of minor presoldiers in mature nests of *Macrotermes michaelseni*.

percentage of minor presoldiers in Figure 15.4. In both cases there is no apparent trend in soldier production with nest size, but the variability seems to be less in larger nests. In each figure, the point for one nest has been ringed. This nest had a large (but not exceptional) percentage of minor presoldiers, and an outstandingly large percentage of major presoldiers. These peculiarities may be explained by the discovery of several hundred head capsules of the soldier caste of *Hodotermes mossambicus* Hagen, the harvesting termite, walled up in the basement. It seems this nest was at war with a neighbouring nest of *Hodotermes*, involving heavy casualties on both sides. It is particularly interesting that the major soldiers were apparently being replaced at a much greater rate than the minor soldiers. *Hodotermes* soldiers are of similar size to the *Macrotermes* major soldiers, so conflict mortality may have fallen most heavily on them. If this difference is real, it again suggests that there is a different mechanism of determination for the two castes; but as before, one cannot rule out the possibility that a peak in production of minor soldiers had already passed. It is also interesting to note that the proportion of larvae in this nest was exceptionally low, 35% of the total population compared with 52–62% usually found in nests of this small size, although the instar ratios were normal. Apparently, the resources necessary to produce large numbers of extra replacement soldiers were obtained by cutting back on worker production. This is the only nest where this has been observed.

The cause of the conflict might be competition for resources since both species are grass feeders. The implications are interesting, since the two species have overlapping distributions in Kajiado District. Perhaps the large, polycalic nests of the *Hodotermes* enable them to exploit gaps between the permanent foraging territories of the *Macrotermes* nests. Each species may be to some extent limiting the population of the other by competitive exclusion.

A series of mature nests sampled at approximately monthly intervals over 2 years showed no seasonal changes in caste ratios or production. The only changes observed were during the 1976 drought when the proportion of larvae

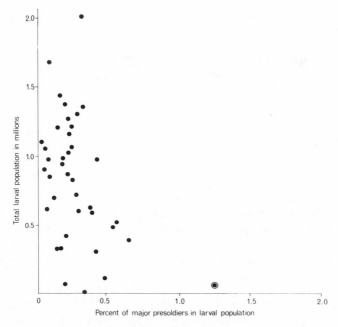

Fɪɢ. 15.3. Percentage of major presoldiers in the larval population plotted against total number of larvae, in nests of *Macrotermes michaelseni*.

in the population declined gradually over 4–5 months from an average of 45% to about 35%. During the same period the soldier replacement rate dropped to a very low level. After the drought ended, the proportion of presoldier in the larval population recovered; in the case of minor presoldiers, indeed, there appeared to be a temporary over-production (Fig. 15.5). No change could be detected in adult caste ratios over the same period.

There are two possible explanations for the observed drop in soldier replacement during the drought. Perhaps a nest under stress of food shortage cannot afford to produce soldiers, which are consumers and not providers. Alternatively, perhaps the drought conditions had so reduced the populations of the predators that no replacements were needed.

The observations on soldier production described above can be explained in terms of a feedback mechanism from soldier numbers, though other possible explanations are also offered. A relationship between numbers of soldiers and of presoldiers could not be demonstrated in the data, but this may be because only the numbers of soldiers inside the nest are known; the shortfall may be in the soldiers which accompany the foragers, upon whom predator pressure is greatest. Such an explanation seems probable, since feedback mechanisms of

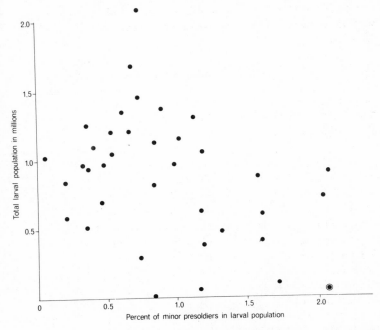

FIG. 15.4. Percentage of minor presoldiers in the larval population plotted against total number of larvae, in nests of the *Macrotermes michaelseni*.

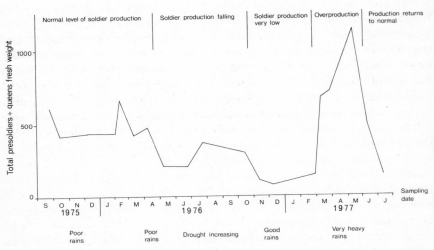

FIG. 15.5. Graph of total numbers of minor presoldiers in mature nest populations divided by queen's fresh weight, plotted against sampling date.

this sort have been demonstrated in laboratory studies on incipient colonies (G. Bühlmann, pers. comm., Okot-Kotber, Chapter 7).

15.3.2 Production of alates

A single large brood of nymphs is produced each year. It is apparently initiated during the long rains (April–May), develops through the long dry season, and is ready to fly in the short rains (November–December). There is often a wide spread of sizes and nymphal instars in the brood, indicating either that there is great variation in growth rates, or that development is initiated over quite a long period. Nymphal broods in adjacent nests can be out of step by up to about 1 month. There is some indication that development may be held back in the last nymphal instar, until the first shower of the short rains triggers the final moult to the alate. This would enable nymphal broods in different nests to synchronize the last stage in their development, so that all the alates are ready to fly at the same time.

In addition to the main nymphal brood, small unseasonal broods of up to a few hundred nymphs may appear in the nest in March or April, before the long rains. These may be initiated by unseasonal showers after the end of the short rains in December or January. Certainly they seemed to be much more common in years when such showers were frequent. Usually these unseasonal broods disappeared after the main brood was initiated in April. However, in years of particularly frequent and erratic rainfall, when the two rainy seasons were hard to distinguish, some nests apparently became confused and not only reared both unseasonal and seasonal broods to maturity, but in a few cases initiated their main brood too early, so that they flew in June instead of November. In dry years, if the short rains were inadequate to trigger flight, the alates remained in the nest up to the beginning of the long rains when they finally flew. This situation seems to be incompatible with the production of unseasonal broods, since any shower large enough to initiate an unseasonal brood would probably be large enough to trigger the flight of the alates still in the nest, whose threshold for flight stimulation becomes lower as time goes on.

The short rains of 1981 were succeeded by a long dry spell with no showers. On 14 February 1982 a heavy shower (22.6 mm) fell over a part of the study area. No further rain fell until the start of the long rains in April. In the same month it was found that a full brood of nymphs had appeared in nests in the area where the shower had fallen, and they were at a stage of development normally reached in about June. Thus, for the first time it was possible to put an exact date to the initiating stimulus, and to be reasonably confident of its nature. The suggestion that the chemical composition of newly sprouting grass might be the stimulus can now be discarded, since this solitary shower did not result in new growth of grass except in valley bottoms and drainage hollows.

Furthermore, the production of the full brood is not the cumulative result of repeated stimuli, for although a single shower initiated this brood, the same wide spread of nymphal instars was observed as in other years. The two-month gap between the triggering shower and the discovery of second, third and fourth instar nymphs in the nests, was just sufficient for them to have been determined at the time the eggs were laid, so that the queen may play some part in initiating the nymphal brood. Where repeated stimuli were involved it had never been possible to be sure if some cumulative effect might have acted at a later stage in development.

Some experiments were carried out in which the primary reproductives were removed and the nest re-opened after an interval. This was done at varying times of year, both when nymphs or alates were present and when they were not. Altogether 79 nests were treated in this way. On no occasion did a brood of nymphs appear which could have been initiated by, or after, the removal of the primary reproductives. This contrasts with the observations of Bordereau (1965) on *M. bellicosus* in West Africa, which he interpreted as showing that the presence of the primary reproductives inhibited the initiation of nymphs. In *M. michaelseni* the presence of primary reproductives does, however, seem to inhibit the development of replacement reproductives from nymphs or alates already present in the nest (Sieber & Darlington, 1982; Darlington, Chapter 13).

15.4 SUMMARY

Observations on intact field colonies showed that there are no seasonal cycles in the production of the sterile castes. Caste ratios in adults and instar ratios in larvae are constant over time and in nests of different sizes. The proportion of larvae in the population, however, is greater in small, growing nests than in full-sized, mature, stable nests.

Workers are produced at a steady rate, but the much less numerous soldiers are produced in bursts. During a prolonged drought the proportion of larvae in mature nests declined, but the replacement rate of soldiers decreased disproportionately. A young nest apparently at war with a colony of *Hodotermes* produced exceptionally large numbers of replacement soldiers but had less than the expected number of other larval instars. A feedback mechanism, of the sort independently observed in the laboratory, would explain most of these observations, but cannot be conclusively proved from the evidence available.

The main brood of reproductives can be initiated by a single rain shower. Once started, the production of nymphs seems to continue for several weeks without any further external stimulus.

15.5 ACKNOWLEDGEMENTS

The observations referred to in this paper were made in the course of a project on the ecological role of termites in semi-arid grassland, sponsored by the United Nations Development Programme and the United Nations Environment Programme.

15.6 REFERENCES

Bordereau C. (1965) Déterminisme des castes chez les termites supérieurs; mise en évidence d'un contrôle royal dans la formation de la caste sexuée chez *Macrotermes bellicosus* Smeathman (Isoptera: Termitidae). *Insects Sociaux* **22**, 363–374.

Darlington J. P. E. C. (1982a) Population dynamics in an African fungus-growing termite. In *The Biology of Social insects*, Proc. Ninth Int. Congr. IUSSI, Boulder, Colorado (eds Breed M. D., Michener C. D. & Evans H. E.), pp. 54–58. Westview Press, Boulder, Co. USA.

Darlington J. P. E. C. (1982b) Underground passages and storage pits used in foraging by a nest of the termite *Macrotermes michaelseni* in Kajiado, Kenya. *J. Zool.*, Lond. **198**, 237–247.

Darlington J. P. E. C. (1984) A method for sampling the populations of large termite nests. *Ann. Appl. Biol.* **104**, 427–436.

Lepage M. G. (1981a) Etude de la prédation de *Megaponera feotens* (F.) sur les populations récoltantes de Macrotermitinae dans un écosystème semi-aride (Kajiado–Kenya). *Insectes Sociaux* **28**, 247–262.

Lepage M. G. (1981b) L'impacte des populations récoltantes de *Macrotermes michaelseni* (Sjöstedt) (Isoptera: Macrotermitinae) dans un écosystème semi-aride (Kajiado–Kenya) I. L'activité de récolte et son déterminisme. *Insectes Sociaux* **28**, 297–308.

Okot-Kotber B. M. (1981) Instars and polymorphism of castes in *Macrotermes michaelseni* (Isoptera: macrotermitinae). *Insectes Sociaux* **28**, 233–246.

Okot-Kotber B. M. (1983) Influence of group size and composition on soldier differentiation in female final larval instars of a higher termite. *Macrotermes michaelseni*. *Physiol. Entomol.* **8**, 41–47.

Sieber R. & Darlington J. P. E. C. (1982) Replacement of the royal pair in *Macrotermes michaelseni*. *Insect Sci. Application* **3**, 39–42.

Section D

Hormones and Caste Determination

CHAPTER 16

The Role of Pheromones in Termite Caste Differentiation

CHRISTIAN BORDEREAU

E.R.A., C.N.R.S. 231, Université de Dijon, Laboratoire de Zoologie, 6 Boulevard Gabriel, 21100 Dijon, France

CONTENTS

16.1 INTRODUCTION

Termite polymorphism appears to be a complication of post-embryonic development processes observed in non-social insects; the environmental, nutritional and neurohormonal individual factors are of major importance. However, the harmonious development of the colony involves a social regulation which is, at least in part, ensured by chemical communication and especially by the distribution of pheromones. The first evidence of social pheromones was obtained in termites (Pickens, 1932; Castle, 1934; Light, 1944; Lüscher, 1955); and Lüscher with others coined the term "pheromone" (Karlson & Butenandt, 1959; Karlson & Lüscher, 1959). According to Wilson & Bossert's terminology (1963), the social pheromones or caste pheromones which induce changes in morphogenesis are called *primer pheromones*.

Several investigations have shown that the production of one caste can be stimulated by another caste. For example, soldier production is stimulated by the reproductives in *Kalotermes flavicollis* (Springhetti, 1970) and in *Prorhino-*

termes simplex (Miller, 1942). In *Reticulitermes lucifugus*, soldier production increases when pseudergates are reared with nymphs (Lenz, 1976). Likewise, soldiers would stimulate the production of the supplementary reproductives in *K. flavicollis* (Springhetti, 1970). An exceptional case has been reported in *Mastotermes darwiniensis* where the supplementary reproductives production would be stimulated by the neotenic reproductives themselves (Watson *et al.*, 1975; Watson & Sewell, Chapter 3).

All these examples show that stimulation certainly occurs in termite caste regulation. However, it is necessary to extend the above studies by investigating the nature of these stimulatory mechanisms, since no data has been furnished supporting the hypothesis of a pheromonal stimulation (Lüscher, 1975).

16.2   REPRODUCTIVE INHIBITION

Very little information is available, but some observations seem to show a royal-pair control. In the lower termites, *Kalotermes* and *Zootermopsis*, evidence suggests that the appearance of nymphs in the alate line may be inhibited by the presence of primary reproductives (Grassé & Noirot, 1957; Springhetti, 1971; Lüscher, 1973). In the higher termite, *Macrotermes bellicosus*, the removal of the royal pair induces the appearance of nymphs (Bordereau, 1975). The nature of this control on the alate production remains unknown.

Data are more available on the differentiation of the supplementary reproductives. Since 1893, Grassi and Sandias have shown that the royal pair of *K. flavicollis* exerts a strict inhibition on the other members of the colony preventing their transformation into supplementary reproductives. The inhibition has been observed in many lower termites with different degrees of extent. In the higher termites, supplementary reproductives often appear in field colonies deprived of their royal pair. In *Astalotermes*, supplementary reproductives are formed in laboratory cultures containing only workers and alates (Noirot, 1956).

The nature of the inhibition exerted by the functional reproductives has been intensively investigated in the lower termites. In *Zootermopsis*, Light (1944) induced retardation in the formation of supplementary reproductives for 3 weeks with methanolic extracts of functional reproductive heads, but after 15 weeks, the percentages of neotenics formed were similar in both controls and experimental tests. So, the author could not affirm the presence of a pheromone. In *K. flavicollis*, Lüscher never obtained inhibition of neotenics with extracts of functional reproductives. From several ingenious experiments, Lüscher (1952a, b, 1955, 1956a, b, 1961, 1974, 1975) proposed the following scheme: two inhibitory pheromones are produced, one by the queen, the other by the king; they are transmitted to the other members of the colony *via* anus during proctodeal feeding. However, this is not the case of *Neotermes jouteli* (Nagin, 1972) nor in *Zootermopsis angusticollis* (Stuart, 1979; Greenberg & Stuart, 1980; Greenberg, 1980, 1982). In these two species, varnishing the anus does not suppress the inhibition, and faeces have no inhibitory effects. In *Z. angusticollis*, Greenberg obtained partial inhibition of neotenics with ethanolic washes of neotenic queens; so, the putative inhibitory substance could be transmitted by licking or grooming. In this context, it may be noted that in *K. flavicollis*, the partial varnishing of the abdominal pleural membrane (segments 4–9) reduces the inhibitory power of the reproductives (Lüscher, 1974). So, it would be certainly interesting to study the ultrastructure of the pleural membranes of the functional reproductives. In physogastric queens of many species of higher termites, cuticular differentiations are observed around the hairs of the abdominal pleural membranes; it may be assumed that they allow the passage of queen substances through the cuticle (Bordereau, unpub. data).

So, if the inhibition exerted by the reproductives is well established, then much complementary information and especially for the chemical composition of the putative inhibitory pheromones should be sought. Lüscher (1972) suggested that the pheromone of the reproductive might be juvenile hormone (JH) itself; this hypothesis recently has been adopted by Myles (1982). However, after experiments with juvenile hormone analogues (JHA), Lüscher (1975) reconsidered this hypothesis and suggested that it is more likely the pheromone of the reproductives is not the hormone itself, but stimulates corpora allata (CA) secretion.

16.3 SOLDIER INHIBITION

There is now good evidence for soldier inhibition. In incipient colonies of *Kalotermes* (Grassé, 1982), *Zootermopsis* (Castle, 1934) and *Reticulitermes* (Light and Weesner, 1955) there is for a long time only one soldier. If this soldier is removed, another appears soon after and the experiment can be repeated many times. The presence of a soldier prevents soldier transformation of the other members of the colony. This inhibition has also been shown in laboratory cultures in several species: *K. flavicollis* (Springhetti, 1969), *Neotermes jouteli* (Nagin, 1972), *Prorhinotermes simplex* (Miller, 1942), *Schedorhinotermes lamanianus* (Renoux, 1975) and *Nasutitermes lujae* (Lefeuve & Bordereau, 1981, 1982). (See also Okot-Kotber, Chapter 21, for *Macrotermes michaelseni*.)

In *N. lujae*, the soldiers develop from small workers of the first instar (Noirot, 1955). The production of soldiers was measured in two types of population. The first one was composed of only small workers, in this group, 30 days after the beginning of the experiment about 15% of soldiers were produced, and near 30% after 60 days; then, the soldier percentage remained almost stable. The second type of population contained initially 20% soldiers. In this group, soldier production was much lower and after 60 days, the two types of population were no longer different in their soldier proportions. The soldiers present in the cultures clearly slowed down the differentiation of more soldiers.

Concerning the nature of this inhibition exerted by the soldiers, only two cases have been studied. In *S. lamanianus*, Renoux (1975) has shown that soldier extracts in methylene chloride prevent or reduce the rate of soldier production. One component of the frontal gland secretion, the tetradecenone, would play the role of an inhibitory pheromone. However, this component increases the mortality in the cultures so that it is difficult to know whether the soldier inhibition is arising from a pheromonal inhibitory mechanism or from a phenomenon of toxicity. In *N. lujae* (Lefeuve & Bordereau, unpub. data) whole soldier extracts in methylene chloride clearly reduce the soldier production in cultures of small workers and in this case, the mortalities in controls and in experiments are not statistically different. Soldier inhibition of *N. lujae* is actually chemical in nature. As in *S. lamanianus*, the frontal gland is the source of the inhibitory pheromone.

The chemical nature of the soldier inhibition pheromone of *N. lujae* is not yet known. Considering that the soldier formation is JH dependent, it can be assumed that the soldier pheromone exerts an anti-JH action, but it is also possible that the soldier inhibition results from an inhibitory action on the prothoracic glands inducing a moult-retarding effect. The two possibilities are not incompatible since interactions between CA and prothoracic glands (PG) secretions are known.

The primer pheromones act through the neuroendocrine system, but we do not know whether they act directly after penetration in the body of the insect, or whether their action is relayed by specialized chemoreceptor sensillae. In *N. lujae*, olfaction is not involved in the transmission of the pheromone, extracts of whole soldiers or of frontal gland secretions are inhibitory only if they are in contact with the workers; in this case, if chemoreception is involved, it must be contact chemoreception.

16.4 CONCLUSION

Termite caste regulation involves a complex set of individual, social and environmental factors. Caste pheromones have certainly an important role in these mechanisms. However, more data must be obtained or confirmed. An important step will be realized with the chemical identification of the inhibitory pheromones. It will be then easier to study the mode of action of these primer pheromones on the neuroendocrine system.

16.5 SUMMARY

The role of pheromones in termite caste differentiation is reviewed. The pheromonal stimulation put forward for the reproductive and soldier production remains entirely hypothetical. Very likely in return, the inhibition exerted by the reproductives on the supplementary reproductive differentiation is pheromonal in nature. However, the chemical composition of these pheromones is not yet known. Also good evidence now exists for an inhibitory pheromone of soldier production. In *Nasutitermes lujae*, the rate of soldier production is reduced by organic extracts of soldier frontal glands. Olfaction is not involved in this phenomenon.

16.6 REFERENCES

Bordereau C. (1975) Déterminisme des castes chez les Termites supérieurs: mise en évidence d'un contrôle royal dans la formation de la caste sexuée chez *Macrotermes bellicosus* Smeathman (Isoptera, Termitidae). *Insectes Sociaux* **22**, 363–374.

Castle G. B. (1934) The damp-wood Termites of the western United States, genus *Zootermopsis* (formerly, Termopsis) in C. A. Kofoid *et al.*, *Termites and Termite Control*, 2nd rev. ed., pp. 273–310. Univ. of Calif. Press, Berkeley.

Grassé P.-P. (1982) *Termitologia. I; Anatomie, physiologie, reproduction des Termites* (ed. Masson), Paris, 676 pp.

Grassé P.-P. & Noirot C. (1957) La société de *Calotermes flavicollis* (Insecte Isoptère) de sa fondation au premier essaimage. *C.R. Acad. Sci.* Paris **246**, 1789–1795.

Grassi B. & Sandias A. (1893–1894) Costituzione e sviluppo della societa dei termitidi. *Atti Accad. Gioenia Sci. Nat. Catania* **6**, 1–75; **7**, 1–76.

Greenberg S. L. W. (1980) Pheromonal inhibition of neotenic reproductive development in a primitive termite. *Amer. Zool.* **20**, 905.

Greenberg S. L. W. (1982) Studies on neotenic reproductive development in a primitive termite. In *The Biology of Social Insects*, Proc. IXth Congr. IUSSI Boulder, Colorado (eds Breed, M. D., Michener, C. D. & Evans, H. E.), Westview Press, 420 pp.

Greenberg S. & Stuart A. M. (1980) Control of neotenic development in a primitive termite (Isoptera: Hodotermitidae). *J. N. Y. Entomol. Soc.* **88**, 49–50.

Karlson P. & Butenandt A. (1959) Pheromones (ectohormones) in insects. *Ann. Rev. Entomol.* **4**, 39–58.

Karlson P. & Lüscher M. (1959) "Pheromones": a new term for a class of biologically active substances. *Nature* **183**, 55–56.

Lefeuve P. & Bordereau C. (1981) Mise en évidence d'une phéromone inhibitrice de soldats chez *Nasutitermes lujae* (Isoptera: Termitidae). *Symp. Sect. Française IUSSI*, Toulouse, pp. 93–96.

Lefeuve P. & Bordereau C. (1982) Regulation of the production of soldiers in *Nasutitermes lujae*. Proc. IXth Congr. IUSSI, Boulder, Colorado.

Lenz M. (1976) The dependence of hormone effects in termite caste determination on external factors. In *Phase and Caste Determination in Insects* (ed. Lüscher M), pp. 73–89, Pergamon Press, Oxford and New York.

Light S. F. (1944) Experimental studies on ectohormonal control of the development of supplementary reproductives in the termite genus *Zootermopsis* (formerly *Termopsis*). *Univ. Calif. Publ. Zool.* **43**, 413–454.

Light S. F. & Weesner M. F. (1955) The production and replacement of soldiers in incipient colonies of *Reticulitermes hesperus* Banks. *Insectes Sociaux* **2**, 135–146.

Lüscher M. (1952a) Die Produktion and Elimination von Ersatzgeschlechstieren bei der Termite *Kalotermes flavicollis* (Fabr.) Z. *Vergl. Physiol.* **34**, 123–141.

Lüscher M. (1952b) New evidence for ectohormonal control of caste determination to termites. *Trans. Ninth Int. Congr. Ent., Amsterdam* **1**, 289–294.

Lüscher M. (1955) Zur Frage der Übertragung sozialer Wirkstoffe bei Termiten. *Naturwiss.* **42**, 186.

Lüscher M. (1956a) Die Entstehung vor Ersatzgeschlechstieren bei der Termite *Kalotermes flavicollis* (Fabr.). *Insectes Sociaux* **3**, 119–128.

Lüscher M. (1956b) Hemmende und fördernde Faktoren bei der Enstehung der Ersatzgeschlechstiere bei der Termite *Kalotermes flavicollis* (Fabr.). *Rev. Suisse Zool.* **63**, 261–267.

Lüscher M. (1961) Social control of polymorphism in Termites. In *Insect Polymorphism* (ed. Kennedy J. S.), pp. 57–67. Symp. R. Entomol. Soc. London.

Lüscher M. (1972) Environmental control of juvenile hormone (J.H.) Secretion and caste differentiation in Termites. *Gen. Comp. Endocrinol. Suppl.* **3**, 509–514.

Lüscher M. (1973) The influence of the composition of experimental groups on caste development in *Zootermopsis* (Isoptera). Proc. VII Congr. IUSSI, London, 253–256.

Lüscher M. (1974) Kasten und Kastendifferenzierung bei niederen Termiten. In *Sozialpolymorphismus bei Insekten* (ed. Schmidt G. H.), pp. 694–739. Wiss. Verlagsges, Stuttgart.

Lüscher M. (1975) Pheromones and polymorphism in bees and termites. In *Pheromones and Defensive Secretions in Social Insects* (eds Noirot Ch., Howse P. E. & Lemasne G.), pp. 123–141. Proc. Symp. IUSSI, Dijon.

Miller E. M. (1942) The problem of castes and caste differentiation in *Prorhinotermes simplex* Hagen. *Bull. Univ. Miami* **15**, 1–27.

Myles T. G. (1982) Pheromonal juvenile hormone polytiterism: the basis of termite polymorphism. Proc. IXth Congr. IUSSI, Boulder, Colorado.

Nagin R. (1972) Caste determination in *Neotermes jouteli* (Banks). *Insectes Sociaux* **19**, 39–61.

Noirot C. (1955) Recherches sur le polymorphisme des Termites supérieurs (Termitidae). *Ann. Sc. Nat. Zool.* **17**, 400–595.

Noirot C. (1956) Les sexués de remplacement chez les Termites supérieurs (Termitidae). *Insectes Sociaux* **3**, 145–158.

Pickens A. L. (1932) Observations on the genus *Reticulitermes* Holmgren. *Pan-Pacific Entomol.* **8**, 178–180.

Renoux J. (1975) Le polymorphisme de *Schedorhinotermes lamanianus* (Sjòstedt) (Isoptera-Rhinotermitidae). *Insectes Sociaux* **23**, 279–494.

Springhetti A. (1969) Influenza dei reali sulla differenziazione dei soldati di *Kalotermes flavicollis* Fabr. (Isoptera). Proc. VI Congr. IUSSI, Bern, 267–273.

Springhetti A. (1970) Influence of the king and the queen on the differentiation of soldiers in *Kalotermes flavicollis* Fabr. (Isoptera). *Monitore Zool. Ital.* **4**, 99–105.

Springhetti A. (1971) Il controllo dei reali sulla differenziazione degli alati in *Kalotermes flavicollis* Fabr. *Boll. Zool.* **38**, 101–110.

Stuart A. M. (1979) The determination and regulation of the neotenic reproductive caste in the lower termites (Isoptera) with special reference to the genus *Zootermopsis* (Hagen). *Sociobiology* **4**, 223–237.

Watson J. A. L., Metcalf E. C. & Sewell J. J. (1975) Preliminary studies on the control of neotenic formation in *Mastotermes darwiniensis* Froggatt (Isoptera). *Insectes Sociaux* **22**, 415–426.

Wilson E. O. & Bossert W. H. (1963) Chemical communication among animals. *Recent Progress Hormone Research* **19**, 673–716.

CHAPTER 17

The Role of Hormones in Social Polymorphism and Reproduction in Kalotermes flavicollis Fabr.

D. LEBRUN

University of Nantes, 2 Rue de la Houssinière, 44072 Nantes Cedex, France

CONTENTS

17.1 MORPHOGENETIC ROLE OF JUVENILE HORMONE

As a result of many studies, it is now established that the juvenile hormone (JH) plays a leading part in the polymorphism and reproduction of the lower termite, *Kalotermes flavicollis* Fabr. Lüscher (1958), in a pioneering study, showed that the implantation of *corpora allata* (CA) into pseudergates usually transforms them, in the course of the two following moults, into presoldiers then into soldiers. Later workers confirmed these findings and showed that JH appears to be the factor controlling differentiation into soldiers and the maintenance of the larval condition.

Extension of Lüscher's (1958) work has shown that the formation of soldiers is induced by the implantation of CA from reproductive termites into pseudergates (Lüscher & Springhetti, 1960). An implantation of CA from adult *Periplaneta americana* (Lebrun, 1964) similarly causes transformation into soldiers. These experiments show that the JH is neither species nor stage-specific. The CA of larval *Periplaneta* are smaller than those of adults. Nevertheless, the simultaneous implantation into pseudergates of three or four

227

ion into soldiers; clearly, soldier development
:ient titre of JH in the haemolymph.

ìtercastes provide further proof of the role
ì of soldiers (Lebrun, 1970). Various types of
lanting a pair of CA into second-stage nymphs
: imaginal moult, such as the whitening of the
pigmentation. The implantations change the
ìs. The maximum effect is obtained on some
ìme fertile soldiers. In these females the first
moult to the presoldier is followed by a moult to a soldier of normal
appearance, but whose ovaries produce eggs of normal form and size (Fig.
17.1). However, the genital ducts remain typically larval and do not allow
eggs to be laid. These individuals are typical soldier–sexual intercastes. This
type of experiment also gives rise to composite individuals in which the
features of one caste are differently pronounced from the other. The individuals whose imaginal features are most pronounced have the least development of soldier traits, and vice versa. Other experiments confirm that
morphogenesis depends on the titre of JH in the haemolymph. Imagos,
neotenics and even soldiers produce a new cuticle when they receive implantation of active prothoracic glands (Lebrun, 1967). Unfortunately, the closed
ecdysial sutures prevent the liberation of the pharate recipient which eventually dies. However, the moult usually involves a new type of morphogenesis.
Following this manipulation, functional neotenics develop soldier-type mandibles. In other neotenics however, the mandibles do not change, but the
compound eyes and wing buds differentiate closer to the imaginal type. The
moulting of soldiers under these conditions, give rise to a new type of
mandibles, more slender than the former pair and almost rectilinear, with
reduced marginal teeth (Fig. 17.2). Thus, the induction of a supernumerary
moult in soldiers or functional neotenics, both of which have active CA does
not produce a replica of the former stage, but emphasizes soldier features; the
induced moult of a neotenic with inactive CA leads back towards the alate.
The morphogenetic changes presumably result from different titres of JH at
the time the moult is induced. Similarly, in *Mastotermes darwiniensis* Froggatt,
JH probably intervenes in morphological differences between the two groups
of soldiers (Watson, 1974).

In natural colonies of *K. flavicollis*, occasional individuals are found that
have evident, but incomplete imaginal features; these individuals do not
swarm and are called pseudoimagos (Grassé, 1949). Similar individuals can be
obtained by implanting a pair of CA into second-stage nymphs with long wing
buds, just before their imaginal moult (Lebrun, 1970). This massive input of
JH prevents the full realization of the imaginal features. These experimentally
produced pseudoimagos have atrophied wings and incomplete pigmentation,

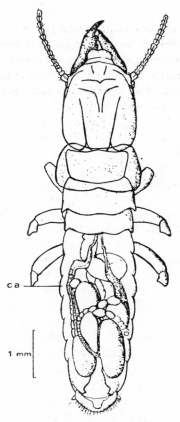

Fig. 17.1. *Kalotermes flavicollis* (Fabr.). Experimental intercaste imago-soldier with developed ovaries and mature eggs. ca = implanted *corpora allata*

and their eyes and genitalia are less developed than those of the imago (Fig. 17.3).

Effects comparable to the implantation of CA have been obtained with JH analogues (JHAs). These substances have been used in various ways. The JHAs usually cause an increase in the number of presoldiers in groups of pseudergates or workers. Their role in morphogenesis has been shown in many studies, particularly by Hrdý (1972), Wanyonyi and Lüscher (1973), Varma (1977) and Okot-Kotber (1980) but in a higher termite (see also reviews by Howard & Haverty, 1979) and Hrdý *et al.*, 1979). The groups of termites treated with JHAs and the synthetic JH II and III also produce a great number of worker–soldier intercastes that are rare in natural colonies (Hrdý *et*

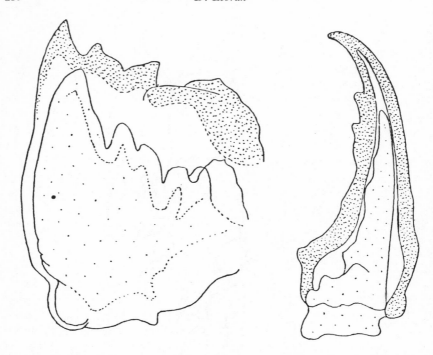

FIG. 17.2 Mandible modifications after soldier moult (right) and neotenic moult (left) experimentally produced.

al., 1979). Similar results obtained by Lüscher (1969), Lenz (1976) and Springhetti (1974) on *K. flavicollis* corroborate the action of synthetic JH and of the JHAs in the formation of soldiers.

17.2 SOCIAL POLYMORPHISM

A colony of *K. flavicollis* is mainly composed of larvae and nymphs almost all which become alates. This normal development requires about seven stages. The larvae do not have wing buds but may moult, first of all, into nymphs with short wing buds (first-stage nymphs) and, afterwards, into nymphs with long wing buds (second-stage nymphs) which subsequently give rise to imagos. However, during the development moulting is not always progressive. For instance, some moults undergone by the nymphs mark the end in the imaginal differentiation in progress. The wing buds remain unchanged or may even regress. Through those peculiar moults, pseudergates are obtained (Grassé & Noirot, 1947). The supplementary reproductives or neotenics which appear

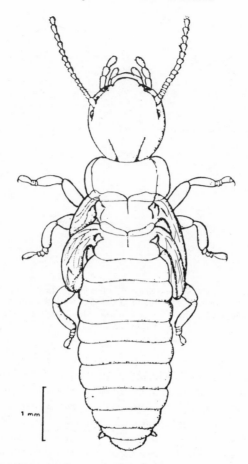

Fɪɢ. 17.3. Pseudoimago of *Kalotermes flavicollis*, produced experimentally.

when the colony loses its primary reproductives, often originate in pseudergates, but also in two nymphal stages or in larvae of the third stages onwards.
Thus, a royal pair is permanently kept in the colony of *K. flavicollis*. The
soldiers are formed from young larvae of second and third stage in newly-
formed colonies. In older colonies, they are formed from advanced larvae,
nymphs and above all pseudergates (Fig. 17.4).

It is well known that the outcome of the moult depends on the titre of JH in
the haemolymph. Lenz (1976) said: "For every developmental stage, a certain
JH titre is characteristic". The society of *K. flavicollis* provides a good example
of the part played by the JH in the determination of castes; along the
developmental line, they keep all potentialities of differentiation. In a series of

D. Lebrun

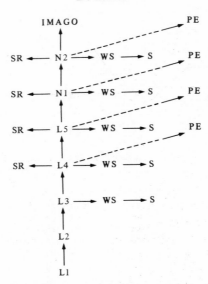

FIG. 17.4. Scheme of development in *Kalotermes flavicollis* (Fabr.). L = larvae; N1 = first-stage nymph; N2 = second-stage nymph; PE = pseudergates; WS = white soldiers (presoldiers); S = soldiers; SR = supplementary reproductives (neotenics). Modified from Grassé & Noirot (1947) and Lüscher (1961).

diagrams Gillot and Yin (1975) have shown the possible relationships between the titre of JH and the outcome of moults in *Zootermopsis angusticollis* (Hagen). Stuart (1979) summarized the scheme in *Zootermopsis angusticollis* (Hagen) in a diagram which is equally applicable to *K. flavicollis* (Fig. 17.5). In this diagram the levels I and II represent the minimal and the maximal titre of JH necessary, respectively, for the transformation into imagos and into soldiers. Between these extreme points the different titres of JH bring about other differentiative moults; in the course of the larval life the titre of JH decreases. The formation of wing buds signifies the onset of imaginal development. Nevertheless, the nymphs keep all their developmental potentiality. The nature of their moults depends on the titre of JH in the haemolymph. The titre of JH may remain unchanged or increases slightly in the nymphs. Probably, in the former case they undergo a stationary moult, while in the latter they undergo a regressive moult. These moults give rise to pseudergates. The pseudergates retain the developmental potentiality of nymphs. The transformation into presoldiers occurs when the JH reaches a particularly high titre (level II). In contrast, a decrease of the titre of JH induces development towards the imaginal form; wing buds develop further at the moult to the second-stage nymph, which then moults to the winged imago (level I). This development can be interrupted in favour of a moult to a

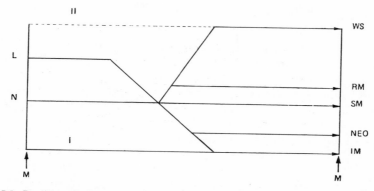

F<small>IG</small>. 17.5. Possible variations of the JH titre in haemolymph related to caste differentiation in *Kalotermes flavicollis* Fabr. I = JH minimum level; II = maximum level; L = larva; N = nymph; WS = white soldier (presoldier); RM = regressive moult (pseudergate); SM = stationary moult (pseudergate); NEO = neotenic reproductive; IM = imago; M = moult. Modified from Stuart (1979).

supplementary reproductive. Probably this event occurs when the titre of JH is slightly more elevated than level I.

17.3 ROYAL CONTROL ON THE DIFFERENTIATION OF CASTES

In a large part, caste differentiation in colonies of *K. flavicollis* is controlled by the reproductive pair. The second-stage nymphs must withdraw themselves progressively from the influence of the royal pair to complete their metamorphosis (Grassé, 1982). On the contrary, the moult of second-stage nymphs isolated from the colony with the pair of reproductives, acquires a regressive or stationary character of pseudergate (Springhetti, 1969). In the presence of a reproductive pair, the production of soldiers in a group of pseudergates (or second-stage nymphs), from which the soldiers have been removed, is stimulated (Springhetti, 1970). The colony forms new reproductives only to replace those that are lost. The presence of reproductive pair inhibit the formation of supplementary reproductives or neotenics (Grassé & Noirot, 1946a; Lüscher, 1951).

The royal control over caste differentiation appears to be pheromonal. According to Lüscher, the reproductives produce pheromones which inhibit the differentiation of pseudergates into supplementary reproductives; the inhibiting pheromones are distributed via the anus (Lüscher, 1961, 1974a). Unfortunately, the existence of these inhibiting pheromones are still not established in the lower termites (Stuart, 1979). How do royal inhibiting pheromones exert their action? These substances may act on CA of larvae,

nymphs and pseudergates to stimulate the JH secretion. It seems that JH
restrains the activities of the moulting glands (Lebrun, 1967, 1980; Gillot &
Yin, 1975). Therefore, the royal pheromones should delay moults while
maintaining JH activity. From disappearance of the reproductives should
result a fall of JH titre, and correlatively, an increased activity of the
prothoracic glands of larvae, nymphs and pseudergates. Activation of prothoracic glands then should induce an anticipated moult. From this moult,
which occurs early in the intermoult period, when the JH titre is still low
(competence period) should result supplementary reproductive.

The presoldier moult which occurs in later stages of moulting interval
(Lüscher, 1974b), when the JH titre is high (competence period) necessitates a
CA-stimulating pheromone probably produced by the reproductives. The
action of this supposed pheromone on competent individuals (i.e. pseudergates) is counteracted by pheromone produced by soldiers existing in colonies
(Springhetti, 1976). The formation of pseudergates requires an "intermediate" titre of JH (Lüscher, 1972) which, probably, is depending on reproductive pheromones.

Some elements of pheromonal–hormonal mechanisms intervening in *K.
flavicollis* castes formation begin to be known; these mechanisms are attributed
to seasonal factors, as shown by Lüscher (1974a).

17.4 REPRODUCTION

The function of reproduction is reserved to the primary reproductives or
the supplementary reproductives (neotenics). The hormone systems (ecdysone
and JH) which control polymorphism are also involved in the control of
reproduction. The role played by JH is better known.

The importance of the imaginal moult in the differentiation of the genital
organs must be underlined. At the imaginal moult, the ovaries become
competent to produce eggs. Ovaries of nymphs or of female soldiers transplanted into young queens do not grow. In contrast, growth and production of
eggs occur if the transplanted ovaries come from young female imagos
(Lebrun, 1973). For young imagos formed in the colony, the first manifestation of sexual instinct is swarming. The flight is short and settling on the
ground is immediately followed by the search for a partner. Once a pair has
formed, the two de-alates start drilling the first cell of the nest. These first
manifestations of sexual instinct are correlated with a high titre of JH in the
haemolymph. Precocious sexual maturation, with all the manifestations
mentioned above, follows the implantation of supernumerary CA into very
young immature imagos, male or female (Lebrun, 1969).

Juvenile hormone is involved in vitellogenesis and oviposition in *K. flavicollis*. An implantation of CA into female nymphs just before the imaginal

moult can lead to the development of fertile soldiers whose ovaries contain numerous eggs, which duly mature (Lebrun, 1970; see above). Supernumerary CA implanted into young paired and probably mated female, increase by 80% the number of eggs laid (Lebrun, 1975). Virgin female imagos, reared separately, do not lay any eggs; after the implantation of supernumerary CA, they lay unfertilized eggs which hatch into parthenogenetic larvae. The larvae survives for only a short time (Lebrun & Vieau, 1978).

Synthetic juvenile hormone (JH I, JH III) have the same effect, on *K. flavicollis*, as the implantation of CA. After dilution in acetone (100 mg HJ in 10 ml acetone), JH I or JH III is applied four times, at about 2 days interval (20 μg of the hormone each time) on the abdominal tergites of artificially dewinged female imagos. The application of JH on isolated virgin females causes the laying of parthenogenetic eggs. For young female imagos in pairs with males the same treatment causes a pronounced increase of the laying (Fig. 17.6). In both types of experiments, the treated females lay more or less the same number of eggs. There is no significant difference between the effect of JH I and JH III in the number of laid eggs (Vieau & Lebrun, 1981).

Juvenile hormone also controls the growth of the male accessory glands. In male imago-soldiers intercastes obtained by the implantation of CA have larger accessory glands than those of normal soldiers; they are also very large in experimental pseudoimagos (Lebrun, 1970). The moult to the imago is accompanied by a stimulation of the accessory glands. Nevertheless, their size does not change in the young unpaired imagos. The implantation of supernumerary CA into such individuals induces an increase in the size of the accessory glands and their epithelium becomes functional. Young male imago accessory glands develop when they are implanted into founding females, in which the JH titre is high. All these experiments show that the JH is involved in the development and functioning of the male accessory glands, whose role, however, is not yet completely understood (Vieau & Lebrun, 1980).

After imaginal or neotenic moult, prothoracic glands degenerate (Herlant-

	CONTROL	EXPERIMENT		
Female imagos (dewinged)		CA	JH I	JH III
Single	0	6,6 ± 0,5	7,4 ± 0,7	7 ± 0,4
paired (♀ + ♂)	4 ± 0,5	7 ± 0,4	7 ± 0,4	7 ± 0,4

Fɪɢ. 17.6. *Kalotermes flavicollis* (Fabr.) egg laying in different types of experiments: Average number of eggs laid by 20 females 30 days after the start of experiment.

Meewis & Pasteels, 1961). The presence of active prothoracic glands seems to be incompatible with vitellogenesis. The implantation of prothoracic glands into a functional female of *K. flavicollis* induces an important diminution of eggs laid (Lebrun, 1977). In the queens of several higher termites, most organs and especially the ovaries contain significant quantities of ecdysone secreted by the follicular cells of the ovary (Bordereau *et al.*, 1976). Ecdysone is transferred into the eggs, but the role it plays there is still unknown. Possibly it plays part in the synthesis of yolk proteins; it has also been suggested that it may influence the future caste of the embryo (Noirot, 1977).

17.5   SUMMARY

In lower termites, and particularly in *Kalotermes flavicollis* (Fabr.) the involvement of hormones on the formation of castes is well established. The outcome of a moult depends on the titre of JH present in the haemolymph. A high titre of JH leads to a moult producing a presoldier; in contrast, the moult to an imago requires a substantial fall in this titre. Other types of moults arise from intermediate titres. Implantation of CA experiments, and also the application of synthetic JH and of chemical substances having similar effects (JHAs) provide convincing proof. The role of the moulting hormone, ecdysone, in the regulation of caste development remains obscure. It is certain that the factors which influence caste formation have some action on the moulting glands by controlling their function. It is necessary to specify the period competence idea.

The important roles of JH in reproduction are supported by the implantation of CA and the application of synthetic JH. The reproductive functions of both male and female require a high titre of JH. Factors involved in the stimulation of the CA of the reproductives remain hypothetical. The part played by ecdysone, recently discovered in the eggs of higher termites, also remains speculative.

In summary, it is clear that hormones play primordial roles in caste determination and reproduction of termites, but the details of these roles are yet to be specified.

17.6   REFERENCES

Bordereau C., Hirn M., Delbecque J.-P. & de Reggi M. (1976) Présence d'ecdysone chez un insecte adulte: la reine de Termite. *C. R. Acad. Sci.* Paris **282** (D), 885–887.
Gillot C. & Yin C. M. (1975) Endocrine control of caste differentiation in *Zootermopsis angusticollis* Hagen (Isoptera). *J. Can. Zool.* **53**, 1701–1708.
Grassé P.-P. (1949). Ordre des Isoptères ou Termites. In *Traité de Zoologie* (ed. Grassé P.-P.), Vol. IX, pp. 408–544. Masson, Paris.

Grassé P.-P. (1982) *Termitologia* (Anatomie Physiologie Reproduction des Termites). (ed. Masson), Vol. I, pp. 1–676.

Grassé P.-P. & Noirot Ch. (1946a) La production des sexués néoténiques chez le termite a cou jaune (*Kalotermes flavicollis* F.): inhibition germinale et inhibition somatique. *C. R. Acad. Sci.* Paris **223**, 869–871.

Grassé P.-P. & Noirot Ch. (1947) Le polymorphisme social du termite à cou jaune (*Kalotermes flavicollis* F.). Les faux ouvriers ou pseudergates et les mues régressives. *C. R. Acad. Sci.* Paris **224**, 219–221.

Herlant-Meewis H. & Pasteels J. M. (1961) Les glandes de mue de *Kalotermes flavicollis* F. (Ins. Isoptère). *C. R. Acad. Sci.* Paris **253**, 3078–3080.

Howard R. W. & Haverty M. I. (1979) Termites and juvenile hormone analogues: a review of methodology and observed effects. *Sociobiology* **4**, 269–278.

Hrdý I. (1972) Der Einfluss von zwei Juvenilhormonanalogen auf die Differenzierung der Soldaten bei *Reticulitermes lucifugus santonensis* Feyt. (Isop.:Rhinotermitidae). *Z. angew. Entomol.* **72**, 129–134.

Hrdý I., Krecek J. & Zuskova Z. (1979) Juvenile hormone analogues: effects on the soldier caste differentiation in termites (Isoptera). *Vestnik Ceskoslovenske Spolecnosti Zoologicke* **XLIII**, 260–269.

Lebrun D. (1964) Le rôle des corps allates dans la formation des castes de *Kalotermes flavicollis*. *C. R. Acad. Sci.* Paris **259**, 4152–4155.

Lebrun D. (1967) La détermination des castes du termite à cou jaune *Kalotermes flavicollis* Fabr. *Bull. biol. Fr. et Belg.* **101**, 139–217.

Lebrun D. (1969) Corps allates et instinct génésique de *Kalotermes flavicollis* Fabr. Le déclenchement de l'activité sexuelle de jeunes imagos ailés de *Kalotermes flavicollis* nécessite la présence dans l'organisme d'un taux élevé d'hormone juvénile. *C. R. Acad. Sci.* Paris **269**, 632–634.

Lebrun D. (1970) Intercastes expérimentaux de *Kalotermes flavicollis* Fabr. *Insectes Sociaux* **27**, 159–176.

Lebrun D. (1973) Résultats de transplantations d'ovaires dans les diverses castes de *Kalotermes flavicollis* Fabr. *C. R. Acad. Sci.* Paris **277**, 2239–2241.

Lebrun D. (1975) Etude expérimentale de la ponte et de son contrôle hormonal chez *Kalotermes flavicollis* Fabr., *C. R. Acad. Sci.* Paris **280** (D), 1265–1267.

Lebrun D. (1977) Glandes de mue et ponte du Termite à cou jaune, *Kalotermes flavicollis* Fabr. *Bull. intérieur Section française Un. Intern. Etude Insectes Soc.* Nantes, 41–42.

Lebrun D. (1980) Effets des hormones juvéniles de synthèse sur la morphogenèse et la ponte de *Kalotermes flavicollis* Fabr. *Bull. intérieur Section française Un. Intern. Etude Insectes Soc.* Toulouse 1981, 90–92.

Lebrun D. & Vieau F. (1978) Corps allates et ponte d'oeufs parthénogénétiques chez *Kalotermes flavicollis* Fabr. *Bull. intérieur Section française Un. intern. étude Insectes Soc.* Besançon, 58–62.

Lenz M. (1976) Die Wirkung von Juvenilhormon-analoga (JHA) auf *Kalotermes flavicollis* und *Coptotermes amanii* (Isoptera:Kalotermitidae, Rhinotermitidae) bei unterschiedlicher Ernährung der Tiergruppen. *Material und Organismen* **3**, 377–392.

Lüscher M. (1951) Uber die Determination des Ersatzgeschlechtstiere bei der Termite *Kalotermes flavicollis* (Fabr.) *Rev. Suisse Zool.* **58**, 404–408.

Lüscher M. (1958) Ueber die Enstsehung der Soldaten bei Termiten. *Rev. Suisse Zool.* **65**, 372–377.

Lüscher M. (1961) Social control of polymorphism in termites. Symp. Insect Polymorphism. *Proc. Roy. Entomol. Soc. London*, 57–67.

Lüscher M. (1969) Die Bedeutung des Juvenilhormons für die Differenzierung des Soldaten bei der Termite *Kalotermes flavicollis*. *Proc. VIth Congr. IUSSI* Berne, 165–170.

Lüscher M. (1972) Environmental control of juvenile hormone (JH) secretion and caste differentiation in termites. *Comp. Endocrinol. Suppl.* **3**, 509–514.

Lüscher M. (1974a) Kasten und Kastendifferenzierung bei niederen Termiten. In: *Sozialpolymorphismus bei Insekten* (ed. Schmidt G. H.), pp. 695–739. Wiss. Verlagsgesellschaft, Stuttgart.

Lüscher M. (1974b) Die Kompetenz zur Soldatenbildung bei Larven (Pseudergaten) der Termite *Zootermopsis angusticollis*. *Rev. Suisse Zool.* **81**, 710–714.

Lüscher M. & Springhetti A. (1960) Untersuchungen über die bedeutung der *Corpora allata* für die differenzierung der Kasten bei der *Kalotermes flavicollis* F. *Journ. Insect. Physiol.* **5**, 190–212.

Noirot Ch. (1977) Various aspects of hormone action in social insects. *Proc. VIIIth Int. Congr. IUSSI*, Wageningen, The Netherlands, pp. 12–16.

Okot-Kotber B. M. (1980) Competence of *Macrotermes michaelseni* (Isoptera:Macrotermitinae) larvae to differentiate into soldiers under the influence of juvenile hormone analogue (ZR-515, Methroprene). *J. Insect Physiol.* **26,** 655–659.

Springhetti A. (1969) Il controllo sociale della differenziazione degli alati in *Kalotermes flavicollis* Fabr. (Isoptera). *Annali del l'Università di Ferrara Biologia animale* **III,** 73–96.

Springhetti A. (1970) Influence of the king and queen on the differentiation of soldiers in *Kalotermes flavicollis* Fabr. (Isoptera). *Monitore Zool. Ital.* **4,** 99–105.

Springhetti A. (1974) The influence of farnesic acid ethyl ester on the differentiation of *Kalotermes flavicollis* Fabr. (Isoptera) soldiers. *Experientia* **30,** 1197–1198.

Springhetti A. (1976) The influence of soldiers on the action of farnesenic acid ethyl ester in *Kalotermes flavicollis* Fabr. (Isoptera). *Monitore Zool. Ital.* (N.S.) **10,** 413–420.

Stuart A. (1979) The determination and regulation of the neotenic reproductive caste in the lower termites (Isoptera): with special reference to the genus *Zootermopsis* (Hagen). *Sociobiology* **4,** 223–237.

Varma R. V. (1977) Influence of juvenile hormone analogue, farnesyl methyl ether on caste differentiation in termite *Postelectrotermes nayari* Roonwal & Varma 1971. *Ind. J. Exp. Biol.* **15,** 564–565.

Vieau F. & Lebrun D. (1980) Etude de certains facteurs qui déterminent l'apparition des oeufs chez le termite *Kalotermes flavicollis* Fabr. *Biologie-Ecologie méditerranéenne* **VIII,** 177–178.

Vieau F. & Lebrun D. (1981) Hormone juvénile, vitellogenèse et ponte des jeunes imagos femelles de *Kalotermes flavicollis* Fabr. *C. R. Acad. Sci.* Paris **293,** 399–402.

Wanyonyi K. and Lüscher M. (1973) The action of juvenile hormone analogues on caste development in *Zootermopsis* (Isoptera). *Proc. 7th Int. Congr. IUSSI,* London, 392–395.

Watson J. A. L. (1974) The development of soldiers in incipient colonies of *Mastotermes darwiniensis* Froggatt (Isoptera). *Insectes Sociaux* Paris, **21,** 181–190.

CHAPTER 18

Hormonal Mechanisms of Soldier Differentiation in Postelectrotermes nayari*

R. V. VARMA

Division of Entomology, Kerala Forest Research Institute, Peechi 680 653, Kerala, India

CONTENTS

18.1 INTRODUCTION

Apart from their great economic importance, termites are of deep biological interest because of the intriguing mechanisms involved in their caste systems. Two important biological agents, hormones and pheromones, are involved in the differentiation of castes in termites. That hormones, especially juvenile hormone (JH), are involved in soldier differentiation both in lower and higher termites, is well established (Lüscher, 1969, 1972, 1974, 1976; Miller, 1969; Hrdý & Krecek, 1972; Hrdý et al., 1979; Springhetti, 1974; Wanyonyi, 1974; Okot-Kotber, 1980).

In recent years, JH and its analogues (JHAs) have been suggested as agents for control of insect pests. Howard and Haverty (1979) have indicated that termites are capable of response to and avoidance of contact with toxic substances, so that compounds like JH which may not deter termites from

*KFRI Scientific publication No. 19.

feeding, would be advantageous, but note Lenz and Westcott (Chapter 20). Information on such aspects of any of the Indian termites has, hitherto, been negligible but, in the present paper, the effect of a JHA on soldier differentiation in a dry-wood termite, *Postelectrotermes nayari* Roonwal and Verma, is described. The investigation is part of the broader studies on the biology and pheromone–endocrine interactions of *P. nayari*.

18.2   MATERIALS AND METHODS

Colonies of *P. nayari* consist of a few hundred termites and can be reared easily in the laboratory. Laboratory cultures comprised 100–200 individuals, including pseudergates, soldiers and a few reproductive forms established in glass troughs. The pseudergate can be distinguished from larvae by its greater pigmentation and by its abdomen, which is comparatively wide and flat dorso-ventrally.

The colony composition and formation of soldiers under ambient conditions were examined.

The effect of the JHA, farnesyl methyl ether (FME), on pseudergates of *P. nayari* was studied. The experimental as well as control animals consisted of a single group of 20 pseudergates each, selected at random from the laboratory cultures, without soldiers.

FME was diluted in acetone and applied topically at the following doses: 0.5, 1.0, 1.5, 2.0, 2.5 and 3.0 μg per pseudergate, using a microsyringe. The control insects were treated with acetone alone. Both experimental and control insects were kept at a temperature of $26 \pm 1°C$ and rh 94% in glass Petri dishes for more than 2 months and were checked daily to note the morphological changes, if any, as well as the incidence of mortality.

The corpora allata (CA) of 10 JHA-treated (2.5 μg) pseudergates was dissected out 15 days after the treatment and processed histologically and *in situ* using modified aldehyde fuchsin stain (Dogra & Tandan, 1964). These were compared with the CA of an equal number of untreated pseudergates and soldiers. For calculation of the volume of the gland, outlines of alternate sections of the corpora allata were drawn on graph paper using a camera lucida. The mean values of alternate sections were substituted for the sections skipped over. The projected area of each section was calculated in μ^3.

18.3   RESULTS

18.3.1   Soldier production in laboratory colonies

In a culture consisting of only 50–60 individuals, soldiers were absent, whereas those cultures comprising more than 100 individuals contained 2–3 soldiers. If the existing soldiers were removed from such colonies a presoldier (white soldier) appeared within 20–25 days. Presoldiers were rarely found in the laboratory cultures.

18.3.2 Soldier production following JHA treatment

None of the pseudergates treated with acetone differentiated into other castes, although stationary moults were observed after 30–40 days. The application of FME, in contrast, induced the development of presoldiers in a dose-dependent fashion (Table 18.1). There was no response to doses of 0.5 and 1.0 μg, and only a worker–presoldier intercaste at 1.5 μg (see below). At higher doses, 20–35% of the pseudergates moulted into presoldiers, within 25–30 days. The presoldiers produced following doses of 2.0 and 2.5 μg FME moulted to soldiers within 10–15 days. These experimentally-induced soldiers were comparable with spontaneously produced soldiers from the laboratory cultures, having castaneous brown heads with darker mandibles 2.37–2.53 mm long and 12–15 segmented antennae. The presoldiers formed in the group treated with 3.0 μg FME per pseudergate did not moult into soldiers. Mortality in this group was about 40%, and occurred mostly during ecdysis, although a few instances of cannibalism were observed.

TABLE 18.1 EFFECT OF FME ON DIFFERENTIATION OF CASTES IN *P. NAYARI*

Dose (μg)	Initial no. of pseudergates	No. of individuals of different castes 40 days after treatment			No. of pseudergates dead during the experimental period
		Presoldier	Intercaste	Pseudo-imago	
0	20	0	0	0	0
0.5	20	0	0	0	0
1.0	20	0	0	2	1
1.5	20	0	1	1	0
2.0	20	4	2	0	0
2.5	20	7	1	0	2
3.0	20	6	0	0	8

Two kinds of intercastes were produced under FME treatment: worker–presoldier and nymph–alate or pseudo–imago. The worker–presoldier intercastes had elongate bodies and the mandibles were poorly developed. The pseudo–imagines had wingpads almost equal in size (2.5 mm) to those of the second stage nymph, but thicker, and the body was reddish brown, like that of the alate. Eye pigmentation became prominent after 25–30 days.

18.3.3   Effects of FME on corpora allata

Corpora allata of the pseudergates of *P. nayari* are paired, spherical, transparent and measure about 60–70 μm in diameter. In some individuals they appear to be unequal in size. Corpora allata of soldiers are elongated and measure 75 μm in length and 55 μm in breadth. In FME-treated pseudergates, the diameter of corpora allata varied from 70–85 μm. A comparison of the volume of the corpora allata of pseudergates, JHA-treated pseudergates and soldiers revealed conspicuous differences. Camera-lucida drawings of outlines of CA of alternate sections of pseudergates, soldiers and JHA-treated pseudergates were made on graph paper and a stage micrometer projected beside the outlines helped in the calculation of the area and volume of CA. The mean values of alternate sections were substituted for the sections skipped over. The projected area of each section was calculated in μ^3. In pseudergates it was 4517 μ^3, in soldiers, it was 7822 μ^3 while in JHA-treated pseudergates it was 7200 μ^3.

18.4   DISCUSSION AND CONCLUSION

The involvement of JH or JHA in the differentiation of soldier castes in the lower termites is well documented. The present studies confirm some of the earlier observations made in other species of termites. In *P. nayari* high doses of FME resulted in the formation of soldiers. It appears therefore that soldier differentiation in *P. nayari* is governed by an increased JH titre. Lüscher (1963) postulated that corpora allata may produce more than one hormone, one of which may induce soldier formation. Miller (1969) suggested that the various castes found in lower termites are equipotent and their formation will be influenced by both social and environmental factors.

In a normal colony of *P. nayari*, the number of soldiers is rather low and if the existing soldiers are removed, presoldiers are formed. Lüscher & Springhetti (1960) suggest that, in lower termites both reproductives and soldiers prevent otherwise competent termites from developing into these castes by secreting pheromones that are ingested, and that may inhibit the corpus allatum. According to Lüscher (1972) the reproductives of termites may produce and give off JH and the soldiers probably an anti-juvenile hormone substance.

The physiological role and changes in the volume of the corpora allata during post-embryonic development in termites have been dealt with in detail by Lüscher (1958, 1960) and Lebrun (1967). Enlargement of the corpora allata prior to soldier differentiation also occurs in *P. nayari*.

Lebrun (1967a,b) observed that implantation of corpora allata from replacement reproductives (and also from sexually mature female cockroaches) into pseudergates of *Kalotermes flavicollis* gave rise to soldiers or soldier–pseudergate intercastes. He also found that soldiers could be produced with more certainty if, after implantation of corpora allata, prothoracic glands were also implanted to facilitate an early moult. The time of moulting cycle when the analogue is applied may also be a deciding factor in the differentiation possibilities. The unmoulted pseudergates in the experimental group in *P. nayari* might be individuals that had undergone a moult before the application of FME.

18.5 SUMMARY

The effect of treatment of FME on pseudergates of *P. nayari* has been studied.

High doses of FME (2, 2.5 and 3.0 μg) resulted in the formation of presoldiers. Low doses (0.5, 1.0 and 1.5 μg) did not produce any presoldiers, although a dosage of 1.5 μg produced pseudergate–presoldier intercastes. Other intermediate forms, pseudo–imagoes, were also obtained from several treated groups.

The possible role of JH in soldier formation in *P. nayari* is discussed on the basis of results obtained in other lower termites.

18.6 REFERENCES

Dogra G. S. & Tandan B. K. (1964) Adaptation of certain histological techniques for *in situ* demonstration of the neuroendocrine system of insects and other animals. *Q. J. micro. Sci.* **105**, 455–466.

Howard R. W. & Haverty M. I. (1979) Comparison of feeding substrates for evaluating effects of insect growth regulators on subterranean termites. *J. Georgia Entomol. Soc.* **141**(1), 3–7.

Hrdý I. & Krecek J. (1972) Development of superfluous soldiers induced by juvenile hormone analogues in the termite, *Reticulitermes lucifugus Santonensis. Insectes Sociaux* **19**, 105–109.

Hrdý I., Krecek J. & Zuskova Z. (1979) Juvenile hormone analogues: effects on the soldier caste differentiation in termites (Isoptera). *Vest. Ceskoslov. Spolec. Zool.* **43**, 260–269.

Lebrun D. (1963a) Implantation de glandes de la mue *Periplaneta americana* dans les sexués neoteniques de *Calotermes flavicollis* Fabr. (Insecta, Isoptera). *Compt. Rendus.* **257**, 2181–2182.

Lebrun D. (1963b) Implantation de glandes de la mue de *Periplaneta americana* dans des soldates de *Calotermes flavicollis* Fabr. *Compt. Rendus.* **257**, 3487–3488.

Lebrun D. (1967) Nouvelles recherches sur le déterminisme endocrinien du polymorphisme de *Calotermes flavicollis. Ann. Soc. Entomol.* France (N.S.) **3**, No. 3, 867–871.

Lüscher M. (1958) Experimentelle Erzeugung von Soldaten bei der Termite *Kalotermes flavicollis. Naturwissenschaften* **45**, 69–70.

Lüscher M. (1960) Hormonal control of caste differentiation in termites. *Ann. N.Y. Acad. Sci.* **89**, 549–563.

Lüscher M. (1963) Functions of the corpora allata in the development of termites. *Proc. 16th Int. Congr. Zool*, Washington DC; Vol. 4. Nat. Hist. Press, New York. pp. 244–250.

Lüscher M. (1969) Die Bedeutung des Juvenilhormons für die Differenzierung der Soldaten bei der Termite *Kalotermes flavicollis*. Proc. VI Congr. IUSSI, Bern. pp. 165–170.

Lüscher M. (1972) Environmental control of juvenile hormone (JH) secretion on caste differentiation in termites. *Gen. Comp. Endocrinol. Suppl.* **3**, 509–514.

Lüscher M. (1974) Die Kompetenz zur Soldatenbildung bei Larven (Pseudergaten) der Termite *Zootermopsis angusticollis*. *Rev. Suisse. Zool.* **3**, 710–714.

Lüscher M. (1976) Evidence for an endocrine control of caste determination in higher termites. In *Phase and Caste Determination in Insects. Endocrine Aspects* (Lüscher M., ed.), pp. 73–89. Pergamon Press, Oxford and New York.

Lüscher M. & Springhetti A. (1960) Untersuchungen über die Bedeutung der Corpora allata für die Differenzierung der Kasten bei der Termite *Kalotermes flavicollis* F. *J. Insect Physiol.* **5**, 190–212.

Miller E. M. (1969) Caste differentiation in the lower termites. In *Biology of Termites*, Vol. 2 (Krishna K. & Weesner F. M., eds), pp. 283–310. Academic Press, New York.

Okot-Kotber B. M. (1980) Competence of *Macrotermes michaelseni* (Isoptera: Macrotermitinae) larvae to differentiate into soldiers under the influence of juvenile hormone analogue (ZR-515, Methoprene). *J. Insect Physiol.* **26**, 655–659.

Springhetti A. (1974) The influence of farnesenic acid ethyl ester on the differentiation of *Kalotermes flavicollis* Fabr. (Isoptera) soldiers. *Experientia* **30**, 541–542.

Wanyonyi K. (1974) The influence of the juvenile hormone analogue ZR-512 (Zoecon) on caste development in *Zootermopsis nevadensis* (Hagen) (Isoptera). *Insectes Sociaux* **21**, 35–44.

CHAPTER 19

The Role of Juvenile Hormones and Juvenoids in Soldier Formation in Rhinotermitidae

IVAN HRDY

Institute of Entomology, Czechoslovak Academy of Sciences, U Šalamounky 41, 15800 Praha, Czechoslovakia

CONTENTS

19.1 INTRODUCTION

The most extensive studies on the effects of the juvenile hormone (JH) and/ or its synthetic analogues (juvenoids) on termites have been devoted to their influence on the formation of the soldier caste. The history of the discovery of the regulatory function of JH in the differentiation of soldiers (Lüscher & Springhetti, 1960; Lebrun, 1967; Lüscher, 1969), and summaries of the effects of juvenoids, have been presented earlier in several papers (Lenz, 1976; El-Ibrashy, 1982). A brief account (*cf.* Hrdý, Křeček & Zusková, 1979) of the influence of juvenoids and JH on soldier caste differentiation in termites of the family Rhinotermitidae is given.

19.2 SCREENING OF JUVENOIDS

The marked effect of the synthetic JH and of the juvenoid hydroprene on

245

the formation of the soldier caste was first shown in *Reticulitermes lucifugus santonensis* (Rhinotermitidae) (Hrdý & Křeček, 1972; Hrdý, 1972). We have generally used this species in our continued screening of juvenoids along with *Prorhinotermes simplex*, another representative of the same family. The results summarized in Table 19.1 were obtained by exposing termite groups to treated filter paper in Petri dishes (for details *cf.* Hrdý, Křeček & Zusková, 1979).

Approximately 60 compounds, mostly aliphatic analogues of farnesic acid, oxa analogues of 4-(geranoxy)-benzoic acid, and 4-(geranylamino)-benzoic acid were tested. The majority of substances were not effective even at high concentrations (0.5%), but a few were toxic at concentrations as low as 0.1%. In Table 19.1 the compounds are listed according to their stimulus on the formation of presoldiers or soldier–worker (pseudergate) intercastes. In tests with termites, synthetic JH III ($C_{16}JH$) (I) proved highly effective as well as the following three juvenoids: hydroprene (Altozar, ZR 512, Zoecon, Cal. USA) (II) and two other compounds prepared in the Institute of Organic Chemistry and Biochemistry of the Czechoslovak Academy of Sciences, Praha:

TABLE 19.1 EFFECT OF JH AND JUVENOIDS ON TERMITES IN LABORATORY TESTS

Compound		Concentration %	Species	Effect	
(I)		0.5	R.l.	(M)	+ + +
		0.05			+ + +
(II)		0.5	R.l.	M	+ + +
		0.05			+ + +
		0.005			0
		0.5	P.s.		+ + +
		0.05			+ + +
(III)		0.5	R.l.	M	+ +
		0.05		(M)	+ + +
		0.005			0
		0.5	P.s.		+ + +
(IV)		0.5	R.l.	M	
		0.05			+ + +
(V)		0.1	P.s.	M	
		0.01			+
(VI)		0.1	P.s.		+
(VII)		0.1	P.s.		+
(VIII)		0.5	R.l.	M	+

R.l.—*Reticulitermes lucifugus santonensis*
P.s.—*Prorhinotermes simplex*
Scale of effects according to formation of soldiers and/or soldier–worker intercastes: + (low) to + + + (high)
M—high mortality, (M)—low mortality.

(III) 11-chlorine analogue of farnesic acid, and (IV) tetrahydrofuryl analogue of methoprene. The juvenoids V–VIII were less effective.

19.3 TERMITE SPECIES AFFECTED BY JUVENOIDS

The influence of juvenoids on soldier caste formation has been demonstrated in both the lower termites (Kalotermitidae, Hodotermitidae, Rhinotermitidae) and the higher termites (Termitidae) (Hrdý *et al.*, 1979). A review of findings on the family Rhinotermitidae is given in Table 19.2.

TABLE 19.2. TERMITE SPECIES DEVELOPING PRESOLDIERS, SOLDIERS AND/OR SOLDIER–WORKER INTERCASTES UNDER THE INFLUENCE OF JHS AND/OR JUVENOIDS

Species	Compound	Reference
Heterotermes convexinotatus (Snyder)	hydroprene	Lenz, 1976
H. indicola (Wasmann)	hydroprene	Lenz, 1976
Reticulitermes flaviceps (Oshima) ·	hydroprene	Chu Hsang-hsoung
	methoprene	*et al.*, 1974
	S-ethyl*	
R. flavipes (Kollar)	hydroprene	Lenz, 1976
	methoprene	
R. lucifugus (Rossi)	hydroprene	Lenz, 1976
	methoprene	
R. lucifugus santonensis Feytaud	JH II	Hrdý, 1972
	JH III	Hrdý & Křeček,
	hydroprene†	1972
Coptotermes amanii (Sjöstedt)	methoprene	Lenz, 1976
	hydroprene	
C. formosanus Shiraki	hydroprene	Hrdý *et al.*,
		1979
C. niger Snyder	methoprene	Lenz, 1976
Prorhinotermes simplex (Hagen)	JH III	Hrdý *et al.*,
	hydroprene	1979

*S-ethyl 11-methoxy-3,7,11-trimethyldodeca-2, 4-dienethioate.
†Other compounds cf. Hrdý *et al.* (1979) and Table 19.1.

19.4 SYNTHETIC JHS AND JUVENOIDS IN STUDIES OF SOCIAL HOMEOSTASIS

The identification and the synthesis of JHs and effective juvenoids has provided an efficient tool for the study of regulatory mechanisms in caste development of termites and other social insects. Knowledge of developmental potentials in the earliest larval stages was perfected, the practicability of juvenoid-induced development toward presoldiers and subsequently to morphologically and functionally-perfect soldiers was assessed. Studies were made on interactions of juvenoids and the effect of nutrition as regulation factors, on the composition of colonies (Lenz, 1976; Hrdý et al., 1979). Inhibitory effects of methoprene on egg hatch and the time of development of larvae were established by Howard (1980) in Reticulitermes flavipes.

In my opinion, there is a need to exploit fully the utilization of juvenoids on one hand, the precocenes on the other (cf. Křeček et al., 1981) as model substances influencing and regulating the development and behaviour in social-insect societies, to unravel further the mechanisms of caste differentiation.

19.5   USE OF JUVENOIDS IN PEST CONTROL

Social insects were recognized relatively early as appropriate targets for the utilization of juvenoids as control agents (Hrdý & Křeček, 1972; Hrdý, 1973). The project, using a new method for controlling the synantropic ant, Monomorium pharaonis, by means of baits with juvenoids (Edwards, 1975a,b; Hrdý et al., 1977; Rupeš et al., 1978) marked a first success. Possibilities of further practical exploitation of juvenoids in the control of harmful social insects have been the subject of frequent discussion (Edwards & Menn, 1981; El-Ibrashy, 1982) and have remained an open question up to the present. For example, mortality in Reticulitermes flavipes after feeding on paper pads impregnated with high concentrations of methoprene resulted from toxicity to the termites and/ or their symbiotic protozoa or from incomplete ecdysis. At lower concentrations mortality was due to starvation from defaunation or production of superfluous soldiers (Howard & Haverty, 1978). On the other hand, in preliminary field trials, when complete colonies of Prorhinotermes simplex inhabiting pine stumps were treated with 1% hydroprene emulsion, methoprene or the compound III failed to prove any effect. Further theoretical study of fundamental problems concerning the regulation of development and behaviour in social insects is needed and may provide decisive stimuli for novel methods in insect-pest management.

19.6   SUMMARY

The effects of JHs and juvenoids on soldier caste formation in Rhinotermitidae are summarized. In screening tests with Reticulitermes lucifugus santonensis and Prorhinotermes simplex JH III and juvenoids hydroprene, 11-chloro farnesoic acid and tetrahydrofuryl analogue of methoprene were found as most active. The soldier caste formation under JHs (II and III) and juvenoids' (methoprene, hydroprene) influence was proved further in *Heterotermes convexinotatus*, *H. indicola*, *Reticulitermes flaviceps*, *R. flavipes*, *R. lucifugus*, *Coptotermes amanii*, *C. formosanus* and *C. niger*.

19.7 REFERENCES

Chu Hsang-hsoung, Tai Tchi-dar, Chen Tse-fu & King Mei-wen (1974) Induction of soldier differentiation in the termite, *Reticulitermes flaviceps* Oshima with juvenile hormone analogues. *Acta ent. sinica* **17**, 161–165.

Edwards J. P. (1975a) The effect of a juvenile hormone analogue on laboratory colonies of Pharaoh's ant, *Monomorium pharaonis* (L.) (Hymenoptera, Formicidae). *Bull. ent. Res.* **65**, 75–80.

Edwards J. P. (1975b) The use of juvenile hormone analogues for the control of some domestic insect pests. *Proc. 8th British Insecticide and Fungicide Conf.*, Brighton 1975, pp. 267–275.

Edwards J. P. & Menn J. J. (1981) The use of juvenoids in insect pest management. In *Chemie der Pflanzenschutz- und Schädlingsbekämpfungsmittel*, Band 6 (Wegler R., ed.), pp. 185–209. Springer-Verlag.

El-Ibrashy M. T. (1982) Juvenoids: Physiological impacts on caste differentiation for practical utilization in termite and ant control. *Assiut J. agric. Sci.* **13**(3), 13–39.

Howard R. W. (1980) Effects of methoprene on colony foundation by alates of *Reticulitermes flavipes* (Kollar). *J. Georgia ent. Soc.* **15**, 281–285.

Howard R. W. & Haverty M. I. (1978) Defaunation, mortality and soldier differentiation: concentration effects of methoprene in a termite. *Sociobiology* **3**, 73–77.

Hrdý I. (1972) Der Einfluss von zwei Juvenilhormonanalogen auf die Differenzierung der Soldaten bei *Reticulitermes lucifugus santonensis* Feyt. (Isoptera: Rhinotermitidae). *Z. angew. Ent.* **72**, 129–134.

Hrdý I. (1973) Effect of juvenoids on termites and honeybees. *Proc. 7th Int. Congr. IUSSI*, London 1973, pp. 158–161.

Hrdý I. & Křeček J. (1972) Development of superfluous soldiers induced by juvenile hormone analogues in the termite *Reticulitermes lucifugus santonensis*. *Insectes Sociaux* **19**, 10–109.

Hrdý I., Křeček J., Rupeš V., Žďárek J., Chmela J. & Ledvinka J. (1977) Control of the pharaoh's ant (*Monomorium pharaonis*) with juvenoids in baits. *Proc. 8th Int. Congr. IUSSI*, Wageningen 1977, pp. 83–84.

Hrdý I., Křeček J. & Zusková Z. (1979) Juvenile hormone analogues: Effects on the soldier caste differentiation in termites (Isoptera). *Vĕst. čs. spol. zool.* **43**, 260–269.

Křeček J., Hrdý I., Jarolím V. & Wimmer Z. (1981) Antagonistic interaction between a juvenile hormone analogue and precocene I in *Prorhinotermes simplex* (Isoptera). *Acta ent. bohemoslov.* **78**, 266–269.

Lebrun D. (1967) La détermination des castes du termite à cou jaune (*Calotermes flavicollis* Fabr.). *Bull. biol. France et Belg.* **101**, 139–217.

Lenz M. (1976) The dependence of hormone effects in termite caste determination on external factors. In *Phase and Caste Determination in Insects, Endocrine Aspects* (Lüscher M., ed.), pp. 73–89. Pergamon Press.

Lüscher M. (1969) Die Bedeutung des Juvenilhomons für die Differenzierung der Soldaten bei der Termite *Kalotermes flavicollis*. *Proc. 6th Int. Congr. IUSSI*, Bern 1969, pp. 165–170.

Lüscher M. & Springhetti A. (1960) Untersuchungen über die Bedeutung der Corpora allata für die Differenzierung der Kasten bei der Termite *Kalotermes flavicollis* F. *J. Insect Physiol.* **5**, 190–212.

Rupeš V., Hrdý I., Pinterová J., Žďárek J. & Křeček J. (1978) The influence of methoprene on pharaoh's ant *Monomorium pharaonis* colonies. *Acta ent. bohemoslov.* **75**, 155–163.

CHAPTER 20

Homeostatic Mechanisms Affecting Caste Composition in Groups of Nasutitermes nigriceps (Isoptera: Termitidae) Exposed to a Juvenile Hormone Analogue

M. LENZ[1] and M. WESTCOTT[2]

[1] CSIRO, Division of Entomology, Canberra, A.C.T. 2601, Australia
[2] CSIRO, Division of Mathematics and Statistics, Canberra, A.C.T. 2601, Australia

CONTENTS

20.1 INTRODUCTION

In the lower termites, juvenile hormone (JH) determines which of the developmental potentials open to an individual is realized at its next moult. The selectivity of this determination depends on the timing of JH secretion by the corpora allata (CA) relative to a series of sensitive periods during the intermoult, and not on JH titre (Nijhout & Wheeler, 1982). The secretory activity of the CA is, in turn, regulated by conditions in the colony, especially the pheromonal environment (Yin & Gillot, 1975).

The best known effect of JH on lower termites is the induction of presoldier development (Howard & Haverty, 1979a; Hrdý et al., 1979; Lüscher, 1974). Although caste determination in higher termites is poorly understood (Lüscher, 1976; Nijhout & Wheeler, 1982), it is clear that JH and its analogues (JHA's) similarly induce the formation of presoldiers (French, 1974; Lenz, 1976b; Lüscher, 1976; Okot-Kotber, 1980). The apparent generality of this mechanism has led to the concept that termite colonies might be controlled by exposing them to JHAs; excessive development of soldiers might so overburden the workers (in addition to decreasing their numbers) that the social integration of the colony would break down, and the colony decline.

However, it is clear that the effects of developmental regulators, as reflected in caste ratios, are modified by many aspects of the environment, whether or not pheromones are the final common path. Thus the number of dependent termites in a colony are related to the number of workers (and, at least in some cases, nymphs) available to keep them, so that the numbers of dependants vary with the size (and age) of a colony, and with its circumstances, e.g. its food supply (Lenz, Chapter 9; cf. Watson et al., 1977) and season (Ferrar, 1982).

Caste ratios in a colony are very effectively regulated through an integrated set of processes, involving a stimulus to the differentiation of further individuals into castes that are inadequately represented, or the inhibition of differentiation towards castes already present in sufficient numbers, or the elimination of termites surplus to needs.

It might be argued that the mechanisms which ensure homeostasis of caste composition should provide a field colony with a defence against the disturbance of caste ratios caused by JHAs. Yet, despite the fact that many studies have been carried out on the effects of JHAs on termites, this aspect has been given little attention. Work has, instead, concentrated on the soldier-inducing effects of various analogues over a range of concentrations, and on other effects of those substances, such as overt toxicity and defaunation of the gut (see review by Howard & Haverty, 1979a). Many of these studies have been based on termite groups composed mainly of workers and nymphs, which in no way reflect the polyphenism of a termite colony. In addition, groups have for the most part been kept on filter paper, which is a poor diet, but makes it easier to administer the analogues, and to observe the termites.

Striking effects on the rate of soldier induction, the incidence of group breakdown and mortality, and the extent of defaunation have been demonstrated under such conditions; and these results have led to optimism about the use of JHAs as termiticides. However, results obtained under such circumscribed laboratory conditions scarcely permit conclusions to be drawn on the likely effects of JHAs on termites in the field. It is, perhaps, not unexpected that the one report on a field application of JHAs against termites showed that this was unsuccessful. There were many possible reasons for this failure, including the instability and high evaporation rate of the compounds (Hrdý *et al.*, 1979) and, at least initially, their repellency, apart from any question of homeostatic mechanisms in the colonies themselves.

In bioassays that have provided conditions better approximating those in the field, the soldier-inducing and other adverse effects of the JHAs were invariably and significantly less pronounced. These better conditions were achieved either by offering a diet more appropriate than filter paper, such as sound wood, artificial diet, decayed wood or, preferably, a choice between treated and untreated timber (Howard & Haverty, 1979b; Lenz, 1976a, b) and/or by including more than one caste in the termite groups. In particular, the addition of soldiers (Afzal & Ahmad, 1982; French, 1974; Lenz, 1976a, b; Springhetti, 1976), or of neotenics (Afzal & Ahmad, 1982) lowered the rate of soldier production, whereas the presence of nymphs could, depending on their age, inhibit or stimulate the moulting of termites to presoldiers (Lenz, 1976b).

In order to evaluate the contribution of various castes to maintaining the caste composition of a termite group, variously composed groups of *Nasutitermes nigriceps* from Central America were exposed to the JHA hydroprene and the changes in caste structure were followed over a period of 8 weeks.

20.2 MATERIALS AND METHODS

The experiments were carried out in 1977, during the senior author's period with the Bundesanstalt für Materialprüfung, Berlin, Germany; the results were analysed in Canberra.

20.2.1 Termites

A species of *Nasutitermes* was chosen since the genus is characterized by a range of clearly identifiable stages, especially in the worker line (Fig. 20.1): two small male workers (SW1, SW2) and up to five large female worker types (LW1–LW5) are known (McMahan & Watson, 1975; Noirot, 1969; Watson & Abbey, 1977). Soldiers develop from SW1 and less commonly from SW2 and, in some species, from LW1 (Fig. 20.1). Under laboratory conditions soldiers (Noirot, 1969) and worker/soldier intercastes (Lenz, 1976b) can develop from older large workers.

It seems that in at least some Central American arboreal *Nasutitermes* there are two small worker stages (SW1, SW2) and only three large worker stages (LW1–LW3) (McMahan, 1970; Noirot, 1969; Watson & Sewell, Chapter 3). *N. nigriceps*, however, has five distinct large worker stages (Lenz, unpubl. results); its developmental pathway for the worker stages thus resembles that of *N. exitiosus* from Australia (Fig. 20.1) (McMahan & Watson, 1975; Watson & Abbey, 1977). To what extent soldier development parallels that of *N. exitiosus* remains to be seen, as the culture of *N. nigriceps* contained only small soldiers derived from SW1.

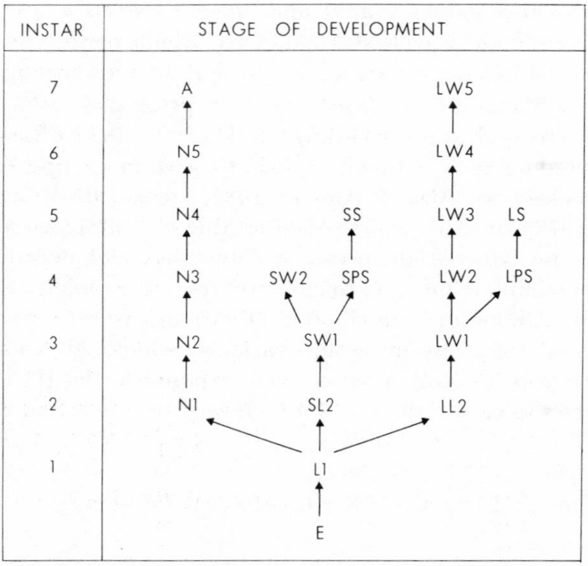

FIG. 20.1. The developmental pathways of *Nasutitermes exitiosus* (reproduced from Watson J. A. L. & Abbey H. M. (1977) *J. Aust. ent. Soc.* **16,** 161–164 with kind permission from the journal).

A combination of size and the extent of pigmentation of the head capsules makes it fairly straightforward to identify the worker stages. However, in assembling groups of older large workers, it sometimes proved difficult to assign every individual to a specific stage (see also McMahan & Watson, 1975; McMahan, 1977). We therefore made no distinction between termites belonging to LW2 or 3, and LW4 or 5; termites of these stages were pooled into "LW2/3" and "LW4/5" groups.

Termites were extracted from the feeding sites of a populous laboratory colony of *N. nigriceps*, originating in Guatemala in 1967, but since then cultured in Berlin at 30°C and 98% r.h. (Becker, 1978; Garcia & Becker, 1975).

In some of the experiments described below, in which small soldiers were added to groups which contained SW1, the precursor stage for small presoldiers, it was necessary to differentiate at the 4-weekly inspections between the added soldiers and those that had developed during the experiments (see Tables 20.2, 20.3 and 20.6). At the time of each inspection, at least some of the newly-formed soldiers were either not yet fully pigmented or had a glossy sheen, and could thus be separated easily from the added soldiers.

With other individuals this distinction may no longer have been apparent. The latter certainly holds true for soldiers present at the inspections after 8 and 12 weeks (Table 20.2). We therefore assumed that neither the initially-present nor newly-formed soldiers died during the experiments. The number of "new" soldiers at each 4-weekly count was, then, the difference between the total number of soldiers and the number of soldiers originally present. Thus, the figures for the numbers of soldiers developed represent a minimum estimate. From results with groups which contained only small soldiers and older workers, unable to produce small soldiers, it was evident that this approach was realistic, for the mortality of the small soldiers after 4 weeks was almost invariably low (Table 20.1).

TABLE 20.1. AVERAGE NUMBER OF SMALL SOLDIERS OF
NASUTITERMES NIGRICEPS (±SE) SURVIVING 4 WEEKS AFTER 20
INDIVIDUALS WERE ADDED TO GROUPS OF 200 WORKERS

Treatment	No. and type of worker	
	200 LW1	200 LW4/5
Control	17 (0.7)	18 (0.0)
JHA	18 (1.7)	19 (0.0)

20.2.2 Application of juvenile hormone analogue

The JHA hydroprene (ethyl (2E,4E)-3,7,11-trimethyl-2,4-dodecadienoate) was offered to the termites on their food, $2.5 \times 1.5 \times 1.2$ cm blocks of *Eucalyptus regnans*. The blocks had been decayed beforehand by the brown rot fungus *Serpula lacrimans* to a mass loss of *ca* 10%, and were heat-sterilized afterwards. The decayed blocks were impregnated for 20 min under vacuum-pressure (7.10^{-1} kPa) with a 0.5% (v/v) acetone solution of technical grade hydroprene (86% A.I.), or acetone alone for controls: the retention was *ca* 1.9 ml solution per block. Blocks were stored for 24 hr in a room at 20°C and 65% r.h. before they were placed with the termites.

20.2.3 Maintenance conditions

Each group was set up in a glass Petri dish, 10 cm in diameter, and given a block on one side of the dish, a pile of 2 g of vermiculite on the opposite side as a matrix and source of moisture (300% water content (v/m)), together with a piece of nest carton as building material and limited alternative food supply.

The experiments were carried out in the same controlled environment in which the parent colony was kept. There were five replicates. Within the first 3 weeks, the location of termites in the dishes and the nature of building activity were recorded every 1–3 days. After 4 weeks the number of each developmental stage were counted and the groups were reset. They were finally examined after 8 weeks. Specific details of individual experiments are given in the results section.

20.2.4 Analysis of results

In all cases, the data initially form a four-way contingency table, the categories represented being the state of a termite after a given number of weeks, the replicate, the number of small soldiers included and the presence or absence of JHA. Inclusion of the replicates is necessary to detect any interaction between number of soldiers and the level of JHA.

The model proposed is a log-linear model for the proportions of termites in the various states of development (Nelder, 1974). That is, the natural logarithm of the proportion p, $\log_e p$, is taken to be a linear function of the various factors under investigation, while the observed numbers in each state follow a multinomial distribution with these proportions. In the special case of just two states (*e.g.* Table 20.5), it is more convenient to use the logit,

$$\log_e \left\{ \frac{p}{1-p} \right\}.$$

The model was fitted using the GLIM package following the procedure described in Nelder (1974). This procedure assumes a Poisson distribution for the observed numbers in each cell of the contingency table, the mean in the cell being the exponential of a linear function in the factor effects. To take account of the fact that some of the marginal totals are fixed *a priori* in the experiment, these are fitted first and the model then reduces to the log-linear one described above.

To investigate the significance of a factor, the model was fitted with and without that factor and the change in deviance d of the model calculated. Associated with this difference is an integer f, the degrees of freedom, indicating the extra number of parameters fitted. If the factor had no effect then the ratio d/f should have a chi-square distribution with f degrees of freedom. However, for reasons mentioned below, the residual variation in the model was nearly always larger than should occur. The remedy adopted was to use the square root of residual mean deviance (residual deviance after fitting the model, divided by residual degrees of freedom) as an estimate of the inflationary scale factor, and to divide all *d*/*f* ratios by this before assessing their significance. The more sophisticated procedure described in Williams (1982) was tried on some data, but made little difference to the conclusions.

Results from an experiment with variously composed groups, differing mainly in the age of the workers and the number of added soldiers, held on untreated wood only, were analysed using the same model.

A number of the termites which moulted into presoldiers and soldiers under the influence of the analogue died during ecdysis or shortly after, especially in situations where few workers remained to attend to them. The disturbance caused by examining and resetting the groups after 4 weeks accelerated the decline in their vigour, already stressed by JHA, and so greatly increased the differences between replicates that only the results after 4 weeks of exposure to hydoprene could be included in the analysis.

The numbers of termites in different stages varied more between replicates than the multinomial error assumption would indicate (see above). In addition, after certain combinations of treatments the numbers in some stages were consistently small, which caused problems with the fitting of models.

Various modifications of the basic analysis were tried, in attempts to reduce the residual variability (deviance) after fitting all terms in the model. Replications which seemed particularly aberrant were discarded, data from different developmental stages were pooled, and replications within treatment regimes were also pooled. These procedures all helped to reduce the variation. Finally, since it was clear that exposure to JHA had a substantial and significant effect on development, only the effect of presence or absence of soldiers on development in the relevant experiments with hydroprene treatment was analysed.

20.3 RESULTS

Only those results for caste differentiation which were statistically significant at the 1% level and below are discussed.

20.3.1 Effect of existing soldiers on the production of additional soldiers in termite groups of varying composition

Groups of 200 LW2/3 or LW4/5 together with 50 SW1 were set up as described under materials and methods, but the termites received only untreated timber as food. Soldiers were added in the numbers 0, 5, 20 or 40 in order to evaluate the effect of various soldier proportions on the pattern of soldier production. The number of presoldiers and new soldiers was assessed at 4-weekly intervals, in this case up to 12 weeks. The method of analysis was the same as for the experiments with hydroprene treatment.

The production of new soldiers was inhibited when the groups contained 20 or 40 soldiers, but was slightly stimulated in groups with only five soldiers initially. However, the inhibitory effect of larger groups of soldiers is not absolute, but is related to the stage of larger workers which they accompany. Inhibition is more pronounced with LW4/5 in the group than with LW2/3 (Table 20.2). This difference was highly significant for the 8 and 12 week data (5 standard errors on the logit scale).

TABLE 20.2. AVERAGE NUMBER OF NEWLY-DEVELOPED PRESOLDIERS AND SOLDIERS IN GROUPS OF *NASUTITERMES NIGRICEPS*, INITIALLY COMPOSED OF 50 SW1, 200 LW 2/3 OR LW 4/5 AND SOLDIERS RANGING IN NUMBERS FROM 0–40, AFTER 4, 8, AND 12 WEEKS

| No. soldiers | 50 SW1 + 200 LW 2/3 | | | 50 SW1 + 200 LW 4/5 | | |
| | No. newly developed presoldiers and soldiers after weeks | | | | | |
	4	8	12	4	8	12
0	15.8	28.0	28.0	16.0	21.7	22.0
5	16.4	32.2	31.8	13.3	22.7	21.6
20	12.8	28.6	26.0	11.0	17.3	14.5
40	7.0	19.6	21.8	10.5	12.0	16.5

20.3.2 Soldier differentiation in termite groups of varying composition exposed to JHA

20.3.2.1 *Morphogenetic response*

The previous experiment indicated that 20 small soldiers in a group of 250 workers could significantly reduce the production of new soldiers. The extent of soldier differentiation under the influence of hydroprene was therefore compared in groups of 200–300 workers with or without the addition of 20 small soldiers.

The response to the JHA was tested on SW1 and on all the large worker stages. Insufficient SW1 were available to set up groups of that stage alone, so 60 SW1 were combined with 150 LW2/3 to build up the group to about 200 termites. In addition, representatives of all the worker stages that had been tested separately, with or without soldiers, were combined, the numbers of each stage reflecting an impression of the proportion in which they were present at the feeding sites (actual ratios were not established). However, there was a deliberate bias towards stages that are precursors of presoldiers under natural conditions (SW1, LW1), to obtain a greater response to JHA.

Since the worker stages were assessed separately in their response to JHA, the presoldiers, soldiers or intercastes into which workers of a particular stage differentiated could be used as reference in identifying the origin of corresponding stages in those experimental groups which contained a mixture of worker types (Table 20.6).

In groups of 60 SW1 and 150 LW2/3, only the SW1 moulted into presoldiers and soldiers when untreated timber was offered (Table 20.3). Addition of soldiers reduced the production of new soldiers. JHA treatment increased the number of SW1 which differentiated into presoldiers and soldiers in groups composed solely of workers, and few presoldiers developed from LW2/3. The presence of soldiers inhibited presoldier differentiation from SW1, but increased it from LW2/3.

TABLE 20.3. PERCENTAGE OF ORIGINAL NUMBER OF WORKERS OF EACH DEVELOPMENTAL STAGE IN GROUPS OF *NASUTITERMES NIGRICEPS*, INITIALLY COMPOSED OF 60 SW1 AND 150 LW 2/3, 4 WEEKS AFTER APPLICATION OF THE JHA HYDROPRENE

Group composition:		60 SW1				150 LW 2/3		
No. soldiers added	Treatment	SW1 →	SPS →	SS	→ SW2	LW2/3→	PS →	S
0	control	60	11	11	2	82	0	0
	JHA	3	1	36	0	54	2	0
20	control	66	8	6	1	83	0	0
	JHA	2	6	21	0	32	14	0

In all groups in which large workers (except LW1) moulted to presoldiers and soldiers, few workers attained full soldier characteristics, most moults resulting in presoldier/worker or soldier/worker intercastes. If viable, these intercastes would probably disturb the caste ratios, and burden remaining workers, in much the same way as fully-formed presoldiers and soldiers.

Hydroprene induced the production of large soldiers in groups of 200 LW1 and lowered the survival rate of the workers in the absence of small soldiers (most deaths probably occurred during the moult from worker to presoldier) (Table 20.4). The main effect of adding small soldiers was that it increased the percentage of workers surviving the treatment with JHA.

Survival was reduced in groups of LW4/5 exposed to JHA, but more live workers were found after 4 weeks when soldiers were present (Table 20.5). No LW4/5 were found moulting into presoldiers.

TABLE 20.4. PERCENTAGE OF ORIGINAL NUMBER OF WORKERS, OF EACH DEVELOPMENTAL STAGE IN GROUPS OF *NASUTITERMES NIGRICEPS*, INITIALLY COMPOSED OF 200 LW1, 4 WEEKS AFTER APPLICATION OF THE JHA HYDROPRENE

Group composition: 200 LW1

No soldiers added	Treatment	Development options			
		LW1 →	LPS →	LS →	LW2
0	control	78	0	0	1
	JHA	23	8	1	0
20	control	50	0	0	0
	JHA	61	4	0	0

TABLE 20.5. PERCENTAGE OF ORIGINAL NUMBER OF WORKERS OF EACH DEVELOPMENTAL STAGE IN GROUPS OF *NASUTITERMES NIGRICEPS*, INITIALLY COMPOSED OF 200 LW 4/5, 4 WEEKS AFTER APPLICATION OF THE JHA HYDROPRENE

Group composition: 200 LW 4/5

No soliders added	Treatment	Developmental options		
		LW4/5 →	PS →	S
0	control	83	0	0
	JHA	53	0	0
20	control	86	0	0
	JHA	77	0	0

In groups with a more natural composition, including SW1 and LW1 to LW5 (a total of 310 termites in each group), JHA induced differentiation to presoldiers, and led to a decline in numbers of all worker stages (Table 20.6). However, survival and the number of undifferentiated termites increased significantly when 20 soldiers were included with the workers. Inhibition of soldier production was, however, gradual: it was complete or almost so for LW2 to LW5, reduced in LW1, but not apparent in SW1 (Table 20.6).

20.3.2.2 *Behavioural response*

Control groups readily accepted the untreated wood as food and concentrated around it; only a few individuals were found in the vermiculite.

JHA-treated wood was avoided at first, and for several days the termites were restricted to the vermiculite. All groups other than those composed solely of LW4/5 used the carton to build a more or less complete wall opposite the piece of treated timber; the wall was 1–2 cm long, and extended from the surface of the vermiculite to the lid of the dish. At times the wall was extended

TABLE 20.6. PERCENTAGE OF ORIGINAL NUMBER OF WORKERS OF EACH DEVELOPMENTAL STAGE IN GROUPS OF *NASUTITERMES NIGRICEPS*, INITIALLY COMPOSED OF 30 SW1, 200 LW1, 50 LW 2/3 AND 30 LW 4/5, 4 WEEKS AFTER APPLICATION OF THE JHA HYDROPRENE

No. soldiers added	Treatment	30 SW1				200 LW1				50 LW 2/3			30 LW 4/5		
		SW1	→ SPS	→ SS	→ SW2	LW1	→ LPS	→ LS	→ LW2	LW2/3	→ PS	→ S	LW 4/5	→ PS	→ S
0	control	51	23	11	0	88	0	0	2	90	0	0	93	0	0
	JHA	0	0	41	0	6	35	1	0	19	37	2	23	13	0
20	control	48	9	3	0	63	0	0	0	72	0	0	70	0	0
	JHA	1	3	36	0	30	17	0	0	49	2	0	62	0	0

Group composition / Developmental options

to form a small chamber. The termites stayed behind the wall (or in the chamber) for several days, but after 3–4 days (in the case of LW1, after 7 days), the workers began to attack the treated wood. Even then, the bulk of the termites remained behind the protective wall.

The LW4/5 spread vermiculite over the floor of the dish, both in the controls and in the groups treated with JHA. However, when exposed to JHA they began this activity only after 4–5 days and used the vermiculite to cover the blocks. However, unlike the other worker stages, they did not build walls out of carton material.

Worker groups which had been supplemented with soldiers abstained from feeding on the treated wood for 2 days longer than soldierless groups. The soldiers positioned themselves in front of or close to the sides of the walls or, when together with LW4/5, on the edge of the vermiculite, facing the JHA source. Only when workers commenced feeding on the wood, were soldiers also seen in other areas of the dishes.

20.4 DISCUSSION

The results throw light on two points mentioned earlier, the importance of caste composition in groups of termites used in studies of homeostatic mechanisms (and, hence, its importance in field colonies), and the use of JHA in studies of termites and termite control.

Group composition clearly influenced the extent of soldier differentiation in workers, the existing soldiers providing the most effective contribution in counterbalancing the effects of the JHA. However, the intensity with which soldiers inhibited production of presoldiers was, in turn, affected by the type of worker present with them (Table 20.6). The response of a worker stage could differ, depending on whether it was on its own, or in the presence of other worker stages, when it was exposed to the analogue (e.g. LW2/3, Tables 20.3 and 20.6; LW4/5, Tables 20.5 and 20.6). It is also interesting to note that the addition of soldiers to groups including all worker stages inhibited the production of presoldiers from the older worker stages far more than it did from SW1 and LW1, which are the precursors of soldiers in the field.

Developmental stages which under natural conditions do not differentiate into presoldiers and soldiers may retain the potential to do so, as in the older worker stages of *N. nigriceps* and the large third instar larvae of *Macrotermes michaelseni* (Okot-Kotber, 1980). The results with groups including a complete set of large worker stages (Table 20.6) indicate that the small soldiers play some part in preventing the older workers developing into presoldiers, and suggest that, in addition to being the guardians of the nest, small soldiers have an important integrative role in a termite colony. We have no data on the effects that large soldiers might have on caste development, but their behaviour is known to differ markedly from that of small soldiers (Kriston *et al.*, 1977).

When groups are exposed to a JHA, several behavioural mechanisms operate, which minimize the potential effects of the analogue. Workers isolate the group by building a protective wall between it and the source of JHA, and cover the treated wood with building material. Similar behaviour is shown towards other repellent and threatening objects, *e.g.*, nest intruders, diseased termites and nest areas contaminated by micro-organisms. These behaviour patterns can be added to other known examples of temporal polyethism in *Nasutitermes*, which include repair and extension of nests, gallery construction and foraging (McMahan, 1970, 1977, 1979; Jones, 1979, 1980). The two castes which are least affected by JHA, the soldiers and the oldest large workers, were the stages that exposed themselves most to the analogue, and provided the most substantial protection to other stages. The behaviour of the soldiers was reminiscent of that described by Eisner *et al.* (1976) and Kriston *et al.* (1977) in small soldiers of *N. exitiosus*: soldiers remain engaged in surveillance of a "threat" for as long as its presence can be perceived, by contact, or by air movement from it, once it has been sprayed with defensive secretion, acting as an alarm pheromone as well. The JHA, being somewhat volatile, might have a similar effect on the soldiers.

Our observations on soldier behaviour can also be interpreted in the light of Traniello's (1981) studies on foraging in some Central and South American species of *Nasutitermes*. Soldiers play a key role in foraging. They scout for new food sources, alone in *N. costalis*, but often in the presence of larger workers in *N. corniger* and *N. ephratae*. In *N. costalis*, workers are recruited to the food source after some delay. In case of danger, *e.g.*, during ant attacks, recruitment of workers can be postponed for longer periods. Our observations suggest that soldiers are more important than workers in determining the suitability of food sources, as indicated by the time difference in feeding on the treated wood between groups with or without soldiers. It is also possible that soldiers actively keep workers away from unsuitable food.

The change in the blocks from being regarded as a "threat" to becoming a tolerable food source was fairly abrupt, although delayed in the presence of soldiers, and could have been related to a decline in the evaporation rate of the analogue and increasing demand for food.

Morphogenetic substances, including JH-mimics, are known to occur naturally in a number of plants, including trees (Jacobson, 1982). Should termite colonies encounter them, they appear to have at their disposal a range of measures to offset potentially disruptive effects on caste composition.

The present observations help to explain why field trials of JHAs can fail, apart from any factors inherent to the chemicals themselves, such as volatility or instability, in that the termites can isolate themselves from the material as described above. Soldier behaviour might reinforce the response in workers that leads them to isolate the affected zone.

High rates of soldier production or mortality in laboratory studies on the effects of JHAs and insecticides may be more a consequence of adverse bioassay conditions than a reflection of the potential effectiveness of the materials in the field. This has been clearly demonstrated in laboratory tests with an insecticide (Esenther, 1979) and a JHA (Lenz, 1976a, b). The more the bioassays approximated field conditions, the higher the levels of termiticide with which the termites could cope. A more natural feeding substrate than filter paper on to which to administer the JHA, the supply of an alternative food source, and the composition of the groups appear to be important elements to consider when assessing the effects of JHAs. However, irrespective of the value of these substances as termiticides, they provide a useful tool for examining caste interactions, the regulative mechanisms of caste homeostasis and questions of polyethism. A better understanding of these aspects of termite biology should aid the search for new methods of control, based more on the biology of the termites than on the characteristics of deleterious chemicals.

20.5 SUMMARY

In groups of *Nasutitermes nigriceps*, small soldiers inhibited the production of presoldiers from small workers (SW1) more effectively in the presence of older large workers (LW4/5) than in the company of the earlier stages LW2/3. Exposure of groups of various worker stages without soldiers, to wood treated with the juvenile hormone analogue hydroprene, increased mortality in all stages and induced presoldier and soldier differentiation (largely presoldier/worker and soldier/worker intercastes) in all stages except LW4/5. Combining all worker stages into one group and feeding the termites hydroprene-treated wood, caused soldier differentiation from all worker stages; when soldiers were added, LW2–LW5 were prevented from becoming presoldiers and LW1 developed into them at a lower rate, but as many developed from SW1 as in groups without mature soldiers. Certain patterns of behaviour were noted which could have isolated the JHA source, rendering it ineffective: older workers covered it with building material, younger workers sealed off the area and soldier behaviour might have reinforced these responses in workers. Soldiers have a key role in maintaining social homeostasis of caste ratios in termite groups. Juvenile hormone analogues provide useful tools for a better understanding of caste interactions, the regulation of caste composition and of polyethism.

20.6 ACKNOWLEDGEMENTS

The senior author is grateful to the Bundesanstalt für Materialprüfung, Berlin, and his former colleagues for providing working space, facilities and various forms of assistance, especially by Dr H. Kühne and Mrs S. Vlacho-georgios-Pantos and U. Kudrhalt. Zoecon Corporation, Palo Alto, California, kindly supplied the JHA. We also appreciated comments by Dr J. A. L. Watson on the first draft of the manuscript.

20.7 REFERENCES

Afzal M. & Ahmad M. (1982) Significance of existent castes on the future caste differentiation of *Bifiditermes beesoni* (Gardner) under the influence of a juvenile hormone analogue. *Mater. Organismen* **17**, 93–116.

Becker G. (1978) Temperatur-Optimum der Frassaktivität verschiedener Termiten-Arten. *Z. ang. Ent.* **86**, 225–259.

Eisner T., Kriston I. & Aneshansley D. J. (1976) Defensive behavior of a termite (*Nasutitermes exitiosus*). *Behav. Ecol. Sociobiol.* **1**, 83–125.

Esenther G. R. (1979) Termite bioassays show greatly varied tolerances to insecticide in bait blocks. *For. Prod. J.* **29**, 55–56.

Ferrar P. (1982) Termites of a South African savanna. II. Densities and populations of smaller mounds, and seasonality of breeding. *Oecologia (Berl.)* **52**, 133–138.

French J. R. J. (1974) A juvenile hormone analogue inducing caste differentiation in the Australian termite, *Nasutitermes exitiosus* (Hill) (Isoptera:Termitidae). *J. Aust. ent. Soc.* **13**, 353–355.

Garcia M. L. & Becker G. (1975) Influence of temperature on the development of incipient colonies of *Nasutitermes nigriceps* (Haldemann). *Z. ang. Ent.* **79**, 291–300.

Howard R. W. & Haverty M. I. (1979a) Termites and juvenile hormone analogues: A review of methodology and observed effects. *Sociobiol.* **4**, 269–278.

Howard R. W. & Haverty M. I. (1979b) Comparison of feeding substrates for evaluating effects of insect growth regulators on subterranean termites. *J. Georgia Entomol. Soc.* **14**, 3–7.

Hrdý I., Krecek J. & Zuskova Z. (1979) Juvenile hormone analogues: effects on the soldier caste differentiation in termites (Isoptera). *Vest. Ceskoslov. Spolec. Zool.* **43**, 260–269.

Jacobson M. (1982) Plants, insects, and man—their interrelationships. *Econ. Bot.* **36**, 346–354.

Jones R. J. (1979) Expansion of the nest of *Nasutitermes costalis*. *Insectes Sociaux* **26**, 322–342.

Jones R. J. (1980) Gallery construction by *Nasutitermes costalis*: polyethism and the behavior of individuals. *Insectes Sociaux* **27**, 5–28.

Kriston I., Watson J. A. L. & Eisner T. (1977) Non-combative behaviour of large soldiers of *Nasutitermes exitiosus* (Hill): an analytical study. *Insectes Sociaux* **24**, 103–111.

Lenz M. (1976a) Die Wirkung von Juvenilhormon-Analoga (JHA) auf *Kalotermes flavicollis* und *Coptotermes amanii* (Isoptera: Kalotermitidae, Rhinotermitidae) bei unterschiedlicher Ernährung der Tiergruppen. *Mater. Organismen, Beih.* **3**, 377–392.

Lenz M. (1976b) The dependence of hormone effects in termite caste determination on external factors. In *Phase and Caste Determination in Insects. Endocrine Aspects* (Lüscher M., ed.), pp. 73–89. Pergamon Press, Oxford.

Lüscher M. (1974) Kasten und Kastendifferenzierung bei niederen Termiten. In *Sozialpolymorphismus bei Insekten. Probleme der Kastenbildung im Tierreich.* (Schmidt G. H., ed.), pp. 694–739. Wissenschaftl. Verlagsges., Stuttgart.

Lüscher M. (1976) Evidence for an endocrine control of caste determination in higher termites. In *Phase and Caste Determination in Insects. Endocrine Aspects.* (Lüscher M., ed.), pp. 91–103. Pergamon Press, Oxford.

McMahan E. A. (1970) Polyethism in workers of *Nasutitermes costalis* (Holmgren). *Insectes Sociaux* **17**, 113–120.

McMahan E. A. (1977) Mound repair and foraging polyethism in workers of *Nasutitermes exitiosus* (Hill): (Isoptera:Termitidae). *Insectes Sociaux* **24**, 225–232.

McMahan E. A. (1979) Temporal polyethism in termites. *Sociobiol.* **4**, 153–168.

McMahan E. A. & Watson J. A. L. (1975) Non-reproductive castes and their development in *Nasutitermes exitiosus* (Hill) (Isoptera). *Insectes Sociaux* **22**, 183–198.

Nelder J. A. (1974) Log linear models for contingency tables: A generalization of classical least squares. *Appl. Statistics* **23**, 323–329.

Noirot Ch. (1969) Formation of castes in the higher termites. In *Biology of Termites*, Vol. I (Krishna K. & Weesner F. M., eds), pp. 311–350. Academic Press, New York.

Nijhout H. F. & Wheeler D. E. (1982) Juvenile hormone and the physiological basis of insect polymorphisms. *Quart. Rev. Biol.* **57**, 109–133.

Okot-Kotber B. M. (1980) The influence of juvenile hormone analogue on soldier differentiation in the higher termite, *Macrotermes michaelseni*. *Physiol. Entomol.* **5**, 407–416.

Springhetti A. (1976) The influence of soldiers on the action of farnesenic acid ethyl ester in *Kalotermes flavicollis* Fabr. (Isoptera). *Monitore Zool. Ital. (N.S.)* **10**, 413–420.

Traniello J. F. A. (1981) Enemy deterrence in the recruitment strategy of a termite: Soldier-organized foraging in *Nasutitermes costalis*. *Proc. Nat. Acad. Sci. USA* **78**, 1976–1979.

Watson J. A. L. & Abbey H. M. (1977) The development of reproductives in *Nasutitermes exitiosus* (Hill) (Isoptera:Termitidae). *J. Aust. ent. Soc.* **16**, 161–164.

Watson J. A. L., Barrett R. A. & Abbey H. M. (1977) Caste ratios in a long-established, neotenic-headed laboratory colony of *Mastotermes darwiniensis* Froggatt (Isoptera). *J. Aust. ent. Soc.* **16**, 469–470.

Williams D. A. (1982) Extra-binomial variation in logistic linear models *Appl. Statistics* **31**, 144–148.

Yin C.-M. & Gillott C. (1975) Endocrine control of caste differentiation in *Zootermopsis angusticollis* Hagen (Isoptera). *Can. J. Zool.* **53**, 1701–1708.

CHAPTER 21

Mechanisms of Caste Determination in a Higher Termite, Macrotermes michaelseni (*Isoptera, Macrotermitinae*)

B. M. OKOT-KOTBER

International Centre of Insect Physiology and Ecology (ICIPE), P.O. Box 30772, Nairobi, Kenya

CONTENTS

21.1   INTRODUCTION

Caste differentiation in termites, as in other social insects, may be determined by changes in hormonal levels, by the direct influence of pheromones on individuals, or indirectly by modulating the behaviour of members of the society (Lüscher, 1972, 1974a, 1976).

In the higher termites, only a limited number of studies have been reported on the various mechanisms involved in caste differentiation. Since hormones are involved, as shown extensively in the lower termites and less so in the higher termites, it is useful to outline some of the important facts about the endocrine system and its role, as established over a period of time by numerous investigators.

21.1.1   Developmental mechanisms

21.1.1.1   *Corpora allata and their functions*
The anatomy of the retrocerebral complex (corpora cardiaca and corpora allata) of termites was first documented early in the century (Holmgren, 1909). This was later expanded on by Hanström (1940) and Cazal (1948). Jucci (1924) described the prothoracic glands, which he named tentorial glands. Later, Pflugfelder (1947) renamed them ventral glands because of their position. Lüscher (1960) called these glands in the *Kalotermes flavicollis* prothoracic glands because one part of the gland is located in the head while the other is in the prothorax. In the present review the latter terminology will suffice.

The corpora allata (CA) are endocrine glands which produce one of the most important hormones for insect development, the juvenile hormone (JH). The physiological role of these glands in termite development was first noted by Lüscher (1958). He found that active CA are necessary for soldier differentiation in *K. flavicollis*. Lüscher and Springhetti (1960) expanded on these ideas and Lebrun (1967a, b) confirmed that if active CA are transplanted, even into nymphs, soldier determination may be induced in the recipients. Lüscher (1965) subsequently noted that CA undergo growth up to the final moult into imagos, but that these glands decrease in size soon after the moult of pseudergates or nymphs. During the formation of neotenics (replacement reproductives), CA grow considerably. Thus, enlargement of the CA is known to occur in *K. flavicollis* during (a) development of the pharate imagos, (b) formation of presoldiers and (c) formation of neotenics.

While studying the morphology and histology of endocrine glands of *Zootermopsis angusticollis*, another species of lower termite, Gillott and Yin (1972) found that the CA of presoldiers and reproductives are much larger than those of larvae and soldiers. It seems, therefore, that changes in CA size during development of castes are not limited to *Kalotermes*, but are perhaps a general phenomenon in the lower termites.

In the higher termites, Holmgren (1909) showed that the CA of *Nasutitermes chaquimayensis* became enlarged in the queen and king. Kaiser (1956) and Pasteels and Deligne (1965) reported similar results in *Anoplotermes pacificus* and *Microcerotermes parvus*, and in *Cubitermes heghi*, respectively. It had also been reported (Pflugfelder, 1938) that the CA of the replacement reproductives of *Microcerotermes amboinensis* became enlarged and Kaiser (1956) showed that in the same species, these glands are progressively larger as neotenics are derived from more advanced nymphal instars, and increase in size during the development of ergatoid reproductives. Similar observations were made by Noirot (1969) on *Termes hospes*. During the development of imagos, Kaiser (1956) noted that *A. pacificus* CA slowly increase in size during the early stages of development, but sharply increase in size in the final stage. This also seems to be the case in *T. hospes* (Noirot, 1969).

There are also observations on the CA in the neuter castes. Small CA were found in workers of *Mi. amboinensis* (Pflugfelder, 1938) and *A. pacificus* (Kaiser, 1956). According to Noirot (1969), the same applies to *Nasutitermes arborum*, *T. hospes* and *Macrotermes bellicosus* (previously called *natalensis*). On the other hand, Kaiser (1956) found that soldier development was associated with marked increase in the size of the CA of *Neocapritermes* sp. and in a species of Nasutitermitinae (Kaiser, 1956). Noirot (1969) made similar observations in *M. natalensis* and *Mimeutermes giffardii*.

21.1.1.2 *Prothoracic glands and their functions*

The other endocrine glands thoroughly investigated in association with caste differentiation are prothoracic glands (PG). Changes in these glands have been noted during the development of *K. flavicollis* (Lüscher, 1960). Herlant-Meewis & Pasteels (1961) found that these glands degenerate in the replacement reproductives of *K. flavicollis*, as they do in the nymphoid and ergatoid replacement reproductives of *Mi. amboinensis* (Kaiser, 1956), as well as of other species of Termitidae (Noirot, 1969). On the other hand,

Springhetti (1957) reported that prothoracic glands undergo regular growth during development of *K. flavicollis* nymphal stages through to imagos. Kaiser (1956) and Noirot (1969) made similar observations on *A. pacificus* and *T. hospes* respectively. These two authors noted as well that these glands persist, poorly developed, in the neuter castes.

21.1.1.3 *The role of juvenile hormones*

Recently, Okot-Kotber (1980a) attempted to elucidate the role of endocrine glands in the caste differentiation of *Macrotermes michaelseni*, as a model of a higher termite. These studies were later extended to obtain direct evidence for the role of JH in soldier differentiation in *M. michaelseni* (Okot-Kotber, 1980b), in the light of earlier findings that soldier formation in *K. flavicollis* could be induced by feeding isolated larvae with food impregnated with juvenile hormone analogue (JHA) or injecting them with synthetic JH (Lüscher, 1969). This had also been shown to be the case in the higher termite, *Nasutitermes* (French, 1974; Lenz, 1976). However, JHA did not, in any of the cases cited above, induce transformation of all the individuals treated into presoldiers: some moulted to workers. Presumably, to ensure the transformation of all individuals other environmental factors are required. To determine what these other factors are, it is of paramount importance to analyse various physiological changes that may be associated with soldier determination and development. Lüscher (1969) has also shown that, in *K. flavicollis,* presoldiers produced by an external source of JH had smaller CA than found in spontaneously produced individuals. In the same species, competence period (an interval in the development of undifferentiated larva during which the individual is prone to hormonal influence to differentiate) was correlated with changes in CA volume (Lüscher, 1974b).

In JHA-treated *Zootermopsis nevadensis* larvae, Wanyonyi (1974) found that there is a differential influence of the analogue on the development of the prothoracic glands, those of larvae differentiating into presoldiers being much larger than the untreated, whereas those of treated individuals not undergoing transformation become even smaller than those of the controls. All this points to a possible interaction between hormones, endocrine glands and differentiating tissues of a larva, which must be well balanced to allow the appropriate effect to prevail.

21.1.1.4 *Group effects—size and composition*

In the lower termites, a number of reports have appeared relating the rate of soldier production to the size of artificial colonies or groups. Springhetti (1968, 1973) reported, in *K. flavicollis,* a greater production of soldiers with increase in the group size. A correlation between the emergence ratio of soldiers and the number of larvae and workers present in artificial colonies of *Reticulitermes speratus* was found by Shimizu (1963). More recently, Haverty (1979) showed similar results in *Coptotermes formosanus,* and Haverty & Howard (1981) in *R. flavipes* and *R. virginicus.* However, such information is lacking for higher termites.

The influence of group composition on soldier production has been investigated in a number of lower termite species. Springhetti (1969) reported that in *K. flavicollis*, the presence of a soldier in a group of pseudergates inhibits development of more soldiers. Similar results have been obtained for *C. formosanus* (Haverty, 1979), and *R. flavipes* and *R. virginicus* (Haverty & Howard, 1981). In the higher termites, only fragmentary data are available. Lenz (1976) showed in *Nasutitermes nigriceps* and French (1974) in *N. exitiosus* that the presence of soldiers inhibits development of more soldiers in a group of workers.

In the lower termites, older larvae are also considered as workers by most authors, hence the mutual influence of larvae on one another cannot be separated from the influence of workers on larvae to differentiate into soldiers. The influence of workers on soldier development in the higher termites is not known. This was investigated in the work reported recently (Okot-Kotber, 1983) on group effects on the differentiation of soldiers in the fungus-growing termite, *M. michaelseni*.

This is one of the higher termites whose scheme of development is relatively rigid (Noirot, 1969; Okot-Kotber, 1981a) with branched developmental pathways first diverging, as far as is known, at the first ecdysis. In the incipient colonies, male larvae moult exclusively into major workers at the third (final) larval instar, whereas females in the same instar have two options: some develop into minor presoldiers, the majority into minor workers (Okot-Kotber, 1981b). We may now turn to specific aspects of caste determination in a representative species of higher termites, *M. michaelseni*.

21.2　ENDOCRINE GLANDS

21.2.1　Larvae and neuter castes

21.2.1.1　*Morphology and histology of CA*

These studies were conducted on field material obtained from Kajiado, approximately 55 km South of Nairobi, Kenya.

The CA of *M. michaelseni* larvae and workers are paired and spherical, whereas those of presoldiers and soldiers are somewhat oval-shaped. They lie . posterior to a pair of large, egg-shaped corpora cardiaca (CC) which are located immediately behind the brain. Nerves connect the two pairs of glands. Transverse histological sections show that CA are in close contact dorso-laterally with the aorta and that there is, apparently, a nerve leading ventrally from each of the glands passing on either side of the oesophagus to join the (ipsilateral relevant) prothoracic gland (PG) (Fig. 21.1). The possible nerve connection between the CA and PG was also shown by Zuberi and Peeters (1964) in *Cubitermes exiguus*. However, more specific staining procedures for nerves need to be carried out to confirm the existence of such a connection.

The CA cell boundaries are as a rule, difficult to see, although in some cases, such as those of the older fourth instars and, occasionally, the presoldiers, the boundaries are fairly prominent. The cells, which are arranged radially, have spherical nuclei usually positioned close to the periphery of the gland. Depending on the size of the glands, the nuclei may be either closely packed as in the small glands of first instars and workers (Figs 21.1, 21.2), or sparsely distributed, as in those of third instars and, more so, in fourth instars and presoldiers (Figs 21.3, 21.4).

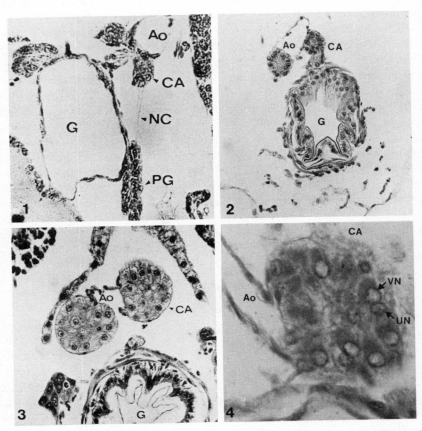

FIG. 21.1. Small corpora allata (CA) of first instar larva with densely packed nuclei. Note the possible nerve connection between CA and the prothoracic gland (PG).

FIG. 21.2. In the workers, CA are also small with densely packed nuclei.

FIG. 21.3. The CA of fourth instar larvae are large with sparsely distributed nuclei and the cell boundaries are fairly well defined.

FIG. 21.4. A transverse section of a presoldier CA showing vacuolated nuclei (VN) and a few unvacuolated nuclei (UN). Note that some parts of the cytoplasm are also vacuolated.

Some of the late stage fourth instar larvae and, more so, the presoldiers, have CA nuclei bearing characteristic and histologically interesting features. Some of these nuclei have large portions which, apparently, do not take up the nuclear stain, thus appearing highly vacuolated with only a thin layer of karyoplasm along the nuclear membrane and a little at one end where the nucleoli are located (Fig. 21.4). Vacuolation is sometimes seen in the cytoplasm. The vacuolated nuclei and cytoplasm react positively to the PAS test for glycogen. PAS-positive reactions were not observed in controls which had been treated with saliva, confirming the presence of glycogen in the vacuoles (Okot-Kotber, 1979). Later, electron-microscopic examinations supported these observations (Okot-Kotber & Owor, unpubl. obs.): the typical rosette-like deposits of glycogen were found in the cytoplasm and nuclei which had appeared vacuolated under the light-microscope. Nuclear glycogen had not previously been known in insect tissues, except in the form of glycoprotein in the nuclei of polyhedral virus-infected lepidopteran *Mamestra brassicae* (Gröner, 1979). The function of glycogen in the nuclei is still unknown.

21.2.1.2 *Changes in CA size during larval development*

During larval development, the nuclei barely increase in size until the later stage of the fourth instar when a drastic increase ensues and they double their size. The number of nuclei within the largest CA transverse sections hardly changes throughout development. This indicates that there is little or no cellular proliferation during the whole period.

However, it was found that the whole glands change in size during larval development (Fig. 21.5). There is a progressive increase in size from the first instar to the third of both minor and major worker lines. A sexual dimorphism is evident, males having larger CA than females of the same instar. However, after the moult to the worker, the CA of both sexes significantly decrease in size, and to the same level, despite the differences in size between males and females. However, the CA of the fourth instar are larger by a factor of 4 than those of a third instar (Fig. 21.5) making them the largest in all developing larvae.

The relationships between CA nuclear and cytoplasmic cross sectional areas (Fig. 21.6) vary much during larval development from first to fourth instar, being smallest in the fourth instar and largest in the first. It is generally believed that the smaller this ratio and the larger the gland, the more active the glands are. Therefore, it seems that the most active CA are those found in the fourth instar larvae which have been shown to be a precursor stage of soldier development (see earlier chapter). This strongly suggests involvement of active CA in soldier determination in *M. michaelseni*.

21.2.1.3 *Changes in CA size during presoldier development*

The size of the CA was also investigated during the intermediate stages of minor and major soldier development. The results are summarized in Figures 21.7 and 21.8. It is clear that although there are changes in the size of the

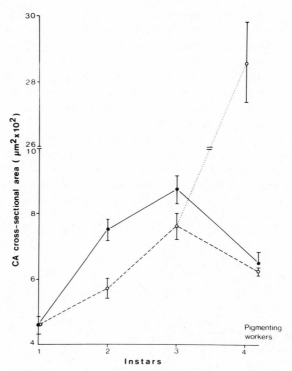

FIG. 21.5. Changes in corpora allata cross-sectional areas during larval development and in teneral workers.

gland during development through the stages, these changes are not significant except during the transition from third or fourth instar to presoldier; they
may be important during the phase of determination. Before third instars
moult into either fourth instars or minor presoldiers, CA are relatively small,
but they increase rapidly in size during the respective moults [more recent
studies using incipient colonies have shown that CA of third instars which
differentiate into presoldiers increase in size drastically about mid-point of the
instar duration (Okot-Kotber, 1982)]. Regarding major soldier development,
CA continue increasing in size in the fourth instar, until they have doubled in
cross-sectional area by the end of the instar.

After the final moult into soldiers, the CA decrease dramatically in size, to
about a quarter.

It seems, therefore, that a relatively high level of CA activity is required
throughout soldier development following the initial stages of determination,
since CA changes in size only slightly during the developmental stages of
soldiers. Lüscher and van Doorn (1976) also showed that the differentiation
characteristics of soldiers in *Zootermopsis* is dependent on the duration of JH or

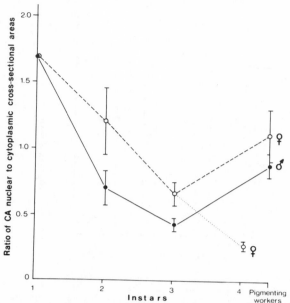

Fig. 21.6. Changes in the corpora allata nuclear/cytoplasmic cross-sectional areas during larval development and in teneral workers.

JHA treatment which seems to support our findings on CA size changes during soldier development.

21.2.1.4 *Morphology and histology of PG of neuter castes*

The paired PG lie in the head capsule ventro-laterally to the oesophagus, extending posteriorly towards the neck region and anteriorly to a position beneath the posterior end of the corpora cardiaca. Each gland comprises double strands of cells attached to muscle fibres on both sides. Some of the PG cells have elongate nuclei barely surrounded by cytoplasm. This is a common appearance among workers and is occasionally observed in the PG of some larvae (in their early stages) (see below). Other larvae (in their later stages) have PG with generally oval-shaped nuclei of varying sizes surrounded by appreciable amounts of cytoplasm. The amount of PG cytoplasm also varies from one larval instar to another, being greatest in the later stages of final instar.

The nuclei diameter, which was measured as an index of activity of the PG from individuals of different instars, increases progressively in size from first instar to a maximum diameter during the final larval instar. The PG nuclei of late fourth instar larvae are the largest (about twice the size of those of third instars). After a moult into presoldiers, the PG decrease overall in size and persist in rudimentary form even in soldiers and workers, which are considered to be adult or terminal castes.

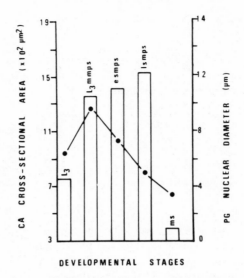

FIG. 21.7. Changes in corpora allata size (columns) and prothoracic gland nuclear diameters (line) during different stages of minor presoldier development. L₃—third instar females, L₃ mmps—minor presoldiers moulting from third instar females, l smps—minor presoldiers in late stage of development and ms—minor soldiers.

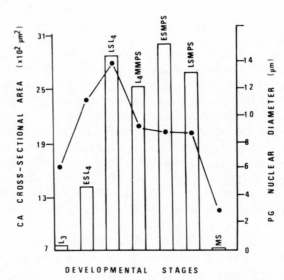

FIG. 21.8. Changes in corpora allata size (columns) and prothoracic gland nuclear diameters (line) during different stages of major presoldier development. L₃—third instar females, ESL₄—early stage fourth instar larvae, LSL₄—late stage fourth instar larvae, L₄MPS—fourth instar larvae moulting into major presoldiers, ESMPS—early stage major presoldiers, LSMPS—late stage major presoldiers and MS—major soldiers.

21.2.2 Nymphs and reproductives

21.2.2.1 *Changes in CA and PG sizes during nymphal development*

The CA of nymphs and reproductives are positioned and arranged in the head capsule like those of the neuter castes.

Measurements of CA volume were made from histological preparations and are shown in Figure 21.9. Although the figure suggests that the CA increases in size during the first four instars, the increase was not significant. However, during the final instar, these glands increased in size about tenfold compared with those of the preceding instar. There is a further increase (about fivefold) soon after the emergence of imagos. It appears that this increase is caused mainly by somatic growth of the glands, as indicated by the sudden increase in the number of nuclei, and has no relevance to activity at this stage. This seems to be a preparation for later events in the life of the adult, when reproduction ensues. The limited increase in size of the glands from first to fourth instars suggests that, unlike in the soldiers, JH may not be necessary for the determination of the reproductives.

The increase in PG volume is more marked during nymphal development than that of the CA (Fig. 21.9). From first instar larvae to first instar nymphs,

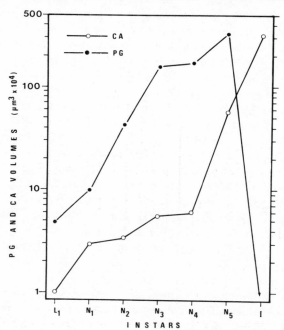

FIG. 21.9. Changes in corpora allata and prothoracic gland volumes during nymphal development. L_1—first instar larvae, N_1–N_5—Nymphal instars and I—imagos.

the PG doubles in volume, but after the first nymphal moult, they increase in volume fourfold. However, there is only a slight increase between third and fourth instars, whereas a significant increase is observed in the fifth instar. Unlike the situation in the neuter castes, these glands degenerate altogether soon after the imaginal moult.

There are two possible explanations for the enlargement of PG during nymphal development. These are: either PG are necessary for the differentiation of nymphs and/or they are needed to meet the requirement for high growth rate particularly in the earlier stages. The role played by PG in the differentiation of the reproductives still remains obscure. There are, however, suggestions by Kaiser (1956) and more recently, by Noirot (1977) that ecdysone may be necessary for differentiation of the reproductives. However, there has been no direct evidence reported to support this view.

21.3 JUVENILE HORMONE IN CASTE DETERMINATION

We have outlined above some circumstantial evidence that JH is an important hormone in caste determination in *M. michaelseni*. Recently, Okot-Kotber (1980b) undertook a series of direct studies to elucidate the role played by JH and JHA in soldier determination in incipient colonies of *M. michaelseni*. The JHA, ZR-515 (methoprene) was applied topically at different dosages on to female third instar larvae. The results showed that JHA induces presoldier production: about 35% of treated individuals transformed into presoldiers, whereas only 15% of the control larvae did so.

Besides presoldier formation, intermediate forms between presoldiers and workers also developed as a result of the treatment. Their morphology ranged from that of workers to that of presoldiers and are here called "worker-like", "presoldier-like", or "soldier-like" according to their form. Pigmentation also varied, ranging from very light amber to dark brown. The analysis of mandible and clypeus forms of some of the individuals in their final stage of development, revealed at least four such intermediate forms (Fig. 21.10) The formation of intermediate forms (intercastes) has been observed in the lower termites following CA implantation (Lüscher & Springhetti, 1960; Lebrun, 1967a, b) or JHA treatment (Lüscher, 1969; Hrdý, 1972; Springhetti, 1974), and even in some higher termites, species of *Nasutitermes* (French, 1974; Lenz, 1976).

Tests were also performed on male third instars which, under normal conditions, develop exclusively into major workers (Okot-Kotber, 1981a, b). Some males were treated with an optimal dose ($2\,\mu$g per animal) of the analogue and the controls received only acetone treatment. Females were treated likewise. Female controls developed as expected (10% into presoldiers and 90% into workers) so did those treated with JHA (overall 36% into

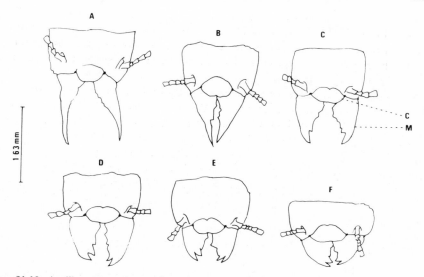

Fig. 21.10. An illustration of mandibles and clypeus from major types of individuals formed under JHA influence. They range from minor soldier type to worker type (A–F).

individuals with presoldier characteristics and 64% into those with worker characteristics) (Figs 21.11a, b). The acetone-treated male larvae developed as expected, exclusively into major workers. However, of those which were JHA-treated, about 30% developed into individuals with presoldier characteristics and 70% into those with worker characteristics (Figs 21.12a, b).

Despite the rigid developmental scheme in *M. michaelseni* (Okot-Kotber, 1981a) and in other species of *Macrotermes* (Noirot, 1955, 1969), with only female larvae capable of developing naturally into soldiers, the present results show that JHA application can induce soldier development even in males. In the lower termites, larvae or pseudergates of both sexes are capable of forming soldiers and it has been assumed that this ability was lost in the course of evolution to the specialized state found in the higher termites (Noirot, 1969). However, the reactivation of soldier-forming genes in the male larvae by exogenously supplied JHA, shows that this ability is not completely lost from the genome, but is secondarily suppressed, supporting the theory of Castle (1934) that caste differentiation is determined by external factors rather than genetic determination.

As mentioned above, topical treatment of third instar larvae with the optimal dose of JHA results in soldier production with an array of intermediate forms (as determined by the shape of their mandibles). Lüscher and van Doorn (1976) reported that the formation of mandibles in presoldiers of *Zootermopsis* was influenced by a regime of JHA application, i.e. a single dose gave rise to presoldiers with short mandibles, whereas repeated application

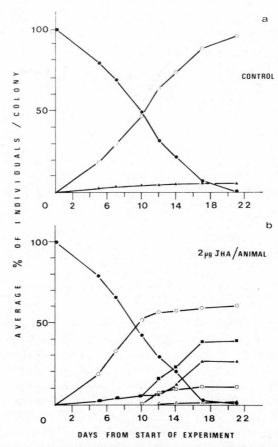

Fig. 21.11a, b. Rates of presoldier formation in groups of female third instars: (a) control groups, (b) JHA treated. Note that intermediate forms were produced only in JHA-treated groups. Workers (open circles), untransformed third instars (solid circles), presoldiers (solid triangles) presoldier-like (open squares), worker-like (open triangles) and total affected individuals (solid squares).

induced formation of normal mandibles (as judged by mandibular index). This led us to determine whether vapour treatment (prolonged JHA effect) would produce presoldiers with perfect mandibles. The results showed that there is a dose-depended response in incipient colonies to JHA supplied in vapour form. At lower doses (1mg JHA/colony) there was no effect on development (15% presoldiers, 45% minor workers and 40% major workers). However, at about 10mg JHA/colony, about 40% of the third instar larvae differentiated into presoldiers, 35% into minor workers and 25% into major workers. Under these conditions intercastes were also formed, but in insignificant numbers.

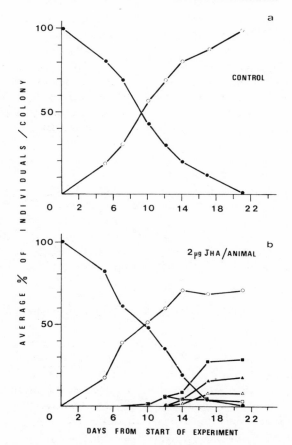

FIG. 21.12a, b. Rates of presoldier formation in groups of male third instars: (a) control groups (b) JHA treated. Note that presoldiers were not produced in control groups, however all forms were induced in the JHA-treated groups: workers (open circles), untransformed third instars (solid circles), presoldiers (solid triangles), presoldier-like (open triangles), worker-like (open squares) and total affected individuals (solid squares).

The analysis of mandibular indices (mandibular length/head capsule length) showed no appreciable differences between presoldiers formed under a single topical dose, those formed under vapour treatment and the controls. The only difference found was in sex specificity, the mandibular index of the males being smaller than those of the females. Partial reactivation of CA of treated individuals might help to explain this lack of difference (Okot-Kotber, 1980c).

Under normal circumstances maximum production of presoldiers is achieved between the 9th and 10th day from third instar (Okot-Kotber, 1981b). However, JHA-treated larvae transform into presoldiers at a maximum rate on day 12 or soon after. This may suggest initial inhibition of moulting of larvae in these latter groups. Masner and Hangartner (1973) showed that the JHA, geranylphenylester or JH may inhibit moulting if supplied continuously to the nymphs of the cockroach *Blattella germanica*. Wanyonyi (1974) also noted similar effects on groups of larvae and nymphs of *Z. nevadensis*. However, in the present experiments, the inhibition seems to be temporary, because after 10 days there was a sudden burst of presoldier formation. It is probable, therefore, that the prothoracic glands go through two phases. First they are inhibited by the exogenous JHA, perhaps to allow a reprogramming of soldier-forming genes, then they are reactivated just before the burst of presoldier moult, after differentiation has occurred.

It is now evident that JH is important not only for soldier differentiation in the lower termites [e.g. in *K. flavicollis* (Lüscher, 1969), *Z. nevadensis* (Wanyonyi, 1974), and *Reticulitermes lucifugus santonensis* (Hrdý, 1972; Hrdý & Křeček, 1972)], but also plays an important role in soldier formation in the higher termites [e.g. in species of *Nasutitermes* (French, 1974; Lenz, 1976) and in *M. michaelseni* (Okot-Kotber, 1980b)]. It appears, therefore, that JH plays a universal role in soldier differentiation in the order Isoptera.

21.4 COMPETENCE OF LARVAE TO DIFFERENTIATE UNDER JHA

Collection of alates and rearing of *M. michaelseni* incipient colonies were basically the same as reported earlier (Okot-Kotber, 1981b). In order to test the potentiality of larvae belonging to different instars to differentiate into presoldiers, female first, second and third (final) larval instars were treated with standard doses (2 μg per animal) of JHA (Okot-Kotber, 1980b). The results showed that only third instars had the potential (competence) to differentiate into presoldiers under these conditions. This is compatible with the earlier observation made on minor presoldier formation in laboratory incipient colonies (Okot-Kotber, 1981b) and in field situations (Okot-Kotber, 1981a). The results also show that the timing mechanism in presoldier formation in *M. michaelseni* is very rigid, unlike the situation in *Prorhinotermes simplex* (a lower termite), where Hrdý et al. (1979) showed that presoldier formation could be induced in the second instar, as opposed to the third instar, from which presoldiers form under natural conditions.

Since only third instar larvae in incipient colonies of *M. michaelseni* have the competence to differentiate into presoldiers, and not even excessive JHA, which can cause death to some individuals, induces 100% presoldier formation, further studies were undertaken to find out whether there is a period of competence within the instar, during which the larvae are most responsive to the analogue. Fig. 21.13 shows that the individuals which responded to the analogue moulted into presoldiers and the array of intermediate forms (intercastes). The rate of presoldier and presoldier-like formation was high

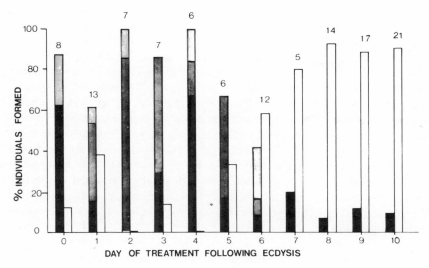

Fɪɢ. 21.13. Formation rates of presoldiers and other individuals from synchronous groups of third instar larvae at different ages after topical treatment with JHA. Presoldier (dark columns), presoldier-like (hatched columns), worker-like (striped columns) and workers (open columns). Figures above the columns represent the total number of individuals observed.

(over 70%) when larvae of five or less days old were treated. Although 6-day-old larvae also responded to the treatment, the rate was relatively low (about 40%) and most of those which responded developed into worker-like individuals. There was no response to the analogue treatment in 7-day-old or older larvae since the rate of presoldier formation was the same as in untreated. It is evident, therefore, that in this species the competence period lies between zero and 6th day of the instar.

Springhetti (1972) showed that pseudergates of *K. flavicollis* also have competence period for differentiation into presoldiers. However, this period is rather short, and occurs in the second half of the approximately 70-day instar, between the 45th and 60th days. Working on another species of lower termites, *Z. angusticollis*, Lüscher (1974b) arrived at the same conclusions when he applied vapours of JH or farnesylmethyl ester to groups of larvae of known age within the intermoult period. These findings contrast with the results of *M. michaelseni*, that the sensitive period is during the first half of the moulting interval and the loss of competence is relatively abrupt. It was also found that intermediate forms develop only during the competence period and that their formation is not correlated with any particular period within the competence interval.

Studies on the CA of presoldiers formed under various conditions have shown that these glands may differ in size and nuclear/cytoplasmic ratio, hence in activity (Okot-Kotber, 1980c). This suggests that glandular activity depends on the conditions under which the presoldiers are formed.

The most active glands are those in spontaneously formed presoldiers from laboratory incipient colonies. The next most active are those formed under laboratory conditions, but from field collected larvae; followed by those minor presoldiers collected from the field (Table 21.1). Minor presoldiers formed under JHA treatment have the least active glands. Lüscher (1969) reported that the CA of spontaneous presoldiers of *K. flavicollis* were larger than those of JHA induced ones. This observation agrees well with the situation in *M. michaelseni*. However, the finding in this latter species that the CA in spontaneously formed individuals from incipient-adopted third instars are much larger than those of presoldiers from field larvae adopted in the same way, and even larger than those of field collected minor presoldiers poses very interesting questions. A possible explanation may be based on royal influence. Springhetti (1969, 1970) reported in *K. flavicollis*, Miller (1942) in *Prorhino-termes simplex* and Lüscher (1973) in two species of *Zootermopsis* that royal couples may enhance soldier formation, although our own observations on *M. michaelseni* have not confirmed these reports (Okot-Kotber, unpubl. obs.).

21.5 CORRELATION BETWEEN LARVAL WEIGHTS, GLANDULAR ACTIVITY AND COMPETENCE

The existence of a competence period during the development of larvae has been documented earlier. The responsiveness of third instar larvae to an exogenous source of JH in the form of an analogue was shown to be stage-dependent; younger larvae showed a response whereas the analogue had no developmental effects on older larvae. Recently, studies were undertaken in an attempt to establish whether there is an association between competence period and changes in endocrine gland volumes, as a measure of activity (Okot-Kotber, 1982). It was also possible to carry out comparative investi-gations on soldier and worker development. Thanks to recent findings that if a pair of female third instars are adopted by the reproductives on day zero, the chance that one of them will develop into a presoldier and the other into a worker is 50% (Okot-Kotber, 1983).

Fresh weights of adopted pairs of female third-instar larvae are shown in Fig. 21.14. There was a clear separation of the pairs of larvae into two distinct groups, namely lighter and heavier individuals, beginning from day 1. The lighter larvae developed into workers whereas the heavier ones moulted into presoldiers.

The rate of increase in weights in the two groups were steady and similar, and peaks were achieved about the same day (day 7). The drop in weights on

TABLE 21.1. MEASUREMENTS OF CORPORA ALLATA, SHOWING DIFFERENT LEVELS OF ACTIVITY IN MINOR PRESOLDIERS FORMED UNDER VARYING EXPERIMENTAL CONDITIONS

Types of individuals	n	Corpora allata cross-sectional area (μm^2) (mean ± S.E.)	Number of nuclei/cross-section (mean ± S.E.)	Nuclear cross-sectional area (μm^2) (mean ± S.E.)	Ratio nuclear/cytoplasmic area
Field minor presoldiers	9	1568.89 ± 216.87	11.47 ± 0.23	34.18 ± 4.51	0.26
Spontaneous laboratory minor presoldiers (produced from adopted field larvae)	12	1939.94 ± 409.52	11.58 ± 0.31	36.06 ± 2.28	0.27
Spontaneous laboratory minor presoldiers (produced from incipient colony larvae)	3	2531.64 ± 288.88	13.00 ± 0.68	41.46 ± 6.52	0.27
Minor presoldiers induced by JHA topical application (incipient colony larvae)	4	1199.19 ± 104.59	12.38 ± 0.38	34.94 ± 0.01	0.56

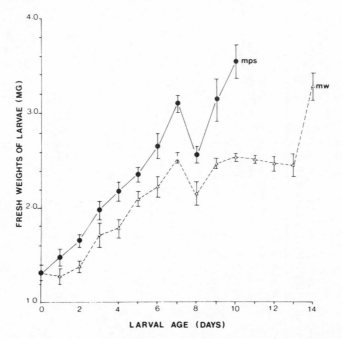

Fig. 21.14. Changes in fresh weights of paired female final-instar larvae during their development into minor presoldiers (mps) from heavier larvae (solid circles) or into minor workers (mw)
lighter larvae (open triangles). Each point represents mean fresh weights of at least 10 larvae and
vertical bars designate ± SE.

day 8 may be explained by the emptying of the gut, and despite the midgut
renovation, feeding may be resumed.

It appears that, from day 1 onwards, there is a differential feeding pattern
associated with the rate of increase in larval weights. It is not clear how this
happens, but it is possible that the pattern may be guided by behavioural
elements of larvae and/or reproductives, leading to recognition.

Light microscopic observations revealed the following: on day 0, all larvae
observed had no stainable gut contents, indicating that they were empty. Both
CA and PG were even in their appearance with, if any, only small vacuoles
present. The prothoracic glands had small rounded nuclei with little cytoplasmic materials. This was also so between days 1 and 3 with the exception that
heavier larvae had already some stainable gut contents, presumably food,
whereas lighter larvae had less. At this stage the PG of the lighter larvae had
not changed much in appearance, but those of the heavier individuals were
staining more heavily and had larger nuclei and more cytoplasmic material.
Between days 4 and 7 the staining intensities of the gut contents were
comparable in the two categories of larvae. However, the PG nuclei of the

heavier larvae became progressively larger and more rounded and cytoplasmic material also increased and stained more intensely, whereas those of lighter larvae did not change greatly. Similar patterns of changes in histological features which occurred in PG were also observed in the CA. In addition from day 6, nuclear vacuolation occurred in the CA, particularly so on days 6–9, when vacuolation was also observed in the cytoplasm. The nuclear vacuolation disappeared only after worker emergence. After day 6, progressively less stainable gut contents could be seen in either type of larvae. The midgut remained empty and the epithelium underwent renewal. During the same period the PG deteriorated progressively in the lighter larvae, but rather abruptly in the heavier larvae.

The association between food intake and activation of CA during soldier differentiation in *K. flavicollis* was postulated by Lüscher (1958). We found a close correlation between increase in CA volume (activity) and differential pattern in larval weight gain from the initial stages of development leading to soldier formation. It appears that once the mechanism of CA activation has been triggered more nutriments are required to boost the activity to the level necessary for soldier determination. This condition seems to be met in the heavier larvae. On the other hand, it appears that, if the initial trophic stimulus has not reached a threshold, however much of the weight may subsequently increase, it will not influence the CA activity significantly. It remains unclear whether CA activation is achieved directly or indirectly through food.

Changes in volume of the CA throughout the developmental period of heavier and lighter larvae into presoldiers and workers, respectively, are illustrated in Figure 21.15. It is evident that the changes in the heavier larvae were more marked than in the lighter individuals. The highest peak in CA volume in both types of larvae was achieved on day 6. The competence period for soldier determination lasts between 0 and 6 days as mentioned earlier. It is clear therefore, that the high level of JH required for soldier differentiation must be achieved at the latest by day 6, after which competence of larvae to differentiate into soldiers is totally lost. The end of competence in the lighter larvae is also marked by the low peak of CA activity, but since there is inadequate JH present, no soldier differentiation takes place. Instead, these larvae take a more direct route of development into workers which does not require high levels of JH as indicated by low CA volume throughout the developmental period. Lüscher (1958, 1974a) reported to have also found a correlation between competence period and increased CA activity (volume) in *K. flavicollis*. However, in his work on a related genus, *Z. angusticollis* he found no such correlation (Lüscher, 1974b). No explanation is offered for this discrepancy.

Changes in prothoracic gland volume (activity) were also monitored during the study. The results are presented in Figure 21.16. As was the case for the

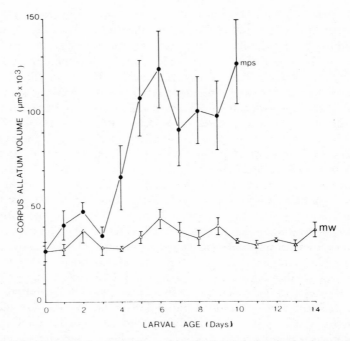

FIG. 21.15. Measurements of corpora allata volume (activity) during the development of paired female final-instar larvae into minor presoldiers (mps) from heavier larvae (solid circles) and into minor workers (mw) from lighter larvae (open triangles). Each point is represented by a mean of 10 measurements and vertical bars designate ± SE.

CA, the prothoracic glands enlarge rapidly in the heavier larvae, whereas in the lighter larvae it was less pronounced. The highest peak in heavier larvae was reached on day 5, preceeding a decline; the volume reached a relatively low level a day before the presoldier moult. In the lighter larvae, however, the peak achieved on the 5th day was maintained as a high plateau until day 8. Fluctuations then followed until a final drop on day 12 to a low level, which was maintained until the worker moult. Since this high peak of PG activity was achieved on day 5, this suggests that ecdysone also may be important during the competence period of soldier differentiation.

Prothoracicotropic effects of JH have been demonstrated by several authors (Williams, 1959; Ichikawa & Nishiitsutsuji-Uwo, 1959; Gilbert & Schneiderman, 1959; Gilbert, 1962; Hiruma et al., 1978; Cymborowski & Stolarz, 1979; Safranek et al., 1980) in a number of insect species. It appears that the same mechanism of prothoracic gland activation may operate in M. michaelseni. This assumption is based on the fact that in the heavier larvae, the first peak in CA volume is followed by a sharp rise in PG volume. It is further supported by Wanyonyi's work on Zootermopsis (1974) in which he demonstrated that larvae

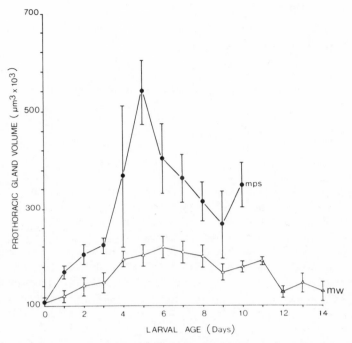

Fɪɢ. 21.16   Measurements of prothoracic gland volume (activity) during the development of paired female final-instar larvae. These measurements were of PG from the same individuals as in Figure 21.15 and the symbols remain unchanged.

treated with JHA and whose development had been channelled into presoldier formation, had enlarged PG. Apparently, the prothoracicotropic effect of JH in *M. michaelseni* depends on the level of CA activity, because in the situation where CA volume increase was small, as in the lighter larvae, there was only a small increase in the volume of the prothoracic gland.

21.6   ECDYSTEROID LEVELS ASSOCIATED WITH EPIDERMAL EVENTS DURING DIFFERENTIATION

The action of JH at cellular level during caste differentiation may be displayed in the form of morphological changes. This is usually associated with changes in the levels of ecdysteroids. We have seen that when CA change in volume during differentiation in the third instar, the prothoracic glands also do so in a phase-like pattern. In order to determine more precisely the involvement of ecdysteroids in soldier development, levels of this group of hormones were monitored during worker and soldier determination (in lighter and heavier larvae), and were associated with epidermal events during development in this crucial instar. These studies were limited to laboratory-reared female third instar larvae.

21.6.1   Ecdysteroid levels in third instars

Ecdysteroid levels measured by radioimmunoassay in the extracts of heavier and lighter paired third instar larvae during their development are shown in Figure 21.17. In both cases two hormonal peaks were observed, the first ones being considerably lower than the second ones. During the first 2–3 days the hormonal levels were low, practically constant and comparable in the two types of larvae (about 75 ng per g fresh weight). The first peaks (125 ng per g fresh weight in both cases) were similar and achieved on the same day (4th day). While the peak for lighter larvae considerably dropped the following day and remained low until day 6, that of heavier larvae remained high for another day and only slightly dropped on the 6th day. A steep rise followed until day 9 in the two types of larvae (Fig. 21.17). This interval was followed by a sudden burst in ecdysteroid level in the heavier larvae achieving the highest peak (560 ng per g fresh weight) on day 10, just before a presoldier moult. In the lighter larvae, however, the tempo continued as before reaching the highest peak (310 ng per g fresh weight) on day 12. Subsequent rapid drops in the levels of ecdysteroids were observed in both cases. The level in the heavier larvae after moulting into presoldiers dropped to about 130 ng per g fresh weight, while that of lighter larvae, after a worker moult, was lower (back to the level at the beginning of third instar).

21.6.2   Morphological differentiation of mandibles in third instars

Mandibles of third instars were used as markers of soldier differentiation. The dentition of larval mandibles does not differ in pattern from that of workers. Each mandible has an apical tooth, two large marginal teeth and a poorly defined molar plate. Presoldier mandibles are more slender, with the apical tooth attenuated and greatly reduced marginal teeth.

Third instar larvae in days 0–3 did not show any sign of mandibular differentiation (Figs 21.18A, B) although differences in larval weights were established during this period. Progressive thickening of mandibular epidermis and underlying tissues, especially toothed edge was evident. In the heavier larvae, epidermal retraction had begun approximately on day 4 and initial morphological differentiation of the larval mandibles into those of a future presoldier was already detectable (Fig. 21.18C). This period coincides with

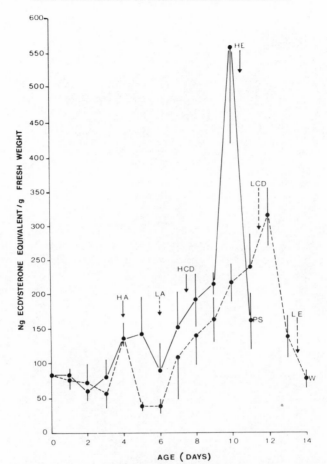

Fɪɢ. 21.17. Changes in ecdysteroid levels during the development of lighter (broken line) and heavier (solid line) larvae into workers (w) and presoldiers (PS), respectively. (HA)—Start of apolysis in heavier larvae; (LA)—start of apolysis in lighter larvae. Heavier larvae cuticular deposition (HCD) and ecdysis (HE). Lighter larvae cuticular deposition (LCD) and ecdysis (LE). Vertical bars designate ± SE of the mean (Five replicates for each point).

the first peak of ecdysteroid level (Fig. 21.17) and with surge of CA activity outlined above. At this stage the mandibles of lighter larvae showed no significant cuticular detachment except on the toothed edge (Fig. 21.18D). It appears, therefore, that while the first peak of ecdysteroids may be important for apolysis (Riddiford & Curtis, 1978) and induction of critical period (change in cellular commitment) as reported in *Manduca sexta* (Bollenbacher *et al.*, 1975; Riddiford, 1978) increased activity of CA (increased JH levels) may modulate the response of target cells to ecdysone as suggested by Schneider-

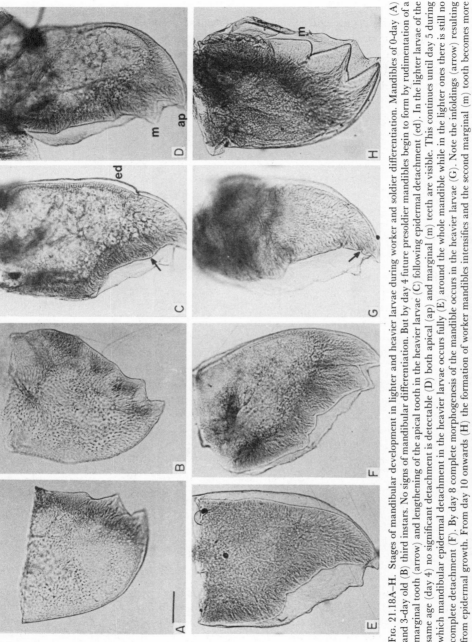

FIG. 21.18A–H. Stages of mandibular development in lighter and heavier larvae during worker and soldier differentiation. Mandibles of 0-day (A) and 3-day old (B) third instars. No signs of mandibular differentiation. But by day 4 future presoldier mandibles begin to form by rudimentation of a marginal tooth (arrow) and lengthening of the apical tooth in the heavier larvae (C) following epidermal detachment (ed). In the lighter larvae of the same age (day 4) no significant detachment is detectable (D) both apical (ap) and marginal (m) teeth are visible. This continues until day 5 during which mandibular epidermal detachment in the heavier larvae occurs fully (E) around the whole mandible while in the lighter ones there is still no complete detachment (F). By day 8 complete morphogenesis of the mandible occurs in the heavier larvae (G). Note the infoldings (arrow) resulting from epidermal growth. From day 10 onwards (H) the formation of worker mandibles intensifies and the second marginal (m) tooth becomes more pronounced. Scale bar represents 50 µm. Magnification is the same for all figures.

man (1969) in other insect systems. Therefore, this early ecdysteroid peak may also be a signal to the end of the competence period in *M. michaelseni*. During the subsequent stages of mandibular development, the future presoldier mandibles continue to develop as epidermal retraction spreads over the mandible (Fig. 21.18E). This period is accompanied by a steep rise in ecdysteroid level indicating that higher levels are required for subsequent developmental events which culminate in deposition of new cuticle (in 8–9-day-old larvae) before a presoldier moult (Fig. 21.18G).

In the lighter larvae, the onset of mandibular cuticular detachment (Fig. 21.18F) occurred during the sudden drop in the first ecdysteroid peak (Fig. 21.17). The subsequent rise in ecdysteroid levels was accompanied by reorganization of larval mandibles into well-defined future worker mandibles (Fig. 21.18H) especially at the major hormonal peak.

21.6.3   Histology of epidermis of third instars

During the first 2 days, there was no significant difference in histological appearance in the two types of larvae. The abdomens appeared shrunken, and the epidermal cells were poor in cytoplasm, and had small nuclei. During the subsequent stage of development, the abdominal segments became stretched, the epidermal cell nuclei and cytoplasm became much more enlarged (Fig. 21.19A), and the pericardial cells appeared prominent before abdominal apolysis.

Epidermal detachment started from the mouthparts on about day 4, then gradually spread to other areas, first to the ventral parts of the abdomen (starting day 4–5 in heavier larvae and day 6–7 in lighter larvae) and quickly extending to the dorsum of the abdomen (Fig. 21.19B), the thorax and the head capsule.

Between days 7 and 8, rapid deposition of new cuticle occurred in the abdominal epidermis of heavier larvae accompanied by cell division evidenced by increased number of nuclei which appeared much smaller and cramped into the limited space within the old cuticle, hence the convoluted appearance of the epidermis (Fig. 21.19C). Deposition of new cuticle intensified for the next 1 or 2 days, coinciding with the highest ecdysteroid peak before a presoldier moult (Fig. 21.17). Similar observations were made for lighter larvae. Intensive cuticular deposition was, however, detected later (day 10–11) and was also accompanied by cell division. Deposition continued more intensively for a further 2 or 3 days, also corresponding with the highest ecdysteroid peak before a worker moult ensued (Fig. 21.17). The development culminating in initiation of new cuticular deposition, ending in a moult, corresponds with the highest ecdysteroid peak (second peak). This has also

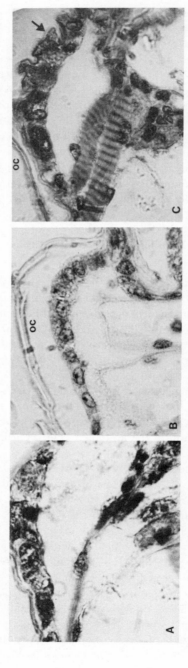

FIG. 21.19A–C. Main features of events taking place in the dorsal abdominal epidermis of lighter and heavier larvae during worker and soldier differentiation. By day 2 there is already nuclear and cytoplasmic increase in size (Fig. 21.19A). Complete apolysis is achieved by day 5 in heavier larvae and by day 7 in the lighter ones (Fig. 21.19B). Heavy deposition of new cuticle (arrow) which follows several days after apolysis is shown in Fig. 21.19C. Pieces of old detached cuticle still visible (oc). Note also convolutions of the epidermis apparently as a result of intensive growth. Scale bar represent 10 µm. Magnification is the same for all figures.

been reported in a number of other insect species, e.g. *Aeshna cyanea* (Schaller & Charlet, 1980); *Locusta migratoria* (Hoffmann *et al.*, 1974; Bouthier, 1975), *Tenebrio molitor* (Delbecque *et al.*, 1978), and *Manduca sexta* (Bollenbacher *et al.*, 1975).

Recently, Safranek *et al.* (1980) reported that JH affects ecdysone-dependent development in the tobacco hornworm, *M. sexta*. They showed that JH accelerated the onset of metamorphosis if administered after the onset of the wandering period. This may explain the observed acceleration of development into presoldiers, since CA in heavier larvae become more active than in the lighter larvae moulting into workers.

21.6.4   Ecdysteroid levels during soldier development

During the development of the presoldier to the soldier, two distinct ecdysteroid peaks were detectable (Fig. 21.20). The first, small peak appeared on day 2 and may be associated with early events of metamorphosis. The second, achieved on day 9 was by far the highest and this late peak, common

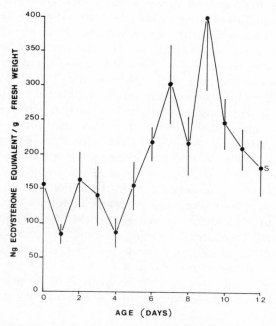

FIG. 21.20. Patterns of ecdysteroid levels during presoldier–soldier transformation. Note the characteristic two clear peaks and transient third one in between. Vertical bars indicate ±SE of the mean.

to many insect species (see above), may be important for the later events leading to ecdysis. Similar peaks were recently reported in the last larval instars of *L. migratoria* (Hirn *et al.*, 1979), another hemimetabolous insect. The results have shown that changes in ecdysteroid levels during the development of *M. michaelseni* follow basically the same pattern reported in a number of other insect orders, despite the polymorphism characteristic of isopteran development.

21.7   INFLUENCE OF GROUP SIZE AND COMPOSITION

21.7.1   Larval group size

The group effect is an important aspect of regulation of caste composition in termites. Recent studies (Okot-Kotber, 1983) with homogeneous groups of third instar female larvae cared for by homosexual female pairs showed that group size did not influence the instar duration for either presoldier or worker development, these being about 9.5 and 13.5 days respectively. This suggests that all larvae had equal moulting opportunities. However, a few larvae remained untransformed after as long as 4 weeks, which far exceeds the period for normal development, even of workers. These untransformed larvae appeared more active than normal, and their guts contained brownish yellow pigment, but were not distended. They were sometimes observed gathering unfertilized eggs laid by their virgin "foster mothers".

The rates of presoldier formation in various sized larval groups are shown in Fig. 21.21. Only with singly isolated larvae was there a greater tendency for transformation into a presoldier than a worker: such produced the highest proportion of presoldiers (about 60%). With two or more larvae, there were an exponential downward trend in presoldier proportion with increasing group size, falling to a minimum of about 7% in groups of 32 larvae. This implies an inherent tendency towards differentiation into presoldiers rather than workers and, hence, that this tendency is suppressed if another larva which has acquired more competence is present (as in the larger groups). The competence to differentiate into presoldier seems to be randomly induced by the acquisition of more food from the parents, and results in the inhibition of presoldier development in the other larvae. It seems that the induction may occur at about the same time in several individuals in the larger groups, since if more than one larva differentiates into a presoldier, they emerge on about the same day.

The levelling off in presoldier formation in the larger groups leads to a proportion (about 7%) similar to that found by J. P. E. C. Darlington (Pers. comm.) for soldiers in field colonies (about 6% of the total adult sterile female

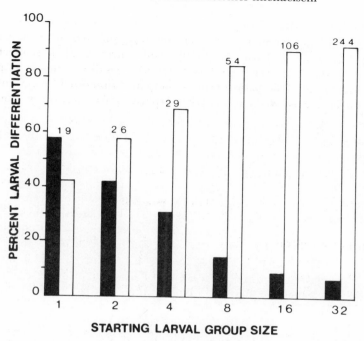

Fig. 21.21. Influence of larval group size on presoldier production shown as percentage of total larval transformation into presoldiers (dark columns) and workers (open columns). Numbers above columns indicate the total of individuals which survived throughout the experimental period in each group size.

population of a mature mound of *M. michaelseni*), a figure also close to those found in other species of *Macrotermes* (Haverty, 1977).

This inverse dependence of soldier proportion on group size does not agree with most of the findings on lower termites. For example, Springhetti (1973) found that the proportion of soldiers formed in groups of 2–25 *K. flavicollis* pseudergates increases with the size of the group, and argued that there was no soldier determination in groups with 2 or 3 pseudergates per colony, any that formed being due to chance determination before the groups were established. In *Coptotermes formosanus* (Haverty, 1979), *R. flavipes* (Haverty & Howard, 1981) and *Cryptotermes brevis* (McMahan, 1966) lower percentages of soldiers were produced in smaller groups than in larger ones; but these findings are in contrast to those of Lüscher (1961) for *K. flavicollis*, which are in agreement with the present findings.

These differences may be partially explained by the fact that, whereas these previous authors worked with pseudergates of unknown age, the present experiments were carried out on synchronized larvae, grouped at such a time that there could have been no prior differentiation and only minimal interaction.

21.7.2 Worker and larval group size

Sets of acceptor colonies consisting of groups with 20, 40 and 80 workers each were established. Each of these sets was sub-divided into three sub-sets; (a) receiving two third instars, (b) receiving four, and (c) eight. They were then checked at regular intervals. The results are given in Figure 21.22. With only two larvae present, there were no significant differences in presoldier formation between the 20, 40 and 80 worker groups, nor between them and groups consisting of two larvae only (see Fig. 21.21). Increasing the number of larvae present to four, reduced the proportion of presoldier formation, and increasing it to eight reduced it still more. On the other hand, there was a tendency for presoldier formation to increase slightly as the number of workers per group increased, at least with four or eight larvae present. In addition, the higher the number of both workers and larvae in a group, the greater the chance that it will form more than one presoldier (Table 21.2).

Higher termites have a definite worker caste distinct from larvae, whereas in some lower termites this distinction is difficult to draw. There are species-specific proportions of soldier caste in both lower and higher termites (Haverty, 1977), including *M. michaelseni* (J. P. E. C. Darlington, Pers.

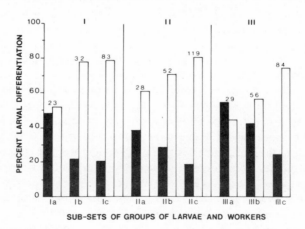

Fig. 21.22. Influence of worker and larval group size on presoldier production shown as percentage of total larval transformations into presoldiers (dark columns) and workers (open columns). Roman numerals I, II and III designate experimental sets, consisting of 20, 40 or 80 workers each, respectively, and each sub-set (a, b, c) with in addition 2, 4 or 8 third instars respectively. Numbers above columns indicate the total of individuals which survived throughout the experimental period.

TABLE 21.2. THE INFLUENCE OF WORKER AND LARVAL GROUP SIZE
ON THE FREQUENCY DISTRIBUTION OF COLONIES FORMING
VARIOUS NUMBERS OF PRESOLDIERS (SEE FIG. 21.22 FOR DETAILS)

Group composition		n*	Frequency of numbers of presoldiers formed/group			
Workers	Larvae		0	1	2	3
20	2	14	3	11	0	0
20	4	9	2	7	0	0
20	8	15	1	11	3	0
40	2	15	5	9	1	0
40	4	15	1	13	1	0
40	8	15	0	8	6	1
80	2	15	1	12	2	0
80	4	15	0	7	7	1
80	8	14	1	5	8	0

*n, number of replicates.

comm.). This suggested that the presence and number of workers may influence the direction of larval differentiation. Varying the number of workers adopted, together with varying the number of final instar larvae of the same age, influenced the outcome of the moults, and showed that there was a tendency towards higher production of presoldiers with increase in the number of workers and larvae per group.

This may indicate that there is a trend towards compensation for original lack of soldiers. Since the natural proportion of soldiers in this species (*ca* 6%) was not achieved even in groups which should have had a maximum influence (80 workers plus 8 larvae), it is conceivable that negative larval interactions might have counteracted the positive influence of workers in promoting presoldier development. The potential influence of the reproductives was irrelevant, since all the groups had an equal number of reproductives. Moreover, our recent experiment in which various numbers of reproductives adopted different-sized groups of third instar larvae failed to show any direct influence on development into presoldiers (Okot-Kotber, unpubl. obs.).

21.7.3 Soldier influence

The influence of soldiers on the formation of other soldiers was assessed by forming groups of eight larvae and introducing a soldier into some groups. No presoldiers were formed in the groups which included a soldier, whereas 13% of the transformations were to presoldiers when no soldier was present (Table 21.3).

In experiments where groups of four larvae were divided into two subgroups by mesh, the results (Table 21.4) show that rates of presoldier production in the absence of a soldier were the same in the two halves at (*ca* 40%) and comparable with those in the unscreened colonies with two larvae (Fig. 21.21). Moreover, even when a soldier was present, the rate of presoldier transformation was still around 40%, provided the larvae were screened off from the soldier. In the other half of the same dishes, however, where the soldier could be in direct contact with the larvae, only 5% of transformations were into presoldiers (P 0.001, x^2, for the 2 × 2 comparison of the two halves). These results show that soldiers exert a strong inhibitory influence on the differentiation into soldiers of unbiased competent larvae. Similar findings have been reported in lower termites, for example, Castle (1934) on *Z. angusticollis*, Springhetti (1969) on *K. flavicollis* and a number of others. In the higher termites, this phenomenon seems not to be limited to *M. michaelseni* and has been demonstrated also in *Nasutitermes* (French, 1974; Lenz, 1976) and in *N. lujae* (Bordereau, Chapter 16).

The mechanisms of this inhibition remains obscure, although the present

TABLE 21.3. SOLDIER PRODUCTION IN GROUPS OF EIGHT THIRD INSTAR LARVAE WITH AND WITHOUT A SOLDIER PRESENT

	n^*	Total no. (%) of transformations	
		To presoldiers	To workers
No soldier present	11	9 (13)	60 (87)
Soldier present	11	0 (0)	50 (100)

*n, number of replicates.

TABLE 21.4. PATTERNS OF PRESOLDIER FORMATION IN SCREENED GROUPS OF LARVAE WITH OR WITHOUT A SOLDIER PRESENT

	n^*	Total no. (%) of transformations	
		To presoldiers	To workers
Soldier present	10		
Left ½ dish + soldier		1 (5)	19 (95)
Right ½ dish − soldier		8 (40)	12 (60)
Total		9 (23)	31 (77)
No soldier present	18		
Left ½ dish		14 (39)	22 (61)
Right ½ dish		15 (42)	21 (58)
Total		29 (40)	43 (60)

*n = number of replicates; 2 × 2 larvae per group, so maximum possible transformation = $4n$.

experiments with the screened groups demonstrate that if a pheromone is involved it must be of very low volatility since it did not traverse the wire mesh to the larvae on the other side of it in a 5 cm diameter Petri dish. Springhetti (1969), working on *K. flavicollis*, and Hewitt *et al.* (1969) with *Hodotermes mossambicus* found similarly that if inhibition is by pheromone, it must be a non-volatile one. It appears, therefore, that inhibition by soldiers of further soldier development may be universal in Isoptera.

In summary, the following scheme of regulatory mechanisms of soldier determination is proposed (Fig. 21.23). The key external factor is food which stimulates the CA of newly-moulted third instars. If the pheromone that inhibits soldier production is weak or absent, then the activated third instar will develop into a presoldier. While it develops, it exerts an inhibitory influence on any other third instar it contacts. The inhibited individuals will develop into workers. Soldiers have an overall inhibiting effect over larvae, to

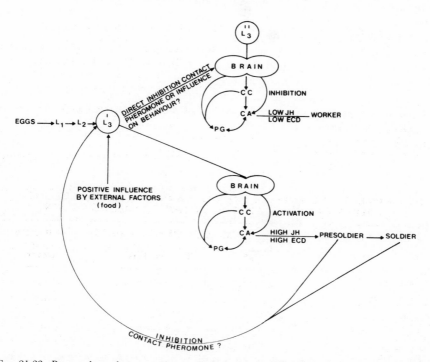

FIG. 21.23. Proposed regulatory mechanisms of soldier determination. L_1, L_2 and L_3 are larval instars. L_3I perceives the influence of external factors (food) more than or earlier than L_3II so develops a potential of exerting inhibitory influence on L_3II. As a result L_3I develops into a presoldier while L_3II develops into a worker. CC—corpus cardiacum, CA—corpus allatum, PG—prothoracic gland, JH—juvenile hormone, and ECD—ecdysteroid.

such an extent that only if the number of soldiers drops, this effect is "diluted" and more soldiers are produced. The cycle is repeated as the colony enlarges and soldier percentage falls, or some soldiers are lost for one reason or another.

21.8 SUMMARY

Caste determination has been shown to be under hormonal control in both higher and lower termites. Enlargement of CA is associated with maturation of the imagos, formation of presoldiers and neotenics. These glands do not change much during worker development. Prothoracic glands have also been shown to undergo changes during caste development in both lower and higher termites. These glands degenerate in replacement reproductives, but undergo regular growth during the development of primary reproductives. It is not clear whether they are important for differentiation in the reproductives or are simply required for somatic growth which is marked in this line of development. In the neuters, they are poorly developed and persist throughout the life span of these individuals.

Juvenile hormones have been conclusively shown to be a key factor in soldier differentiation in both lower and higher termites. In *M. michaelseni* externally-applied JHA may induce soldier differentiation in the larvae (males) which normally develop exclusively into workers. There are also indications that JHA may reactivate CA of individuals treated with it. The analogue treatment was also shown to delay metamorphosis and this is discussed in some details.

Competence period to differentiate into soldiers has been demonstrated in a number of termite species. In the lower termites studied, competence is apparently acquired in the second half of the instar while it is the reverse in a higher termite species, *M. michaelseni*. Active CA have been associated with this period in both cases. In *M. michaelseni* PG also become activated during this period. Differential increase in larval weights in this species has been demonstrated. The heavier larvae have been shown to differentiate into presoldiers, while lighter ones differentiate into workers. *Corpora allata* and PG were found to be more active in the heavier individuals than in the lighter ones and the peak of their activity marks the end of the competence period.

Other factors which regulate caste composition in the lower termites are known. Some of these factors are the group size of the developing individuals, the number and type of mature castes present. In the lower termites, the proportion of presoldiers produced is positively related to the size of the group formed. However, in *M. michaelseni* this seems to be the opposite. This discrepancy is discussed in some detail. The number of workers present positively influence the proportion of presoldiers formed in groups of female third instars, while the presence of soldiers inhibits the development of other soldiers. The inhibition seems to be pheromonal through contact. It appears food (food factor) is important in the activation of CA during soldier determination. In turn CA then activate PG. A scheme of regulatory mechanisms for soldier determination is proposed.

21.9 REFERENCES

Bollenbacher W. E., Vedeckis W. V., Gilbert L. I. & O'Connor J. D. (1975) Ecdysone titers and prothoracic gland activity during the larval-pupal development of *Manduca sexta. Dev. Biol.* **44**, 33–45.

Bouthier A., Pennetier J. L., Mauchamp B. & Lafont R. (1975) Variation due taux de β-ecdysone circulante chez *Locusta migratoria cinerascens* Fabr. (Orthoptères, Acrididae) au cours du dernier stade larvaire. *C.r. Hebd, Seanc. Acad. Sci.*, Paris **280**, 1837–1840.

Castle G. B. (1934) An experimental investigation of caste differentiation in *Zootermopsis angusticollis*. In *Termites and Termite Control* (Kofoid C. A., ed.), 2nd ed., pp. 292–310. Univ. Calif. Press, Berkley, California.

Cazal P. (1948) Les glandes endocrines retrocérébrales des insectes. Etude morphologique. *Bull. Biol. France Belg. Suppl.* **32**, 1–228.

Cymborowski B. & Stolarz G. (1979) The role of juvenile hormone during larval-pupal transformation of *Spodoptera littoralis*: Switchover in the sensitivity of the prothoracic gland to juvenile hormone. *J. Insect Physiol.* **25**, 939–943.

Delbecque J. P., Hirn M., Delachambre J. & De Reggi M. (1978) Cuticular cycle and moulting hormone levels during the metamorphosis of *Tenebrio molitor* (Insecta, Coéleoptére). *Dev. Biol.* **64**, 11–30.

French J. R. J. (1974) A juvenile hormone analogue inducing caste differentiation in the Australian termite, *Nasutitermes exitiosus* Hill (Isoptera: Termitidae). *J. Aust. ent. Soc.* **13**, 353–355.

Gilbert L. I. (1962) Maintenance of the prothoracic gland by juvenile hormone in insects. *Nature, Lond.* **193**, 1205–1207.

Gilbert L. I. & Schneiderman H. A. (1959) Prothoracic gland stimulation by juvenile hormone extract of insects. *Nature, Lond.* **184**, 171–173.

Gillott G. & Yin C. M. (1972) Morphology and histology of endocrine glands of *Zootermopsis angusticollis* Hagen (Isoptera). *Can. J. Zool.* **50**, 1537–1545.

Gröner A. (1979) Machweis von Glycoproteinen in Kernpolyedern. *Naturwiss.* **66**, 208–209.

Hanström B. (1940) Inkretorische Organe, Sinnesorgane und Nervensystem des Kopfes einiger niederer Insektenordnungen. *Kgl. Svenska Vetenskapsakad. Handl.* **18**, 1–265.

Haverty M. I. (1977) The proportion of soldiers in termite colonies: A list and a bibliography (Isoptera). *Sociobiol.* **2**, 199–216.

Haverty M. I. (1979) Soldier production and maintenance of soldier proportions in laboratory experimental groups of *Coptotermes formosanus* Shiraki. *Insectes Sociaux* **26**, 69–84.

Haverty M. I. & Howard R. W. (1981) Production of soldiers and maintenance of soldier proportions by laboratory experimental groups of *Reticulitermes flavipes* (Kollar) and *Reticulitermes virginicus* (Banks) (Isoptera: Rhinotermitidae). *Insectes Sociaux* **28**, 32–39.

Herlant-Meewis H. & Pasteels J. M. (1961) Les glandes de mue de *Calotermes flavicollis* F. (Insectes: Isopteré). *Comp. Rend. Acad. Sci. Paris* **253**, 3078–3080.

Hewitt P. H., Nel J. J. C. & Conradie S. (1969) Preliminary studies on the control of caste formation in the harvester termites *Hodotermes mossambicus* (Hagen). *Insectes Sociaux* **16**, 159–172.

Hirn M., Hetru C., Lagueux M. & Hoffman J. A. (1979) Prothoracic gland activity and blood titres of ecdysone and ecdysterone during the last larval instar of *Locusta migratoria* L. *Insect Physiol.* **25**, 255–261.

Hiruma K., Shimada H. & Yagi S. (1978) Activation of prothoracic gland by juvenile hormone and prothoracicotropic hormone in *Mamestra brassicae*. *J. Insect Physiol.* **24**, 215–220.

Hoffman J. A., Koolman J., Karlson P. & Joly P. (1974) Moulting hormone titer and the fate of injected ecdysone during the fifth larval instar and in adults of *Locusta migratoria* (Orthoptera). *Gen. Comp. Endocrinol.* **22**, 90–97.

Holmgren N. (1909) Termitenstudien. 1. Anatomische Untersuchungen. *Kgl. Svenska Vetenskapsakad. Handl.* **44**, 1–215.

Hrdý I. (1972) Der Einfluss von zwei Juvenilhormonalogen auf die Differenzierung der Soldaten bei *Reticulitermes lucifugus santonensis* Feyt. (Isoptera: Rhinotermitidae). *Z. angew. Entomol.* **72**, 129–134.

Hrdý I. & Křeček J. (1972) Development of superfluous soldiers induced by juvenile hormone analogues in termite, *Reticulitermes lucifugus santonensis. Insectes Sociaux* **19**, 105–109.

Hrdý I., Křeček J. & Zuskova Z. (1979) Juvenile hormone analogues: effects on the soldier caste differentiation in termites (Isoptera). *Vest. Ceskoslov. Spol. Zool.* **43**, 260–269.

Ichikawa M. & Mishiitsutsuji-Uwo I. (1959) Studies on the role of the corpus allatum in the Erisilk worm, *Philosamia Cynthia ricini. Biol. Bull. mar. biol. Lab., Woods Hole* **116**, 88–94.

Jucci C. (1924) Sulla differenciazione delle caste nella società dei termitidi. 1, Neotenici Reali veri e neotenici—l'escrezione nei reali neotenici—la fisiologia e la biologia. *Atti Accad. Nazl. Lincei Rend., Classe Sci. Fis., Mat. Nat.* **14**, 269–500.

Kaiser P. (1956) Die Hormonalorgane der Termiten mit der Enstehung ihrer Kasten. Mitt. *Hamburgischen Zool. Museum Inst.* **54**, 129–178.

Lebrun D. (1967a) Hormone juvenile et formation des soldats chez le termite à cou jaune *Calotermes flavicollis* Fabr. *Comp. Rend. Acad. Sci. Paris* **265**, 996–997.

Lebrun D. (1967b) La détermination des castes du termite à cou jaune *Calotermes flavicollis* Fabr. *Bull. Biol. France Belg.* **101**, 139–217.

Lenz M. (1976) The dependence of hormone effects in termite caste determination on external factors. In *Phase and Caste Determination in Insects*: (Endocrine aspects) (Lüscher M., ed.), pp. 73–89. Pergamon Press, Oxford.

Lüscher M. (1958) Experimentelle Erzeugung von Soldaten bei der Termite *Kalotermes falvicollis* (Fabr.). *Naturwiss.* **45**, 69–70.

Lüscher M. (1960) Hormonal control of caste differentiation in termites. *Ann. N.Y. Acad. Sci.* **89**, 549–563.

Lüscher M. (1961) Social control of polymorphism in termites. In *Insect Polymorphism* (Kennedy J. S., ed.), pp. 57–67. Roy. Entomol. Soc., London.

Lüscher M. (1965) Functions of the corpora allata in the development of termites. Proc. 16th Intern. Congr. Zool. Washington DC. 4, pp. 244–250. Nat. Hist. Press, Garden City, New York.

Lüscher M. (1969) Die Bedeutung des Juvenilhormons für die Differenzierung der Soldaten bei der Termite *Kalotermes flavicollis*. Proc. Congr. IUSSI, Bern, pp. 165–170.

Lüscher M. (1972) Environmental control of juvenile hormone (JH) secretion and caste differentiation in termites. *Gen. Comp. Endocrinol.* (Suppl. 3), 509–514.

Lüscher M. (1973) The influence of the composition of experimental groups on caste development in *Zootermopsis* (Isoptera). Proc. VII Congr. IUSSI, London, pp. 253–256.

Lüscher M. (1974a) Kasten und Kastendifferenzierung bei nie deren Termiten. In *Sozialpolymorphismus bei Insecten* (Schmidt G. H., ed.), pp. 694–739. Wissenschaftl. Verlagsanst, Stuttgart.

Lüscher M. (1974b) Die Kompetenz zur Soldatenbildung bei Larven (Pseudergaten) der Termite *Zootermopsis angusticollis. Rev. suisse Zool.* **81**, 710–714.

Lüscher M. (1976) Evidence for an endocrine control of caste determination in higher termites. In *Phase and Caste Determination of Insects*: Endocrine Aspects (Lüscher M., ed.), pp. 91–103. Pergamon Press, Oxford.

Lüscher M. & Springhetti A. (1960) Untersuchungen uber die Bedeutung der corpora allata fur die Differenzierung der Kasten bei der Termite *Kalotermes flavicollis* F. *J. Insect Physiol.* **5**, 190–212.

Lüscher M. & van Doorn J. (1976) Die Abhängigkeit der Soldatenbildung bei der Termite *Zootermopsis* von der Dauer der Einwirkung des Juvenilhormonanalogons Altozar. *Rev. suisse Zool.* **83**, 939–942.

Masner P. & Hangartner W. (1973) Ecdysone: Antagonist of juvenile hormone in the control of cutis synthesis in the German cockroach, *Blattella germanica. Experientia* **29**, 1550–1552.

McMahan E. A. (1966) Food transmission within the *Cryptotermes brevis* colony (Isoptera: Kalotermitidae). *Ann. ent. Soc. Am.* **59**, 1131–1137.

Miller E. M. (1942) The problem of caste and caste differentiation in *Prorhinotermes simplex* Hagen. *Bull. Univ. Miami* **15**, 3–27.

Noirot Ch. (1955) Recherches sur le polymorphisme des termites supérieurs (Termitidae). *Ann. Sci. Nat. Zool. Biol. Animale* **17**, 399–595.

Noirot Ch. (1969) Formation of castes in higher termites. In *Biology of Termites* (Krishna K. & Weesner F. M., eds), pp. 283–310. Academic Press, New York & London.

Noirot Ch. (1977) Various aspects of hormone action in social insects. Proc. VIII Congr. IUSSI, Wageningen, pp. 12–16.

Okot-Kotber B. M. (1979) Polymorphism and the role of hormones on caste differentiation of a higher termite species, *Macrotermes michaelseni* (Isoptera—Macrotermitinae). Ph.D. Thesis, Univ. Dijon, France, pp. 1–218.

Okot-Kotber B. M. (1980a) Histological and size changes in corpora allata and prothoracic glands during development of *Macrotermes michaelseni* (Isoptera). *Insectes Sociaux* **27**, 361–376.

Okot-Kotber B. M. (1980b) The influence of juvenile hormone analogue on soldier differentiation in the higher termite, *Macrotermes michaelseni. Physiol. Entomol.* **5**, 407–416.

Okot-Kotber B. M. (1980c) Competence of *Macrotermes michaelseni* (Isoptera: Macrotermitinae) larvae to differentiate into soldiers under the influence of juvenile hormone analogue (ZR-515, Methoprene). *J. Insect Physiol.* **26**, 655–659.

Okot-Kotber B. M. (1981a) Instars and polymorphism of castes in *Macrotermes michaelseni* (Isoptera, Macrotermitinae). *Insectes Sociaux* **28**, 233–246.

Okot-Kotber B. M. (1981b) Polymorphism and the development of the first progeny in incipient colonies of *Macrotermes michaelseni* (Isoptera, Macrotermitinae). *Insect Sci., Applicat.* **1**, 147–150.

Okot-Kotber B. M. (1982) Correlation between larval weights, endocrine gland activities and competence period during differentiation of workers and soldiers in *Macrotermes michaelseni* (Isoptera: Termitidae). *J. Insect Physiol.* **28**, 905–910.

Okot-Kotber B. M. (1983) Influence of group size and composition on soldier differentiation in female final larval instars of a higher termite, *Macrotermes michaelseni. Physiol. Ent.* **8**, 41–47.

Pasteels J. M. & Deligne J. (1965) Etude du système endocrine au cours du vieillissement chez les "reines" de *Microcerotermes parvus* (Haviland) et *Cubitermes heghi* (Sjöstedt) (Isoptéres, Termitidae). *Biol. Gabonica* **1**, 325–336.

Pflugfelder O. (1938) Untersuchungen über die histologischen Veränderungen und das Kernwaschtum der "Corpora allata" von Termiten. *Z. Wiss. Zool.* **150**, 451–467.

Pflugfelder O. (1947) Ueber die Ventraldrusen und einige andere inkertorische Organe des Insektenkopfes. *Biol. Zentr.* **66**, 211–235.

Riddiford L. M. (1978) Ecdysone-induced changes in cellular commitment of the epidermis of the tobacco hornworm, *Manduca sexta*, at the initiation of metamorphosis. *Gen. Comp. Endocrinol.* **34**, 438–446.

Riddiford L. M. & Curtis A. T. (1978) Hormonal control of epidermal detachment during the final feeding stage of the tobacco hornworm larva. *J. Insect Physiol.* **24**, 561–568.

Safranek L., Cymborowski B. & Williams C. M. (1980) Effects of juvenile hormones on ecdysone-dependent development in the tobacco hornworm, *Manduca sexta. Biol. Bull. mar. biol. Lab., Woods Hole* **158**, 248–256.

Schaller F. & Charlet M. (1980) Neuroendocrine control and rate of ecdysone biosynthesis in larvae of a paleopteran insect: *Aeshna cyanea* Müller. In *Progress in Ecdysone Research* (Hoffman J. A., ed.), pp. 99–110. Elsevier/North-Holland Biomedical Press, Amsterdam, New York and Oxford.

Schneiderman H. A. (1969) Control systems in insect development. In *Biology and Physical Sciences* (Devons W., ed.), pp. 186–208. Columbia University Press, New York.

Shimizu K. (1963) Studies on caste differentiation in termites. III. Emergence of soldiers and supplementary reproductives of the Japanese termites *Leucotermes* (*Reticulitermes speratus*) (Kolbe). *Japan. J. of Appl. Entomol. Zool.* **7**, 207–212.

Springhetti A. (1957) Ghiandole tentoriali (ventrali, protoraciche) e corpora allata in *Kalotermes flavicollis* Fabr. *Symp. Genet. Biol. Ital.* **5**, 333–349.

Springhetti A. (1968) La fertilita dei reali di sostituzione di *Kalotermes flavicollis* Fabr. *Ann. Univ. Ferrera, Biol.* **3**, 49–64.

Springhetti A. (1969) Influenza dei reali sulla differenziazione dei soldati di *Kalotermes flavicollis* Fabr. (Isoptera). *Proc. VI Congr. IUSSI, Bern,* pp. 267–273.

Springhetti A. (1970) Influence of king and queen on the differentiation of soldiers in *Kalotermes flavicollis* Fabr. (Isoptera). *Monitore Zool. Ital.* (N.S.) **4**, 99–105.

Springhetti A. (1972) The competence of *Kalotermes flavicollis* pseudergates to differentiate into soldiers. *Monitore Zool. Ital.* (N.S.) **6**, 97–111.

Springhetti A. (1973) Group effects in the differentiation of the soldiers of *Kalotermes flavicollis* Fabr. (Isoptera). *Insectes Sociaux* **20**, 333–342.

Springhetti A. (1974) The influence of farnesenic acid ethyl ester on the differentiation of *Kalotermes flavicollis* Fabr. (Isoptera) soldiers. *Experientia* **30**, 541–543.

Wanyonyi K. (1974) The influence of the juvenile hormone analogue ZR-512 (Zoecon) on caste development in *Zootermopsis nevadensis* Hagen (Isoptera) *Insectes Sociaux* **21**, 35–44.

Williams C. M. (1959) The juvenile hormone. 1. Endocrine activity of the corpora allata of the adult Cecropia silkworm. *Biol. Bul. mar. biol. Lab., Woods Hole* **116**, 323–338.

Zuberi H. & Peeters P. (1964) A study of neurosecretory cells and endocrine glands of *Cubitermes exiguus.* In *Etudes sur les Termites Africains* (Bouillon A., ed.), pp. 87–105. Masson, Paris.

CHAPTER 22

Titres of Juvenile Hormone and Ecdysteroids in Reproductives and Eggs of Macrotermes michaelseni: Relation to Caste Determination?*

B. LANZREIN, V. GENTINETTA and R. FEHR

Department of Zoophysiology, University of Berne, Erlachstrasse 9A, CH-3012 Berne, Switzerland

CONTENTS

22.1 INTRODUCTION

In higher termites of the family Termitidae the caste system is very rigid

*This paper is dedicated to the late Professor Martin Lüscher

(Noirot, 1969, 1974) as compared to the high flexibility observed in at least some lower termites, where the larvae and nymphs are able to undergo differentiation in various directions including regressive development (Lüscher, 1974). In *Macrotermes michaelseni*, the species studied here, two categories of individuals are discernible after the first moult: larvae of the neuters, without any trace of wing development and with rudimentary gonads, and nymphs of the reproductives, with very small wing pads and with gonads which have undergone a definite development (Noirot, 1969; Okot-Kotber 1981a). The production of nymphs is not continuous, but shows a seasonal rhythm (Lüscher, 1976; Darlington, 1982) as also observed in many other species of higher termites (Noirot, 1969). Neuter development is different for the two sexes: minor workers as well as minor and major soldiers are females, whereas major workers are males. For minor soldiers, determination is initiated in third instar larvae and for major soldiers in fourth instar females (see Lüscher, 1976; Okot-Kotber, 1981a). The development of the first progeny has been described in detail for incipient colonies by Okot-Kotber (1981b).

Caste proportions are precisely adapted to both the environmental conditions and the demands of the society. It has been shown for lower termites that pheromones play an important role in the regulation of caste differentiation and it has been suggested that they exert their effects by acting on the endocrine system (Lüscher, 1974). The juvenile hormone (JH) seems to be of paramount importance (Lüscher, 1974; Wanyonyi, 1974) since implantation of corpora allata (CA) or application of JH or JH analogues significantly influences the development of particular castes; high JH or JH analogue (JHA) doses always favour soldier development. In higher termites, however, there is no direct evidence for the existence of pheromones acting on caste differentiation, but certain observations indicate that some mechanisms might be similar to those in lower termites. In *Macrotermes bellicosus* removal of the royal pair led to the production of nymphs during a season when normally no nymphs develop which demonstrates an inhibitory action of the royal pair upon the development of nymphs (Bordereau, 1975). A comparable inhibiting action of soldiers on soldier development has been observed in *M. michaelseni* (Bühlmann, pers. comm.; Okot-Kotber, Chapter 21). With regard to the role of hormones in caste differentiation in higher termites, very little is yet known. In the case of soldier differentiation, measurements of CA volumes in *Odontotermes* (see Lüscher, 1976) and in *M. michaelseni* (Okot-Kotber, 1977) as well as JHA application experiments in *M. michaelseni* (Okot-Kotber, 1980a, b) suggest (similar to the findings in lower termites) a stimulating action of JH on soldier development.

The factors inducing neuter or reproductive development have not yet been elucidated, but it is known that determination occurs either during oogenesis, embryogenesis or in the first larval instar (Noirot, 1969; Lüscher, 1976).

Genetic determination can probably be excluded since the existence of nymphal-soldier intercastes has been observed (see Noirot, 1969). As far as the role played by hormones is concerned, the following observations should be mentioned. The moulting hormones (ecdysteroids) could be of importance since prothoracic glands are larger in nymphs than in larvae in three different species of higher termites (Kaiser, 1956; Noirot, 1969; Okot-Kotber, 1980c). It is interesting to note that a role for ecdysteroids in caste differentiation has been suggested for the ant *Pheidole pallidula*, because the ecdysteroid level is higher in worker-biased eggs than in queen-biased eggs (Suzzoni *et al.*, 1980). On the other hand, involvement of JH has been suggested in *M. michaelseni*: the observation of relatively low JH titres in eggs collected in a season when normally eggs of reproductives are laid, led Lüscher (1976) to propose that eggs with a low JH content are predetermined to develop into reproductives. However, few data are available at present and interpretation is impeded by the limited knowledge of the physiology and endocrinology of reproduction and embryonic development in higher termites in general and *M. michaelseni* in particular.

Physogastric queens seem to differ in many ways from reproducing non-social female insects. In the majority of the latter, including cockroaches, which are closely related to termites, the yolk proteins (vitellogenins) are synthesized under the influence of JH in the fat body, released into the haemolymph and then taken up under the action of JH into the growing oocytes (for a review see Engelmann, 1970, 1979; Lanzrein *et al.*, 1981). In contrast, it is assumed that physogastric queens of *M. michaelseni* synthesize vitellogenin mainly in the ovarian follicle and not in the "royal fat body" (Wyss-Huber & Lüscher, 1975) and the function of the enormous and variable quantities of JH–III (Meyer *et al.*, 1976; Lanzrein *et al.*, 1977), which is produced in the highly enlarged CA (Lüscher, 1976; Lanzrein *et al.*, 1977) is not yet clear, although a role in stimulating vitellogenin synthesis and/or uptake is strongly suggested. The presence of ecdysteroids in reproducing non-social female adults has been ascertained in several insect species (see Hoffmann *et al.*, 1980) and different hypotheses on their functions have been proposed. Hagedorn *et al.* (1975) assumed that ecdysteroids stimulate vitellogenin synthesis in the fat body of mosquitoes; Beckemeyer and Lea (1980) showed that injection of 20-hydroxy-ecdysone prematurely induced separation of the incipient follicles in the ovarioles of mosquitoes; and Hoffman *et al.* (1980) postulated that ovarian ecdysteroids are destined to be used by the embryo during early phases of embryogenesis. In a species closely related to the termites, namely the cockroach *Nauphoeta cinerea*, we found 20-hydroxy-ecdysone to be predominant and to increase in the ovary and the haemolymph shortly before chorion formation; we thus suggested an involvement of ecdysteroids in chorion formation and also a role in inactivating the CA (Lanzrein *et al.*, 1981; Zhu *et al.*, 1982). In queens of *M. michaelseni* we have demonstrated the presence of mostly ecdysone together with some 20-hydroxy-ecdysone in ovaries and to a far lesser extent also in the haemolymph (Delbecque *et al.*, 1978); however, the biological function of these ecdysteroids in the queen remains unclear.

Eggs and embryos of some non-social insect species have recently been reported to contain variable and stage-specific quantities of ecdysteroids (see Hoffmann *et al.*, 1980) and JH's (see Bergot *et al.*, 1981). For embryonic ecdysteroids a role in cuticle formation and embryonic moulting is suggested, but little is known of the role of embryonic JH. In *N. cinerea*, where simultaneous measurements of JH and ecdysteroids have been performed, we have found large quantities of JH–III and ecdysteroids in older embryos at the time of cuticle deposition (Imboden *et al.*, 1978), whereas young embryos have revealed only a small ecdysteroid peak before dorsal closure, and JH was undetectable (Imboden & Lanzrein, 1982). From these data it is evident that JH and ecdysteroids are a normal occurrence in eggs and embryos of insects and that they serve functions which are not related to caste determination. Association of JH or ecdysteroid titres in eggs of social insects with the development of a particular caste is thus very difficult.

In order to understand better the role of JH and ecdysteroids in reproduction and to investigate their possible involvement in determining the seasonal development of reproductives, we measured and compared various parameters of queens, kings and eggs of *M. michaelseni* collected from medium-sized mounds in different seasons between 1976 and 1979. In queens, we measured the fresh weight, the egg-laying activity, the dry weight of the CA and their JH production rate, the haemolymph and anal fluid JH titre and the ecdysteroid content of haemolymph and of oocytes at different developmental stages. In kings, we determined the fresh weight of the testes, the *in vitro* production of JH by the CA and the haemolymph JH titre, and in newly-laid eggs we measured the ecdysteroid and JH titres.

22.2 MATERIALS AND METHODS

Macrotermes michaelseni (formerly thought to be *Macrotermes subhyalinus*) queen cells were collected from closed mounds characteristic of this species near Kajiado, Kenya. In this region, nymphs appear in about April and the imagos are ready to fly in the short rains of November and December (Darlington, 1982). We selected mounds of medium size inhabited by mature colonies, which regularly produce winged imagos. A correlation between mound measurements and population parameters has been demonstrated by Darlington (1982). The mean weight of the queens was 13.9 ± 4.8 g (SD).

Embryonic development lasts approximately 36 days in incipient colonies (Okot-Kotber, 1981b) but is shorter in field colonies (Darlington, 1982), while each larval stage lasts between 5 and 10 days in incipient colonies (Okot-Kotber, 1981b) and takes longer in the field (Darlington, 1982).

The 48 queen cells with the living queens and kings and some members of other castes were either directly prepared at ICIPE, Nairobi, or at its Kajiado Field Station (18 cells) or else flown to Berne where they usually arrived 20 to 32 hours after having been dug out (30 cells). We observed that the queen loses about 20% of her weight during transport to Berne, and since the majority of investigations were made in Berne the weight of the queens studied in Kenya was converted to a hypothetical "Bernese" weight for comparative purposes. In general, one queen and king were present; in exceptional cases, two queens with one king (6 cells), or four queens with one king (1 cell), or one queen with two kings (1 cell) were found.

In order to measure the CA weight, the glands were dried and weighed with a Cahn 4700 electrobalance. *In vitro* culture of CA was performed according to the method of Tobe & Pratt (1974) using tissue culture medium M-199 containing methyl-^{14}C-methionine (Amersham, England); 300 μl of medium were used for queen CA and 100 μl for king CA. The culture medium was changed every 6, 12 and 24 hr and extracted with ethylacetate. The extract was spotted on thin layer plates (Silicagel 0.25 mm, F-254) together with JH–III as a reference compound. After development in ethylacetate/hexane 1:1 (v/v), zones of 1 or 1.5 cm were scraped and counted in a liquid scintillation counter. The methods of extraction, purification and titre determination of JH were essentially the same as described by Lanzrein *et al.* (1975) using one thin layer chromatography (TLC) step for purification and the *Galleria* bioassay (De Wilde *et al.*, 1968) for titre determination. Under our conditions, 1 *Galleria* unit (GU) corresponds to 5–8 pg of JH–III (Calbiochem).

Ecdysteroids were extracted with 65% methanol/water and purified by TLC (1 × diisopropylether, 1 × chloroform/ethanol 96%, 80/20) as described by Imboden *et al.* (1978). After TLC purification, the ecdysone and 20-hydroxy-ecdysone zones were assayed separately in a radioimmunoassay (RIA), carried out according to the method of Borst & O'Connor (1974) and Horn *et al.* (1976). Ecdysone and 20-hydroxy-ecdysone used as standards were purchased from Simes (Milan). Results are expressed as ng of ecdysone or 20-hydroxy-ecdysone equivalents. For measuring ecdysteroid production *in vitro* ovaries or oocytes were cultured for 16–24 hr in tissue culture medium M-199. After incubation, the medium and the tissue were extracted separately with 65% methanol/water and ecdysteroid titres were measured as described above. Statistical evaluations were made according to Sachs (1974).

22.3   RESULTS

22.3.1   JH and ecdysteroid titres in eggs and JH titres in the haemolymph of queens and kings

Since the decision between neuter and reproductive development is possibly taken during oogenesis (Noirot, 1969), and since it has been suggested that ecdysteroids (Kaiser, 1956; Noirot, 1969; Okot-Kotber, 1980c) and/or JH (Lüscher, 1976) are involved in this determining step, we measured the content of these two hormones in batches of newly-laid eggs 10–32-hours old collected from the isolated queen cells of different colonies (Fig. 22.1). Analyses were made during different seasons because reproductive development is not continuous throughout the year; in the region where the *M. michaelseni* were collected, a single annual brood of reproductives is initiated in about April (Darlington, 1982) and, taking into account the time of development, one can calculate that eggs destined to develop into reproductives are laid in February/March. In Figure 22.1 we can see that the JH titre of newly-laid eggs collected from different queen cells shows a great variability, even when the eggs were collected at the same time. The mean values fluctuate throughout the year, but do not show a regular pattern, which makes it difficult to draw conclusions concerning a relationship between egg JH titre, season, and the development of reproductives. Interpretation is also impeded

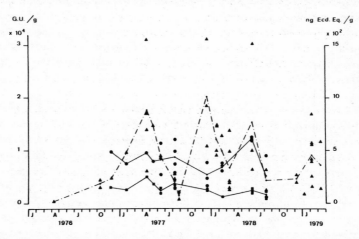

Fig. 22.1. Titres of JH (triangles and broken line for mean values), ecdysone (dots and continuous line for mean values) and 20-hydroxy-ecdysone (squares and continuous line for mean values) in 0–32 hr old eggs over the course of 3 years. For JH determination approx. 100 mg of eggs were extracted and measured by *Galleria* bioassay and results are expressed as *Galleria* units (GU) per gram. For ecdysone and 20-hydroxy-ecdysone determinations, 50–100 mg of eggs were extracted and measured with RIA. Results are expressed as ng ecdysone equivalents and ng 20-hydroxy-ecdysone per gram.

by the fact that measurements were made on pools of eggs (100 mg), and at irregular intervals throughout the year, and that we do not know whether and how many reproductives would have developed in a particular colony. The titres of free ecdysone and 20-hydroxy-ecdysone show much less variation than the JH titre between different mounds and during the course of the year, and ecdysone is always the predominant ecdysteroid. The variability in the JH titre and the uniformity in the ecdysteroid titre of newly-laid eggs suggest that, at this stage, JH but not ecdysteroids might play a role in caste determination; however, a clear-cut correlation between a given JH titre and the development of a particular caste is impossible to ascertain at this stage.

The JH in the newly-laid eggs could arise from different sources, such as the queen's anal fluid or haemolymph; these two possibilities were therefore investigated. Measurements of JH titres in anal fluid gave values lower than 800 GU/ml in 16 out of 19 cases, which excludes the possibility that the presence of JH in the newly-laid eggs is due to contamination with anal fluid. The haemolymph JH titres of queens and kings, the "parents" of the eggs analysed in Figure 22.1, are given in Figure 22.2. The titre in the queen is very high and is always higher than that in the king; it shows great variability and a

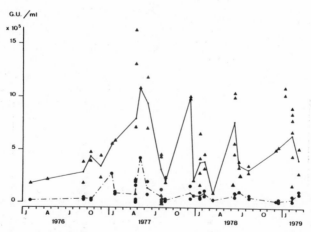

Fig. 22.2. Haemolymph JH titre in CU/ml in queens (triangles and continuous line for mean values) and kings (dots and broken line for mean values) over the course of 3 years.

similar trend to the JH titre in the newly-laid eggs (see Fig. 22.1). In Figure 22.3 the haemolymph JH titre of the queen and the JH titre of her eggs are plotted; calculation reveals that the two parameters are vaguely correlated, $r = 0.436$, $0.01 < P < 0.05$, according to Fisher (see Sachs, 1974). This suggests that the JH found in the newly-laid eggs arises from the queen's haemolymph, which might be due to accidental contamination of the maturing oocytes with

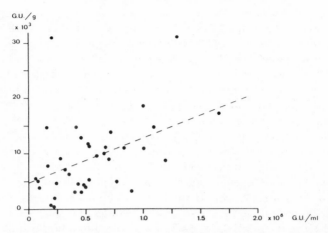

FIG. 22.3. Correlation between the JH titre in the haemolymph of the queen (abscissa) and in her eggs (ordinate); r = 0.436, 0.01 < P < 0.05.

haemolymph JH, or else to selective uptake. The latter seems more likely since newly-laid eggs of other insects have been shown to be devoid of JH, even when the haemolymph JH titre of the females was high (see Imboden *et al.*, 1978; Bergot *et al.*, 1981).

In order to assess the reproductive state of the queens and to examine whether the haemolymph JH titre is correlated with egg production, we estimated the egg-laying activity during 0.5–1 hr after opening the queen cell. Since it was not feasible to count the number of eggs laid precisely, we classified the queens into three categories (high, medium and low) of egg-laying activity. It was seen that 58% of the queens displayed a high, 34% a medium and 8% a low egg-laying activity; no relationship was found with the haemolymph JH titre.

We have also investigated whether the JH titre in the haemolymph of the queen and the king from the same colony are correlated (Fig. 22.4) Calculation reveals r = 0.359 and 0.01 < P < 0.05, meaning that the two parameters are only vaguely correlated. This could be interpreted as an indication that the haemolymph JH titre of queen and king are to some extent dependent on similar environmental or social factors. Parameters related to reproduction in king and queen are further analysed and compared below.

22.3.2 Comparison of the fresh weight of the queen with the dry weight of her CA and with the fresh weight of the king's testicles

Since we always investigated mounds of roughly similar dimensions, one

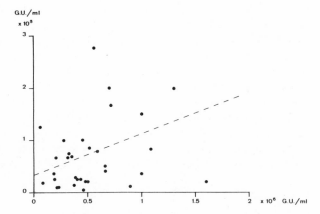

Fig. 22.4. Correlation between the haemolymph JH titre in queens (abscissa) and king (ordinate). Only colonies with 1 king and 1 queen were used; $r = 0.359$, $0.01 < P < 0.05$.

could expect a similar population size and caste distribution according to Darlington (1982), and possibly also a similar reproduction rate. In order to know whether the reproductive organs are at a similar stage of development in king and queen of the same mound, we measured the fresh weight of the testes of the king, the fresh weight of the queen (which largely depends on the weight of her ovaries) and the dry weight of her CA. The results with the correlation coefficients are given in Table 22.1, and show that no correlation exists between the queen's weight and the weight of the king's testes, nor between the queen's weight and the dry weight of her CA. Lack of correlation between queen weight and testicular weight could be interpreted in several ways. Either the reproductive organs of the queen and king are still in a stage of development of which the rate is different, or the queen or the king is often replaced during the growth of the colony, or else testicular weight and ovarian weight are not related to the age of a colony nor to the reproduction rate.

TABLE 22.1. COMPARISON OF THE FRESH WEIGHT OF THE QUEEN WITH THE FRESH WEIGHT OF THE KING'S TESTES AND OF THE FRESH WEIGHT OF THE QUEEN WITH THE DRY WEIGHT OF HER CA

	Mean ± SD	n	Coefficient of correlation r
Weight of queen vs.	12.4 g ± 3.7	27	−0.028
Weight of testes	29.7 mg ± 11.4		
Weight of queen vs.	11.2 g ± 2.4	29	−0.123
Weight of CA	58.4 µg ± 23.8		

With present knowledge, it is impossible to decide between these different possibilities. Lack of correlation between fresh weight of the queen and the dry weight of her CA can also be explained in different ways. Either the weight of the CA is not correlated to the degree of physogastry, or CA and ovary are still growing, but at non-synchronous rates, or the CA weight at a certain stage of physogastry is variable and mainly related to the JH production rate. The third possibility is investigated below. If one compares the weight of the king's testes with the dry weight of the queen's CA (Fig. 22.5) a slight $(r = -0.559, \ 0.01 < P < 0.05)$ inverse correlation can be observed. This means that queens with larger CA are associated with kings having relatively light testes, a finding which is difficult to interpret.

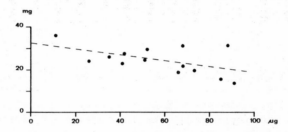

FIG. 22.5. Correlation between the dry weight of the queen's CA (abscissa) and the fresh weight of her king's testes (ordinate); $r = -0.559, \ 0.01 < P < 0.05$

22.3.3 Relationship between CA dry weight, CA activity and haemolymph JH titre in the queen and between CA activity and haemolymph JH titre in the king

The CA are very enlarged in physogastric queens (Lüscher, 1976) and we have seen that their dry weight and the queen's weight are not correlated (Table 22.1). We have also shown that the haemolymph JH titre varies greatly from one queen to another (Fig. 22.2) and have therefore investigated in individual queens whether the CA dry weight, the JH production rate by the CA and the haemolymph JH titre are correlated (Fig. 22.6). Obviously, all three parameters show a great variability and calculation of correlations reveals $r = 0.060$ for CA weight vs CA activity and $r = -0.157$ for CA activity vs JH titre in haemolymph, which demonstrates the absence of correlation in either case. This is true for both queens examined directly in Nairobi (marked with an asterisk) and queens transported to Berne, and indicates that lack of correlation is not caused by transporting the queens. These data show that the dry weight of the CA is not indicative of its JH production rate. They also suggest that either the haemolymph JH titre is dependent on several factors

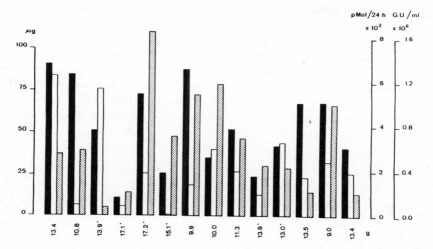

FIG. 22.6. CA dry weight in μg (black bars), CA *in vitro* activity in pMol JH-III/24 hr (white bars) and haemolymph JH titre in GU/ml (dotted bars) of individual queens. The fresh weight of the queens is given underneath each set of bars, asterisks denote queens prepared in Nairobi.

and not only regulated by the JH production rate, or else that CA produce JH in pulses and not continuously. Comparison of the CA *in vitro* activity in the king with the JH titre in its haemolymph (Fig. 22.7), gave a similar result; no correlation between CA activity and haemolymph JH titre (r = −0.243) was found. There is also no correlation between CA activity or haemolymph JH titre and the testicle weight. A comparison of the CA activity of queen and

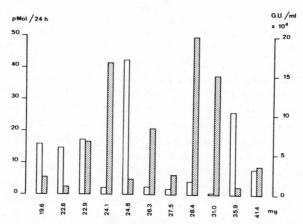

FIG. 22.7. CA *in vitro* activity in pMol JH-III/24 hr (white bars) and haemolymph JH titre in GU/ml (dotted bars) in individual kings. The fresh weight of the king's testes is given underneath each set of bars.

king from the same mound again reveals no correlation (r = 0.409 P > 0.05). It is obvious from the data shown here that the reproductive parameters such as ovary and testicle weight, CA weight and activity and JH titre in haemolymph show a great variability in different queens and kings and are not related to each other.

22.3.4 Ecdysteroids in the haemolymph of the queen, in oocytes of different developmental stages and in eggs

We have already demonstrated (Delbecque *et al.*, 1978) that the ovaries and eggs of *M. michaelseni* contain ecdysone and 20-hydroxy-ecdysone. Since the function of ecdysteroids in queens is still unknown, and since in a closely-related species (namely, the cockroach *Nauphoeta cinerea*) ecdysteroid production by the ovary is limited to the time before chorion formation (Zhu *et al.*, 1982), we investigated the ecdysteroid content and production of oocytes at different stages of development (Tables 22.2 and 22.3, respectively) Table 22.2 shows that small and large oocytes contain similar quantities of both ecdysone and 20-hydroxy-ecdysone. The concentrations in the ovary (oocytes of various sizes) and particularly in the newly-laid eggs are somewhat

TABLE 22.2. CONTENT OF FREE ECDYSONE AND 20-HYDROXY-ECDYSONE IN OVARY, OOCYTES OF DIFFERENT SIZE, NEWLY-LAID EGGS AND HAEMOLYMPH

	Ecdysone in ng/g or ml	n	20-hydroxy-ecdysone in ng/g or ml	n
Ovary	368 ± 123	12	144 ± 73	11
Small oocytes < 900 μ	233 ± 202	11	90 ± 107	11
Large oocytes > 900 μ	240 ± 110	11	106 ± 51	10
Newly-laid eggs	457 ± 274	25	173 ± 108	21
Haemolymph	13 ± 8	15	7 ± 4	15

Data are expressed in ng ecdysone and 20-hydroxy-ecdysone equivalents respectively and are means ± SD.

TABLE 22.3. PRODUCTION OF ECDYSTEROIDS *IN VITRO* BY OVARY AND SMALL AND LARGE OOCYTES

	ng/g/24 h	n
Ovary	292 ± 168	11
Small oocytes < 900 μ	174 ± 142	6
Large oocytes > 900 μ	207 ± 71	6

Data are expressed in ng ecdysone equivalents and are means ± SD.

higher, while the titre in haemolymph is very low. The larger amount of the ecdysteroids is thus not released into the haemolymph, but retained in the oocytes. In all cases, ecdysone is the predominant free ecdysteroid.

If the ecdysteroids are produced in the oocyte, it follows that little is released into the haemolymph. In order to determine if oocytes produce ecdysteroids, a portion of oocytes was directly extracted while another portion was cultured for 16–24 hours *in vitro*. Then the medium and the tissue were extracted and assayed for ecdysteroids. The increase in ecdysteroids (quantity at the end of incubation minus quantity before incubation) is given in Table 22.3. We do not know, however, whether oocytes synthesize ecdysteroids, or whether the ecdysteroid production is due to hydrolysis of conjugates. The production rate is similar for large and small oocytes, indicating that in termite queens, unlike in other insects, oocytes of various stages are capable of producing free ecdysteroids.

22.4 DISCUSSION

The data presented here indicate that the morphological and endocrine parameters investigated differ greatly from one colony to another and that they are scarcely related to each other or to the changing seasons. This points to there being markedly individual patterns in each colony despite the fact that we only used mounds of similar dimensions, which might be expected to contain comparable, mature colonies (Darlington, 1982). It should be mentioned, however, that recolonization of mounds is 5–10% per year (Darlington, 1982) and that the royal pair is sometimes replaced (Sieber & Darlington, 1982). The possible roles of JH and ecdysteroids in reproduction and in caste determination in *M. michaelseni* are compared below with actions of JH and ecdysteroids in other insects.

The JH and ecdysteroid titre measurements performed in 0–32 hr old eggs collected from different colonies and during different seasons (Fig. 22.1) show that the JH content is extremely variable, whereas the content of ecdysone and 20-hydroxy-ecdysone is relatively uniform. From this it seems unlikely that the content of free ecdysteroids in 0–32 hr old eggs play a role in determining neuter or reproductive development. Measurements of free ecdysone and 20-hydroxy-ecdysone in the course of embryonic development, carried out in eggs collected in July 1978 revealed fluctuations in both ecdysone and 20-hydroxy-ecdysone and higher titres in later stages of embryogenesis (unpublished results obtained in collaboration with Dr M. Lepage). Similar observations have been made by J. P. Delbecque (pers. comm.), who measured total ecdysteroid content with an RIA. In other non-social insects, comparable fluctuations in the titre of free ecdysteroids during embryogenesis have been observed and the ecdysteroid peaks have been correlated with the formation of embryonic and larval cuticles (Imboden *et al.*, 1978; Hoffman *et al.*, 1980; Imboden & Lanzrein, 1982). The similarity in the changes in embryonic free ecdysteroids in *M. michaelseni* and other insects suggests that these ecdysteroids exert similar functions in embryogenesis in non-social and social insects. Since we have no data on ecdysteroid titre fluctuations during embryogenesis in eggs collected during the season when reproductives normally develop, it is still possible that the ecdysteroid titre changes are different in embryos of reproductives and thus decisive in determining reproductive development. This possibility is discussed below in connection with the JH content of the eggs.

Concerning the JH, the titres in 0–32 hr old eggs are extremely variable from one colony to another and the mean values show significant, but irregular changes during the 3 years (Fig. 22.1). The JH active material has been tentatively identified as JH–III, using high pressure liquid chromatography combined with *Galleria* bioassay (Lanzrein, unpublished). The titres in 0–32 hr old eggs are high compared with those in newly-laid eggs of other insects, where low or undetectable quantities are present (Imboden *et al.*, 1978; Bergot *et al.*, 1981). We found variable and decreasing quantities of JH during the course of embryonic development in *M. michaelseni* (unpublished results obtained in collaboration with Dr M. Lepage), while in other insects high JH titres have been observed in later stages of embryogenesis (Imboden *et al.*, 1978; Bergot *et al.*, 1981). Thus, the variability of JH titres observed in 0–32 hr old eggs of *M. michaelseni* collected from different colonies during different seasons and particularly the fact that the JH titre and its fluctuation are completely different from that in eggs of non-social insects, may indicate that the JH content of the eggs plays a role in caste determination in *M. michaelseni*. This is, however, a purely hypothetical assumption since we measured batches of eggs (100 mg) containing an unknown percentage of infertile eggs at irregular intervals, and since we never knew into which castes and to what extent the eggs would have developed. The number of reproductives produced in a colony in 1 year can be substantial, and varies from 3000 to 73,000 with a mean of 34,000 (8 observations) according to Darlington (1982). It is not known how JH might, if at all, influence caste determination; but a concerted action with the ecdysteroids seems conceivable since the prothoracic glands have been found to be larger in nymphs than in larvae in three species of higher termites (Kaiser, 1956; Noirot, 1969; Okot-Kotber, 1980c) and since application of JH to larvae of *Zootermopsis* has been observed to influence the early ecdysteroid peak (König and Lanzrein, unpublished). We do not know where and in what form the JH is present in the egg nor whether it is bound to a protein such as vitellin. Contamination by anal fluid seems very unlikely since its JH content was found to be very low. The similarity of the JH titre fluctuation in the eggs (Fig. 22.1) to that in the queen's haemolymph (Fig. 22.2), and the slight positive correlation between these two parameters (Fig.

22.3), suggest that the JH of the newly-laid egg arises from the queen's haemolymph.

Physogastric queens have very variable haemolymph JH titres (Figs 22.2 and 22.6, Lanzrein *et al.*, 1977), which are higher than those in non-social reproducing insects (Lanzrein *et al.*, 1978; Rembold, 1981; De Kort and Granger, 1981). Since queens produce an enormous number of eggs (up to 40,000 or 4 g per day) a role for JH in oocyte maturation seems very likely. However, the reproductive physiology of physogastric queens is only partly understood and they differ significantly from other insects in the reproductive stage. In most non-social insects, vitellogenin is synthesized under the influence of JH in the fat body, then released into the haemolymph from where it is taken up under the control of JH into the maturing oocytes (see Engelmann, 1970, 1979; Wilhelm & Lüscher, 1974), whereas it has been suggested for physogastric queens of *M. michaelseni* that vitellogenin is synthesized in the follicle cells (Wyss-Huber & Lüscher, 1975). It is not known whether JH stimulates vitellogenin synthesis or uptake or both processes in this case. Association of JH with particular processes in oocyte maturation is complicated by the fact that, unlike the situation in many other insects, oocytes at all stages of maturation are present at any given time. No correlation between the rate of oviposition and the haemolymph JH titre has been found. According to our observations, one function of the queen's JH may be to provide the eggs with JH (Fig. 22.3); but JH probably fulfils multiple functions and its titre is possibly related to various endogenous, environmental and social factors.

In the development of physogastry, a correlation between the volume of the CA and the length of the abdomen has been observed (Sieber & Leuthold, 1982a), while in queens that have reached the physogastric stage, there is no correlation between the weight of the queen (largely decided by the weight of her ovaries) and the dry weight of the CA (Table 22.1). This could mean that the weight of the CA is not related to the degree of physogastry, or that CA and ovary grow at non-synchronous rates. It is not known whether and at which stage the growth of the ovaries and of the CA ceases. A comparison of the dry weight of the CA with their *in vitro* production of JH, and the latter with the haemolymph JH titre (Fig. 22.6), reveals no correlation, as already indicated (Lanzrein *et al.*, 1977). This can be best interpreted by a fluctuating rather than a continuous production of JH by the CA since the degradation of JH in queen haemolymph is low (Lanzrein *et al.*, 1977). The absence of correlation between CA volume, CA *in vitro* activity and haemolymph JH titre has also been observed in individual females of *N. cinerea* (Lanzrein *et al.*, 1978); thus it seems questionable to use the CA volume as a measure of its activity as proposed by Sieber and Leuthold (1982a) for partially physogastric queens of *M. michaelseni*. The size of the CA might be correlated with its potential activity, but is certainly not correlated with its actual biosynthetic activity.

In the king, the haemolymph JH titre is high (Figs 22.2, 22.4 and 22.7) compared to that in other male insects such as *N. cinerea*, where only 100–200 GU per ml were found (Lanzrein, unpublished), and the activity of the CA is also high (Fig. 22.7) if one compares it with that in *Diploptera punctata* (Szibbo & Tobe, 1982). It is known that the king copulates repeatedly (Sieber & Leuthold, 1982b) and that he has very enlarged testes (Fig. 22.5; also Sieber & Leuthold, 1982b); from this it seems conceivable to assume that JH plays a role in the reproductive physiology of the king. The precise function of JH in the king is, however, not known. In the rather small number of insect species investigated so far, spermatogenesis, which in most insects takes place during the premetamorphic stages, is often correlated with high ecdysteroid titres in the absence of JH (see Dumser, 1980). In contrast, spermiogenesis in the adult leaf-hopper *Draeculacephala crassicornis* seems to be controlled by JH, since application of JHA was found to accelerate spermiogenesis (Reissig & Kamm, 1975). Thus it may well be that in the mature king, JH regulates spermiogenesis. Nothing is known on the physiology of accessory glands and their possible control by JH. The JH production rate by the CA of the king is not correlated with the haemolymph JH titre (Fig. 22.7), suggesting that JH is released in pulses and not continuously, as already observed in the queen (Fig. 22.6).

The haemolymph JH titre in king and queen from the same mound show slight positive correlation (Fig. 22.4), which could mean that the JH titre of the queen and the king depend to some extent on the same environmental and/or social factors. The fresh weight of the king's testes is not correlated with the fresh weight of the queen from the same mound (Table 22.1), which might be due to replacement of either the king or the queen during the development of a colony, since it is known that reproductives can occasionally be replaced (Sieber & Darlington, 1982). No correlation exists between the fresh weight of the testes and the king's haemolymph JH titre (calculated from Fig. 22.7). However, there is a weak inverse correlation between the king's testicular weight and the dry weight of the queen's CA (Fig. 22.5). These observations show that the sizes of the reproductive organs and of the CA in kings and queens of mature colonies are very variable and that they are scarcely related to each other or to the haemolymph JH titre.

Measurement of free ecdysone and 20-hydroxy-ecdysone in small and large oocytes, newly-laid eggs and haemolymph (Table 22.2) reveals that ecdysone is always predominant, as already shown (Delbecque *et al.*, 1978). The titre of ecdysteroids is comparatively high in newly-laid eggs, but it is very low in the haemolymph. Small and large oocytes contain (Table 22.2) and produce (Table 22.3) similar quantities of ecdysteroids. These findings are remarkably different from those in a related non-social species, namely the cockroach *N. cinerea* (Zhu *et al.*, 1982) In the latter, 20-hydroxy-ecdysone is always predominant and it shows strictly stage-specific changes of titres in the ovary, being high only before and during chorion formation and low in the newly-formed eggs. In *Locusta migratoria*, on the other hand, the ecdysone titre rises in the ovaries at the end of oocyte maturation and remains high in the newly-laid eggs (Hoffman *et al.*, 1980). The presence of ecdysteroid conjugates, which seem to be of paramount importance in locusts (Gande *et al.*, 1979; Hoffman *et al.*, 1980) has not been investigated in *M. michaelseni*. The biological function of ecdysteroids in reproducing female insects is still controversial and several hypotheses have been proposed (see Introduction). From the data available, it is impossible to say which role is played by ecdysteroids in queens of *M. michaelseni*; but the fact that both small and large oocytes produce and contain similar quantities of ecdysteroids suggests a function in oocyte maturation, and their presence in the newly-laid egg could indicate that some of the ecdysteroids are destined to be used during embryonic development, as proposed for *L. migratoria* (Hoffmann *et al.*, 1980). Ovarian ecdysteroids in *M. michaelseni* probably exert multiple biological functions as we have suggested for *N. cinerea* (Zhu *et al.*, 1982).

To sum up, the queen and king of *M. michaelseni* are certainly very exceptional cases of reproductive insects, considering their longevity and their reproductive output. Owing to the fact that there is only one pair of reproductives per colony and that they only survive under the continuous care of their nest-mates, it is almost impossible to carry out the necessary experiments to provide conclusive information concerning their reproductive physiology and endocrinology. The following statements are thus very hypothetical and speculative and are mainly based on the comparison with findings in other insects. The high quantities of JH found in both queen and kings suggest that JH is necessary for oogenesis as well as for the production of sperm. The precise functions of JH, however, are not known. The presence of rather high quantities of ecdysteroids in oocytes at younger and older stages of maturation infers a function of ecdysteroids in oocyte maturation. The great variability in JH production rates and titres and the difference in size of reproductive organs and CA observed in the different queens and kings collected from mounds of similar sizes, indicate that each colony is ruled by its own dynamic principles.

As far as the function of JH and ecdysteroids in determining neuter or reproductive development is concerned, we venture to put forward the following hypothesis. During oogenesis, the oocytes receive from the queen variable quantities of JH which to some extent predetermines the presumptive caste. JH influences the development of the prothoracic gland, and modulates ecdysteroid titres. The development of a particular caste could thus result from a concerted action of JH and ecdysteroids; however, many more investigations will be necessary before we can define precisely the role of these hormones in caste determination in *M. michaelseni*.

22.5 SUMMARY

Various endocrine and morphological parameters of queen, king and eggs of *Macrotermes michaelseni* were measured in 48 colonies collected from medium-sized mounds during different seasons in order to understand better functions of JH and ecdysteroids in reproduction and in the seasonal appearance of reproductives.

The JH and ecdysteroid measurements performed in 0–32 hr old eggs show that the JH content is extremely variable from one colony to another and that the mean value fluctuates during the year, whereas the content of ecdysone and 20-hydroxy-ecdysone is more or less constant.

The JH titres in the haemolymph of the king and particularly the queen are extremely high and show a great variability, and the two show a weak positive correlation. The haemolymph JH titre of the queen is slightly correlated with the JH titre of her eggs but not with the egg-laying activity. Only little JH is found in the anal fluid. A comparison in the queen of the dry weight of the CA with the *in vitro* production of JH and the haemolymph JH titre, reveals no correlation between these parameters and similarly no correlation between CA *in vitro* activity, and haemolymph JH titre is found in the king. The dry weight of the queen's CA is not correlated with her fresh weight (which is largely dependent on the weight of her ovaries), neither is this correlated with the fresh weight of the king's testicles.

Measurements of free ecdysone and 20-hydroxy-ecdysone in small and large oocytes and in the queen's haemolymph, reveals that ecdysone is always predominant and that haemolymph contains little ecdysone, whereas both small and large oocytes contain similar and substantial (approximately 235 ng/g) quantities of ecdysome. Small and large oocytes also produce comparable quantities of ecdysteroids when kept *in vitro*.

The data presented here show that the morphological and endocrine parameters of queen, king and eggs differ greatly from one colony to another and that they are hardly related to each other or to the changing seasons. Obviously, each colony is ruled by its own dynamic principles. The high quantities of JH found in the queen and king suggest a function in oocyte maturation as well as in sperm production and from the presence of remarkable quantities of ecdysteroids in small and large oocytes as well as in eggs, a function of ecdysteroids in both oocyte maturation and embryogenesis is inferred. The rather high and variable quantities of JH in 0–32 hr old eggs suggest that JH has a function in predetermining neuter or reproductive development; however, this remains to be proven.

22.6 ACKNOWLEDGEMENTS

We would like to express our thanks to Prof. T. R. Odhiambo, Nairobi, for allowing us to use the ICIPE's facilities for collection and preparation of *Macrotermes michaelseni* and to Dr M. Lepage, Paris, for collecting and extracting eggs. Thanks are also due to Prof. J. D. O'Connor, Los Angeles, for ^{3}H-ecdysone and ecdysone antibody and to Mr M. Kaltenrieder for drawing the graphs. In addition, we are grateful to all the friends who very kindly agreed to bring back termites with them at the end of their holidays in Kenya. Financial support from the Swiss National Science Foundation (grants nos 3.411.74 and 3.188.77) is also gratefully acknowledged.

22.7 REFERENCES

Beckemeyer E. F. & Lea A. D. (1980) Induction of follicle separation in the mosquito by physiological amounts of ecdysterone. *Science Wash.* **209,** 819–821.

Bergot J. B., Baker F. C., Cerf D. C., Jamieson G. & Schooley D. A. (1981) Qualitative and quantitative aspects of juvenile hormone titers in developing embryos of several insect species: discovery of a new JH-like substance extracted from eggs of *Manduca sexta*. In *Juvenile Hormone Biochemistry* (Pratt G. E. & Brooks G. T., eds), pp. 33–45. Elsevier/North Holland Biomedical Press, Amsterdam.

Bordereau C. (1975) Déterminisme des castes chez les termites supérieurs: mise en évidence d'un contrôle royal dans la formation de la caste sexuée chez *Macrotermes bellicosus* Smeathman (*Isoptera, Termitidae*). *Insectes Sociaux* **22,** 363–374.

Borst D. W. & O'Connor J. D. (1974) Trace analysis of ecdysones by gas–liquid chromatography, radioimmunoassay and bioassay. *Steroids* **24,** 637–656.

Darlington J. P. (1982) Population dynamics in an African fungus-growing termite *Macrotermes michaelseni*. In *The Biology of Social Insects* (Breed M. D., Michener C. D. & Evans H. E., eds) Proc. 9th Congr. IUSSI, 1982, pp. 54–58. Westview Press, Boulder, Colorado.

De Kort C. A. D. & Granger N. A. (1981) Regulation of the juvenile-hormone titer. *Ann. Rev. Entomol.* **26,** 1–28.

Delbecque J. P., Lanzrein B., Bordereau C., Imboden H., Hirn M., O'Connor J. D., Noirot C. & Lüscher M. (1978) Ecdysone and ecdysterone in physogastric termite queens and eggs of *Macrotermes bellicosus* and *Macrotermes subhyalinus*. *Gen. Comp. Endocr.* **36,** 40–47.

De Wilde J., Staal G. B., De Kort C. A. D., De Loof A. & Baard G. (1968) Juvenile hormone titer in the haemolymph as a function of photoperiodic treatment in the adult Colorado beetle (*Leptinotarsa decemlineata* Say) *Proc. Kon. Ned. Akad. Wetensch.*, Ser. C. **71,** 321–326.

Dumser J. B. (1980) Regulation of spermatogenesis in insects. *Ann. Rev. Entomol.* **25,** 341–369.

Engelmann F. (1970) *The Physiology of Insect Reproduction*. Pergamon Press, Oxford.

Engelmann F. (1979) Insect vitellogenin: identification, biosynthesis and role in vitellogenesis. *Advan. Insect Physiol.* **14,** 49–108.

Gande A. R., Morgan E. D. & Wilson I. D. (1979) Ecdysteroid levels throughout the life cycle of the desert locust, *Schistocerca gregaria*. *J. Insect Physiol.* **25,** 669–675.

Hagedorn H. H., O'Connor J. D., Fuchs M. S., Sage B., Schlaeger D. A. & Bohm M. K. (1975) Ovary as a source of α-ecdysone in an adult mosquito. *Proc. Nat. Acad. Sci. U.S.* **72,** 3255–3259.

Hoffmann J. A., Lagueux M., Hetru C., Charlet M. & Goltzené F. (1980) Ecdysone in reproductively-competent female adults and in embryos of insects. In *Progress in Ecdysone Research* (Hoffmann J., ed.), pp. 431–465. Elsevier-North Holland Biomedical Press, Amsterdam.

Horn D. H. S., Sage B. & O'Connor J. D. (1976) A high affinity antiserum specific for the ecdysone nucleus. *J. Insect Physiol.* **22,** 901–905.

Imboden H. & Lanzrein B. (1982) Investigations on ecdysteroids and juvenile hormones and on morphological aspects during early embryogenesis in the ovoviviparous cockroach *Nauphoeta cinerea*. *J. Insect Physiol.* **28,** 37–46.

Imboden H., Lanzrein B., Delbecque J. P. & Lüscher M. (1978) Ecdysteroids and juvenile hormone during embryogenesis in the ovoviviparous cockroach *Nauphoeta cinerea. Gen. Comp. Endocr.* **36**, 628–635.

Kaiser V. P. (1956) Die Hormonalorgane der Termiten im Zusammenhang mit der Entstehung ihrer Kasten. *Mitt. Hamburg Zool. Mus. Inst.* **54**, 129–178.

Lanzrein B., Gentinetta V. & Lüscher M. (1977) *In vivo* and *in vitro* studies on the endocrinology of the reproductives of the termite *Macrotermes subhyalinus. Proc. VIII Congr. IUSSI*, Wageningen, pp. 265–268.

Lanzrein B., Hashimoto M., Parmakovich V., Nakanishi K., Wilhelm R. & Lüscher M. (1975) Identification and quantification of juvenile hormones from different developmental stages of the cockroach *Nauphoeta cinerea. Life Sci.* **16**, 1271–1284.

Lanzrein B., Gentinetta V., Fehr R. & Lüscher M. (1978) Correlation between haemolymph juvenile hormone titer, *corpus allatum* volume, and *corpus allatum in vivo* and *in vitro* activity during oocyte maturation in a cockroach (*Nauphoeta cinerea*). *Gen. Comp. Endocr.* **36**, 339–345.

Lanzrein B., Wilhelm R. & Buschor J. (1981) On the regulation of the *corpora allata* activity in adult females of the ovoviviparous cockroach *Nauphoeta cinerea*. In *Juvenile Hormone Biochemistry* (Pratt G. E. & Brooks G. T., eds), pp. 147–160. Elsevier-North Holland Biomedical Press, Amsterdam.

Lüscher M. (1974) Kasten und Kastendifferenzierung bei niederen Termiten. In *Sozialpolymorphismus bei Insekten* (Schmidt G. H., ed.), pp. 694–739. Wiss. Verlagsgesellschaft mbH, Stuttgart.

Lüscher M. (1976) Evidence for an endocrine control of caste determination in higher termites. In *Phase and Caste Determination in Insects, Endocrine Aspects* (Lüscher M., ed.), pp. 91–104. Pergamon Press, Oxford.

Meyer D., Lanzrein B., Lüscher M. & Nakanishi K. (1976) Isolation and identification of a juvenile hormone (JH) in termites. *Exper.* **32**, 773.

Noirot C. (1969) Formation of castes in the higher termites. In *Biology of Termites*, Vol. 1, (Krishna K. & Weesner F. M., eds), pp. 311–350. Academic Press, New York and London.

Noirot C. (1974) Polymorphismus bei höheren Termiten. In *Sozialpolymorphismus bei Insekten* (Schmidt G. H., ed.), pp. 740–765. Wiss. Verlagsgesellschaft mbH, Stuttgart.

Okot-Kotber B. M. (1977) Changes in *corpora allata* volume during development in relation to caste differentiation in *Macrotermes subhyalinus. Proc. VIII Congr. IUSSI*, Wageningen, pp. 262–264.

Okot-Kotber B. M. (1980a) The influence of juvenile hormone analogue on soldier differentiation in the higher termite, *Macrotermes michaelseni. Physiol. Entomol.* **5**, 407–416.

Okot-Kotber B. M. (1980b) Competence of *Macrotermes michaelseni* (*Isoptera, Macrotermitinae*) larvae to differentiate into soldiers under the influence of juvenile hormone analogue (ZR-515, methoprene) *J. Insect Physiol.* **26**, 655–659.

Okot-Kotber B. M. (1980c) Histological and size changes in corpora allata and prothoracic glands during development of *Macrotermes michaelseni. Insectes Sociaux* **27**, 361–376.

Okot-Kotber B. M. (1981a) Instars and polymorphism of castes in *Macrotermes michaelseni* (Isoptera, Macrotermitinae). *Insectes Sociaux* **28**, 233–246.

Okot-Kotber B. M. (1981b) Polymorphism and the development of the first progeny in incipient colonies of *Macrotermes michaelseni* (*Isoptera, Macrotermitinae*). *Insect Sci. Applic.* **1**, 147–150.

Reissig W. H. & Kamm J. A. (1975) Effect of synthetic juvenile hormone on reproduction of adult male *Draeculacephala crassicornis. Ann. Entomol. Soc. Am.* **68**, 353–354.

Rembold H. (1981) Modulation of JH III titer during the gonotrophic cycle of *Locusta migratoria*, measured by gas chromatography-selected ion monitoring mass spectrometry. In *Juvenile Hormone Biochemistry* (Pratt G. E. & Brooks G. T., eds), pp. 11–20. Elsevier-North Holland Biomedical Press, Amsterdam.

Sachs L. (1974) *Angewandte Statistik*, 4th Edition. Springer-Verlag, Berlin.

Sieber R. & Darlington J. P. (1982) Replacement of the royal pair in *Macrotermes michaelseni. Insect Sci. Applic.* **3**, 39–42.

Sieber R. & Leuthold R. H. (1982a) Development of physogastry in the queen of the fungus-growing termite *Macrotermes michaelseni* (*Isoptera, Macrotermitinae*). *J. Insect Physiol.* (In press.)

Sieber R. & Leuthold R. H. (1982b) Repeated copulation and testes enlargement in *Macrotermes michaelseni. Physiol. Entomol.* (In press.)

Suzzoni J. P., Passéra L. & Strambi A. (1980) Ecdysteroid titre and caste determination in the ant, *Pheidole pallidula. Exper.* **36,** 1228–1229.

Szibbo C. M. & Tobe S. S. (1982) Intrinsic differences in juvenile hormone synthetic ability between *corpora allata* of males and females of the cockroach *Diploptera punctata. Gen. Comp. Endocr.* **46,** 533–540.

Tobe S. S. & Pratt G. E. (1974) The influence of substrate concentrations on the rate of insect juvenile hormone biosynthesis by *corpora allata* of the desert locust *in vitro. Biochem. J.* **144,** 107–113.

Wanyonyi K. (1974) The influence of the juvenile hormone analogue ZR 512 (Zoecon) on caste development in *Zootermopsis nevadensis* (Hagen) (*Isoptera*). *Insectes Sociaux* **21,** 35–44.

Wilhelm R. & Lüscher M. (1974) On the relative importance of juvenile hormone and vitellogenin for oocyte growth in the cockroach *Nauphoeta cinerea. J. Insect Physiol.* **20,** 1887–1894.

Wyss-Huber M. & Lüscher M. (1975) Protein synthesis in "fat body" and ovary of the physogastric queen of *Macrotermes subhyalinus. J. Insect Physiol.* **21,** 1697–1704.

Zhu X. X., Gfeller H. & Lanzrein B. (1982) Ecdysteroids during oogenesis in the ovoviviparous cockroach *Nauphoeta cinerea. J. Insect Physiol.* (In press.)

Section E

Caste Differentiation in Other Social Insects

CHAPTER 23

Soldier Determination in Ants of the Genus Pheidole

L. PASSERA

Laboratoire Associé au CNRS no. 333, Recherche Coopérative sur Programme du CNRS no. 645, Laboratoire de Biologie des Insectes, Université Paul-Sabatier, 118, route de Narbonne, 31062 Toulouse Cedex, France

CONTENTS

23.1 INTRODUCTION

In social insects, the term polymorphism is usually applied to a discontinuous, non-genetic variation within a population, involving the appearance of several castes. For example, Wilson (1971) defined polymorphism as the coexistence of two or more functional castes within the same sex.

Two basic female castes are found in ants: one or more fully developed reproductive females—queens—and ordinary sterile females—workers. The workers may be subdivided into several additional castes according to size:

MINOR, MEDIA, and MAJOR workers. In the absence or (the disappearance or the) rarity of MEDIA workers, leaving only the MINOR and MAJOR
workers, the MAJOR are called SOLDIERS.

These three female castes (queen, workers and soldiers) are known to exist
in a few genera belonging to the sub-families Myrmicinae and Formicinae:
Acanthomyrmex, Ischnomyrmex, Oligomyrmex, Cryptocerus, Pheidole and Colobopsis.

The determination of queen-appearance in ants is now well-documented
(Brian, 1979; Passera, 1982; Suzzoni, 1983). On the other hand, the mechanisms of soldier determination is still unknown. What little information we
possess concerns the genus Pheidole.

Pheidole is a cosmopolitan genus. Most species, e.g. P. pallidula in Europe or
P. bicarinata in North America, show a complete worker dimorphism. For
example we can see in Figure 23.1 a histogram of the head length of the
worker castes of a P. pallidula colony collected in the South of France. There is

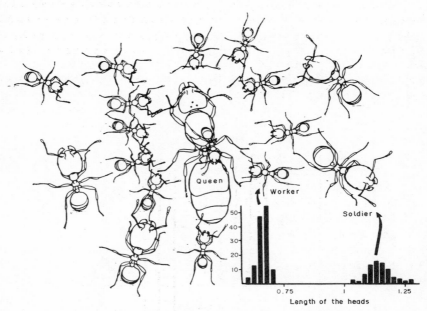

FIG. 23.1. Complete dimorphism in Pheidole pallidula. Abscissa: length of the heads (less the
mandibles) of a single colony.

a large discontinuity in the measurements of the two castes; workers range
from 0.57 to 0.67 mm, and soldiers from 1.04 to 1.29 mm (Passera, 1974).

23.2 LARVAL DIFFERENTIATION INTO SOLDIERS

Light microscope examination of larvae taken from developing colonies of

P. pallidula societies allowed three larval instars to be recognized in the minor worker line.

Instar 1: length of larvae: 0.4 mm. The mandible with one-pointed tooth looks like a very large paddle; low pilosity; on dorsal abdomen two lines of five or six fairly thick short hairs characteristic of the first instar.

Instar 2: length of larvae: 0.40 to 0.75 mm. The mandible with three-pointed teeth is fairly elongated; thick pilosity with single hairs and two lines of five or six thick forked hairs on the dorsal abdomen, characteristic of the second instar.

Instar 3: length of larvae: 0.75 to 1.50 mm. The three-pointed mandible has asperities. Pilosity is less than in the preceding instar but single hairs and forked thin hairs are present but scarce on the entire surface of the body. On the dorsal face of the abdomen, two lines of five to eight long flexuous (springlike) forked hairs replace the second instar's forked hairs.

A histogram of the diameters of the first thoracic spiracle clearly shows three peaks corresponding to the three instars (Fig. 23.2).

Soldier larvae are larger, up to 3.5 mm long. Their teguments have the same

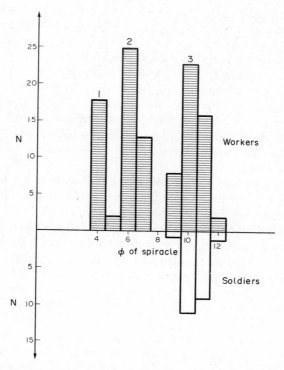

Fig. 23.2. Histogram of the diameter (μm) of the first thoracic spiracle of the three larval instars in *Pheidole pallidula*. Hatched columns show worker-biased larvae. Open columns show soldier-biased larvae. Numbers above the columns designate instars.

characteristics as the third instar worker larvae, and the same spring-shaped hairs are present.

The histograms of the diameter of the first thoracic spiracle are the same for the soldier and third instar worker. Larvae, i.e., the spiracle diameters of the oldest worker larvae and those of soldier larvae of all ages belong to the same population (Fig. 23.2). Thus the soldier larvae are of the third instar: the increased growth of soldier larvae is accomplished without a supplementary moult, but by cuticle extension. This phenomenon is well-known in many arthropods (Bordereau, 1982).

The time at which soldier larvae become visibly different from worker larvae was identified in a detailed study of the third instar larvae (Passera, 1973, 1974; Suzzoni et al., 1982). When the worker larvae reach 1.30 mm they are orange, because of the colour of the gut contents. Their development temporarily ceases on emptying the hindgut, resulting in the acquisition of a grey colour before pupation (Fig. 23.3), which occurs when the larvae are 1.5 mm long and 0.4 to 0.5 mg in weight. The resulting worker pupae develop through the following stages: first, white pupae with white eyes; second, white pupae with coloured eyes; then yellow pupae. However, the larvae may continue to grow, and reach 3.5 mm in length and 2.5 to 3 mg in weight before emptying the hindgut, and pupating as before, but to form soldier pupae (Fig. 23.3). Thus orientation towards soldiers takes place when the coloured orange third instar larvae reach a length slightly over 1.5 mm.

The American species, P. bicarinata, shows similar development: three larval instars with soldier differentiation at the end of the last instar (Wheeler & Nijhout, 1981a).

Larval development into soldier is characterized by the existence of a pair of mesothoracic wing discs. This phenomenon was discovered by Wheeler & Nijhout (1981a) in Pheidole bicarinata and later confirmed in P. pallidula (Suzzoni et al., 1982).

Imaginal wing discs in Pheidole pallidula do not become apparent until the orange-coloured larvae begin to differentiate into soldiers (Fig. 23.4). The discs are dense, compact masses which have a spherical shape in larvae and become ellipsoid in the pupae. Their external cells are rather elongated and tall and the central cells are more rounded; the nucleus is $3\,\mu$ by $5\,\mu$m. The development of the discs is shown in Figure 23.5. From the orange larvae stage to the grey larvae stage they grow slightly, the surface area increasing from 0.01 to 0.0135 mm^2. During pupation they emerge from the body in the form of a minute bud behind and above each mesothoracic spiracle (Fig. 23.4). Their size then decreases and by emergence they have disappeared.

Metathoracic imaginal wing discs have not been observed in larvae of either species. However, we did once find two pairs of wing buds in a pupa of Pheidole pallidula infected by Mermis larvae (Nematoda). It has already been shown that mermithization causes important morphological alterations in P. pallidula (Passera, 1976); when the infecting larvule enters an orange larva it disturbs

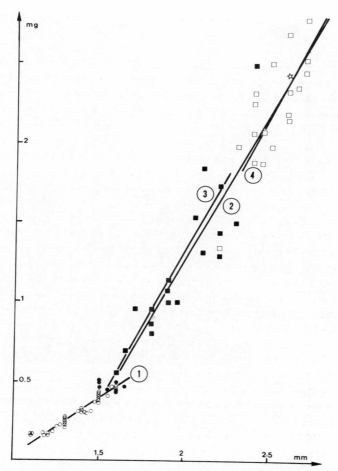

FIG. 23.3. Relationship between weight and length of worker and soldier larvae in *Pheidole pallidula*. Abscissa: length in mm; ordinate: weight in mg. ○ = orange worker larvae; ● = grey worker larvae; ■ = orange soldier larvae; □ = grey soldier larvae; 1 = regression line for worker larvae; 2 = regression line for soldier larvae; 3 = regression line for orange soldier larvae; 4 = regression line for grey soldier larvae. (From Suzzoni *et al.*, 1982.)

the worker/soldier differentiation. The result is an ant with morphology intermediate between that of a worker and of a soldier, i.e., an intercaste. Moreover some intercastes develop a queen-like character in certain morphological features, such as the presence of ocelli, gynecoidy of the thorax, and indeed the presence of two pairs of wing buds. During the imaginal ecdysis these buds disappear, as they do in healthy soldiers. However, Tinaut & Millan (1981) have reported the presence of wing stumps in some adult mermithized intercastes of *P. pallidula* collected in Spain.

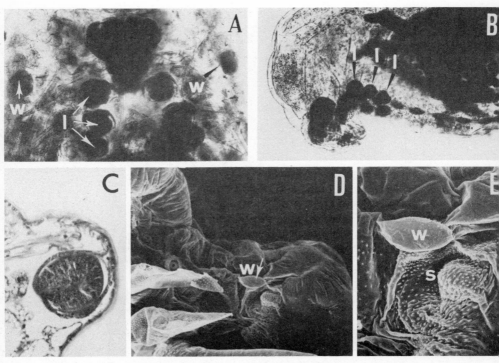

FIG. 23.4. Wing discs in *Pheidole pallidula*. A: orange soldier larva; ventral view (whole mount); B: orange worker larva; lateral view (whole mount); C: mesothoracic wing disc of an orange soldier larva; D: Scanning electron micrograph of the thorax of a white soldier pupa; E: Scanning electron micrograph of the mesothoracic region of the same pupa (soldier); l = leg imaginal disc; w = wing imaginal disc; s = mesothoracic spiracle.

Workers of neither of the species possess wing imaginal discs at any time (Wheeler & Nijhout, 1981a; Suzzoni *et al.*, 1982). This is surprising because, as a general rule, workers of ants have two pairs of wing imaginal discs where development is synchronized with leg discs. However, these wing discs are always smaller than those of the soldiers and disappear before pupation (Wheeler & Nijhout, 1981a).

23.3 DIFFERENTIATION OF THE SOLDIERS: FACTORS INTERNAL TO THE SOCIETY

23.3.1 Social factors

This work was conducted on *Pheidole pallidula* in the South-West of France (Passera, 1974, 1977).

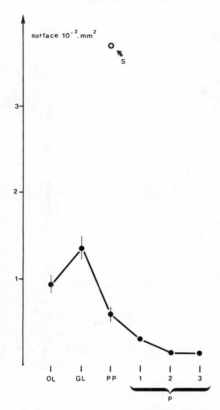

FIG. 23.5. Relationship between surface area of mesothoracic discs to development of larvae and pupae during soldier differentiation in *Pheisole pallidula*. OL = orange larvae; GL = grey larvae; PP = prepupae; Pl = white pupae with white eyes; P2 = White pupae with black eyes; P3 = yellow pupae; S = queen prepupae. (From Suzzoni *et al.* 1982.)

Counting the number of adults in colonies in the field showed that the percentage of soldiers varies greatly. Colonies coming out of hibernation had 1.5 to 13% soldiers (mean = 5.58%). As the season progresses, the number of soldiers increases to a maximum of 10 to 30% in the autumn and beginning of winter (mean = 18.38%).

These variations in the adults are the result of variations found in the brood. When colonies were collected in the field, until 20th June when the first brood of the year pupated, a mean of 1.89% of soldier pupae was found. Between 20 June and 12 July, the percentage increased to 3.78, on 12 August it was 6.92, and on 28 August 8.43. At the end of the season, on 27 September, the percentage reached a maximum of 18.51. Then the soldier pupae, which are rare in the first brood, become more and more frequent as the season progresses (Fig. 23.6).

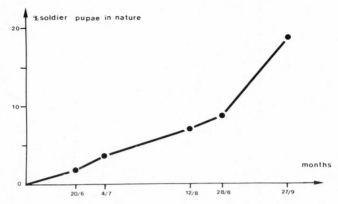

FIG. 23.6. The percentage of soldier pupae of *Pheidole pallidula* collected in the field. Along the abscissa dates of the gathering.

It is possible to reproduce these rates in the laboratory. Societies with 5% of adult soldiers were cultured at the end of hibernation. Every month, the pupae were counted. From the 30th to the 90th day after the beginning of experimentation, the average percentage of pupae soldiers increased from 0.25 to 4.42 (Fig. 23.7). The factors that influence the numbers of soldiers during the year was therefore, studied in such a laboratory group.

23.3.1.1   *Physiological variations of nurse workers*

The physiological state of the nurse workers seems to have no effect on the differentiation of the soldiers: workers just coming out of hibernation are equally able to rear soldiers as those that have left hibernation for several weeks.

23.3.1.2   *Egg bias*

The eggs are usually bipotential in spite of seasonal changes in size. Even the eggs of queens just coming out of hibernation are able to give rise to soldiers. Therefore, the direction in which the eggs develop depends on larval feeding and not on a blastogenetic factor (Passera, 1977).

23.3.1.3   *Number of workers*

The abundance of nurse workers favours the production of soldiers; there is a direct relationship between the number of adult workers and that of soldiers produced. Societies with one queen and less than 550 workers give rise to 3.55% soldiers in 30 days. If there are 750 to 2500 workers, the percentage of soldiers is doubled to about 7.52% (Passera, 1977). These results corroborate the studies of Nakao (1973) on the Japanese species *Pheidole nodus*.

23.3.1.4   *Number of soldiers*

This is the most critical factor: societies with thousands of workers but a high proportion of soldiers are unable to give rise to new soldiers. In laboratory tests, at the end of hibernation, the first brood produced contains

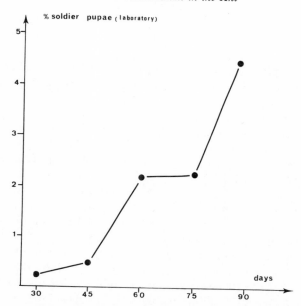

FIG. 23.7. The percentage of soldier pupae of *Pheidole pallidula* in experimental colonies. Along the abscissa number of days after emergence from hibernation.

only worker pupae if the proportion of adult soldiers is greater than about 4%. In nature, at the same time, colonies have more than 5% adult soldiers so their production of soldiers is inhibited; these societies give rise to workers alone in the first brood. The emergence of these workers lowers the percentage of soldiers, thus reducing the inhibition and leading to the development of the first soldiers of the season (Passera, 1977).

Gregg (1942) for *Pheidole morrisi* and Nakao (1973) for *P. nodus* indicate clearly that a similar social regulation exists in these species.

23.3.2 Climatic and trophic factors

In the laboratory the rearing of soldiers is only possible at high temperatures (Passera, 1974). A colony cultured at about 21 to 22°C give rise to workers. Although soldiers develop at 24°C they do so readily only above 26°C.

In the field, the effect of temperature—low at the end of hibernation and higher in the summer months—adds to the effect of colony composition in influencing soldier differentiation.

Animal prey seems to be necessary for soldier production in the brood (Goetsch, 1937, 1953). A colony gives rise to workers alone if it is fed on honey (Passera, 1974).

23.4 DIFFERENTIATION OF THE SOLDIERS: INDIVIDUAL INTERNAL FACTORS

The physiological basis of the determination of queen differentiation is relatively well-known in *P. pallidula* (Passera & Suzzoni, 1978; Suzzoni *et al.*, 1980; Suzzoni, 1983).

At the end of hibernation, the first eggs laid by most queens are queen-biased. The ecdysteroid and juvenile hormone (JH) levels of the queens and of the eggs they lay are very low during this period. Later in the season, only worker/soldier biased eggs are laid and ecdysteroid and JH levels are very high.

The application of higher doses of JHA lowers the ecdysteroid level and the endogenic JH level by feed-back effect. The summer queen thus treated returns to the state of an early spring queen and lays queen-biased eggs.

On the assumption that queen caste determination is under endocrine control, Suzzoni *et al.* (1982) studied the role of JH in soldier differentiation in *P. pallidula*. JH1 (Ayerst Laboratories) was administered to colonies in the way as follows: Societies of 1000 workers and one queen, without soldiers, received twice a week a *Tenebrio* larva injected with JH in olive oil solution. In the first group of experiments, colonies are fed with *Tenebrio* larva which has received 200 μg of JH (high dosage). In a second group of experiments, *Tenebrio* has received 5 μg of JH (low dosage). Three or four weeks later, the first pupae appeared. The pupae were either left in the culture or removed depending on the experimental design. The results are summarized in Figure 23.8.

23.4.1 High dosage of JHA (200 μg)

This concentration induces high mortality in workers and queens. The surviving colonies gave rise to 35% soldiers. Control colonies fed with *Tenebrio* injected with pure olive oil gave rise to only 9.4% soldiers.

23.4.2 Low dosage of JHA (5 μg)

None of the colonies died. The experimental groups in the 1981 series gave rise to 21.7% soldiers compared with 9.5% for the controls. In 1982 we obtained 7.8% soldiers in treated colonies compared with 3.8% in control societies; in these experiments the pupae were removed weekly. Thus the number of soldiers increased two- or three-fold when the ants were fed JH.

The studies of Edwards *et al.* (1981) showed similar phenomena. The use of bait containing 0.5% JHA (Methoprene ZR 515) for the control of the widespread species *Pheidole megacephala* results in a great increase in the number

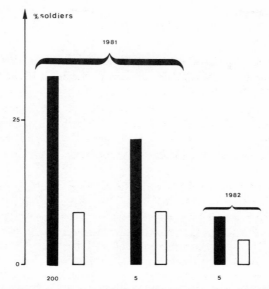

FIG. 23.8. Developmental alternative of *Pheidole pallidula* larvae when the colonies are fed on prey with JHA. Ordinate: the percentage of soldier pupae produced; black bars: societies treated with 5 or 200 μg of JHA; white bars: control societies without JHA. (From Suzzoni *et al.* 1982.)

of soldiers. However, the authors speculate over the reason for this increase, it may simply reflect a difference in longevity of soldiers and workers, since soldiers survive better.

The titres of ecdysteroids in worker-biased and soldier-biased larvae have been studied by radioimmunoassay to investigate the possible role of these hormones during the caste differentiation (Suzzoni *et al.*, 1982). In worker larvae the titre increases progressively, reaching 5.1 pmoles/mg at a weight of approximately 420 μg, then decreases to a minimum reached just before pupation (Fig. 23.9). A second peak occurs during the pupal period, at the stage when the white pupae have black eyes. Soldier differentiation is characterized by high titres before the larval weight reaches 1 mg. Then a second peak is achieved near pupation, when the larvae weigh approximately 2.2 mg. During the pupal period there is a third peak, when the pupae are white with black eyes. Thus the changes in ecdysteroid titres just before prepupation and during the pupal period are the same in the worker-biased and soldier-biased individuals. These variations are due simply to ecdysis. However, the low level of ecdysteroids in 300–400 μg worker-biased larvae and the high level in 600–900 μg soldier-biased larvae at the beginning of differentiation may be significant and should be checked by other RIA titrations. Unfortunately it is at present impossible to separate worker-biased and soldier-biased larvae when they weigh less than 500 μg.

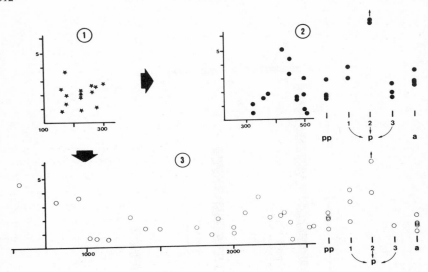

Fig. 23.9. Ecdysteroid levels during soldier and worker differentiation in *Pheidole pallidula*; 1 = undifferentiated stage; 2 = workers; 3 = soldiers; Every point represents a titration; abscissa: the weight (μg) or the stage; ordinate: ecdysteroids equivalent (pmoles/mg); PP = prepupae; P2, P3 = pupae; a = adult. (From Suzzoni *et al.*, 1982.)

Ono (1982) performed a comparable study in a Japanese species *Pheidole fervida*. The larvae of the three instars were painted with various solutions of 0.02 μl to 20 μl of ZR515 in 150 μl of acetone: the exact amount of JHA topically applied was unknown. The lower doses failed to cause differentiation of soldiers in the brood. The higher doses (2 and 20 μl) killed many larvae but more soldiers differentiated from the survivors than in the control. In Ono's opinion, the third instar larvae had the competence to differentiate into soldiers, and are sensitive to JHA.

The JH target could be the third instar larvae as suggested by Wheeler & Nijhout (1981a, b) and Nijhout & Wheeler (1982) in their studies on the effects of topical applications of JHA in *P. bicarinata*. Third instar larvae, classified according to their size, were treated with Methoprene (ZR 515). Results (Fig. 23.10) show that treatment with high doses of JHA (100 to 250 μg) induce soldier differentiation in 75% of the larvae. Treatment with low dosage (20 to 50 μg) shows that the larvae react only if they are between 0.9 and 1.2 mm long. This length must coincide with the sensitive period of hormonal action.

Moreover, Ono (1982) provides data on the volume of the *corpora allata* (CA) through the third instar and prepupal stage. It seems that future soldiers have larger CA than future workers. For instance, during the prepupal stage CA of future soldiers were about twice as large as that of future workers. This

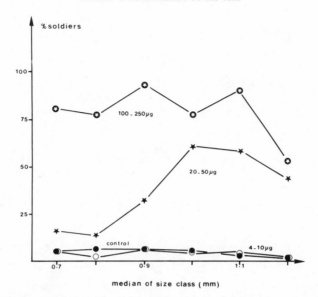

Fig. 23.10. Developmental alternative of larvae after topical application of JHA (*Pheidole bicarinata*); abscissa: the percentage of the treated larvae (mm); ordinate: the percentage of soldier pupae produced. (From Wheeler & Nijhout, 1981b.)

suggests that endogenous JH from the CA has a role in soldier determination in *P. fervida*.

Suzzoni *et al.* (1982) studied the same phenomenon in *P. pallidula*. Batches of second instar larvae (20–80 μg) or third instar larvae of various sizes (100–200, 200–300, 300–400 and 400–500 μg) were given to groups of queenless workers. Each larva received a topical application of JHA (Ayerst). According to experiments, the doses differ from 133 to 2000 μg with the aim of founding the threshold of response. Out of 817 treated larvae, 553 developed into worker pupae and 7 into soldier pupae (1.3%). On the other hand, 160 control larvae treated with only pure acetone gave rise to 97 workers and 4 soldiers (3.9%). Thus the JHA failed to induce soldier differentiation. However, it did affect the weight of the worker pupae. The earlier the topical application, the heavier the resulting pupae: second instar larvae produced pupae of 470 μg (mean weight) whereas the oldest third instar larvae produced pupae of 284 μg (mean weight) (Fig. 23.11).

Wheeler & Nijhout (1981b) also obtained longer workers, but it is perhaps a secondary effect of JH: the hormone increases the nutrition period by extending larval life.

Measurements of the CA volume of the orange worker and soldier larvae also provided ambiguous data in *P. pallidula* (Suzzoni, 1983). It is only late in development, during the prepupal and pupal stages, that the differences

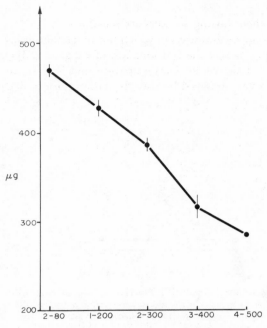

FIG. 23.11. Relationship between the weight of JHA treated larvae and the weight of the resulting pupae (*Pheidole pallidula*); abscissa: larval weight in μg; ordinate: pupal weight in μg. (From Suzzoni *et al.*, 1982.)

between allatal volume of soldiers and workers become statistically signifi-cant. By this time, however, the differentiation is already completed.

It is certain that in *P. bicarinata* and in *P. fervida* the third instar is the JH target, but this has not been confirmed in *P. pallidula* even though *P. pallidula* is sensitive to JH. If other JH analogues, applied at different concentrations or at different times in the larval intervals within instars, prove to be ineffective, we must envisage that JH acts through other routes, the nursing workers, for example.

23.5   DISCUSSION

Despite the scarcity of data, experiments on larvae of ants in the genus *Pheidole* allow some conclusions to be drawn on the roles of hormonal and social factors in regulating the development of soldiers. Soldier differentiation is first subject to factors within the colony. It is only when the number of adult soldiers falls below a threshold, which varies with the season, that soldier differentiation begins. This social regulation seems to be trophogenetic. The best fed larvae become soldiers, as shown by the lack of differentiation into soldier larvae when nursing workers are scarce.

We can envisage several ways in which hormonal factors are involved. In *P. bicarinata* or in *P. fervida* the introduction of exogenous JH could lead to a higher JH titre. This would delay pupation and lead to an increase in the weight of the larvae, followed by transformation into soldier pupae.

We may also suppose that exogenous JH supplied in the food acts first on the nursing workers, modifying their trophic behaviour and inciting them to give more food to the third instar larvae. This hypothesis could explain the failure of JH to act when applied topically to larvae, as we have observed in *P. pallidula*. This situation would be easier to explain if we could distinguish worker-biased larvae from soldier-biased larvae early in the third instar and, by so doing, permit study of growth hormones before major morphological differentiation has occurred.

23.6 SUMMARY

In ants, the soldiers originate from the same brood as the workers. In the genus *Pheidole*, the differentiation of the larvae of soldiers takes place at the end of the third instar as there is no supplementary moult.

Larval development of soldiers is characterized by the presence of a pair of mesothoracic wing imaginal discs. Wing buds can be seen on pupal teguments, then they disappear. In worker-biased larvae however, the wing discs have not been found.

Soldier-biased larvae arise only in colonies well-fed by many nursing workers. On the other hand the production of soldiers is inhibited when the percentage of adult soldiers is greater than a threshold which depends on the time of the year. At the end of hibernation this threshold is about 4 to 5%.

Colonies of *P. pallidula* fed on prey injected with JHA result in differentiation of two or three times more soldier pupae than in controls. However, topical applications of JHA on larvae are ineffective in this species. But in other species (*P. bicarinata* and *P. fervida*) it is possible to induce soldier development by topical applications of JHA. Soldier differentiation is therefore sensitive to the level of JH.

Polymorphism is also associated with changes in ecdysteroid levels. Using radio-immunoassay, ecdysteroid concentrations were measured in worker and soldier larvae of *P. pallidula*. Differences are observed between the two ways of development although their significance does not seem very clear yet.

All in all, differentiation of soldiers is the result of two types of events: environmental (social and climatic) factors and hormonal control.

23.7   REFERENCES

Bordereau C. (1982) Extension et croissance cuticulaires en l'absence de mue chez les Athropodes. *Bull. Soc. Zool. Fr.* **107**, 427–432.

Brian M. V. (1979) Caste differentiation and division of labour. In *Social Insects*, Vol. 1 (Hermann H. R., ed.), pp. 122–222, Academic Press; (1980) Social control over sex and caste in bees, wasps and ants. *Biol. Rev.* **55**, 379–415.

Edwards J. P., Pemberton G. W. & Curran P. J. (1981) The use of juvenile hormone analogues for control of *Pheidole megacephala* and other house-infesting ants. In *Regulation of Insect Development and Reproduction* (Kloza M., ed.), pp. 769–779. Wroclau Techn. Univ. Press.

Goetsch W. (1937) Die Entstehung der "Soldaten" im Ameisenstaat. *Naturwiss.*, **25**, 803–808; (1953) *Die Staaten der Ameisen*, Springer-Verlag Berlin (traduction française, Hachette édit., Paris, 174p., 1959).

Gregg R. (1942) The origin of castes in ants with special reference to *Pheidole morrisi* Forel. *Ecology* **23**, 295–308.

Nakao S. I. (1973) Colony development of *Pheidole nodus* Smith in artificial nest (Hymenoptera, Formicidae), *Mushi* **47**, 19–29.

Nijhout H. F. & Wheeler D. E. (1982) Juvenile hormone and the physiological basis of insect polymorphisms. *Quart. Rev. Biol.* **57**, 109–133.

Ono S. (1982) Effect of juvenile hormone on the caste determination in the ant *Pheidole fervida* Smith (Hymenoptera, Formicidae). *Appl. Entomol. Zool.* **17**, 1–7.

Passera L. (1973) Origine des soldats dans les sociétés de *Pheidole pallidula* (Nyl.) (Formicidae, Myrmicinae). *C.R. VIIème Congr. I.U.S.S.I., London*, pp. 305–309.

Passera L. (1974) Différenciation des soldats chez la Fourmi *Pheidole pallidula* (Nyl.) (Formicidae, Myrmicinae) *Insectes Sociaux* **21**, 71–86.

Passera L. (1976) Origine des intercastes dans les sociétés de *Pheidole pallidula* (Nyl.) (Hymenoptera Formicidae) parasitées par *Mermis* sp. (Nematoda, Mermithidae). *Insectes Sociaux* **23**, 559–575.

Passera L. (1977) Production des soldats dans les sociétés sortant d'hibernation chez la Fourmi *Pheidole pallidula* (Nyl.) (Formicidae, Myrmicinae). *Insectes Sociaux* **24**, 131–146.

Passera L. (1982) Endocrine regulation of caste determination in ants. In *Social Insects in the Tropics* (Jaisson P., ed.), pp. 41–62. Presses de l'Université de Paris XIII.

Passera L. & Suzzoni J. P. (1978) Traitement des reines par l'hormone juvénile et sexualisation du couvain chez *Pheidole pallidula* (Nyl.) (Hymenoptera, Formicidae *C.R. Acad. Sc. Paris* **287**, D, 1231–1233.

Suzzoni J. P. (1983) Le Polymorphisme et son déterminisme chez deux espèces de Fourmis: *Plagiolepis pygmaea* Latr. (Formicinae) et *Pheidole pallidula* (Nyl.) (Myrmicinae). Rôle des hormones du développement. *These d'Etat*, Toulouse, No. 1077, 420p.

Suzzoni J. P., Passera L. & Strambi A. (1980) Ecdysteroid titre and caste determination in the ant *Pheidole pallidula* (Nyl.) (Hymenoptera, Formicidae). *Experientia* **36**, 1228–1229.

Suzzoni J. P., Passera L. & Strambi A. (1982) Etude morpho-anatomique et physiologique de la "soldatisation" chez la Fourmi *Pheidole pallidula* (Nyl.). *Bull. int. Sect. franç. U.I.E.I.S.*, Barcelone, pp. 147–156.

Tinaut-Ranera A. & Millan J. F. Estudo de various ejemplares de *Pheidole pallidula* (Nyl.) (Hym. Formicidae) parasitados por Mermitidoes. *Rev. Iber. de Parasitol.* **40**, 527–537.

Wheeler D. E. & Nijhout H. F. (1981a) Imaginal wing discs in larvae of the soldier caste of *Pheidole bicarinata vinelandica* Forel (Hymenoptera:Formicidae). *Int. J. Insect Morphol. and Embryol.* **10**, 131–139.

Wheeler D. E. & Nijhout H. F. (1981b) Soldier determination in ants: New role for juvenile hormone. *Science* **213**, 361–363.

Wilson E. O. (1971) *The Insect Societies*. Cambridge, Mass., The Belknap Press of Harvard University Press, 548p.

CHAPTER 24

Sequence of Caste Differentiation Steps in Apis mellifera

H. REMBOLD

Max Planck Institute for Biochemistry, Martinsried near Munich, West Germany

CONTENTS

24.1 INTRODUCTION

Caste formation and especially hormonal control of morphogenesis within the framework of sociality in insect colonies offers many fascinating questions to the biochemist. Some of them can be approached only now after micro-chemical methods of appropriate sensitivity have become available. Such physical methods as gas or high-performance liquid chromatography, usually in combination with mass spectrometry, can identify and quantify hormones in the femtomole range. With the necessary precautions in mind, immunologi-cal techniques like the radio or the viro-immunoassay can also be used. However, cross reactivity with biological material other than the compound under consideration must be carefully excluded. It is more convenient, therefore, if after an extensive purification of the biological probe, a physical instead of an immunological method is used.

Social polymorphism, if analysed on the basis of our present knowledge of molecular biology, can be discussed as a sequential expression of genetic programmes. The genes responsible for programming the morphological expression must be switched on by the appropriate hormones. From what is known in this most speculative field, this switch involves a receptor protein. Obviously the affinity of such a hormone receptor, which may be located on the cell surface or within the chromosomes of the responsive organ, determines the amount of hormone necessary for releasing a signal. Such a signal may be the second messenger (cyclic-AMP, for example) which switches on an organ-specific reaction such as synthesis of a caste-specific protein. As an example, the synthesis of cytochrome c and its correlation with caste-specific respiration will be discussed in some detail.

Concerning the receptor-hormone complex, its dissociation constant (K_D) can only be measured by use of the pure proteins which are not yet available. Their K_D value is estimated to be, at an average, between 10^{-8}M (ecdysone) and 10^{-11}M [juvenile hormone (JH)]. In biological terms, this means that a JH concentration of 10^{-11}M may be enough for inducing a 50% response of the sensitive organ, an amount which corresponds to about 3 pg. g^{-1} of haemo-lymph! There is no doubt that such low concentrations are beyond the sensitivity of a biological test such as the *Galleria* assay and, because of its high cross-reactivity with components usually contained in the biological probe, also of the JH radio-immunoassay (RIA). As exemplified in Table 24.1, a physical method, which works in the femtomole range, can easily use insect material of 100 mg and less, depending upon the amount of JH(s) present. The JH-III titre of the honey-bee larval stages will be discussed as an example later on.

TABLE 24.1. LIMIT OF DETECTION FOR ECDYSONE (SPINDLER *ET AL.*, 1978), JUVENILE HORMONE (REMBOLD *ET AL.*, 1980) AND CYTOCHROME C (EDER *ET AL.*, 1977) ASSAY

Ecdysones	
Radio-Immunoassay (RIA)	50 pg (10^{-14}M)
Juvenile hormones	
Gas chromatography–mass spectrometry (GC–MS–MIS)	2 pg (10^{-15}M)
Cytochrome c	
Viro-Immunoassay	15 pg (10^{-15}M)

There has been much speculation about the mechanisms inducing caste formation in the honey bee (for reviews, see Townsend and Shuel, 1962; Rembold, 1964, 1965, 1969, 1974, 1976; Weaver, 1966; de Wilde and Beetsma, 1982). However, even after more than 50 years of endeavour, neither the biological phenomenon of insect caste formation nor its biochemical events can be explained in terms of present molecular biology. From the studies of Zander and Becker (1925) and of Weiss (1978), who transferred worker larvae of different ages into queen cells, and vice versa, and followed their further development, it is known that the female honey bee larva is susceptible to queen induction until the end of its third larval stage. After this sensitive phase, determination of a worker larva to a queen is no longer possible under colony conditions. Beyond this rather narrow developmental gate, nutrition of the worker is changed from a mixture of glandular secretion and honey, released by the nurse bees, to a food which is primarily a mixture of pollen with honey. Worker larvae are fed poorer quality food than queen larvae which continue being fed royal jelly exclusively. This food change after third instar may be another safety provision in the system of honey-bee caste induction.

It is obvious from the preceding arguments that food quality might have an important function. This will be discussed first and evidence will be given for the decisive role of food as the external factor which switches on the developmental programmes in the sensitive larva. The manifestation of an initial difference in food quality by the larval neuroendocrine system will then be described. Under neuroendocrine control the secretory activity of the peripheral hormone glands [corpora allata (CA) and prothoracic gland (PG)] and, by that, the modulation of hormone titre in a caste-specific way will then be discussed as a consequence of the primary interaction of food quality and the neuroendocrine system of the larval brain. Finally, the caste-specific hormone titres switch on caste-specific protein syntheses which interact with physiological events. This will be exemplified by a caste-specific synthesis of cytochrome c, which is directly correlated with the characteristic oxygen consumption of the queen and the worker larva.

24.2   STEP 1: FOOD AND CASTE FORMATION

Queen larval food (royal jelly) is found in abundance in the queen cells. Chemical analysis has shown that food composition is fairly constant (Rembold, 1965). As an example, cation contents of seven different samples of royal jelly, all purchased from commercial dealers, are given in Table 24.2. It is highly remarkable how similar the data are; there is only a deviation from the average by 5% or less! Another remarkable result from this study is the quantitative distribution of the cations: potassium amounts to almost 90% of all the cations contained in the royal jelly samples, followed by sodium and magnesium with about 5%. All the other cations are present only in subordinate or even trace amounts. Similar results were found by Rembold and Lackner (1978) for the water, protein and sugar contents. The total amount of nucleotides was also found to be fairly constant. The quantitative analysis of 12 different nucleotides and nucleosides, however, showed remarkable differences which cannot be explained exclusively by the degradation of

TABLE 24.2. CATION CONTENTS OF SEVEN DIFFERENT COMMERCIAL
ROYAL JELLY SAMPLES. THE DATA WERE OBTAINED FROM FLAME
PHOTOMETRIC MEASUREMENTS AND ARE PRESENTED AS $\mu g.g^{-1}$
FRESH WEIGHT (REMBOLD & LACKNER, 1978)

Sample	K	Na	Mg	Ca	Zn	Fe	Cu	Mn
Bulgaria 11/77	4400	221	304	131	26.5	10.58	5.40	0.60
Yugoslavia 7/75a	4620	190	283	122	24.5	9.55	5.55	—
7/75b	4160	209	271	122	26.5	10.28	5.20	0.48
Taiwan 3/76	4460	278	287	124	25.0	9.62	5.23	0.75
5/76a	4100	208	273	116	26.5	8.95	4.28	0.70
5/76b	4180	239	284	135	27.5	9.75	4.80	0.80
5/76c	4410	217	321	160	30.5	10.85	5.33	0.83
Average	4339	223	289	130	26.7	9.94	5.11	0.69

labile nucleotides. Moreover, the quantitative nucleotide pattern of royal jelly as contained in supersedure queen cells differs markedly in some compounds from that of the commercial samples. The ratio AMP to adenosine, for example, can be used as a very sensitive marker for food quality. If tested by rearing larvae in the incubator, a ratio of more than 10 indicates a high capacity of the royal jelly to induce a high rate of queen-bee formation. It is clear from these data, that there are at least some quantitative differences within different royal jelly samples, which are responsible for their different queen-inducing capacity.

Can this capacity be improved by adding other nutrients to a given royal jelly sample? This is indeed the case as shown by Rembold and Lackner (1981), who reared first instar honey bee larvae *in vitro* under controlled conditions. The yield of adults was 70–80%, and 10% of them were queens if a particular sample of royal jelly was used, diluted 1:1 with water and supplemented with D-glucose and D-fructose. If yeast extract was added to this basic food, larval growth and queen determination was considerably increased, at the same rate of survival. An amount of 1.25 and 2.5% of yeast extract increased the percentage of queens developing from 10% (basic food) to 30% (1.25% yeast extract added) and 50% (2.5% yeast extract added), respectively, without any change in the high rate of survival. However, if the yeast extract was fractionated into a salt and an amino acid fraction and these were added instead of the yeast extract in the feeding test, the result was a dramatic change in survival as well as in the rate of queen production. The salt component reduced the yield of adults to about 50%, but it increased larval growth and queen differentiation from 10% (basic food) to 20%. The amino acid fraction reduced the rate of survival to about 30%; growth rate and differentiation of queens were below those of the basic food. Addition of the recombined fractions gave the same result as addition of the original yeast extract. It emerged from this study, that the average gain in weight of fourth and fifth instar larvae was related to the degree in caste formation. Only an optimum nutritional balance can induce an optimum growth rate during a critical period of development. In other words, food quality controls endocrine mechanisms which then in turn switch on a caste-specific developmental programme. It appears as though the queen-determining principle of the royal jelly is no more than an optimum balance of nutrients during a critical developmental period, and that the labile factor, which has been described in the literature, merely reflects an increasing chemical change in the food during storage. However, the possibility cannot be ruled out that a determinator, as a chemically defined compound, could still be present in the queen larval food. The very few chemical differences between worker and royal jellies, such as biopterin, neopterin, and pantothenic acid (see Rembold, 1965), are not involved in the queen-bee determining process. However, a final answer can only come from the formulation of a completely synthetic diet, which is not yet available.

24.3   STEP 2: THE NEUROSECRETORY SYSTEM DURING THE SENSITIVE PHASE

It is now generally accepted that morphogenesis in higher organisms, including the insects, is under hormonal control. It is also common knowledge that the peripheral hormones (ecdysone and JH) are under neurosecretory control in insects. However, neither the prothoracotropic hormone (PTTH) which controls the prothoracic gland in its ecdysone synthesis, nor the allatotropic hormone (ATH) which controls the CA and therefore the synthesis of JH, have been isolated and structurally identified. Both these factors are peptides, as their activity is lost after treatment with proteolytic enzymes. Both peptide hormones are released from the neurosecretory cells of the pars intercerebralis, are transported through axons to the corpus cardiacum and are then released, after final structural modification, into the haemolymph. From there they are transported in a passive way to their target organs (prothoracic gland, corpus allatum), which possibly recognize them through specific receptors which then initiate a specific hormone synthesis. We must keep in mind, however, that the pathway neurosecretory cells—axons (nervi corpori cardiaci)—corpus cardiacum—haemolymph—hormone gland is still fairly speculative and may vary in detail from species to species. The fact, however, that antibodies raised against brain material from *Locusta* could interfere with this information transfer (Rembold *et al.*, 1980a), speaks in favour of the scheme.

It was very surprising indeed, when Dogra *et al.* (1977) showed that, in the first instar honey-bee larva, the neurosecretory cells of the brain, the corpora cardiaca, the CA, and the prothoracic glands are all in an embryonic or incomplete stage of development. The neurosecretory cells, especially, differentiate during further larval life in a caste-specific way, faster in queen larvae than in the worker. In first instar larvae the neurosecretory cells are without axons. In the queen larvae, outgrowth of the axons begins in the second instar and is completed at the end of third instar. In the worker larvae, onset (third instar) and termination (fourth instar) of axonal outgrowth is one larval instar later. Injection of tritium-labelled uridine, a precursor of RNA and as such an indicator of cellular activity, showed that transcription of genetic information begins near the end of the third instar in the queen and only in the fifth instar of the worker larva (Rembold & Ulrich, 1982; Ulrich & Rembold, 1983). Stainable neurosecretory material is detectable in late fifth instar queen larvae but not until the pupal stage of the worker.

These data, together with the information on the histology of the hormone glands, clearly prove that there is a caste-specific maturation of the endocrine system in the honey bee. If the larvae are supplied with an optimal diet, queen larvae differentiate and activate their endocrine tissues earlier than the worker larvae. As the neurosecretory cells in the brain of the young bee larvae are inactive, it may be postulated that a neurosecretory system, which may be located in the ventral ganglia, is active and controls the peripheral hormone glands. The queen larvae would then switch over from the early larval system to that of the brain earlier than the workers. They gain a developmental advantage by this earlier switch-over from one regulatory system to another, which is probably stimulated by optimal nutrition of the sensitive third instar larvae. A caste-specific developmental programme is switched on as a consequence of different maturation rates of the neuroendocrine system. Such cellular effects at the neurosecretory level are reflected by changes in the peripheral hormonal glands and finally by a caste-specific modulation of hormone titre, as will be discussed in the next section of this paper. We now perceive the mechanisms of caste determination in the third instar honey-bee larvae as a combination of an external stimulus (food quality) with an endogenous, genetically programmed event, i.e., the switch-on of the neurosecretory system in the brain of the female larvae.

24.4   STEP 3: MORPHOGENETIC HORMONES AND CASTE DETERMINATION

The moulting hormones (ecdysone and ecdysterone) control some important enzymatic steps during the process of ecdysis, but not much is known about processes such as gene activation, egg maturation or behaviour. The average concentration of moulting hormone is in the range of nanograms per gram body weight. However, concentrations two orders of magnitude lower may saturate the hormone receptor and, in doing so, induce a signal. Even more sensitive is the hormonal control of morphogenesis through JH. Four homologues have been found in nature, JH–O, –I, –II, and –III. From the holometabolous insects only the Lepidoptera seem to synthesize JH–I and –II in abundance, whereas JH–III seems to be the more general form elsewhere in the insect kingdom. Its concentration is usually much lower than that of the moulting hormone. On average, JH is present in a concentration of nanograms per gram body weight, and the same holds true as has been discussed for the ecdysteroids: this concentration exceeds by far the level needed to saturate the hormone receptor, which is in the range of three orders of magnitude lower.

How can such minute amounts of substance be identified and quantified? As shown in Table 24.1, a RIA for ecdysone is sensitive in the picogram range. Due to high cross-reactivity of the antiserum it is necessary to purify the sample by high-performance liquid chromatography (HPLC) in order to come to a reliable result. Much more critical is the situation with JH, the concentration of which is about three orders of magnitude lower than that of ecdysone. Only at very high concentrations, which are usually found only in the Lepidoptera, can the *Galleria* or radio-immunoassays be used. For the extremely low JH levels which are usual in many insect species, only a direct method is reliable; a method which is sensitive in the picogram range is now available (Rembold *et al.*, 1980b) and it has been successfully used for the establishment of a JH-titre curve for the first time in female honey-bee larvae of both castes.

Before we discuss the hormone titres, let us consider some morphological events which have been studied by use of light-microscopical techniques (Dogra *et al.*, 1977; Rembold & Ulrich, 1982; Ulrich & Rembold, 1983). The corpora cardiaca are embryonic in both the castes until the end of third instar. In the fourth instar, which is a stage after the sensitive phase, they begin to grow and to differentiate. At the end of this instar and in the worker only in the last larval stage, labelled uridine is incorporated into this neurohaemal organ, thus demonstrating its metabolic activity.

The retardation of worker larvae is also shown in the development of the CA. The queen CA are always larger from the third instar onward. During larval development, the nuclei of the CA undergo several stages of endomitosis and, again, the queen larva gains a time advantage of about one instar. The caste- and growth-specific changes in volume and DNA synthesis seem to be connected with each other. This is shown by different levels of incorporation of tritiated thymidine, a DNA precursor, during the phase of condensed nuclei (no incorporation) and decondensed nuclei (incorporation). This again demonstrates that there are several steps of endomitosis in the larval CA and that the organ is only mature in the last larval instar.

The JH-titre curve (Fig. 24.1) reflects the caste-specific morphological and histological events in this hormone gland (Rembold and Hagenguth, 1981). During the first larval instars, including the fourth, no JH was detectable in extracts from a total of 1 g of larvae. The high titres which Wirtz (1973) found in the fourth instar queen larva by means of the *Galleria* bioassay are not supported by our data and may be due to factors, such as cross-reactivity, which have been discussed already. The same holds true for the values found by Lensky *et al.* (1978) who used a RIA for JH quantification. Because of the exact dating of larval stages, which has already been described (Rembold *et al.* 1980c), each JH value measured by GC–MS-technique has high statistical significance even at low JH concentrations. We can, therefore, state the early larval stages may be under the control of such minute JH-titres, that they are below the limit of sensitivity of our method. The overall events in growth and polyploidization of the larval CA do not reflect an elevated JH-titre, but reflect a process of maturation which becomes important in the last larval instar. Immediately after the queen larva has passed through its penultimate instar, the JH titre increases to maximum values of 50 ng JH–III g^{-1} larval

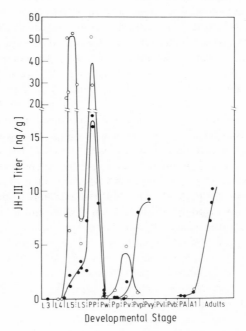

FIG. 24.1. JH–III titres in developmental stages of the queen (●) and worker (○) of the honey bee (from Rembold and Hagenguth, 1981). Larvae and pupae are staged as follows. L3–L5 = 3rd to 5th larval instar; L5, PP = 5th larval instar, spinning larva and prepupa, resp.; Pw–Pvb = pupae with differences in eye (w: white, p: pink, v: violet) and thorax (p: pale, y: yellow, l: light, b: brown) colour. PA = pharate, A1 = 1 day old adult.

fresh weight and then drops before the queen larva starts spinning its cocoon. The worker larva, however, has only a slight increase in its JH titre during its feeding stage. A second JH peak then builds up with a maximum of approximately 20–40 ng JH–III per g fresh weight, this time in both castes. This peak disappears in the newly-formed pupa with values of 1 ng and less per g. No JH-homologue other than JH–III could be detected at any larval stage of the honey bee.

Incorporation of labelled uridine into the prothoracic glands is found at the second stage and at similar levels in both castes. Labelling of the gland is fairly constant until the end of the third instar. It then decreases during the following larval periods and reaches a zero level at the end of the fifth larval instar, which indicates that synthesis of RNA has ceased (Rembold & Ulrich, 1982). The ecdysteroid titres, as measured by Hagenguth and Rembold (1978), do not differ significantly between the castes. The titre decreases from about $500\,\mu\text{g g}^{-1}$ during the fifth larval instar to a minimum of 50 (queen) and 10 (worker) $\mu\text{g g}^{-1}$ in the pharate pupa. Immediately before ecdysis to the pupa, the hormone titre increases again and comes to a level near $1\,\mu\text{g}$ ecdysterone per gram of body weight. As in the histological picture, there is again a clear time shift in the reactivation of ecdysterone synthesis, with a reversal period during the spinning phase in the queen and in the pharate worker pupa. Both castes reach the same moulting hormone titre soon after pupation.

24.5   STEP 4: CASTE-SPECIFIC PROTEIN SYNTHESIS

Morphogenesis is, in terms of molecular biology, the translation of a DNA sequence, which represents the blueprint of a developmental programme, into a protein sequence, which may then act as an enzyme and synthesize such structural elements as lipids or polysaccharides. Gene expression is under hormonal control in higher organisms, most likely through a receptor-hormone complex of high affinity. Such a switching on signal must be reversible and a fairly high turnover of the hormone must be postulated. Catabolic enzymes which rapidly inactivate their respective hormones are well known.

With this reversible activation of genetic information in mind, and from the fact that ecdysone and JH-titre are modulated during the last larval instar, a caste-specific synthesis at least of some proteins can be expected. Rembold and Graf (1972) demonstrated such a modulated protein synthesis. They generated antibodies against a purified worker protein and used them for a quantitative estimation. This protein was found to be present during the last larval stage only in the worker. The queen synthesizes the same protein only from the pupal stage onward. As another example for a caste-specific protein synthesis, cytochrome c has been measured. The protein is present in the mitochondria of the worker larvae in limiting amounts (Osanai & Rembold, 1968). This may be the explanation for the well known physiological difference in oxygen consumption between worker and queen larvae (Melampy & Willis, 1939). By use of the highly sensitive viro-immunoassay, we estimated the cytochrome c content of worker and queen larvae. Oxygen consumption and the respiratory quotient (R) had been measured before by use of the Warburg technique. The product of respiration (R) times the logarithm of larval cytochrome c content, divided by the body weight (W), yields a caste-specific constant (K):

$$K = \frac{R \cdot \log \text{cyt c}}{W}$$

The queen-specific value K_q is about 3 and that of the worker (K_w) about 0.8 (Eder, Kremer, and Rembold, 1983). Interesting enough, from a series of experimental larvae which had been reared *in vitro*, some had a queen-value, some that of a worker, and some were in between, indicating that they were intercastes.

24.6 CONCLUSION

I have tried to give a biochemist's view of what is called caste determination in the honey bee. What has come out from our own work during more than 20 years of endeavour, can be summarized in an admittedly simplified way as follows.

The development of both the castes follows the general scheme of a hymenopteran insect with one exception. A change in the hormonal information transfer from the neurosecretory system to the peripheral hormone glands is used to trigger a caste-specific developmental programme. Four steps in the expression of a caste-specific morphogenesis have been demonstrated. In the first, the role of nutrition becomes clear. Only under optimal conditions, which are reflected by an intensive weight gain in the fourth instar larva, is the queen-forming response of the female honey-bee larva switched on during the third instar. By a difference in food in the colony, or by feeding an imbalanced diet *in vitro*, the activation of the controlling system in the larval brain is delayed by more than one instar in the worker. The second step, therefore, is a time difference in the initiation of hormonal regulation. During this period both worker and queen larvae start with a phase of intensive growth which is not under the control of JH. The third step is a caste-specific maturation of the peripheral hormone glands, especially the CA. Only in the last larval instar, caste induction during the third larval stage is reflected by a modulated hormone synthesis, primarily of JH. The fourth important step is, then, a queen-specific JH–III peak which coincides with the maintenance of the female gonads and with a breakdown of most of the ovarioles in the worker larva. With this important event, the caste-specific programming comes to its end. In a last step, the queen and worker developmental programmes are expressed during the pupal phase.

Much of this clear chain of events is still purely model for other social insects. The establishment of intercastes may lead to a better understanding of the complicated mechanisms which control caste formation in such social insects like the termites.

A final remark on the results of Wirtz (1973), who induced queen-like characteristics in adults after topical application of JH–I to third instar worker larvae. Although the author used the inappropriate hormone (JH–I instead of JH–III, which is much less active) and unphysiological amounts (1000 ng JH–I per larva against 50 ng JH–III present in a queen larva), he may have stimulated the queen-specific JH–III peak in the fifth instar and, in doing so, averted the degradation of larval ovarioles, at least in part. It is possible that the same explanation holds true for the experimental effects of JH–I on other social insects, and also for those of the JH-analogues (for review see de Wilde and Beetsma, 1982).

24.7 SUMMARY

The biochemical basis of honey bee caste formation can be separated into a sequence of time-dependent developmental events.

Step 1—the newly hatched female larva is fed a high-quality food in abundance through the first three larval instars. After the sensitive phase, nutrition of the workers is maintained with a food of lower quality (a mixture of glandular secretion, honey, and pollen). The queen larva is offered royal jelly throughout the whole feeding period.

Step 2—Maturation of the neurosecretory system in the pars intercerebralis is initiated in a caste-specific way. As a consequence of optimal nutrition, the differentiation of the neurosecretory cells and RNA synthesis starts in the queen larva at the end of the third instar and in the worker at the fifth instar. The queen's CA become active at the end of the fourth, those of the worker in the fifth instar.

Step 3—The caste-specific maturation of the endocrine organs results in titre differences of the peripheral hormones. The ecdysteroids decrease in their concentration at the end of the prepupal stage from 400 ng.g^{-1} (L4) to less than 40 ng.g^{-1} (L5) both in worker and queen larvae. During pupal development, both castes maintain an ecdysteroid level of about 1 μg.g^{-1}. The titres of JH–III are modulated in a caste-specific way. Only the queen builds up, at the beginning of L5, a sharp peak of 50 ng JH–III.g^{-1}. Another peak later in the prepupa is formed in both castes.

Step 4—A caste-specific modulation of hormone titres, primarily of JH–III, in the last larval instar controls the maintenance and respectively the breakdown of the ovaries. A typical example which combines biochemical with physiological events is the regulation of cytochrome c pools during L5. A caste factor K, which connects cytochrome c concentrations, respiration, and body weight, is discussed. The values measured for the queen and the worker L5 stages are $K_q = 3$ and $K_w = 0.8$, respectively.

The four sequential steps in honey-bee caste formation are discussed as a special example for the hormonal control of insect morphogenesis in general. The key event seems to be the switching on of the neurosecretory system at the end of the sensitive phase of larval development. Due to a time shift in this event, only the queen larva can preserve its ovaries, which are degraded in the worker during L5, and thus become the reproductive female.

24.8   REFERENCES

De Wilde H. & Beetsma J. (1982) The physiology of caste development in social insects. *Adv. Insect Physiol.* **19,** 167–246.

Dogra G. S., Ulrich G. M. & Rembold H. (1977) A comparative study of the endocrine system of the honey-bee larvae under normal and experimental conditions. *Z. Naturforsch.* **32c,** 637–642.

Eder J., Kremer J. P. & Rembold H. (1983) Correlation of cytochrome c titer and respiration in *Apis mellifera*: adaptive response to caste determination defines workers, intercastes and queens. *Comp. Biochem. Physiol.* **76B,** 703–716.

Eder J., Osanai M., Mane S. & Rembold H. (1977) Immunoassay for honey-bee cytochrome c in single animals with cytochrome c-coated bacteriophages: A sensitive tool for the study of caste formation in the honey-bee, *Apis mellifera. Biochim. Biophys. Acta* **496,** 401–411.

Hagenguth H. & Rembold H. (1978) Kastenspezifische Modulation des Ecdysteroid-Titers bei der Honigbiene. *Mitt. dtsch. Ges. angew. Ent.* **1,** 296–298.

Lensky Y., Baehr J. C. & Porcheron P. (1978) Dosages radio-immunologiques onnoire chez les ouvrières et les reines d'abeille. *C.R. Acad. Sci.* Paris **287D,** 821–824.

Melampy R. M. & Willis F. R. (1939) Respiratory metabolism during larval and pupal development of the female honey-bee (*Apis mellifera* L.) *Physiol. Zool.* **42,** 302–311.

Osanai M. & Rembold H. (1968) Entwicklungsabhängige mitochondriale Enzymaktivitäten bei den Kasten der Honigbiene. *Biochim. Biophys. Acta* **162,** 22–31.

Rembold H. (1964) Die Kastenentstehung bei der Honigbiene. *Naturwiss.* **51,** 49–54.

Rembold H. (1965) Biologically active substances in royal jelly. *Vitams. Horm.* **23,** 359–382.

Rembold H. (1969) Biochemie der Kastenentstehung bei der Honigbiene. *Proc. VI Congr.* IUSSI, pp. 239–246.

Rembold H. (1974) Die Kastenbildung bei der Honigbiene aus biochemischer Sicht. In *Sozialpolymorphismus bei Insekten* (Schmidt J. H., ed.), pp. 694–793. Wissenschaftl. Verlagsgesellschaft, Stuttgart.

Rembold H. (1976) The role of determinator in caste formation in the honey-bee. In *Phase and Caste Determination in Insects* (Lüscher M., ed.), pp. 21–34. Pergamon Press, Oxford.

Rembold H. & Graf H. (1972) Isolierung und Charakterisierung eines kastenspezifischen Proteins aus der Honigbiene. *Z. Physiol. Chem.* **353,** 1615–1624.

Rembold H. & Hagenguth H. (1981) Modulation of hormone pools during postembryonic development of the female honey bee castes. In *Regulation of Insect Development and Behaviour* (Sehnal F., ed.), pp. 427–440. Wrozlaw Techn. Univ. Press, Wrozlaw.

Rembold H. & Lackner B. (1978) A comparative analysis of different commercial royal jelly samples. *Mitt. dtsch. Ges. allg. angew. Ent.* **1,** 299–301.

Rembold H. & Lackner B. (1981) Rearing of honey-bee larvae *in vitro*: effect of yeast extract on queen differentiation. *J. apicult. Res.* **20**, 165–171.

Rembold H. & Ulrich G. (1982) Modulation of neurosecretion during caste determination in *A. mellifera* larvae. In *The Biology of Social Insects* (Breed, M. D., Michener Ch. D. & Evans H. E., eds), pp. 370–374. Westview Press, Boulder.

Rembold H., Eder J. & Ulrich G. (1980c) Inhibition of allatotropic activity and ovary development in *Locusta migratoria* by anti-brain-antibodies. *Z. Naturforsch.* **35c**, 1117–1119.

Rembold H., Hagenguth H. & Rascher J. (1980a) A sensitive method for detection and estimation of juvenile hormones from biological samples by glass capillary combined gas chromatography—selected ion monitoring mass spectrometry. *Anal. Biochem.* **101**, 356–363.

Rembold H., Kremer J. P. & Ulrich G. (1980b) Characterization of postembryonic developmental stages of the female castes of the honey-bee, *Apis mellifera* L. *Apidologie* **11**, 29–38.

Spindler K. D., Beckers C., Groeschel-Stewart V. & Emmerich H. (1978) Radioimmunoassay for arthropod moulting hormone, introducing a new method of immunogene coupling. *Z. Physiol. Chem.* **359**, 1269–1275.

Townsend G. F. & Shuel R. W. (1962) Some recent advances in apicultural research. *Ann. Rev. Entomol.* **7**, 481–499.

Ulrich G. & Rembold H. (1983) Caste-specific maturation of the endocrine system in the female honey-bee larva. *Cell Tiss. Res.* **230**, 49–55.

Weaver N. (1966) Physiology of caste determination. *Ann. Rev. Entomol.* **11**, 79–102.

Weiss K. (1978) Zur Mechnik der Kastenentstehung bei der Honigbiene. *Apidologie* **9**, 223–258.

Wirtz P. (1973) Differentiation in the honey-bee larva. Ph.D. Thesis, Agricult. Univ., Wageningen, Meded. Landb. Hogesch., pp. 73–75.

Zander E. & Becker F. (1925) Die Ausbildung des Geschlechtes bei der Honigbiene. *Erlanger JB Bienenk.* **3**, 163–223.

CHAPTER 25

Extrinsic Control of Caste Differentiation in the Honey Bee (Apis mellifera L.) and in other Apidae

J. DE WILDE*

Department of Entomology, Agricultural University, Wageningen, The Netherlands

CONTENTS

25.1 THE ABERRANT CASTE

Lukoschus (1956) raised the question, "which of the two female castes of the honey-bee has to be considered most aberrant from the normal pattern of female development in the solitary Apidae?" His conclusion, that the worker caste is most deviating, is supported by very convincing evidence. Indeed, the development of a mass-rearing system for female worker individuals with a reduced reproductive system which is extrinsically inhibited by the presence of a queen and the exuberant diversity in behaviour, including the potential learning capacity of these workers, is the real novelty in the evolution of the social Apidae (de Wilde, 1976).

In contrast to the mass-provisioning of the larvae of reproductive females (which is a common pattern in the Apidae), the worker larvae are fed piecemeal, but nevertheless sufficient to allow for the first four larval moults of both castes to occur synchronously. This means that the period of indispensable nutrition is met in worker larvae, and this fact alone points to a very close

*The late Dr J. De Wilde suddenly passed away on 5 October 1983.

interaction between the feeding nurse bees and the developing worker larvae. In queen larvae, on the contrary, it is the abundant nourishment of larvae which solely allows the moulting to be fulfilled.

25.2 THE ENDOCRINE BASIS

Wirtz (1973) has proved beyond doubt that the inner factor which presides over the direction of caste development is the juvenile hormone (JH) titre prevailing around the end of the third day of larval development. He showed that in worker larvae, after 72 hr of larval development, the JH titre increases by a factor of 100, while in queen larva, at the critical time, the JH titre increases by a factor of 1000. This evidence was supported by biometric measurement of the size of the corpus allatum (CA) in both castes (Fig. 25.1) by transfer experiments whereby worker larvae were transferred from worker into queen cells and vice versa, and, ultimately, by topical application of JH to worker larvae at the critical time, resulting in the development of queen characters (Figs 25.2, 25.3). Conclusive confirmation was obtained by Ebert (1980) who showed that caste specific behaviour is already shown by the pupating larvae, and that this behaviour is JH-dependent. As specific JH esterases have not been demonstrated in honey-bee larvae (de Kort et al., 1977), the CA activity is the main factor determining the JH titre.

Very remarkable is the effect of JH on the development of larvae studied by Naisse (Pers. Comm.) in our laboratory. In the early larval stage, the ovarian an-lagen contains about 160 ovariole primordia. In larvae raised in a queen cell these ovarioles will differentiate during the third day of larval life, into tubular ovarioles. In a worker cell larvae will start atrophying almost all ovariole primordia at the end of the third day, leaving only 2–4 to differentiate into tubular ovarioles. When JH is applied to these larvae in the middle of the third day, ovarian atrophy will not take place, but once this atrophy has occurred on the fourth day of larval life the process becomes irreversible.

The above results extended the observations originally made by Lüscher (1958), that the development of presoldiers in the termite, *Kalotermes flavicollis* is initiated by a rise in CA activity and, as a consequence, an increased JH titre. After the discovery of the role of JH in caste development in the honey bee (Wirtz & Beetma, 1972; Wirtz, 1973) (Fig. 25.4), similar findings have been made in other Apidae.

Velthuis and Velthuis-Klupell (1975) topically applied JH and JHA to 4-day-old or spinning larvae of *Melipona quadrifasciata* reared in vitro. Mass-provisioning being the way these larvae are normally fed by the workers, *in vitro* rearing could be performed the same way. Even very minute doses of *Cecropia* JH ($2.10^{-3}\,\mu g$/larva) applied to spinning larvae induced growth development in all female individuals.

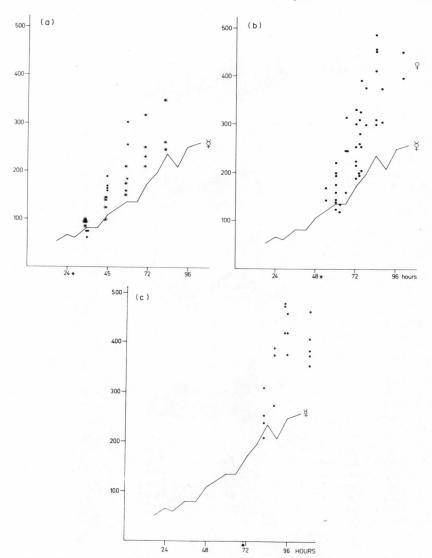

Fig. 25.1. Surface aerea (arbitrary planimeter values) of CA of honey bee larvae after being transferred to queen cells on the 1st (a), 2nd (b) and 3rd day of larval development (c).

The very steep rise of CA growth after transfer on the 3rd day indicates the reactivity during the critical period for caste induction.

The solid line represents the surface area of CA of worker larvae transferred to 3-day-old queen cells. The other data refer to younger queen cells. (After de Wilde & Beetsma, 1982.)

J. de Wilde

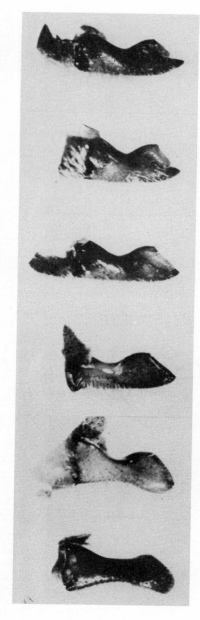

FIG. 25.2. Effect of JH on queen expression in mandibular development of the honey bee. The mandible of a normal worker is shown on the left, that of a normal queen on the right. The cases in between refer to different degrees of queen expression by JH treatment on the 3rd day of larval worker development. (After de Wilde & Beetsma, 1982.)

FIG. 25.3. Effect of JH on the expression of queen characteristics in the shape and structure of the sting of the honey bee: (1) queen, (2) JH treated worker and (3) worker. (After de Wilde & Beetsma, 1982.)

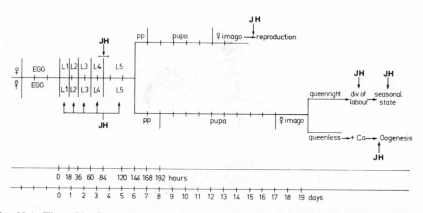

FIG. 25.4. Timetable of stages and instars in queen and worker development in the honey bee. At the top, the involvement of JH in determining stage morphogenesis and oogenesis is indicated. At the bottom, effects are shown on caste morphogenesis and worker function. (After de Wilde & Beetsma, 1982.)

Also in the bumble-bee *Bombus hypnorum* studied by Röseler and Röseler (1974) and Röseler (1976), the larval stage proved to be the JH-sensitive phase in caste induction. In experiments made in queen-right colonies, topical application of 15 μg *Cecropia* JH within a day during the last larval instar resulted in the development of large queens. In *Bombus terrestris* treated under similar conditions, there are indications that the dominance of the queen inhibits queen differentiation and even redetermines presumptive queen larvae into workers of large size (Röseler, 1976) (Fig. 25.5). Recently, it was shown by Wheeler and Nijhout (1981) that an increase in JH titre during a critical period in the last larval instar induces soldier formation in the ant *Pheidole bicarinata*.

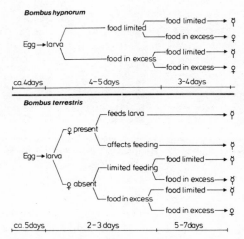

FIG. 25.5. Schematic representation of the factors involved in caste determination of *Bombus hypnorum* and *Bombus terrestris*, as found by Röseler (1975). Note that in *B. hypnorum* excess of food is all-important for queen determination, while in *B. terrestris* the dominance of the queen is a strong inhibiting factor in this process. (After de Wilde & Beetsma, 1982.)

25.3   THE EXOGENOUS TRIGGER STIMULI

In contrast to Rembold and Hanser (1964) who for many years tried to find a determinant factor in royal jelly inducing queen differentiation, we have felt, for reasons mentioned (in the above paragraph), that the inhibition of (CA) activity during the critical period in larvae destined to become workers, is the process to which our research efforts should be directed. Such inhibition can be experimentally performed by administering precocene II, and indeed worker characters are induced by this treatment (Goewie *et al.*, 1978).

It has long been known (Johansson, 1958) that the nutritive state of an insect has an important influence on CA activity, and that starvation for proteins has an inhibitory effect. In this respect, however, little difference has been found between the protein content of worker and royal jellies. Recent work by Brouwers (Pers. Comm.) in our laboratory confirms the absence of such difference. In this respect, it is important to realize that the composition of dry weight of both jellies is the relevant factor to study. The extremely small quantities of hypopharyngeal gland secretion deposited in worker cells are subject to very rapid desiccation. It is emphasized that, when the linear size of a droplet of larval food decreases tenfold, its rate of oxidation and desiccation increases by about the same factor. For this reason, worker jelly present in the cell is always qualitatively inferior to royal jelly.

In vitro rearing of larvae has contributed to some interesting information. Dietz and Lambremont (1970) found in their experiments that larvae consuming a high amount of food developed into queens, but when smaller amounts were consumed, workers resulted. Asencot and Lensky (1976) obtained mostly queens and intercastes when they added 200 mg of glucose and 200 mg of fructose per gram worker jelly. However, analysis of the sugar content in worker and royal jelly, performed by Brouwers (Pers. Comm.) revealed no difference during the critical period of caste determination.

25.4 RECENT WORK ON BROOD-REARING ACTIVITY IN WORKER CELLS

Lindauer (1952) has counted the feeding frequency of worker larvae and queen larvae by the worker bees, and found that right from the beginning of larval life, the visits to queen cells are overwhelmingly more frequent. This has recently been confirmed by Brouwers (Pers. Comm.) in our laboratory, making use of very sophisticated infra-red video recordings of individual worker cells. In addition to the frequency, the duration of each visit was measured. It was shown that many visits are merely an inspection and apparently serve to register the internal situation of the brood cells and the feeding condition of the larvae. The number of feeding visits is extremely reduced during the first three days of larval life, amounting to an average of four during the first 24 hr, the same number during the second 24 hr, and around eight during the third 24 hr. Thereafter, the feeding frequency greatly increases, amounting to an average of 30 during the fourth 24 hr, and thereafter increasing further. In contrast, queen larvae are visited right from the beginning at a rate of one visit every 3 min. The considerably long intervals between feeding visits to worker larvae undoubtedly allow the deposited worker jelly to oxidize and desiccate, rendering food intake by the worker larvae much more cumbersome, especially during the first 3 days of larval life.

It is concluded that the pattern of feeding behaviour displayed by nurse bees with regard to worker larvae is essentially different from that displayed with respect to queen larvae. Although inspection visits assure a reliable food supply to enable a well-timed larval mount to occur, the food provision of worker larvae is kept in check and the food becomes "stale", while in queen cells, the larvae swimming on their food store, are allowed to feed freely on jelly with a much higher degree of freshness. Queen cells apparently release a behaviour sequence in nurse bees resulting in food storage, while worker combs release a pattern of behaviour leading to piecemeal feeding, steered by feedback stimuli obtained from the larvae and probably from the quantity of food still present. The resulting difference in the state of nutrition may result in the endocrine differences responsible for the differential activation of caste-related genes.

The work is still in progress, and will be published more extensively elsewhere.

25.5 SUMMARY

A brief account is given of "the state of that art" in the study of extrinsic control of caste differentiation in the honey-bee; a control which is mediated by the titre of JH at around 72 hr of larval life. Attention is drawn to the worker caste, since apparently development most strongly deviates from the normal pattern in solitary Apidae.

The point of view argued here is that the specific feeding pattern which nurse bees practice, resulting in piecemeal feeding of worker larvae guided by feedback during "test visits" is the factor controlling the activity of the CA and thereby keeping the JH titre at "worker level".

Specific data on feeding duration and frequency, as well as their effect on the quality of "worker jelly" are discussed.

The effect of JH on queen induction in stingless bees, bumble-bees is highly maintained; and here, the critical period is in the last larval instar.

25.6 REFERENCES

Asencot M. & Lensky Y. (1976) The effect of sugars and juvenile hormone on the differentiation of the female honey-bee larvae (*Apis mellifera* L.) to queens. *Life Sci.* **18**, 693–700.

De Wilde J. (1976) Juvenile hormone and caste differentiation in the honey bee (*Apis mellifera* L.). In *Phase and Caste determination in Insects* (Lüscher M., ed.), pp. 5–20. Pergamon Press, Oxford.

De Wilde J. & Beetsma (1982) The physiology of caste development in social insects. *Advances in Insect Physiology* **18**, 163–246.

De Kort C. A. D., Wieten M., Kramer S. J. & Goewie E. A. (1977) Juvenile hormone degradation and carrier proteins in honey-bee larvae. *Proc. Kon. Ned. Akad. Wet.* **C80**, 297–301.

Dietz A. & Labremont E. N. (1970) Caste determination in honey-bees II. Food consumption of individual honey bee larvae, determined with 32 P-labelled royal jelly. *Ann. ent. Soc. Am.* **63**, 1342–1345.

Ebert R. (1980) Influence of juvenile hormone on gravity orientation in the female honey-bee larva (*Apis mellifera* L.). *J. Comp. Physiol.* **A137**, 7–16.

Goewie E. A., Beetsma J. & de Wilde J. (1978) Wirkung von Precocene II auf die Kastendifferenzierung der Honigbiene (*Apis millifera* L.). *Mitt. Dtsch. Ges. allg. angew. Ent. Giessen* **1**, 304–305.

Johansson A. S. (1958) Relation of nutrition to endocrine reproductive functions in the Milkweed Bug, *Oncopeltus fasciatus* (Dallas) (Heteroptera, Lygaeidae). *Nytt. Mag. Zool. (Oslo)* **7**, 1–132.

Lindauer M. (1952) Ein Beitrag zur Frage der Arbeitsteilung im Bienenstaat. *Z. Vergl. Physiol.* **34**, 299–345.

Lukoschus F. (1956) Die Kastenentwicklung bei der Honigbiene: Avitaminose oder endokrine Aplasie? *Verh. Dtsch. Zool. Ges. Hamburg* **278**.

Lüscher M. (1958) Experimentelle Erzeugung von Soldaten bei der Termite *Kalotermes flavicollis* (Fabr.). *Naturwiss.* **45**, 1–2.

Rembold H. & Hanser G. (1964) Ueber den Weiselzellenfuttersaft der Honigbiene VII. Nachweiss des determinierenden Prinzips im Futtersaft der Königinnenlarven. Hoppe. *Seyler's Z. Physiol. Chem.* **339**, 251–254.

Röseler P. F. (1975) *Die Kasten der Sozialen Bienen*. Steiner Verlag, Wiesbaden.

Röseler P. F. (1976) Juvenile hormone and queen rearing in bumble-bees. In *Phase and Caste Determination in Insects* (Lüscher M., ed.), pp. 55–61. Pergamon Press, Oxford.

Röseler P. F. & Röseler J. (1974) Morphologische und physiologische Differenzierung der Kasten bei den Hummelarten *Bombus hypnorum* (L.) und *Bombus terrestris* (L.). *Zool. Jb. Physiol.* **78**, 175–198.

Velthuis H. H. W. & Velthuis-Kluppell F. M. (1975) Caste differentiation in a stingless bee, *Melipona quadrifaciata* Lep., influenced by juvenile hormone. *Proc., K. Ned. Akad. Wet.* **C78**, 81–94.

Wheeler D. E. & Nijhout H. F. (1981) Soldier determination in ants: New role for juvenile hormone. *Science* **213**, 361–363.

Wirtz P. (1973) Differentiation in the honey-bee larva. *Meded. Landb. Hogeschool*, Wageningen, pp. 73–5, 155.

Wirtz P. and Beetsma J. (1972) Induction of caste differentiation in the honey-bee (*Apis mellifera* L.) by juvenile hormone. *Ent. exp. appl.* **15**, 517–520.

CHAPTER 26

Physiological Aspects of Caste Differentiation in Social Wasps

ALAIN STRAMBI

CNRS, Institut de Neurophysiologie et Psychophysiologie BP 71, 13277 Marseille Cedex 9, France

CONTENTS

26.1 INTRODUCTION

Of all social insects, probably the least well known are social wasps. This is especially true of the mechanisms of caste determination and the regulation of reproductive functions in the wasp colony. This lack of knowledge is undoubtedly due, for the most part, to difficulties involved in making experimental observations. Except in the least evolved sub-families, all wasps' nests are wrapped in an envelope which impedes direct observation and renders access inconvenient. Until now, very few Vespinae nest foundations have been obtained in a laboratory environment.

Nevertheless, articles or books enumerating the main problems have been published in the last decade (Richards, 1971; Wilson, 1971; Spradbery, 1973; West-Eberhard, 1978; Brian, 1979, 1980; Jeanne, 1980; Edwards, 1980; de Wilde & Beetsma, 1982; Akre, 1982).

The Vespid family contains three sub-families of social wasps according to the classification of Richards (1971): Stenogastrinae, Polistinae and Vespinae. Stenogastrinae is a primitive sub-family about which little is known as to the caste system and its determination. The most varied group is Polistinae which is sub-divided into Polistini, Ropalidiini and Polybiini. The latter two dwell in tropical and sub-tropical climates, while Polistini (genus *Polistes* and *Sulcopolistes*) live also in temperate zones. Vespinae are widely found in temperate regions.

26.2   CASTE DIFFERENCES

Vespid colonies go through characteristic yearly cycles. Even in tropical conditions with a more or less stable climate, the colony changes in size and above all in composition. These cycles are all the more visible in temperate zones.

In these regions, the colony disappears at the beginning of winter when the nest is abandoned. Only future foundresses are able to survive the winter and found a new colony the following spring. When it becomes warm again the nest is founded by a single female in Vespinae as opposed to several as is often the case for Polistinae. In the tropical Polybiini family, new nests are founded by a swarm of workers accompanying one or more founding females (Jeanne, 1980).

The foundation of a nest is therefore the most significant event in the definition of caste.

The terms "queen" and "worker" used to describe castes in bee societies are not readily applicable to wasp societies in general and in particular to Polistinae which do not often exhibit any external morphological feature on which to base such a distinction.

26.2.1   Vespinae

It is in Vespinae that morphological differences between queens and workers are the most pronounced. The queen is always visibly larger than the workers even though workers do vary in size (Archer, 1972; Spradbery, 1972). In addition to this difference in size, there are often slight variations in colour. The species exhibiting the most pronounced polymorphism is *Vespula squamosa* (Drury): in this type of wasp, the queen is deep orange and nearly two times longer than the worker which has black and yellow stripes.

In temperate zones wasps, the fatbody of the young adult queen stores reserves of fat and other materials (Spradbery, 1973). Egg-laying is not exclusively limited to founding females, but unfertilized workers can only lay eggs which hatch into males.

26.2.2 Polistinae

In the Polistinae family, morphological differences between castes are, however, very small and sometimes even non-existent. The queens have a tendency of being larger in size, but size distribution overlaps in most species. Instead, moderate seasonal variations in size have been reported for *Polistes exclamans* (Eickwort, 1969), *Polistes fuscatus* (West-Eberhard, 1969) and *Polistes gallicus* (Turillazzi, 1980). Only in *Polistes fuscatus* a statistical slight difference between workers and foundresses has been pointed out.

Of all the Polistinae, the Polybiini wasp, *Stelopolybia areata* appears to be the species with the greatest polymorphism (Jeanne & Fagen, 1974). The gaster, especially the first segment, is ostensibly larger in queen wasps to make room for its more voluminous ovaries. The petiole is larger in *S. flavipennis* queens. Jeanne and Fagen (1974) report that caste differences are most conspicuous in species living in large colonies. There is however one notable exception: queen *Polybia dimidiata* wasps (Richards, 1971) are smaller than workers of the species.

In the Polistes, the only reliable criteria by which castes may be defined are biological or ethological in nature. For those species living in temperate zones only founding females are able to hibernate. It is widely believed that although workers are endowed with a complete set of sexual organs including a spermatheca and attract males, they refuse to copulate and are wholly responsible for finding food and wood fibre, constructing the nest and feeding the brood. However, once the nest is firmly established, the queen remains in the nest and lays eggs while the workers assume the outside work and feed the brood and often the queen itself.

In the tropical wasp *Polistes canadensis* (West-Eberhard, 1969) copulation is in some cases postponed and nest building may begin before the female is fertilized.

26.3 SOCIAL PARASITISM

It should be mentioned that, in some species of social vespids, females are not divided into castes. They are called cuckoo wasps. Among Vespinae, *Vespula austriaca* live on the nests of *Vespula rufa*. The female parasite enters an already established nest containing brood and takes the place of the host queen. Its descendants are raised by workers born from the brood existing before its arrival. Only males and females of the parasitic species are hatched (Archer, 1978). *Dolichovespula integra* and *Dolichovespula adulterina* are the two other European parasite species. Greene *et al.* (1978) report on the behaviour of an American species, *D. arctica*, which invades the nests of *D. arenaria* and replaces the queen after several days. The morphology of the social parasites of Vespinae wasps is very close to that of their hosts. In Polistine wasps, however, the difference is more apparent and parasites have been classified into a different genus: *Sulcopolistes*. The parasite is able to impose itself on a polygynous colony of *Polistes* by means of its dominant behaviour (Demolin & Martin, 1980), but the eggs which it deposits in the nest are sometimes destroyed even by females from the lowest ranks of the social hierarchy.

Finally, we should mention some intermediary cases of parasitic activity. Certain species are known to be capable of either building a nest of its own or invading a nest already established by another species. In case of invasion the worker caste continues to exist. Examples of this duality are *Vespa dybowskii* (Sakagami & Fukushima, 1957) in Japan and *Vespula squamosa* in North America (MacDonald & Matthews, 1975).

26.4 PHYSIOLOGICAL EVENTS RELATED TO CASTE DETERMINATION

We have seen above that wasp societies are subject to regulation from ecological, biological and social conditions which together bring about differentiation of females into worker and foundress castes. These interactions have often been studied; we have listed here a few examples. Pheromones, food or perhaps other sensorial information affect ovarian physiology in larvae or young adults and thereby determine their caste by means of endocrine factors. These questions have received less attention and knowledge is fragmentary.

26.4.1 Vespinae

In Vespine wasps, caste dimorphism is clear-cut. The queen alone can found a nest and then give birth to a very large population (one queen can have several thousand descendants in *Vespa crabro, Paravespula germanica* or *P. vulgaris* (Spradbery, 1973). Females are endowed with 12 ovarioles instead of six as in the other vespid females. This gives them a much greater degree of fertility.

The Vespinae are also the only wasp group in which the queen emerges from larger cells located in the lower part of the nest, i.e. in the last combs to be constructed. The queen induces these cells to be built just before the end of the colony life cycle. As there is no transition, they contrast with the appearance of the rest of the nest. Once they have started construction of large cells, it is exceptional to see workers resume building small ones. In *Vespa orientalis* (Ishay, 1975) these larger cells are not built if the queen is removed beforehand. In *Vespula vulgaris*, Potter (1965, quoted from the literature) proved that a queen taken from an old colony producing future foundresses and placed in a newer nest, immediately, induces the workers to construct large cells. Conversely a young queen transferred to an old colony in the process of constructing large cells, induces the workers to resume construction of small cells.

In *V. orientalis*, Ishay (1975) observed that if a queen is transferred from a new nest in which worker cells are being built into one in which construction of the larger cells is in progress, the workers will reduce the size of the opening of the larger cells to approximately the same diameter as worker cells. The larvae fed in these downsized cells, hatch into workers.

Ishay (1975), also succeeded in displacing eggs inside the nest. When the eggs extracted from queen-producing cells are glued into smaller cells they develop into workers. Conversely, eggs from small cells transferred into queen-cells at the end of the season turn into queens. The same sort of transfer can be made with larvae. The same results are obtained as long as the larvae are not older than the third larval instar. In other words larvae from worker-cells transferred into large cells at the end of the cycle become queens. Queen larvae become workers if transferred to small cells during the first to the third instar. In contrast, at the fourth and fifth instars, it is too late and larvae become workers and not queens in spite of transfer to larger cells. The same results have been recorded for *P. germanica*.

Two basic factors in the understanding of female caste determination in Vespidae are outlined below:

(1) Castes are determined before the end of the third larval instar. Larvae which will become large-sized queens, able to found new nests and lay hundreds and thousands of eggs are raised in larger cells where they are fed more and richer food as indicated below. Montagner and Courtois (1963) have shown that worker larvae are fed less than queen larvae. Montagner (1966) further adds that queen larvae receive a much greater quantity of the salivary gland secretions which impregnate the regurgitations of exogenous origin. The size of the cells containing the larvae appears to signal to the workers the quality and quantity of food to be supplied. Fischl and Ishay (1971) have recorded differences in carbohydrate metabolism between the two caste larvae.

(2) The construction of small or large cells by the workers according to

degree of completion of the nest seems to be under the control of the queen. Ishay (1975) reports that in absence of a queen, oriental hornet workers do not build any queen cells at the end of the season. Potter (1965) has shown in *V. vulgaris* that the age of the queen is an important factor in the type of cell constructed. In their experiments, Ishay *et al.* (1965) and Ikan *et al.* (1969) have been able to isolate a pheromone which, when placed in a queenless nest on a piece of cotton wool, is very attractive to workers and triggers the construction of large cells. This substance which is obtained from cephalic glands was identified as a lactone with 16 carbon atoms (δ-n hexadecalactone).

Fertility, however, is not the absolute characteristic of the queen. Under certain conditions, workers are capable of laying eggs. This is the case when the queen is removed from the nest (Montagner, 1963; Ishay, 1964; Spradbery, 1973). In a study of *P. vulgaris* and *P. germanica*, Montagner (1966) showed that if a group of workers is deprived of their queen, their ovaries begin to develop after 10 days if they come from a young colony and after only two if they are taken from an old nest in which male larvae have already appeared. Grouping is an important stimulating factor for the growth of ovaries in workers without a queen. An isolated worker exhibits no such development (Motro *et al.*, 1979). In larger nests, the queen occupies the large cell-combs and the workers sometimes lay eggs in the upper combs. A queen which has used all spermatozoa which it received can no longer lay diploid eggs. In this case, the responsibility for egg laying falls on the workers (Montagner, 1963, 1966). Workers can therefore become the main source of males in ageing colonies.

We can thus assume that in Vespinae, at least in some species, the queen maintains the coherence of the colony by preventing workers from reproducing. Towards the end of the cycle, a pheromone is produced and serves as a signal to begin the construction of large cells. Workers, probably guided by the size of the opening, supply the larvae inside with more and richer food which is determinant in the development of the future queens.

Such a scheme is not so easy to establish for Polistinae colonies.

26.4.2 Polistinae

Certain genera of Polistinae, although considered as social, do not exhibit caste differentiation. One such example is *Belonogaster griseus*. In an important study of this species, Marino-Piccioli and Pardi (1970), Pardi and Marino-Piccioli (1970) performed measurements on the population of a nest with fertilized and unfertilized females and uncovered certain statistical differences. On one hand, fertilized females tended to have larger thoraces as well as more fully developed ovaries. They were more dominant and oophagic, did more construction work and stayed most often close to the brood. Unfertilized females, on the other hand, were less dominant and stayed away from the nest longer in search of food. However, they were capable of great fecundity and could rise to the highest ranks of the hierarchy and even founded a nest on their own. The question of whether the caste of a fertile or unfertile female is already determined at the preimaginal instars is left unanswered by these authors.

It is equally difficult to establish the existence of castes and assign them to Polistinae in general and *Polistes* in particular, for which there are two mechanisms affecting female reproduction: a real caste separation between workers and foundresses and a phenomenon of social hierarchy which separates foundresses into queen and auxiliaries.

26.4.2.1 *Workers and foundresses*

In view of the less and, in many cases, absence of morphological differences, authors have generally relied on behavioural differences as a basis for assigning castes. The progeny of *Polistes* in temperate zones, where only future foundresses survive the winter, normally have underdeveloped ovaries in summer. Furthermore, it is widely accepted that while workers are more active and attract males, they can not be fertilized. Conversely future foundresses work less and can be fertilized (Pardi, 1946; Deleurance, 1946, 1952; West-Eberhard, 1969). West-Eberhard (1969) suggests that in *P. fuscatus* and *P. canadensis* only those females with mature ovaries actually construct new cells whereas workers with undeveloped ovaries simply extend the cell. Under certain conditions, workers can however develop their ovaries (Pardi, 1946, 1951; Haggard & Gamba, 1980). In foundresses, the developmental cycle of the ovaries is of course under the control of the complex neuroendocrine system.

Juvenile hormone (JH) injection or corpora allata (CA) implantation have been seen to stimulate ovarian growth in *P. metricus* and *P. gallicus* (Bohm, 1972; Girardie & Strambi, 1973). Ecdysone can be found in large amounts in the ovaries and also circulating in the haemolymph (Strambi *et al.*, 1977). If the ovaries of a mature queen are removed, the CA first increase, then decrease in size (Strambi, 1967a, 1969), while neurosecretory material accumulates in the cisternae of rough endoplasmic reticulum of medial neurosecretory cells. This material is probably a precursor of a neurosecretion (Strambi, 1967a; Strambi & Strambi, 1973a).

Castration is caused naturally by the Strepsipteron *Xenos vesparum* Rossi, the presence of which also affects the neuroendocrine system (Strambi, 1965a, b, 1966, 1967b, 1969). In newly-emerged parasitized females which have smaller than normal ovaries, the CA greatly decrease in size, while a rapid discharge from the neurosecretory cells of the pars intercerebralis is observed (Strambi & Strambi, 1973b). In newly-emerged females, the haemolymph protein level is low and no depletion is detected in parasitized females up to the 10th day of imaginal life. After that, in some normal females, circulating proteins increase in amount. Such an increase is never observed in stylopized wasps for which protein level remains unchanged (Strambi *et al.*, 1982). In spite of castration, the qualitative composition of haemolymph proteins is the same in both normal and parasitized wasps, even for the female specific fraction (Roux, 1973).

The implantation of CA induces the growth of the ovaries even in such stylopized females (Girardie & Strambi, 1973). Probably endocrine factors are responsible for both ovarian physiology and reproductive behaviour; *Polistes* queen whose ventral nerve cord is severed does not integrate information coming from the ovarian area. Such a wasp, even ovariectomized is able to show the whole sequence of egg-laying behaviour (egg deposition being of course excluded; Deleurance, 1963).

Several authors have used physiological criteria to distinguish between females castes. Eickwort (1969) approached the caste problem in *P. exclamans* on the basis of internal structure. She reports that the parietal fatbody is highly developed in certain females and in her opinion, this feature enables them to survive the winter. She therefore classifies such females as foundresses. This postulation seems not to apply to *P. gallicus* females parasitized by *Xenos*, which have very thin yellowish fatbody and nevertheless overwinter as well as normal females.

Pratte *et al.* (1982) use physiological criteria (fatbody, ovary size, haemolymph levels of ecdysone and proteins, and ethological criteria, nest presence, brood care) to divide a population of *P. gallicus* females into two groups which may correspond to castes. Females with small fatbody seem to spend more time on nest maintenance, while females with large fatbody can remain on a nest without brood. In spite of an obvious analogy, these two groups seem not to coincide perfectly with the two female castes.

The photoconductivity of the cuticle has also been utilized as a criterion for caste distinction by Perna *et al.* (1978). Bohm (1972) used environmental factors for *P. metricus*. The ovaries of newly-emerged wasps raised in June-like conditions (26°C, 16 hr daylight) grew in size, while females raised in July-like conditions (22°C, 14 hr daylight) had smaller ovaries. The latter females are the future foundresses with diapausing ovaries. The "June group" consists of workers, the ovaries of which developed normally in the absence of a queen, but which would have been stunted in a queen right colony. Turillazzi and Conte (1980) do not agree with the results of Deleurance (1952) who reported that chilling the nurse-workers at 5°C during the night induced the larvae they fed during the day to hatch into workers. West-Eberhard (1969) suggests that the determination of castes takes place at the larval stage and depends on the amount of food the larvae receive according to the season and their location in the nest.

26.4.2.2 *Social hierarchy*

In Polistinae, at least in most species, there is another mechanism of regulation of reproduction which functions at the time of polygynous foundation. Generally a nest is started by a foundress which is joined by other foundresses and they all work in the same nest.

Hierarchy is set up in this small society or before the beginning of nest building and leads progressively to a functional monogynous arrangement (Pardi, 1940, 1941, 1946, 1947, 1951; Deleurance, 1946, 1952; Gervet, 1964a, b, 1965, 1968; West-Eberhard, 1969). Social rank depends on behaviour which has been described in detail for many species, but which can be outlined as follows: When two females meet, the dominated one assumes a motionless posture with its antennae folded down and the dominant one holding itself high on its legs, moves around and strikes the dominated one with its antennae.

Usually, the foundresses which are attracted to a nest under construction have mature, functional ovaries and can lay eggs. However, Gervet (1962) reports that the dominant female is the most prolific. He further notes that dominance in a nest is related to fecundity, i.e. the number of eggs laid per day. Eggs laid by lower-ranked females are detected and destroyed by the dominant female. In this way, although the nest is polygynous, the only eggs which hatch are those of the dominant female known as the queen. The others are called auxiliaries.

Gamboa (1980) reports as an advantage of association that in such multiple-foundress colonies of *P. metricus*, the first workers hatch earlier than in single-foundress colonies.

Along with this behaviour-related regulation, there is also a physiological phenomenon at work since the number of eggs deposited by auxiliaries gradually decreases and their ovaries regress (Pardi & Cavalcanti, 1951).

The dominant female is able to increase its egg production (Gervet, 1968; Hermann & Dirks, 1975). At normal temperatures, the queen's ovaries produce more oocytes than the number of eggs it actually lays (Strambi, 1962, 1963, 1965; Gervet & Strambi, 1965). This fact explains how the quantity of eggs laid can be quickly and easily increased or decreased according to the needs of the colony.

Juvenile hormone would also appear to play a role in the phenomenon of dominance. In a worker population of *P. annularis*, Barth *et al.* (1975) revealed that experimentally administered JH not only stimulated ovarian growth, but also strengthened dominant behaviour to such a point that the whole social order was disrupted. In multiple foundresses of *P. gallicus*, queens are larger than their auxiliaries (Turillazzi & Pardi, 1977).

Foundresses of the species *P. gallicus* (Röseler *et al.*, 1980) were subjected to measurements to determine the volume of the CA and the amount of JH synthesized by them. During the activation period the amount of JH synthesized was seen to be correlated to the volume of the CA (Fig. 26.1). Vitellogenesis was also observed to be linked to an increase in the volume of

Alain Strambi

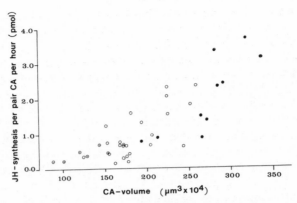

FIG. 26.1. Relationship between CA volume and JH synthesis by single pairs of CA from egg-maturing females of *P. gallicus*. ● dominant females; ○ subordinated females; ○ undefined rank (after Röseler *et al.*, 1980).

the CA. Moreover, the CA of subordinate females were smaller and less active than the dominant ones. It was therefore interesting to know if the CA of the subordinate females shrank as a result of the dominant behaviour of the queen or if, subordination was the result of low hormonal titres suggested by the small size of CA. In order to answer this question, foundresses just emerging from hibernation were divided into small groups of two and three. As soon as the social hierarchy was established in each group, the insects were dissected. In all cases a connection between the volume of the CA and the social hierarchy was established. The dominant ones always had the largest CA, while the most dominated female always had the smallest.

Moreover, it could be shown experimentally that in fact, the dominant female in such small societies causes a decrease in the CA volume of the most dominated ones. The CA of these most dominated females were found to be smaller than the glands dissected from the females they had dominated one week before. Therefore CA of the newly subordinated must have shrunk. In contrast, the glands of the dominant wasps continue to increase in size during the time (Table 26.1; Röseler *et al.*, in preparation). In already established field colonies of *P. gallicus*, Turillazzi *et al.* (1982) corroborate the correlation between hierarchy and CA volume. In such associated wasps, they show that CA and ovaries of equally ranked females vary according to the number of foundresses in each nest. The females in multi-foundress nests have larger CA than females in two-foundress nests which in turn have larger CA than single foundresses. The β females of multifoundress nests have larger CA than β females of two foundress nests. Thus the inequality exists prior to the social hierarchy and it is accentuated by dominant/subordinate behaviour and finally becomes established.

In further experiments, Röseler *et al.* (in prep.) found that injection of either JH or 20-hydroxyecdysone increased clearly the percentage of females

TABLE 26.1. CA VOLUME IN FOUNDRESS ASSOCIATIONS IN RELATION TO SOCIAL WORK (Values are means ± standard deviation)

One day after hibernation the social hierarchy was determined, the subordinated females were dissected and the volume of their CA measured. The three more dominant were left together. After 6 days they were dissected and the size of their CA compared to those of subordinated females investigated before. The CA of the γ females were found to be smaller than those of the lower ranked females which they dominated 6 days before. Therefore the sizes of the CA of the γ females have decreased. (After Röseler *et al.*, in preparation.)

Rank	CA volume ($\times 10^4 \mu m^3$) 1 day after hibernation	N	Rank	CA volume ($\times 10^4 \mu m^3$) 7 days after hibernation	N
α	?		α	501 ± 89	10
β	?		β	437 ± 113	10
γ	?		γ	307 ± 61	10
δ	374 ± 38	10			
ε	340 ± 43	10			
ζ	292 ± 38	10			
η	283 ± 54	5			
θ	227 ± 60	5			

for getting a dominant rank. Table 26.2 shows the extreme case in which the injected females were of smaller size, had smaller ovaries and smaller CA.

26.5   GENERAL CONCLUSIONS AND SUMMARY

Vespids are divided into two zoological categories. This distinction is underlined by their rather different biological characteristics. Vespinae exhibit a monogynous foundation. In the progeny, the two female castes are well distinguishable. The queen inhibits the ovaries of the workers and is able to provoke caste differentiation by means of pheromones which it secretes. So it maintains the yearly regulation of the colony.

In contrast, Polistinae, at least in certain species, are borderline examples of social insects. Castes are often morphologically indistinguishable. The polygynous foundation of their nests necessitates social regulation even within the foundress caste. It is not yet known if any pheromones are involved in the regulation of their social activity. Their physiology and especially endo-

TABLE 26.2. INFLUENCE OF HORMONE INJECTIONS IN FEMALES WHICH WERE SMALLER, HAD SMALLER OVOCYTES AND SMALLER CA THAN SHAM OPERATED

	Number of foundresses	Number of foundresses which became dominant	%
Untreated controls	75	3	4
Injected with JH	25	5	20
Injected with 20-hydroxyecdysone	37	16	43
Injected with JH + 20 hydroxyecdysone	20	6	30

crinology is, however, a little better known and we are beginning to understand the endocrine regulation of their society.

26.6 REFERENCES

Akre R. D. (1982) Social wasps. In *Social Insects*, Vol. IV, (Hermann H. R., ed.), pp. 1–105. Academic Press.

Archer M. E. (1972) The significance of worker size in the seasonal development of the wasps *Vespula vulgaris* (L.) and *Vespula germanica* (F.). *J. Entomol.* **46**, 175–183.

Archer M. E. (1978) The cuckoo wasp, *Vespula austriaca* (Panzer) (Hymen. Vespidae) in Yorkshire. *Naturalist. Hall* **103**, 133–134.

Barth R. H., Lester L. J., Sroka P., Kessler T. & Hearn R. (1975) Juvenile hormone promotes dominance behaviour and ovarian development in social wasps (*Polistes annularis*). *Experientia* **31**, 691–692.

Bohm M. K. (1972) Effects of environment and juvenile hormone on ovaries of the wasp *Polistes metricus*. *J. Insect Physiol.* **18**, 1875–1883.

Brian M. V. (1979) Caste differentiation and division of labor. In *Social Insects*, Vol. I (Hermann H. R., ed.), pp. 121–22. Academic Press.

Brian M. V. (1980) Social control over sex and castes in bees, wasps and ants. *Biol. Rev.* **55**, 379–415.

Deleurance E. P. (1946) Une régulation sociale à base sensorielle périphérique; l'inhibition de la ponte des ouvrières par la présence de la fondatrice chez les Polistes (Hyménoptères Vespidae). *C.R. Acad. Sci.* **223**, 871–872.

Deleurance E. P. (1952) Le polymorphisme social et son déterminisme chez les Guêpes. *Coll. Int. CNRS* **34**, 141–155.

Deleurance E. P. (1963) Analyse segmentaire du comportement de ponte chez les Polistes (*P. gallicus* L., *P. nimpha* Christ, Hyménoptères Vespides). *C.R. Acad. Sci.* **257**, 2175–2177.

Demolin G. & Martin J. C. (1980) Biologie de *Sulcopolistes semenowi* (Morawitz) parasite de *Polistes nimpha* (Christ.), Hyménoptera Vespidae. *Biol. -Ecol. medit.* **7**, 181–182.

de Wilde J. & Beetsma J. (1982) The physiology of caste development in Social Insects. *Adv. Insect Physiol.* **17**, 167–246.

Edwards R. (1980) *Social wasps*, 398 p. Rentokil Ltd, East Grinstead.

Eickwort K. (1969) Separation of the castes of *Polistes exclamans* and notes on its biology (Hym. Vespidae). *Insectes Sociaux* **15**, 67–72.

Fischl J. & Ishay J. (1971) The glucose levels and carbohydrate autolysis in *Vespa orientalis* haemolymph. *Insectes Sociaux* **18**, 203–314.

Gamboa G. J. (1980) Comparative timing of brood development between multiple and single-foundress colonies of the paper wasp, *Polistes metricus*. *Ecol. Entomol.* **5**, 221–225.

Gervet J. (1962) Etude de l'effet de groupe sur la ponte dans la société polygyne de *Polistes gallicus* L. (Hymen. Vesp.). *Insectes Sociaux* **9**, 231–263.

Gervet J. (1964a) Le comportement d'oophagie différentielle chez *Polistes gallicus* L. (Hymen. Vesp.). *Insectes Sociaux* **11**, 343–382.

Gervet J. (1964b) La ponte et sa régulation dans la société polygyne de *Polistes gallicus* L. Ann. Sci. Nat. Zool. 12e série **6**, 601–778.

Gervet J. (1965) La ponte et sa régulation dans la société polygne de *Polistes gallicus* L. *Behaviour* **25**, 221–233.

Gervet J. (1968) L'effet de groupe dans la société polygyne de Polistes (Hymen. Vesp.). *Coll. Int. CRNS, L'effet de groupe chez les animaux* **173**, 77–103.

Gervet J. & Strambi A. (1965) Dynamique de la fonction ovarienne chez les Polistes (Hymen. Vesp.). Cas de l'ouvriére. *C.R. Acad. Sci.* **260**, 4599–4601.

Girardie A. & Strambi A. (1973) Effet de l'implantation de corpora allata actifs de *Locusta migratoria* (Orthoptére) dans les femelles de *Polistes gallicus* L. (Hyménoptére) saines et parasitées par *Xenos vesparum* Rossi (Insecte, Strepsiptére). *C.R. Acad. Sci.* **276**, 3319–3322.

Greene A., Akre R. D. & Landolt P. J. (1978) Behaviour of the yellow jacket social parasite *Dolichovespula arctica* (Rohwer) (Hymenoptera Vespidae). *Melanderia* **29**, 1–28.

Haggard M. & Gamboa G. J. (1980) Seasonal variation in body size and reproductive condition of a paper wasp, *Polistes metricus* (Hymenoptera, Vespidae). *Can Ent.* **112**, 238–248.

Hermann H. R. & Dirks T. F. (1975) Biology of *Polistes annularis* (Hymenoptera, Vespidae). I. Spring Behavior. *Psyche* **82**, 97–108.

Ikan R., Gottlieb R., Bergmann E. D. & Ishay J. (1969) The pheromone of the queen of the oriental Hornet, *Vespa orientalis*. *J. Insect Physiol.* **15**, 1709–1712.

Ishay J. (1964) Observations sur la biologie de la guêpe orientale *Vespa orientalis* F. *Insectes Sociaux* **11**, 193–206.

Ishay J. (1975) Caste determination by social wasps; cell size and building behavior. *Anim. Behav.* **23**, 425–431.

Ishay I., Ikan R. & Bergmann E. D. (1965) The presence of pheromones in the oriental Hornet, *Vespa orientalis* F. *J. Insect Physiol.* **11**, 1307–1309.

Jeanne R. L. (1980) Evolution of social behavior in the Vespidae. *Ann. Rev. Entomol.* **25**, 371–396.

Jeanne R. L. & Fagen R. (1974) Polymorphism in *Stelopolybia areata* (Hymenoptera, Vespidae). *Psyche* **81**, 155–166.

MacDonald J. F. & Matthews R. W. (1975) *Vespula squamosa* a yellow jacket wasp evolving towards parasitism. *Science* **190**, 1003–1004.

Marino-Piccioli M. T. & Pardi L. (1970) Studi sulla biologia di *Belonogaster* (Hymenoptera, Vespidae). 1. Sull' etogramma di *Belonogaster griseus* (Fab.). *Monit. Zool. Ital. N.S.* Suppl. **3**, 197–225.

Montagner H. (1963) Contribution à l'étude du déterminisme des castes chez les Vespides. *C.R. Soc. Biol.* **157**, 147–150.

Montagner H. (1966) Sur le déterminisme des castes femelles chez les guêpes du genre Vespa. *C.R. Acad. Sci.* **263**, 547–549.

Montagner H. & Courtois G. (1983) Données nouvelles sur le comportement alimentaire et les échanges trophallactiques chez les Guêpes sociales. *C.R. Acad. Sci.* **256**, 4092–4094.

Motro M., Motro U., Ishay J. A. & Kugler J. (1979) Some social and dietary prerequisites of oocyte development in *Vespa orientalis* L. workers. *Insectes Sociaux* **26**, 155–164.

Pardi L. (1940) Poliginia vera ed apparente in *Polistes gallicus* L. *Atti. Soc. Tosc. Sci. Nat.* **49**, 3–9.

Pardi L. (1941) Ricerche sui Polistini. 3. Ancora sulla poliginia iniziale di *Polistes gallicus* L. e sul comportamento delle femmine associate fino alla schiusa delle prime operaie. *Atti. Soc. Tosc. Sci. Nat.* **50**, 3–15.

Pardi L. (1946) Ricerche sui Polistini. VII. La dominazione e il ciclo ovarico annuale in *Polistes gallicus* L. *Boll. Ist. Entomol. Univ. Bologna* **15**, 25–84.

Pardi L. (1947) Beobachtungen über das interindividuelle Verhalten bei *Polistes gallicus* L. *Behaviour* **1**, 138–172.

Pardi L. (1951) Ricerche sui Polistini. 12. Studio della attività e della divisione di lavoro in una società di *Polistes gallicus* L. dopo la comparsa delle operaie. *Arch. Zool. Ital.* **36**, 365–431.

Pardi L. & Cavalcanti M. (1951) Esperienze sul meccanismo della monoginia funzionale in *Polistes gallicus* (L.) (Hymenopt., Vesp.) *Boll. Zool.* **18**, 247–252.

Pardi L. & Marino-Picciolo M. T. (1970) Studi sulla biologia di *Belonogaster* (Hymenoptera, Vespidae). 2. Differenziamento castale incipiente in *B. griseus* (Fab.) *Monit. Zool. Ital. N.S.* suppl. **3**, 235–265.

Perna B., Croitoru N. & Ishay J. S. (1978) Dominance and hierarchy in *Polistes gallicus* colonies attained through photo-electric properties. *Experientia* **34**, 1022–1023.

Perna B. & Ishay J. S. (1980) Dominance and hierarchy in Polistes colonies. Correlation with photoelectric properties of their yellow strips. *Insectes Sociaux* **27**, 312–327.

Potter N. B. (1965) A study of the biology of the common wasp, *Vespula vulgaris* L., with special reference to the foraging behaviour. *Ph.D. Thesis*, Bristol Univ.

Pratte M., Strambi C., Gervet J. & Strambi A. (1982) Paramètres physiologiques et éthologiques dans un guêpier de *Polistes gallicus* L. *Insectes Sociaux* **29**, 383–401.

Richards O. W. (1971) The biology of the social wasps (Hymenoptera, Vespidae). *Biol. Rev.* **46**, 483–528.

Röseler P. F., Röseler I. & Strambi A. (1980) The activity of corpora allata in dominant and subordinated females of the wasp *Polistes gallicus. Insectes Sociaux* **27**, 97–107.

Roux C. (1973) Etude comparée de la protéinémie chez les imagos de Polistes (Hyménoptères Vespides) sains ou parasitées par le Strepsiptère *Xenox vesparum* Rossi. *C.R. Acad. Sci.* **276**, 3159–3162.

Sakagami S. F. & Fukishima K. (1957) *Vespa dybowskii* André as a facultative temporary social parasite. *Insectes Sociaux* **4**, 1–12.

Spradbery J. P. (1972) A biometric study of seasonal variation in worker wasps (Hymenoptera: Vespidae). *J. Ent.* **47**, 61–69.

Spradbery J. P. (1973) *Wasps*, 408 pp. Sidgwick and Jackson, London.

Strambi A. (1962) Sur le fontionnement de l'ovaire chez la quêpe Poliste. Determination du temps de croissance ovocytaire (*Polistes gallicus* L. et *P. nimpha* Christ). *C.R. Acad. Sci.* **255**, 2012–2014.

Strambi A. (1963) Action différentielle de la température sur le débit ovarien et la ponte chez la guêpe Poliste (*Polistes gallicus* L. et *Polistes nimpha* Christ., Hyménoptères Vespides). *C.R. Acad. Sci.* **256**, 5642–5643.

Strambi A. (1965a) Essai d'analyse de la dynamique ovarienne chez les Polistes. (*P. gallicus* et *P. nimpha* Christ) en activité reproductrice. *Insectes Sociaux* **12**, 1–17.

Strambi A. (1965b) Influence du parasite *Xenos vesparum* Rossi (Strepsiptère) sur la neurosécrétion des individus du sexe femmelle de *Polistes gallicus* L. (Hyménoptères Vespides). *C.R. Acad. Sci.* **260**, 3768–3769.

Strambi A. (1966) Action de *Xenos vesparum* Rossi (Strepsiptère) sur la neurosécrétion des fondatrices-filles de *Polistes gallicus* L. (Hymenoptère, Vespide) en diapause. *C.R. Acad. Sci.* **263**, 533–535.

Strambi A. (1967a) Quelques effects de la castration sur la neurosécrétion protocérébrale des femelles de Polistes (Hyménoptères, Vespides). *C.R. Acad. Sci.* **264**, 2031–2034.

Strambi A. (1967b) Effets de la disparition du parasite Xenos (Strepsiptère) sur la neurosécrétion protocérébrale de son hôte Polistes (Hymen. Vespides). *C.R. Acad. Sci.* **264**, 2646–2648.

Strambi A. (1969) La fonction gonadotrope des organes neuroendocrines des guêpes femelles du genre *Polistes* (Hyménoptères). Influence du parasite *Xenos vesparum* Rossi (Strepsiptères). *Thèse Doct. Sci. Nat. Paris.*

Strambi A. & Strambi C. (1973a) Etude histochimique et ultra-structurale des sécrétions élaborées par les péricaryons neurosécréteurs de la pars intercérébralis chez la guêpe *Polistes. Acta histochem.* **46**, 101–119.

Strambi A. & Strambi C. (1973b) Influence du développement du parasite Xenos vesparum Rossi (Insecte, Strepsiptère) sur le système neuroendocrinien des femelles de Polistes (Hyménoptère, Vespide) au début de leur vie imaginale. *Arch. Anat. Micr. Morphol. exp.* **62**, 39–54.

Strambi C., Strambi, A. & Augier R. (1982) Protein level in the haemolymph of the wasp *Polistes gallicus* L. at the beginning of imaginal life and during overwintering. Action of the Strepsipterian parasite *Xenos vesparum* Rossi. *Experientia* **38**, 1189–1191.

Strambi A., Strambi C. & De Reggi M. (1977) Ecdysones and ovarian physiology in the adult wasp *Polistes gallicus. Proc. VIIth Congr. I.U.S.S.I.*, Wageningen, Netherlands.

Turillazi S. (1980) Seasonal variations in the size and anatomy of *Polistes gallicus* L. (Hymenoptera, Vespidae). *Monit. Zool. Ital.* **14**, 63–75.

Turillazzi S. & Conte A. (1980) Influence of temperature on caste differentiation in *Polistes foederatus* (Kohl) (Hymenoptera Vespidae). *Monit. Zool. Ital.* **14**, 116.

Turillazzi S., Marino-Piccioli, M. T., Hervatin L. & Pardi L. (1982) Reproductive capacity of single foundress and associated foundress females of *Polistes gallicus* (L.) (Hymenoptera Vespidae). *Monitore Zool., Ital.* **16**, 75–88.

Turillazzi S. & Pardi L. (1977) Body size and hierarchy in polygynic nests of *Polistes gallicus* L. (Hymenoptera, Vespidae). *Monit. Zool. Ital.* **11**, 101–112.

West-Eberhard M. J. (1969) *The Social biology of Polistine wasps.* Miscellaneous publications of the Museum of Zoology, Univ. Michigan, **140**, 1–101.

West-Eberhard M. J. (1978) Polygyny and the evolution of social behavior in wasps. *J. Kans. Entomol. Soc.* **51**, 832–856.

Wilson E. O. (1971) *The Insect Societies*, 548 pp. Harvard Univ. Press.

CHAPTER 27

Comparative Aspects of Caste Differentiation in Social Insects

M. V. BRIAN

Department of Biological Sciences, Exeter University, U.K.

CONTENTS

27.1 INTRODUCTION

This chapter attempts to compare caste morphogenesis in the various groups of social insects—a very speculative subject. Most of the illustrations are drawn from ants because this group has not been discussed in the foregoing chapters of this book. To make useful comparisons between two such diverse groups as ants and termites has only recently become possible, but in recent decades a large body of research and information has come to exist on the subject of caste polymorphism, morphogenesis and endocrinological and social control. The main theme will be that these two groups, neither of which includes solitary forms, have followed similar evolutionary paths and converged on similar designs for their societies; this in spite of their originating in such different stocks with different levels of complexity, and even though the termites started to evolve sociality long before the ants, perhaps even in late palaeozoic times.

Termites and ants are both in essence soil insects. Both use winged imagos for reproduction and dispersal and in both the sexuals shed their wings after flight and return to the soil. In both the work is usually done by wingless individuals with, in ants and at least some termites, pigmented and toughened skins. The nymphs of termites and the larvae of ants have either wing buds or discs that are external in termites and internal in ants; both are capsules in which the future wing membranes are produced prior to being inflated with haemolymph. Termites almost always have a defensive caste that is so highly specialized that it is totally dependent. Such an extreme specialization is unusual in ants where the major workers are used for heavy jobs like cutting vegetation, milling seeds or transporting large prey. Commonly, in ants, the largest workers are used as stores for liquid foods. A policy that avoids undue specialization may well be sound but extreme specialization does not appear to have hindered the termites in their global spread and evolution.

Bees and wasps are aerial or arboreal insects that pollinate flowers or feed on honey-dew on small insects. Their ecology has necessitated the retention of wings in workers (they have no soldiers; in defence, workers take their turn). This has important consequences in caste morphogenesis. Along with ants, they have all-female societies, and males, which are rarely polymorphic, are not socialized. Perhaps their haploid chromosome state gives too little scope for facultative polymorphism which is at root genetic and is the essential basis of castes.

27.2 CASTE DIFFERENCES

The larval termite is a mobile sensory-motor unit that lacks only the systems that confer flight and reproduction. This in fact gives it a very functional shape for soil living close to the typical apterygote shape of soil inhabiting primitive insects. A "worker" or pseudergate is formed by halting the developmental progress of these larvae so that they have stationary moults and can be used whilst they queue to become imagos. That is in most primitive forms; further on in evolution (e.g. *Mastotermes*, some *Kalotermes* and *Schedorhinotermes*) this block to full realization of their potentiality is inserted earlier and earlier in ontogeny. In the Termitidae it may even be found in the mother's ovary (Noirot, 1969, 1974). From the point where sterile and fertile paths diverge the former must be able to acquire the means to venture outside the nest and its tunnels. They are rendered adultoid without being made imaginoid. Flight and reproductive systems are arrested while the rest of the organism differentiates and matures. The individuals as a result become terminal, developmentally end-products that have lost their potential for full-scale maturation. One option does remain to them however: to form, in two moults, a soldier. During this change their anterior region may be totally reshaped. Either their mandibles become grossly exaggerated or vanish almost entirely; in the latter case a snout develops in the median line above the mouth which is used to jet the toxins of the frontal gland on to the foe. The soldier is thus a product of the sterile path plus a reorganized head morphology.

In ants, whose larvae are legless and vermiform, the use of juveniles for mechanical work is not possible. They do contribute to the social welfare by producing enzymes that workers lack and by storing oils (in their blind gut) and, above all, they supply silk from their salivary glands that can be used to seal nests and make communal cocoons (*i.e.* nests). Their immobility may not be much of a drawback for it prevents them intruding and makes them easy to move into appropriate chambers with a suitable microclimate. It is virtually certain that the workers can distinguish quite a number of categories of larvae from their surface chemistry and hairiness. There is a tendency for hairs to increase and become more varied in size and shape with each instar. Pupae have a very different shape once they have come out of the larval skin (Brian, 1970). In *Myrmica* the last stage larvae actually produce a liquid pheromone from their venters when they are ready to embark on their final growth phase that takes them into the gyne from (Brian, 1973a). It is quite likely that workers of this genus can also recognize male larvae, just as honeybees can (even in the wrong cells). In many advanced species, such as *Monomorium*, sexual female larvae are more spheroidal in shape and less hairy in texture than worker larvae (Petersen-Braun, 1977; Edwards, 1982).

In termites, moults are the obvious events with which to start the progressive development of the juvenile into the adult. In ants two difficulties arise: first, there are fewer moults and much growth takes place by the expansion of the cuticle after softening and plasticization; second, the growth of the embryonic adult (strictly the post-embryonic growth of the adult rudiments) takes place whilst they are still inside the larval sub-organism. Differentiation starts whilst the larva is still feeding and growing so that, strictly speaking, the metamorphic process is telescoped into the larval growth process. The periodism of growth is thus represented less by ecdysis and more by apolysis and cuticular extension after softening. In *Myrmica*, a well studied genus of uncomplicated ants, there are only three instars but the last is very long and includes a great increase in size of body without any commensurate growth of the head capsule. It contains the rudiments of at least one moult, possibly more than one, and is important as it is the one in which caste differences first become visible. Some of these processes can be seen through the cuticle, *e.g.* the gradual movement of the brain from the head capsule into the thorax. During the first and second instars it stops half-way and a moult ensues which enables it to return to the enlarged head capsule. In the third instar at this half-way point, no moult ensues, but the larva stops growing and may hibernate; but a rise in temperature of a few degrees or a fresh lot of vigorous worker nurses start it growing again. Under these circumstances it has no alternative but to produce a worker adult after metamorphosis, but this is because it has either a worker bias from the egg stage or is prevented from diapause by the warmth and food. If it diapauses it finds itself growing and storing food concentrates in its fat body but not developing: it remains quiescent. After winter (or experimental chilling for some weeks) its corpora allata (CA) are reorganized and it is able to show sustained growth with not more than minimal activity on the part of the embryonic adult until it has rendered all its parts including flight and genital systems competent to respond to the moulting and metamorphosis hormones. But there are several stages between post-diapause and maturity in which the "embryo" can assert dominance and guide the organism along a worker-forming path. These are not discrete enough to prevent the ultimate worker size distribution from being unimodal, but they point towards a possible division into soldier-forming and worker-forming schism later in evolution (in Fig. 27.1 see c, a and e types of worker).

I think worker determination is a hidden moult; more strictly, I think the moult sequence has evolved into a worker-determination sequence (Brian, 1974, 1979, 1980). It involves an unusual growth of the "embryo", a growth that is suppressed entirely in normal ontogenesis of gynes. This growth fades and ceases unless it occurs very late, just before metamorphosis is due, but even so it has given the "embryo" a greater growth potential; the "embryo" is able to take up more of the food solutes digested in the larval gut and reach metamorphosis sooner by stopping food intake. This gives it a smaller size but the greater size of gynes may also arise from greater plasticization of the cuticle. At the same time as the "embryo" enlarges, it also dissociates the growth of its flight + genital systems though they have a "momentum" that lasts longer the larger they are. So, I suggest that the hidden "moults" in the last instar of *Myrmica* (and maybe other ants will be the same) are used to test the stability of the organism; to assess the coherence of its organization so that only the most stable are allowed to proceed towards gyne formation. Males, by the way, are entirely stable all the way.

A word is needed about ant major workers and soldiers. Until detailed studies of ontogeny have been made we can only ask the question: are they formed from worker-determined individuals or are they simply very late divergents from the main female stem? Almost certainly the former, for late divergence gives wingless gynes with perfect genital systems (c types in Fig. 27.1). Soldiers appear to be sterile individuals whose anterior region hypertrophies (in a structured way) at a later stage due no doubt to resuscitated growth rather than residual growth (Nijhout & Wheeler, 1982).

In the few bees and wasps that are social, caste differences are set-up by inter-individual action. This takes place during the few days or weeks after eclosion (West-Eberhard, 1969, 1977). In some advanced *Bombus* the workers are substantially smaller than the gynes but both have wings that work well, and ovaries and spermatheca. Only in the honeybee *Apis* have the workers

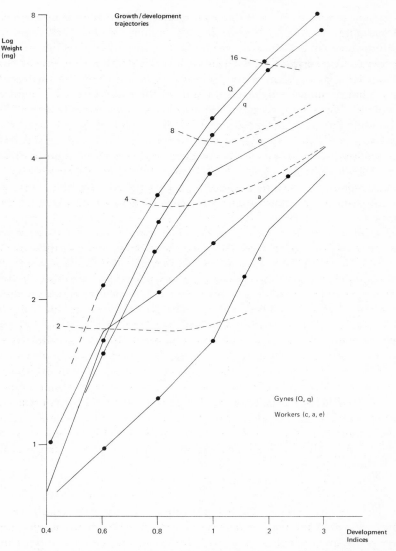

FIG. 27.1. Mean growth/development trajectories for larvae in the ant *Myrmica*. The ordinate is log scale weight in mg, the abscissa is a series of developmental events roughly 2 days apart; first movement of the brain into the thorax starting not at the start of the instar but when it is 4 tenths over; then the number of transverse segments in the leg buds. These are development indices. Queen-forming larvae either diapause (broken line) and hibernate, which boosts their growth or they hibernate before diapause and then omit it. Workers designated *e* are from worker-biased eggs, designated *a* are from labile eggs where larvae were reared by workers under queen influence, designated *c* are from hibernated larvae that have failed to achieve the normal queen-producing programme for some reason [see Brian, 1974 in Schmidt (ed.)]. Wing sizes are marked by broken line contours and black circles are days.

evolved a major structural and behavioural difference from the gyne without a commensurate size difference. I am thinking of their pollen-collecting equipment, their food glands, their informational dances and their reduced longevity. In neither wasps nor bees is there yet any evidence that the egg is caste-biased and determination depends on a switch of the food supply, dictated through a code of discrete cell types (Beetsma, 1979). The food given to larvae in worker cells (and in drone cells) is adequate for growth but does not enable them to metamorphose. For this sugars are needed, but I do not need to go into this in detail here. The main point that I want to make is that the "worker" larva at first seems to be no more than a starvation variant of the gyne: it builds up ovaries with almost (but not quite) as many ovarioles as the gyne but most of these later degenerate; even after this, *Apis* has a remarkable number of ovarioles in its workers (Wirtz and Beetsma, 1972; de Wilde, 1976). I suggest that the *Apis* worker travels all the way up the female stem to attain competence for its wings and that once these are developed, it can adjust its other features by reorganization.

In all these social Hymenoptera, as in termites (see earlier chapters), juvenile hormone (JH) is used as a control of caste morphogenesis (Brian, 1976); not necessarily by its concentration in the haemolymph, more likely by its timing (Nijhout & Wheeler, 1982). Its presence restrains the embryonic adult and stabilizes its tissues, in particular those of the flight and genital systems. It may not only allow them to continue in linkage with the other organ rudiments (in *Myrmica*), but prevent their destruction (in *Apis*).

27.3   SOCIAL CONTROL OVER MORPHOGENESIS

The point of interest in this section is whether or not the workers recognize incipient moults in social Hymenoptera and take an active part in the developmental decision or whether they are merely purveyors of food to larvae whose fate is fixed by an interaction between genetic, blastogenic (maternal) and trophogenic factors.

27.3.1   Termites

In termites it is well known that the reproductive pair can stop the formation of substitutes from workers or nymphs; it must be recorded that the discovery and analysis of this system was largely due to Lüscher, 1974a, b, 1976). In the lower termites some individuals are fully competent to develop a reproductive (though not a flight) system if they are released from the inhibition of the resident reproductive pair. It has been suggested that either

JH is absorbed by this couple after being collected in glandular food by nursing workers, or that they emit a chemical signal that switches off the CA of sensitive individuals (Lüscher, 1974b). Females are stronger and more effective than males and can inhibit sexual development in both males and females. Even pairs of the same sex do better than the corresponding single individual but are not as inhibitory as a heterosexual pair (Nagin, 1972). It looks as though some sort of communication between imagos in a "language" that only they can speak develops their powers of control, presumably their glandular system. The would-be reproductives are thus held up.

An interesting point brought out by Lüscher's work is that though a surplus of replacements may be formed "automatically" from sensitive individuals, all but one couple are exterminated later on. They fight each other, apparently recognizing not just the sex but also the individual identity of an opponent. The wounded are finally dispatched by workers (Lüscher, 1974b). This lesson should make ethologists and their like cautious about underestimating the sensory and behavioural complexity of termites.

Along with the less flexible divergence of a sterile from a fertile (but labile or metastable) stem in higher termites has come a limitation on the ability to produce substitutes from wingless workers (Noirot, 1969, 1974). In this they closely resemble the ants. Where one is needed to replace a lost reproductive, it may be recruited from an imago by dealation, again as in ants, or from late-stage nymphs by precocious metamorphosis. The "flow" of individuals along the imaginal stem is very much influenced by season, though how this is regulated is not yet known. The caste bias which may, perhaps, be given blastogenically to the egg whilst in the mother's ovary could be imparted by JH from her haemolymph (Lüscher, 1976). Seasonal variation in this would presumably arise from a physiological change in her nurses which might also be involved in the survival of lines of sterile and fertile offspring.

Soldiers are well known to inhibit the creation of more soldiers (Lüscher, 1974a, b) and since experimental excess of JH produces soldiers from workers or nymphs, the natural way may be to either absorb and destroy free JH (unless there is a use for it as in reproductive physiology) or to stop its production by circulating an anti-CA chemical (Lenz, 1976). This could, of course, interfere with the reproductives if they actively collect JH from workers and larvae in order to supplement their own manufacture (in spite of the fact that they have very well developed glands of their own). Again, if soldiers destroy free JH their abundance in a society could interfere with reproduction, apart from the fact that they are individually unproductive.

27.3.2 Ants

Primitive ants may well have a reproductive control system analogous with that of primitive termites. Wingless queens are frequently encountered and one may guess that many others are never recognized since they look so like workers. Their thorax is unsutured but their ovaries and spermatheca are normally developed. They can be formed from main stem females if the queen is removed, because workers then relax their rule of not feeding adequately (Colombel, 1978). In one major sub-family of ants, the Dorylinae, these females are the normal queens.

Higher ants have evolved a maternal control like that of the Termitidae (Passera and Suzzoni, 1978). Young queens produce worker-biased eggs in the main but, as they age, more queen-biased or unbiased eggs are formed (Petersen-Braun, 1977; Brian, 1980). On top of this course tuning is a system that fine tunes the production of female castes. This is operated by the workers under the "surveillance" of queens and, in the crudest cases, they weed out the caste that is not needed (gynes if queens are adequate, workers if queens are inadequate). There is also growing evidence that the workers in a colony are conditioned to its queen status during the first few weeks after they emerge from the pupal skin, and less intensively later on (Brian and Evesham, 1982). This depends on the frequency of contact between any worker and its caste-mates relative to contact with its queens. The queens produce a lipid-soluble pheromone not so far identified except in the case of *Monomonium pharaonis*: neocembrene (Edwards, 1982).

In *Myrmica* the production of sexual adults is seasonally variable with a peak in spring. At this time the larger older foraging workers actively massage larvae destined to become gynes. They are so vigorous at this that brown scars are formed, showing that they have pierced the epicuticle (though penetration is no deeper, and the larvae are rarely killed). This comes just in time to divert them into large workers. This, then, is a case of worker determination at the very last moment, just before the features of the gyne caste are irrevocably determined. The chemical signal from larvae "at risk" has the opposite effect on worker behaviour if there are no queens, or if the workers are young and irresponsive: they then cosset the same larvae and lavish great care on them, and feed them copiously. However, it should not be confused with the mechanism, also queen-conditioned, that switches them from normal feeding to feeding dilute food. This has different transmissivity: it does not get far from the queen and is targeted on to young nurse workers. The massage effect travels far through a population, under less favourable conditions, and is targeted on to the older foragers. Furthermore, male larvae are affected by the "no feed" command but not by the "massage" command (Brian, 1981). To sum up, even in the uncomplicated ant *Myrmica*, workers play a considerable part in influencing the fate of larvae: young nurses dilute food and old foragers massage if female larvae reach a critical stage in development and threaten to become gynes in societies in which they would be detrimental.

This is not the only, nor the most important, queen-regulated worker-operated control in *Myrmica*. In fact it may only represent a "safety net". The main switch away from gynes occurs earlier in ontogeny. This is at the point, already alluded to, when the brain is half-way into the thorax and growth has stopped, as if prior to a moult. Instead of moulting, the larva either undergoes worker determination or settles into a pre-diapause sequence of slow growth and storage (Brian, 1980). The evidence here is that queens stimulate the regurgitation of food digests, probaby dilute, to these larvae, and that this prevents the diapause (Brian, 1975). Young workers that are insensitive to queens induce diapause. Thus queens actively encourage feeding and actively deflect larvae away from diapause, with regeneration of the CA and returned growth potentiality. Those that are impervious to this and go on to diapause are dealt with at the next cryptomoult, the safety net. An interesting point about this pre-diapause switch is that it enables the colony to work hard without risk of producing gynes before they are ready, rather like the blastogenic maternal effect.

To sum up for females in ants: there are at least three stages which affect caste. The first is the maternal blastogenic influence which is very important in colonies with young queens. The second is the pre-diapause switch which probably affects the bulk of the unbiased eggs. The third follows diapause and though dual in its action (under-feeding by young, massaging by old workers), may merely be a last fine tune to the main process of suppressing gynes if queens are sufficient and fostering gynes if queens are inadequate.

Males in Hymenoptera are, of course, not social but their production can be a drain on the society and needs to be restrained until their release is actually beneficial, in the sense that it removes congestion by exporting ant material instead of building up more through production of workers. Male Hymenoptera are haploid and produced without sperm, unlike those of Isoptera which are formed by the usual XY chromosome mechanism. If workers have ovaries that can produce viable eggs they must be restrained whilst the colony grows strong. This means that in social bees and wasps the queen is constantly vigilant and will destroy and eat any worker-laid egg she can find and recognize. The queen and workers, it need hardly be said, dispute the right to produce males and do not always "agree" on the sex investment ratio. Male control is thus very important in societies of a social insect.

In the ant *Myrmica* (and probably others in which workers regularly lay viable reproductive eggs when young and when queenless), the inhibition by the queen is only partial: an egg is still made and laid but it is small, weakly chorionated and with a different yolk. It is at once used as food by queens and workers or is stored in the egg mass until larvae hatch and eat it *in situ*. The main way in which inhibition seems to be exercised is by laying eggs and making an egg cluster: even the cluster or reproductive eggs that a set of workers without a queen can lay will react back on them and induce trophic eggs (Brian and Rigby, 1978). These trophic eggs thus represent additional yolk for the new embryo; they help the survival of the queen's female (fertilized) eggs and detract from the production of male eggs (except when queens are few or absent).

The conversion of a reproductive into a trophic egg must surely represent an ideal compromise between controlling workers and yet using them as food refiners and condensers. Its evolution is carried a stage further in ants that do not enclose a yolk in thin shells but extrude it on demand. Thus the ovary becomes a food gland rather than a reproductive organ, or, strictly, can switch from one function to another under the influence of queens. A similar situation with trophic and reproductive eggs has been evolved in stingless bees (Meliponini).

Yet in many ants, workers have become so much smaller than their queens that they have lost their ovaries altogether, and use oral glands for feeding. In primitive bees the trophic egg has not evolved but in the advanced genus *Bombus* the worker ovary is developmentally inhibited by the queen, by means of a pheromone that affects the worker CA. These workers also rear brood in a queen-dependent way (Röseler, 1977; Röseler and Röseler, 1977, 1978). The control appears to depend on rate of delivery of food, not on massage or other special treatment, though primer chemicals are not yet ruled out.

In the honeybee *Apis* a long series of investigations by many insect sociologists has established beyond doubt that the queen inhibits gynes by stopping workers, making the special cells. If she is removed they turn a worker cell with a larva or egg in it through a right-angle and make it into a gyne cell. Of the many substances in her mandibular gland it is the oxygenated unsaturated short chain fatty acid (9-oxo-dec-2-enoic acid) that is effective, and it appears to have come to be used in the hive for worker control after a much longer evolutionary history as a sex attractant. It is not volatile and is dispersed by "messenger" bees that contact her and are left with the material on their mouth parts (Seeley, 1979). Nevertheless it is not all-powerful and, in the right season, it is difficult to stop gyne formation even with larger doses (Velthuis, 1977; Beetsma, 1979). Part of the difficulty is that a material left in queen footprints is also inhibitory (perhaps a conditional reflex?); and as queens frequent the lower rims of combs, where gyne cells are made, this could be very important in congested hives where she might well have difficulty in patrolling effectively (Lensky, 1977). Also, in spring colonies the mass of young bees that creates the congestion may be unresponsive to queen actions, as are the young workers of *Myrmica*. Moreover, there is a pheromone from the queen's abdomen which plays a part in this process (Velthuis, 1977). Thus for several reasons, a large colony with a poor queen, a colony that is congested and full of young bees, will start making queen cells and, once the queen has laid in these, there is no stopping the workers from feeding the larvae. Only when new pupae mature and the cells are sealed is there a chance that the queen (or her gyne successor if she has left in a swarm) will attack and kill them with her sting. In large colonies that need to swarm the workers may protect the pupae or young gynes so that many survive (Simpson, 1974). Honeybees can also replace a living queen, usually in late summer, by making a few gyne cells and allowing the new gyne to take over from the queen either before or after copulating.

Males are formed in the honeybee by a process that also involves interaction between the queen and her workers (Free, 1977; Free and Williams, 1975). It only happens in moderate to large colonies where presumably the queen is less prominent; then the large worker-shaped cells are made low down on the rims, often followed by gyne cells. The queen lays a sequence of eggs without fertilizing any, and the workers rear them. If "drone" cells are left over from a previous year and the queen lays in them, the workers don't necessarily rear them, *i.e.*, they have the final decision. The interesting thing is that in some way there is a balanced ratio of drone to worker cells, a pressure against males by the queen and for them by the workers. So the process again represents a conflict between the two female castes, a counteraction by workers against the queen's influence. Such a system is evidently common in the maturation of insect societies.

27.4 SUMMARY

In this chapter, I have tried to compare the morphogenetic mechanisms that generate castes in termites, where they affect both sexes, and in ants where only the female sex is affected. Bees and wasps are mentioned in passing for further comparison.

In both termites and ants, though one is exo- and the other endopterygote, the reproductive and flight systems mature last in ontogeny and there is some evidence that, compared with the male (in ants), they are retarded as part of the mechanism generating polymorphism. Thus the main stem of development which leads to a winged dispersive imago has gaps from which the metastable norm can leave and develop without reproductive or flight systems or, later on, with reproductive but without a flight system. Such openings are not present in male ontogenies in social Hymenoptera.

Worker determination in ants (as passing from the metastable stem can be called) is a loss of developmental potential and is irreversible. It can be induced artificially by starvation and, seen through the larval cuticle, appears as a growth of leg buds without any commensurate growth of wing buds (discs). In fact these are dropped (along with the germarium) from the growth ensemble or embryonic adult. This change is due to an arrest of CA activity, for JH prolongs the symmetry of development.

In natural conditions these deviations occur at several stages in the last larval instar of the ant and these stages have been compared with the moults of termites; in ants there is no moult and the moulting machinery appears to be used for worker determination and, if gyne formation persists, for plasticization and expansion of the cuticle. Workers are determined by successive application of this "moulting test", some at the beginning of the third instar, some at a stage when the next moult would be expected, and some later still, just prior to metamorphosis (leg bud segmentation). Only the very stable configuration of genes can survive these three tests. The workers produced get larger but in *Myrmica* make a single moded frequency distribution. In ants with "soldiers" they may form from the last to diverge, but probably need to retain a special capacity for selective, anterior enlargement.

Apart from these intrinsic factors, the workers, under queen surveillance actively intervene in larval growth. They regurgitate liberally at stage 2 and prevent diapause and they withhold and dilute food at stage 3 after diapause (which redevelops CA activity). They also massage post-diapause larvae and induce worker determination endocrinologically. The underfeeding and the massage controls are undertaken by different classes of worker and have different penetration potentials in the society, but they achieve the same end.

In the honeybee, which has the greatest caste differences found in bees and wasps, the control of caste is entirely nutritive; there is no blastogenic effect as in ants and, perhaps, in termites. It is based on the use of distinct cell types and either a steady programme of balanced food (growing gynes) or one which is switched halfway from a growth- to a metamorphosis bias. Worker bees need to retain wings and it is found that they have to build up a large ovary in order to achieve wing competence (since the flight system apparently cannot be developmentally manoeuvred into an earlier stage). The ovary is then destabilized with absence of JH, and its material translocated during metamorphosis.

JH is the operator in all caste development systems whether Isopteran or Hymenopteran. Its withdrawal is used to destabilize the normal development programme and cause precocious fixation of the set of organ systems that characterize apterygote insects. Later it can be used in a local regrowth phase to generate soldiers in termites and ants.

27.5 REFERENCES

Beetsma J. (1979) The process of queen-worker differentiation in the honeybee. *Bee World* **60**, 24–39.

Brian M. V. (1970) Communication between queens and larvae in the ant *Myrmica. Anim. Behav.* **18**, 467–472.

Brian M. V. (1973a) Caste control through worker attack in the ant *Myrmica. Insectes Sociaux* **20**, 87–102.

Brian M. V. (1973b) Feeding and growth in the ant *Myrmica. J. Anim. Ecol.* **42**, 37–53.

Brian M. V. (1974) Kastendetermination bei *Myrmica rubra* L. In *Sozialpolymorphismu bei Insekten* (Schmidt G. H., ed.), pp. 565–589. Wiss Verlagsges, Stuttgart.

Brian M. V. (1975) Caste determination through a queen influence on diapause in larvae of the ant *Myrmica rubra. Entomol. exp. appl.* **18**, 429–442.

Brian M. V. (1976) Endocrine control over caste differentiation in a myrmicine ant. *Int. Congr. Entomol. 15th Washington D.C.,* pp. 63–70.

Brian M. V. (1979) Caste differentiation and division of labor. In *Social Insects* 1 (Hermann H., ed.), pp. 121–222. Academic Press, New York.

Brian M. V. (1980) Social control over sex and caste in bees, wasps and ants. *Biol. Rev.* **55**, 379–415.

Brian M. V. (1981) Treatment of male larvae in ants of the genus *Myrmica. Insectes Sociaux* **28**, 161–166.

Brian M. V. & Evesham E. J. M. (1982) The role of young workers in *Myrmica* colony development. *Congr. Int. IUSSI 9th Colorado,* pp. 228–232.

Brian M. V. & Rigby C. (1978) The trophic eggs of *Myrmica rubra* L. *Insectes Sociaux* **25**, 89–110.

Colombel P. (1978) Biologie d'*Ontomachus haematodes,* determinisme de la caste femelle. *Insectes Sociaux* **25**, 141–151.

De Wilde J. (1976) Juvenile hormone and caste differentiation in the honeybee (*Apis mellifera* L.). Symposium on "Phase and Caste Determination in Insects" (Lüscher M., ed.) *Congr. Int. Entomol. 15th Washington D.C.,* pp. 5–20.

Edwards J. P. (1982) Control of *Monomorium pharaonis* (L.) with methoprene baits: implications for the control of other pest species. *Int. Congr. IUSSI 9th Colorado,* pp. 119–123.

Free J. B. (1977) The seasonal regulation of drone brood and drone adults in a honeybee colony. *Int. Congr. IUSSI 8th Wageningen,* pp. 207–210.

Free J. B. & Williams I. H. (1975) Factors determining the rearing and rejection of drones by the honeybee colony. *Anim. Behav.* **23**, 650–675.

Lensky U. (1977) Queen cup and cell construction in queen-right honeybee colonies. *Int. Congr. IUSSI 8th Wageningen,* addenda 3–5, p. 162.

Lenz M. (1976) The dependance of hormone effects in termite caste determination on external factors. *Int. Congr. Entomol. 15th Washington D.C.,* pp. 73–90.

Lüscher M. (1974a) Die Kompetenz sur Soldatenbildung bei larven (Pseudergarten) der Termite *Zootermopsis angusticollis. Rev. Suisse Zool.* **81**, 710–714.

Lüscher M. (1974b) Kasten und Kastendifferenzierung bei niederen Termiten. In *Sozial polymorphismus bei Insekten* (Schmidt G. H., ed.), pp. 694–762. Wiss. Verlagsges., Stuttgart.

Lüscher M. (1976) Evidence for an endocrine control in higher termites. *Int. Congr. Entomol. 15th Washington D.C.,* pp. 91–104.

Nagin R. (1972) Caste determination in *Neotermes jonateli* (Banks) *Insectes Sociaux* **19**, 39–61.

Nijhout H. F. & Wheeler D. E. (1982) Juvenile hormone and the physiological basis of insect polymorphisms. *Quart. Rev. Biol.* **57**, 109–133.

Noirot C. (1969) Formation of castes in the higher termites. In *Biology of Termites* (Krishna K. and Weesner F. M., eds), Vol. 1, pp. 311–350. Academic Press, New York.

Noirot C. (1974) Polymorphismus bei Hoheren Termiten. In *Sozialpolymorphismus bei Insekten* (Schmidt G. H., ed.), pp. 740–765. Wiss. Verlagsges., Stuttgart.

Passera K. & Suzzoni J. P. (1978) Traitement des reines par l'hormone juvenile et sexualisation du couvain de la fourmi *Pheidole pallidula. C.R. Acad. Sci.* Paris, **287**, 1231–1233.

Petersen-Braun M. (1977) Studies on the endogenous breeding cycle in *Monomorium pharaonis, Int. Congr. IUSSI 8th Wageningen,* pp. 211–212.

Röseler P. F. (1977) Juvenile hormone control of oogenesis in bumblebee workers, *Bombus terrestris. J. Ins. Physiol.* **23**, 985–992.

Röseler P. F. & Röseler I. (1977) Dominance in bumblebees, *Congr. Int. IUSSI 8th Wageningen,* pp. 232–235.

Röseler P. F. & Röseler I. (1978) Studies on the regulation of the juvenile hormone titre in bumblebee workers, *Bombus terrestris. J. Ins. Physiol.* **24**, 707–713.

Seeley T. D. (1979) Queen substance dispersal by messenger workers in honeybee colonies. *Behav. Ecol. Sociobiol.* **5**, 391–415.

Simpson J. (1974) The reproductive behaviour of European honeybee colonies. Lecture in Central Association of Beekeepers, 14 March 1974.

Velthuis H. H. W. (1977) The evolution of honeybee queen pheromones. In *Conr. Int. IUSSI 8th Wageningen,* pp. 220–222.

West-Eberhard M. J. (1969) The social biology of polistine wasps *Misc. publ. Mus. Zool. Univ. Michigan*, **140**, 1–101.

West-Eberhard M. J. (1977) The establishment of reproductive dominance in social wasp colonies. *Int. Congr. IUSSI 8th Wageningen*, pp. 223–227.

Wirtz P. & Beetsma J. (1972) Induction of caste differentiation in the honeybee (*Apis mellifera*) by juvenile hormone. *Ent. exp. appl.* **15**, 517–520.

Index